Washington, DC

timeout.com

Time Out Digital Ltd
Universal House
251 Tottenham Court Road
London W1T 7AB
United Kingdom
Tel: +44 (0)20 7813 3000
Fax: +44 (0)20 7813 6001
Email: guides@timeout.com
www.timeout.com

Published by Time Out Digital Ltd, a wholly owned subsidiary of Time Out Group Ltd.
Time Out and the Time Out logo are trademarks of Time Out Group Ltd.

This edition first published in Great Britain in 2013 by Ebury Publishing.
A Random House Group Company
20 Vauxhall Bridge Road, London SW1V 2SA

Random House Australia Pty Ltd 20 Alfred Street, Milsons Point, Sydney, New South Wales 2061, Australia

Random House New Zealand Ltd 18 Poland Road, Glenfield, Auckland 10, New Zealand

Random House South Africa (Pty) Ltd Isle of Houghton, Corner Boundary Road & Carse O'Gowrie, Houghton 2198, South Africa

Random House UK Limited Reg. No. 954009

Distributed in the US and Latin America by Publishers Group West (1-510-809-3700)

For further distribution details, see www.timeout.com.

ISBN: 978-1-84670-397-3

A CIP catalogue record for this book is available from the British Library.

Printed and bound in Great Britain by Butler Tanner & Dennis, Frome, Somerset.

The Random House Group Limited supports the Forest Stewardship Council® (FSC®), the leading international forest-certification organisation. Our books carrying the FSC label are printed on FSC-certified paper. FSC is the only forest-certification scheme supported by the leading environmental organisations, including Greenpeace. Our paper procurement policy can be found at www.randomhouse.co.uk/environment.

Contents

Arts & Entertainment 154

Escapes & Excursions 190

In Context 204

Essential Information 224

Maps 244

Introduction

Washington, DC is different from most cities. It didn't develop organically. Instead, it began life as a planned capital, designed in neo-classical style to reference Ancient Greece, apt for a fledgling democracy. Today its real personality can be hard to pin down because, in the popular imagination, at least, the real city is still dominated by the monumental city – hub of government power. The rational layout remains, along with a collection of neo-classical buildings, with the National Mall at its heart. The buildings add to the resonance of 'Washington' as a concept: a hallowed space to some, the root of all liberal, big-government evil to others. But while the monuments are a reminder that this is a government town, that phrase doesn't define the city. DC is emphatically not one of those planned capitals that doesn't quite make it in its own right. Step just a few blocks away from the Mall and you will discover a different, engaging and independent city: in fact, fewer than 20 per cent of the area's workers are government employees.

If non-monumental Washington's recent history has a theme, it's regeneration. From a mid 20th-century slump, exacerbated by damage caused by riots following the assassination of Martin Luther King in 1968, Washington has been reborn, with dozens of new residential buildings springing up in remade neighbourhoods and a continuing process of gentrification. In the face of nationwide recession, Washington is doing pretty well. It hasn't been a bonanza for all, however. The new urbanites, along with the area's other prosperous inhabitants, who live principally in the suburbs, have very different lives from the working-class, mainly African American residents on the city's east side.

The urban-urban and urban-suburban divide is very real, and remains a defining characteristic of the city. But taken as a whole, DC's education and income levels are now above the United States average, and increasing. So it's not surprising that today Washington has excellent restaurants, with some of the nation's best chefs making a mark. The theatre scene is vibrant and DC has a musical heritage all of its own. Add in the city's wonderful national museums, which are free, and the fact that much of the city is easily accessible using the clean and efficient Metrorail service, and you'll discover a city that is highly rewarding to visit. *Ros Sales, Editor*

About the Guide

GETTING AROUND

The back of the book contains street maps of Washington, DC, as well as an overview map of the city and its surroundings. The maps start on page 244; on them are marked the locations of restaurants (❶), bars (❶) and hotels (❶). Most businesses listed in this guide are located in the areas we've mapped; the grid-square references in the listings refer to these maps.

THE ESSENTIALS

For practical information, including embassies, visas, disabled access, emergency numbers, lost property, useful websites and local transport, please see the Essential Information. It begins on page 226.

THE LISTINGS

Addresses, phone numbers, websites, transport information, hours and prices are all included in our listings, as are selected other facilities. All were checked and correct at press time. However, business owners can alter their arrangements at any time, and fluctuating economic conditions can cause prices to change rapidly.

The very best venues in the city, the must-sees and must-dos in every category, have been marked with a red star (★). In the Sights chapters, we've also marked venues with free admission with a FREE symbol.

PHONE NUMBERS

The area code for Washington, DC is 202 and you need to use this, even when dialling within the city. The code is also needed for calls to and from Virginia and Maryland, or for long-distance calls within the US. Codes vary for Virginia and Maryland; they are included in listings in this guide.

From outside the US, dial your country's international access code (00 from the UK) or a '+' symbol, followed by the number as listed in this guide; here, the initial '1' serves as the US country code. So, to reach the International Spy Museum, dial +1-202 393 7798. For more on phones, *see p236.*

FEEDBACK

We welcome feedback on this guide, both on the venues we've included and on any other locations that you'd like to see featured in future editions. Please email us at guides@timeout.com.

Time Out Guides

Founded in 1968, Time Out has grown from humble beginnings into the leading resource for anyone wanting to know what's happening in the world's greatest cities. Alongside our influential weeklies in London and New York, we publish more than 20 magazines in cities as varied as Beijing and Beirut; a range of travel books, with the City Guides now joined by the newer Shortlist series; and an information-packed website. The company remains proudly independent, still owned by Tony Elliott four decades after he launched *Time Out London*.

Written by local experts and illustrated with original photography, our books also retain their independence. No business has been featured in this guide because it has advertised, and all restaurants and bars are visited and reviewed anonymously.

ABOUT THE EDITOR

Ros Sales studied in Washington, DC and has edited various city guides for Time Out.

A full list of the book's contributors can be found on page 11.

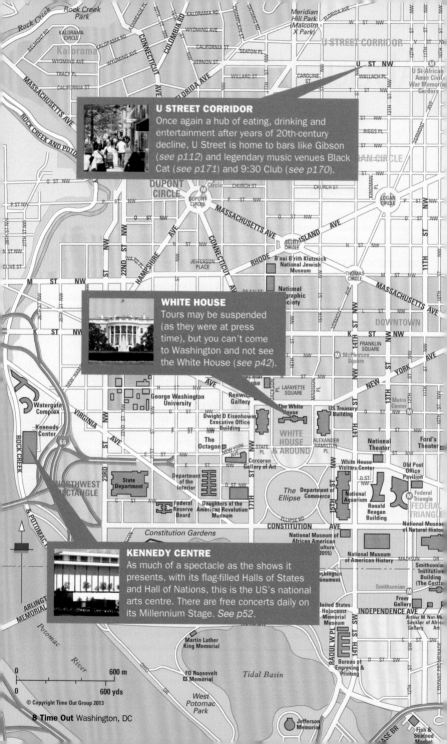

U STREET CORRIDOR
Once again a hub of eating, drinking and entertainment after years of 20th-century decline, U Street is home to bars like Gibson (see p112) and legendary music venues Black Cat (see p171) and 9:30 Club (see p170).

WHITE HOUSE
Tours may be suspended (as they were at press time), but you can't come to Washington and not see the White House (see p42).

KENNEDY CENTRE
As much of a spectacle as the shows it presents, with its flag-filled Halls of States and Hall of Nations, this is the US's national arts centre. There are free concerts daily on its Millennium Stage. See p52.

© Copyright Time Out Group 2013

0   600 m
0   600 yds

NEWSEUM
A modern and highly interactive museum devoted to journalism and free speech, the Newseum (*see p58*) also has one of the city's best views from the terrace on Level 6.

UNITED STATES CAPITOL
Explore the corridors of power with a free tour of the Capitol (*see p45*). The highlight is the famous rotunda, containing nine million tons of iron.

NATIONAL MALL
Epicentre of the city and symbolic national space, the iconic National Mall (*see pp28-39*) is the place for memorials and museums – and they're all free. Check out the new Martin Luther King Memorial (*see p30*).

Time Out Washington, DC

Editorial
Editor Ros Sales
Listings Editor Katie Pearce
Proofreader Tamsin Shelton
Indexer Ros Sales

Editorial Director Sarah Guy
Management Accountant Margaret Wright

Design
Senior Designer Kei Ishimaru
Designer Darryl Bell
Group Commercial Senior Designer Jason Tansley

Picture Desk
Picture Editor Jael Marschner
Deputy Picture Editor Ben Rowe
Freelance Picture Researcher Isidora O'Neill

Advertising
Sales Director St John Betteridge
Advertising Sales Melissa Keller, Christine Legname, Christy Stewart

Marketing
Senior Publishing Brand Manager Luthfa Begum
Head of Circulation Dan Collins

Production
Production Controller Katie Mulhern-Bhudia

Time Out Group
Chairman & Founder Tony Elliott
Chief Executive Officer Aksel Van der Wal
Editor-in-Chief Tim Arthur
UK Chief Commercial Officer David Pepper
International Managing Director Cathy Runciman
Group IT Director Simon Chappell
Group Marketing Director Carolyn Sims

Contributors
Introduction Ros Sales. **Los Angeles Today** Katie Pearce. **The Lobbying Industry** Mark Jenkins. **Diary** Trey Graham. **Sightseeing** Steve Ackerman, Ros Sales. **Hotels** Kelly diNardo, Denise Kersten, Ros Sales (*Hotels are Healthy* Kelly di Nardo). **Restaurants** Denise Kersten, Amanda McClements, Caroline Schweiter, Jessica Dawson (*Lunch on the Move, Power Points* Amanda McClements; *Union Market* Denise Kersten). **Bars** Sophie Gilbert. **Shops & Services** Nicole Aguirre, Caroline Schweiter, Brad McKee (*Vintage on U Street, Man Style* Nicole Aguirre). **Children** Patrick Foster. **Film** Mark Jenkins. **Gay & Lesbian** Steve Gdula. **Nightlife** Mark Jenkins, Christopher Porter. **Performing Arts** Trey Graham, Mark Jenkins. **Sports & Fitness** Cathryn Connolly. **Escapes & Excursions** Cathryn Connolly. **History** Mark Jenkins (*The Star-Spangled Banner* Ros Sales; *Parallel Lives* Steve Ackerman). **Architecture** Mark Jenkins. **Directory** Cathryn Connolly.

Maps john@jsgraphics.co.uk

Cover photograph Detail of Capitol Building by VisionsofAmerica/Joe Sohm
Back cover photography Shutterstock.com, Poste at Monaco Hotel.

Photography 3, 6, 8 (middle), 12/13, 22, 23, 24, 26/27, 38 (right and bottom), 41, 49, 51, 57, 64, 74, 76, 77, 79 (top), 159, 190/191, 197, 224/225 Shutterstock.com; 8 (top), 9 (middle and bottom), 29, 33, 34, 35, 36, 38 (top), 42, 45, 46, 54, 61, 69, 72, 78 (top), 111, 156, 166, 171, 176, 184, 185, 186, 189, 192, 194, 196, 198, 199, 200, 201, 202, 203, 210, 217, 219, 220, 221, 244/245 Elan Fleisher; 8 (bottom) Douglas Litchfield; 9 (top), 58 (left) Sam Kittner/kittner.com; 14, 83, 93, 94, 98, 99, 106, 110 (top), 126, 130, 131, 172, 177 Susana Raab; 18, 213, 216 Getty Images; 21 Rena Schild; 25, 163 Metro Weekly; 30 Dave Newman; 39 Wolf Design; 52 (right) Tim Hursley; 58 (right), 59 Frontpage; 63 Freer Gallery of Art; 82 Darko Zagar; 84 Ron Blunt; 90 Paul Burk; 100, 101 EDENS; 103 Ken Goodman; 104 Dakota Fine; 212 TPWP guide; 122 (top) Charlie Heck; 147 Isaac Maiselman; 151 Robert Reck; 154/155, 168 John Shore/www.johnshorephoto.com; 161 Alamy; 164 Ward Morrison/Metro Weekly; 167, 170 Mark Maskell, Panorama Productions; 179 Janet Macoska; 183 Chris Gieckel; 204/205 Joe Gough; 206 Medford Historical Society Collection/CORBIS; 215 Gamma-Keystone via Getty Images; 223 James P Blair/Newseum.

The following images were supplied by the featured establishments: pages 17, 52 (left), 53, 78 (bottom), 79 (bottom), 80/81, 87, 89, 95, 107, 108, 109, 110 (bottom), 113, 114, 115, 120, 122 (bottom), 125, 135, 136, 137, 138, 139, 140, 143, 145, 146, 148, 149, 152, 153, 157, 162, 165, 173, 175, 178, 180, 209.

In Focus

Washington Today

Regeneration continues but divisions remain.

TEXT KATIE PEARCE

Washington, DC is both pristine and gritty, stodgy and savvy, small-town and cosmopolitan. It's conservative in demeanour but progressive in mindset. Poverty and unrest live next door to affluence and power. The real personality of Washington can be hard to pin down, not only because of these dualities but also because the local city lives so much in the shadows of its identities as tourist mecca and federal seat of power. Both tinge the day-to-day lives of every Washingtonian. There's a static in the air, an awareness that Important Decisions Are Made Here.

RECESSION, WHAT RECESSION?

The city's personality is only getting harder to define as DC enjoys its clout as a rare recession success story. While employment and real-estate prices tumbled all over the country after the 2008 crash, Washington continued full steam ahead with the urban regeneration that has been in progress for decades. Commercial and residential real-estate prices are among the highest in the nation, and the job market has remained buoyant – in part due to the engine of government employment. The city has also shed an unfortunate old nickname – 'Murder Capital'. In 2012, the city saw its lowest murder rate in the last 50 years.

Glassy condo buildings and gleaming new grocery stores are popping up in formerly downtrodden neighbourhoods, new young residents are arriving in hordes, and more and more families are choosing the city over the suburbs. New rooftop bars, farmers' markets, gyms and bike lanes dot the landscape, reshaping the city of row houses into something bigger and brasher.

The Nationals Stadium, built for $611 million a few years ago, started out with dwindling attendance but now regularly draws big crowds to a former industrial zone – particularly after the Nats made it to the postseason in 2012. The waterfront areas of Southwest DC and around the Navy Yard are now prepped for massive redevelopment, with developers finally taking advantage of the appeal of both the Potomac and Anacostia riverfronts. And, after years of delays, controversy and construction rubble, the $700-million City Center DC redevelopment of the old Convention Center site is slated to start opening sometime in 2013.

With all this growth come conspicuous shifts in demographics. The nickname 'Chocolate City' – coined in the 1970s, when DC was over 70 per cent black – is no longer a real fit. Though black culture continues to define the essence and real character of residential Washington, today only around half of its 630,000-some population is black. About 39 per cent of residents are white, nine per cent are Latino and 3.5 per cent are Asian.

These shifts are obvious in areas that have moved upscale. Take the 14th Street Corridor. Following the 1968 riots that trampled the city after the assassination of Dr Martin Luther King, the once-lively strip was desolate and sketchy, then edgy and artsy in the 1980s and '90s. Now it's straight-up posh, with new luxury condo buildings, chic galleries and furniture stores, and trendy bars and restaurants opening every week, it seems. On the other side of the town, by Union Station, the H Street, NE, corridor is following a similar development track – albeit in an earlier phase now, as a hipster nightlife destination with a streetcar set to start running next year.

A DIVIDED CITY

A tired but accurate way to describe Washington is as 'a tale of two cities'. On the one hand, it has high levels of income (with top-earning households averaging over $470,000 a year) and education. Washington has an abundance of masters and law degrees, a ranking as the most literary city in the nation, and a reputation as 'Nerdopolis'. However, the bottom fifth of wage earners in the city average just over $9,000 per year, and unemployment rates among those without college degrees and African Americans remain higher than before the recession hit. In 2012, DC ranked bottom in the nation in high school graduation rates, and almost one in five residents over 16 is functionally illiterate. Efforts are under way in this area, however. Reform of the city's public schools is seeing a new type of aggression, spearheaded a few years ago by the nationally recognised efforts of Chancellor Michelle Rhee.

Racial and class divisions are nothing new in Washington – the leafy neighbourhoods in Northwest DC have never shared much common ground with the urban poverty east of the Anacostia River. What's newer are the population shifts and the way these are shaking up the core of the city. Neighbourhoods long known as majority-black, such as the 14th Street and U Street corridors, H Street, Columbia Heights and Petworth, are now mixed; in Adams Morgan, the

IN CONTEXT

Hispanic population is declining. This brings tension. It can be revealed through smaller quibbles like those over Sunday parking around longstanding African American churches, or in big-picture stuff like city elections and politics.

In 2010, the young one-term mayor Adrian Fenty was defeated by City Council Chairman Vincent Gray, whose political base is in the poorer areas of the city. Some Gray critics tried to cast the election as a return to the 'old guard politics' exemplified by the city's former mayor Marion Barry – best known for getting busted for smoking crack in the '90s. (Barry, by the way, remains an active member of the city government – which has seen a spate of new ethics scandals in the past couple of years, including prison terms for two council members and questions over the legitimacy of Mayor Gray's election campaign.)

The dwindling availability of affordable housing remains a concern for many. Low-income residents face a difficult housing market, widely regarded as one of the most expensive (by some studies, the most expensive) in the country. Some have cited the city's building height law – in general, buildings can't be taller than about 130 feet – as one reason why housing stock is so limited. The city government continues to explore a number of policies to try to combat the growing problem, including a zoning law that requires developers to include affordable units in new projects.

CAPITAL CITY AND TOURIST HOTSPOT

The monuments, memorials and National Mall that form an aesthetic backdrop for locals also attract millions of visitors. In 2011, a record-breaking 17.9 million came to town, spending $6 billion. The tourism machine inevitably colours life in the city, especially in summer, when visitor numbers skyrocket, along with the number of double decker buses and hot dog stands around the Mall.

For Washingtonians, the presence of the White House and Congress is part of the fabric of everyday life. By and large, DC

residents are more informed about and involved in national politics than those in any other part of the country: this is a town of policy wonks, formal state dinners and big-money fundraisers. It's certainly not a love-love relationship, though, between the local city and the federal government. Maybe that's best exemplified by the fact that standard-issue licence plates in DC come printed with a message of protest: 'Taxation Without Representation'. Though it's treated as a state in most federal legislation, Washington, DC is not, of course, one of the 50 US states. The District has no voting representation in Congress, which can overturn any local city legislation. DC residents, however, still pay taxes, unlike those in US territories like Guam and Puerto Rico. The city has a long history of advocacy for voting rights and autonomy. A number of proposals have been debated, including absorbing the District into the state of Maryland or making it a new state, but all have been stymied by political resistance or constitutional challenges. Still, local activism for the cause remains hot, with protestors scoring a potentially big victory in spring 2013 by finding a way to detach the city's budget from Congressional approval (at press time, this law change was pending).

Despite the wonkishness of many local residents, there's not a lot of partisan conflict here. DC proper is overwhelmingly liberal, with over 75 per cent of residents registered as Democrats; 91 per cent of voters went for Obama in the 2012 election. In the suburbs, the majority of voters also lean left, but there's more variation. Northern Virginia in particular includes active pockets of Republicanism.

Defined as it is by the federal government, the government sector actually accounts for only 29 per cent of the area's jobs – which has proved enough to safely cushion the area's economy. But the majority of DC's workers are in the private sector, with hospitality, education, construction and technology leading the pack. Of course, many of those jobs have ties to the feds – there's an abundance of contractors, consultants, lobbying firms, and the like.

The District also hosts nearly 200 foreign embassies, with about 10,000 employees in the diplomatic corps. Major universities, including Georgetown – the largest private employer in the city proper – account for many jobs. There's also a new drive to lure high-tech firms to the city. Mayor Gray paved the way by crafting a major tax break last year for LivingSocial, an online daily deals company that now employs over 4,000 – possibly the highest-profile home-grown tech company in DC since AOL, which started here as a military project.

DC'S DEFINING METRO
The Metro system is another great definer of both the city and its suburbs. The 106 miles of track of the network serve a regional population of nearly six billion. It's the second-largest heavy rail transit system in the country, after New York City's – despite the great disparity in size between DC and New York (and the DC system has notably fewer rats). Given that the District of Columbia itself is relatively compact – only around 68 square miles – a large number of the city's workers, and Metro's riders, are suburban commuters from Maryland and Virginia. Commuters swell the daytime population of the city, crowding the Metro system for a good five hours or so of rush hour each weekday morning and evening. They also clog the roads; the DC region is a notoriously bad place to drive, consistently ranking second to Los Angeles for the worst conditions.

A CITY FOR LIVING
Commuting trends have also affected demographic change (and vice versa). Though the suburbs are largely stable and affluent – seven of the richest counties in the nation surround DC – for some, the hassle and expense of commuting is no longer worth it; and even some with jobs in the suburbs are choosing to live in the city and do a reverse commute. Living in the city is now a desirable option for many who want to ditch reliance on their cars – as well as having the Metro, DC is also known as one of the country's most walkable cities – and live closer to culture, dining and entertainment. At the heart of the city, this means new residents chasing the urban lifestyle are either living alongside or displacing families who have lived in DC for generations. It's a chaotic, sometimes tense, blending of interests, but a diversity that drives the culture of the city today.

The Lobbying Industry

How to make friends and influence people.

TEXT MARK JENKINS

The Washington area's economy, like any other region's, experiences booms and busts. But there's one industry that grows as much during retreats as advances: lobbying. There's always some person, company or interest group that wants something from the federal government, and is willing to pay a legislative or regulatory specialist to get it.

It was in 19th-century Washington that 'lobby' became a verb, to describe the influence peddling that occurred in the Willard Hotel. Petitioning the government didn't start there, of course, and occurs in every country and every political system. But the American way has some unusual features that make its 'lobby shops' particularly active. There are more than 13,000 registered lobbyists in Washington – and thousands more whose activities probably should require them to register.

Lobbyists are often called 'K Streeters', after the DC thoroughfare. The term was immortalised in *K Street*, a 2003 HBO series produced by George Clooney and directed by Steven Soderbergh. Yet many of these political mechanics never had offices on K Street, and by the time Clooney got there, nearly all were located elsewhere in the city.

The 'K Street' name sticks, however, even among those who work in the field. In 1995, with Democrat Bill Clinton in the White House, prominent Republicans Rep Tom Delay and Grover Norquist announced the 'K Street Project'. The plan was to force major lobbying concerns (and law firms involved in that trade) to put Republicans in top positions. This would benefit both the party and the corporations that support it. The first would get permanent political control, while the latter would have more power to rewrite laws and regulations to its liking.

The K Street Project succeeded, but not for very long. One of its most prominent players, Jack Abramoff, was found to be cheating his clients, notably American Indian tribes who operate casinos. (Indian tribes can operate casinos in US states that don't otherwise permit them, as long as they do so on reservations.) Abramoff and his allies played tribes against each other, and collected millions in fees.

In 2006, Abramoff pleaded guilty to felony charges of fraud, conspiracy and tax evasion. He was required to pay at least $25 million in restitution to former clients. Many of his associates and political allies fell along with him. Delay is still appealing his conviction for money laundering and conspiracy. Another Republican Congressman, Bob Ney, went to jail on separate but related charges. Both Delay and Ney benefited from Abramoff's frequent expenses-paid excursions, including golfing vacations in Scotland.

The Abramoff scandal inspired the Legislative Transparency and Accountability Act of 2006. It put new restrictions on the relationships between lobbyists and elected officials, but included enough loopholes to allow the influence business to continue more or less as before.

Representing Indian gambling interests was an exotic gig for Washington lobbyists, but far from the only controversial cause or person to find a DC spokesperson. Many foreign dictators, including some the US ultimately helped depose, have employed the city's persuaders.

Former Assistant Secretary of Defense Richard Perle, one of the architects of the 2003 American invasion of Iraq, was hired in 2006 to improve the image of Libya's then-ruler, Muammar Gaddafi. Such repressive countries as Saudi Arabia, Nigeria and Zimbabwe have benefited from the efforts of American lobbyists.

'We know how to refocus negative or unsubstantiated stories so our clients can avoid embarrassment, economic hardship or a governmental investigation,' promises the website of the Livingston Group. Its founder, former Rep Robert Livingston, does have experience with negative stories. At the height of the furore over Bill Clinton's affair with Monica Lewinsky, Livingston called for the president's resignation. Clinton didn't step down, but Livingston did, after admitting his own extramarital dalliance.

SHOW ME THE MONEY

Personal friendships and political alliances are vital to lobbying, which is why so many former politicians and bureaucrats pursue second careers in the trade. When no such kinship exists, as Abramoff once noted, lobbyists can usually develop one by assisting with campaign fundraising.

One of the hallmarks of American politics is that election cycles are long and expensive. When members of Congress announce their retirements – often to become lobbyists or trade-association officials – they usually complain about the pressures of fundraising. Soliciting cash for the next campaign is a non-stop task, especially for members of the House of Representatives, who must run for re-election every two years.

Potentially lessening this burden is a frequent topic of conversation in political Washington. But the nine-member US Supreme Court, dominated by its five conservative justices, has done the opposite. It holds that spending money to support candidates is a free-speech right protected by the US Constitution. In the 2010 'Citizens United' case – notorious in liberal circles – the court struck down limits on campaign spending by corporations and other associations.

MINORITY PARTY POWER

Another unusual aspect of the American system is divided government. Unlike

IN FOCUS

under a parliamentary system, in the US the chief executive and one or both branches of the legislature can be controlled by different parties. In recent years, the Democrats have held the White House and the Senate, while the Republicans run the House.

Such circumstances give the out-of-power party a lot of power. At present, the Republicans may not be able to accomplish much legislatively, but they can obstruct bills that certain interest groups want blocked. So there's always reason to lobby members of both parties.

Such large, profitable enterprises as oil, gas and coal companies are always working Washington, lobbying for tax breaks and against environmental regulations. But smaller ones can be just as effective, once their representatives acquire a reputation for political savvy and determination.

CHANGING AGENDAS

The best example is the National Rifle Association (NRA), nominally an organisation of hunters, target shooters and gun collectors. To its opponents, the NRA's political clout is a matter of distress and even awe. But while the NRA's power has grown, its agenda has changed.

After 20 six-year-olds and six adults were massacred by a lone gunman at a school in Connecticut in 2012, gun-control advocates made another attempt to tighten the country's famously loose gun laws. The bill couldn't even pass the Democratic-controlled Senate.

The majority of NRA dues-payers actually supported the added restrictions, and the organisation itself had endorsed similar proposals in the past. These days, however, the NRA is no longer controlled by its ordinary members. Its primary role is to advance the interests of gun manufacturers. There's a term in American politics for an organisation that pretends to represent a grassroots membership, but was actually founded by a powerful special interest: astroturf. In the case of the NRA, what was once a genuine grassroots group seems to have mutated into an astroturf one.

Periodically, some upstart industry announces that the federal government is irrelevant. Many of the internet businesses

that began in Seattle or Silicon Valley at first kept their distance. But gradually Microsoft, Apple and Google opened Washington offices to handle what many companies term 'government relations'. Recently, boyish Facebook founder Mark Zuckerberg began to dabble in political persuasion – and quickly alienated environmentalists by supporting a controversial bid to construct a pipeline to bring tar-sands oil from Canada to the US.

Wall Street moguls also used to declare their disregard for the national government, but they've been quiet on that subject since 2008, when the Federal Reserve bailed out the country's major investment banks. There's still more money to be made trading securities than regulating them, but New York financiers are paying attention to Washington these days.

That's not only because of the 2008 near-collapse, and the new banking regulations that resulted from it. The corporate sector is also pondering the Affordable Care Act, often called simply 'Obamacare'. As new health-insurance requirements are phased in, businesses strive to understand – and, in some cases, resist – them.

POLITICAL INTELLIGENCE

In the spring of 2013, controversy erupted over a new sort of K Street-ish firm, dealing in 'political intelligence'. The field may have doubled in size in the past decade, the *Washington Post* reported. Such companies as the four-year-old Height Securities don't try to influence federal law- and rule-making. They attempt to understand it, for the benefit of their clients. After reporting that a pending decision about the Affordable Care Act would favour private healthcare insurers, shares traders stampeded toward those companies. It's another example of the growing synergy between two symbolic streets: K and Wall.

A federal investigation into that stock scramble is already under way, but it probably won't stop the growth of the political intelligence business. After all, if these new companies want to stall attempts to limit their activities, they can just hire a lobbyist.

IN FOCUS

Diary

A city for all seasons.

Washington, DC offers all the state ceremonies you would expect of a capital, and the Mall, Capitol and White House provide the background to great national events such as presidential inaugurations. Happily, it also has a calendar bursting with less formal occasions, from events associated with the big cultural institutions to lively weekends of streetside fun celebrating the diverse neighbourhoods where the District's real people live – Anacostia, Adams Morgan, Chinatown, Dupont Circle, Mount Pleasant, and many more.

You can keep track of events with the *Washington Post*'s Friday 'Weekend' section (www.washingtonpost.com/weekend), the *Washington City Paper* (www.washingtoncitypaper.com), or the events database at the www.washington. org tourist site. Note that most events are free unless otherwise stated. For information on Washington's various film festivals, *see p162*. For a list of national holidays, *see p237*.

SPRING

St Patrick's Day Celebrations
Constitution Avenue, NW, from 7th to 17th Streets, The Mall & Tidal Basin (1-202 637 2474, www.dc stpatsparade.com). Smithsonian, Federal Triangle, L'Enfant Plaza or Archives-Navy Memorial Metro. **Date** close to 17 Mar. **Map** p253 J6.
Washington's St Patrick's Day revelries draw the crowds with a parade of dancers, bands, bagpipes and floats along Constitution Avenue. In true Irish style, the partying continues well into the night in pubs around the city. When 17 March doesn't fall on a Sunday, the festivities take place on the previous Sunday. St Patrick's Day celebrations are also held in Alexandria in Virginia, where they're organised by a charity called Ballyshaners (1-703 237 2199, www.ballyshaners.org). *Photo p22.*

Annual White House Easter Egg Roll
White House South Lawn, 1600 Pennsylvania Avenue, NW, between 15th & 17th Streets (information 1-456 2200/2322, www.whitehouse. gov/eastereggroll). McPherson Square Metro. **Date** 1st Mon after Easter. **Map** p252 H6.
Since 1878, when Congress kicked them off the Capitol lawn, kids aged three to six have been invited to hunt Easter eggs – the egg count is up to 24,000-plus these days – hidden on the South Lawn of the Executive Mansion. A festival on the Ellipse features storytelling, children's authors, even astronauts sometimes – and, crucially for cranky parents, food. The event kicks off at the Southeast Gate at the corner of East Executive Avenue and E Street; it gets very crowded, so arrive early. Make sure the kids are with you around 7-7.30am, when the tickets are handed out (though the actual festivities run from 10am to 2pm).

Blossom Kite Festival
Washington Monument Grounds, The Mall & Tidal Basin (information 1-877 442 5666, www. nationalcherryblossomfestival.org). Smithsonian Metro. **Date** Sun in late Mar. **Map** p252 H7.
Kite-lovers of all ages proudly show off their hand-made contraptions (and the serious ones even take part in competitions). There are also demonstrations with novelty and sport kites by 'kite-making masters'. Usually held on the first day of the National Cherry Blossom Festival (*see below*).

National Cherry Blossom Festival
Headquarters at Union Station, 50 Massachusetts Avenue NE; Welcome Center at the Tidal Basin (1-877 442 5660, www.nationalcherryblossom festival.org). **Date** late Mar-mid Apr.
Cherry blossom time is a big deal in Washington. In 1912, 3,000 cherry trees were donated to the city by Mayor Yukio Ozaki of Tokyo as a symbol of

friendship between Japan and the United States. These original trees were planted along the Tidal Basin; today, the path that rings the basin becomes clogged with visitors during bloom time. The city has become famous for the immigrant blossoms, and celebrates them with near-pagan worship and a weekend of special events, including a National Cherry Blossom Festival Parade and the Sakuri Matsuri Street Festival, a celebration of Japanese art, food and culture held on 12th Street between Pennsylvania and Constitution Avenues. To witness this explosion of colour, try to visit between late March and mid April; the atmosphere is congenial and the blossoms are truly glorious.

Memorial Day

Date Memorial Day weekend (last Mon in May).
On the Sunday evening, the National Symphony Orchestra performs a free concert on the West Lawn of the US Capitol (there's another one on Labor Day in September; details on 1-800 444 1324 or www. kennedy-center.org/nso). On Monday, the presidential wreath-laying and memorial services take place at Arlington National Cemetery (*see p77*), the Vietnam Veterans Memorial (1-202 426 6841) and the US Navy Memorial (1-202 737 2300 ext 768). Rolling Thunder's Ride for Freedom, a massive motorcycle parade on Sunday morning, remembers POWs/MIAs and honours servicemen who died in wars. *Photo p24.*

Memorial Day Jazz Festival

Alexandria, VA (1-703 746 5592, www. alexandriava.gov/recreation). King Street Metro. **Date** around Memorial Day (last Mon in May).
Quaint Old Town Alexandria is the location for this day-long affair, which features half a dozen or so jazz artists, plus food stalls.

Black Pride

Multiple venues (1-202 347 0555, www.dcblack pride.org). **Date** Memorial Day weekend (last Mon in May).
Exhibitions, workshops and concerts over four days, when around 10,000 African American gays and lesbians hit the city for Black Pride.

Capital Pride

Multiple venues (1-202 719 5304, www.capitalpride.org). **Date** early June.
Washington's GLBT community marks Capital Pride Week with parties, pageants, political forums, a Pennsylvania Avenue street festival, the inevitable parade – and even a mini film festival. *Photo p25.*
▶ *For more on gay life in DC, see pp181-84.*

SUMMER

Also check out the two-week **Shakespeare Free For All** festival (www.shakespeare theatre.org/about/ffaheld) at the Carter Barron Amphitheatre in Rock Creek Park.

Fort Reno Summer Concert Series

Fort Reno Park, NW, between Wisconsin & Nebraska Avenues, Upper Northwest (www. fortreno.com). Tenleytown-AU Metro. **Date** June-Aug.
Both up-and-coming and well-known bands take to the outdoor stage at Fort Reno Park, on a hill overlooking Washington. Concerts are free and bands play for nothing; not surprisingly, long-term funding is a concern for the popoular event. Come along, bring a picnic and soak up the music. No booze or glass bottles allowed.

Marine Band's Summer Concert Series & Evening Parades

West Terrace of the US Capitol, Capitol Hill, The Capitol & Around. Capitol South or Smithsonian Metro. **Date** Wed in June-Aug. **Map** p253 K7.
US Marine Corps War Memorial Arlington, VA. Rosslyn Metro. **Date** Tue in June-Aug.
Both *1-202 433 4011, 6060, www.marineband.usmc.mil.*
'The President's Own' – once led by John Phillip Sousa – performs free, twice weekly outdoor con certs at the Capitol and/or on the Mall during the summer months; the band's repertoire ranges from classical music to brass-band favourites, and the action starts at 8pm. (See website for days and locations.) On summer Fridays, the band is also a featured element of the showy Evening Parade, which includes impressive precision formation drills; it begins at 8.45pm on the manicured grounds of the Marine Barracks (8th & I Streets, SE), the corps' oldest post. Reservations are

St Patrick's Day parade. *See p21.*

National Cherry Blossom Festival. *See p21.*

required, though unclaimed seats are sometimes available at the time. The affiliated Commandant's Own drum and bugle corps performs a weekly Sunset Parade at the Iwo Jima memorial statue, adjacent to Arlington Cemetery; start time is 7pm and reservations are not required.

Capital Jazz Fest
Merriweather Post Pavilion, Columbia, MD (1-301 780 9300, www.capitaljazz.com/fest). **Date** early June.
Billed as 'the Woodstock of jazz festivals', this outdoor extravaganza in Columbia, Maryland, serves up food, crafts, and, of course, some of the best jazz musicians around. Dave Koz, Eric Benét, Walter Beasley, David Benoit, Incognito and India Arie are among past headliners.

Dupont-Kalorama Museum Walk Weekend
1-202 387 4062 ext 12, www.dkmuseums.com. **Date** early June.
Hidden-treasure museums and historically important houses in Dupont Circle and the neighbouring Kalorama area take part in an 'off the Mall' museum day for the public. Free food, music, tours and crafts are added bonuses.

Susan G. Komen Race for the Cure
Starts at Constitution Avenue, NW, at 9th Street for runners and 12th Street for walkers, The Mall & Tidal Basin (1-877 465 6636, ww5.komen.org). Federal Triangle Metro. **Date** early June. **Map** p252 H6.
It's said to be the biggest five-kilometre run/walk in the world. The Race for the Cure draws tens of thousands of participants to raise money for and awareness of breast cancer.

DanceAfrica DC: The Annual Festival
Dance Place, 3225 8th Street, NE, at Monroe Street, Northeast (1-202 269 1600, www.dance place.org). Brookland-CUA Metro. **Date** late May-early June. **Map** p251 M2.
A week of masterclasses culminates in a weekend festival celebrating African and African American dance, with free outdoor performances, crafts and food, plus ticketed main stage events indoors. Note that an admission price is charged for some events.

National Capital Barbecue Battle
Pennsylvania Avenue, NW, between 9th & 14th Streets, Federal Triangle (1-202 828 3099, www.bbqdc.com). Metro Archives-Navy Memorial. **Date** late June. **Map** p252/p253 J6.
For more than two decades, barbecue wizards have gathered to compete for titles that now, astonishingly, carry more than $40,000 in prize money. Tens of thousands throng the nation's Main Street to sample glorious ribs, chicken and every other form of barbecue imaginable. Celebs, music, children's activities and much more to go with the food.

Smithsonian Folklife Festival
National Mall, between 10th & 15th Streets, The Mall & Tidal Basin (1-202 357 2700, recorded information 1-202 633 9884, www.folklife.si.edu). Smithsonian Metro. **Date** late June & early July. **Map** p252 H7.
This monster festival celebrates the arts, crafts and food of selected US states and other countries. Food and demonstration booths stretch down the National Mall, and there are evening celebrations and music performances. The atmosphere is cheerful, the weather usually hot and sticky. The themes for 2013 were Hungarian heritage, endangered languages, and African American dress and adornment.

IN FOCUS

Independence Day

*Various venues (information 1-202 789 7000,
www.washington.org).* **Date** 4 July.

Steer clear of this one if you hate crowds (nearly
700,000 people generally turn up), or if the now
rather pervasive security makes you think of Mr
Orwell (the legacy of 9/11 means that Fourth of July
revellers now encounter a fenced-off National Mall,
with checkpoints through which to enter). Official
events begin at 10am at the National Archives,
with a dramatic reading of the Declaration of
Independence, demonstrations of colonial military
manoeuvres, and more. Just before noon, the
Independence Day parade starts to wind its way
down Constitution Avenue (from the National
Archives to 17th Street), and later (5-9.15pm) the
grounds of the Washington Monument host entertainment – folk music, jazz, marching bands, military singers – and hordes of revellers. The National
Symphony Orchestra performs a concert on the
West Lawn of the US Capitol building at 8pm, traditionally concluding with a battery of cannons
assisting in the finale of Tchaikovsky's 1812
Overture; then, at roughly 9pm, a stupendous array
of fireworks is set off over the Washington
Monument. Logistical hassles or no, it's a grand
sight: the monuments are lovely in the summer dusk,
and the barrages involve thousands of rounds of
explosives. Walk to the festivities if you can: Fourth
of July crowds eat up parking spots and test the limits of the public transport system. Check local listings for smaller celebrations.

Memorial Day. *See p22.*

AUTUMN

Adams Morgan Day

*18th Street, NW, between Columbia Road &
Florida Avenue, Adams Morgan (1-202 328
9451, www.adamsmorgandayfestival.com).
Dupont Circle or Woodley Park Metro.* **Date**
2nd Sun in Sept. **Map** p250 G2.

For over a quarter of a century, thousands of DC residents have come out to celebrate this community,
home to large Latino, white, African and African
American populations. Musicians, crafts and ethnic
foods are in ample supply.

National Book Fair

*National Mall, NW, between 7th & 14th Streets
(1-202 888 714 4696, www.loc.gov/bookfest).
Archives-Naval Memorial or Federal Triangle
Metro.* **Date** late Sept or early Oct. **Map** p252 H7.

Sponsored by the Library of Congress, the Book Fair
features dozens of authors, illustrators, poets and sto-
rytellers, all reading, performing and signing in block
after block of pavilions themed around 'Fiction and
Imagination', 'History and Biography', 'Mysteries and
Thrillers' and so on. Admission is free.

Annual High Heel Race

*17th Street, NW, between S & P Streets, Dupont
Circle (information from JR's bar 1-202 328
0090, www.jrswdc.com). Dupont Circle Metro.*
Date on or around 31 Oct. **Map** p250 H4.

Dupont Circle residents and gawkers from across
the city swarm to 17th Street to catch this ultimate
drag race, which features outrageously costumed
contestants promenading up and down – then
sprinting down a two-block stretch in the heart of
the capital's gay ghetto. The event itself lasts only
minutes, but the street-party atmosphere is festive
and the scenery fabulous.

Marine Corps Marathon

1-800 786 8762, www.marinemarathon.com.
Date late Oct.

The 'Marathon of Monuments' draws around 30,000
runners from around the world, and no wonder: the
course winds along the banks of the Potomac, through
Georgetown and Rock Creek Park, past the city's most
famous sites and monuments, finishing at the Iwo
Jima memorial in Arlington. Spectators and supporters turn the route into a 26-mile street party.

Veterans' Day ceremonies

*Arlington National Cemetery, Memorial Drive,
Arlington Drive, VA (1-703 607 8000, www.
arlingtoncemetery.org). Arlington Cemetery
Metro.* **Date** 11am Veterans' Day (11 Nov).

A solemn ceremony with military bands, in honour
of the country's war dead. Ceremonies are also held
at the Vietnam Veterans Memorial (details on 1-202
426 6841), Mount Vernon (1-703 780 2000) and the
US Navy Memorial (1-202 737 2300).

Capital Pride. *See p22.*

WINTER

National Christmas Tree Lighting

The Ellipse, The Mall & Tidal Basin (1-202 426 6841). Federal Triangle Metro. **Date** early Dec. **Map** p252 H6.

The president kicks off the holiday season by switching on the lights on the giant National Christmas Tree. (There's a National Menorah, too, which gets lit on the appropriate night.) For a seat in the enclosure, you'll need a ticket: apply at least six weeks in advance as they run out fast. The ticketless, though, can usually get a glimpse from the other side of the fence. The ceremony begins at 5pm; arrive early. From now until New Year's Day, the Ellipse hosts Christmas performances as part of the annual Pageant of Peace.

New Year's Eve celebrations

Events around town range from relatively inexpensive celebrations at the Kennedy Center (music and dancing in the Grand Foyer) to dinners at some of the area's more upscale dining establishments costing hundreds of dollars. Restaurants and clubs often offer jazz, dinner and a champagne toast for a fixed but generally substantial price (most start taking reservations early); check ads in the *Washington City Paper* and the *Washington Post*.

Martin Luther King Jr's Birthday Celebrations

1-202 727 1186, WPAS concert information 1-202 833 9800, www.wpas.org. **Date** 3rd wk in Jan.

A birthday celebration is held on the steps of the Lincoln Memorial, where Dr King gave his famous 'I have a dream' speech in 1963. That's just one of many, many commemorations in DC. Among others: the Washington Performing Arts Society (WPAS) hosts an annual children's concert with Sweet Honey in the Rock, who combine gospel, African rhythms and rap into a cappella combinations. A tremendous show.

Chinese New Year

Chinatown, H Street, NW, between 6th & 9th Streets, Downtown. Gallery Place-Chinatown Metro. **Date** from 31 Jan 2014, 19 Feb 2015. **Map** p253 J5.

Celebrations kick off with a bang – dancers, dragons, firecrackers and parades – and continue, a bit more muted, for ten days. Look out for details near the time or contact the Chinese Consolidated Benevolent Association at 1-703 851 5685.

Black History Month

Date Feb.

The Smithsonian Institution holds special events, exhibitions and cultural programmes throughout the month. For more information on the activities on offer, check newspaper listings or contact the Martin Luther King Library (*see p232*).

Famous birthdays

Information Lincoln 1-202 426 6841, Washington 1-703 780 2000, Douglass 1-202 426 5960. **Date** Feb.

A trio of famous men's birthdays. A celebration of Abe Lincoln's birthday (12 February) is held at the Lincoln Memorial; Lincoln's Gettysburg Address is read and a wreath is laid. For hardcore history buffs only. George Washington's birthday celebration, with a patriotic military programme and a George Washington impersonator, is held (on the third Monday in February) at Mount Vernon, Virginia (*see p200* **Presidents in Residence**). The Frederick Douglass birthday tribute is held on or near 14 February at the Frederick Douglass National Historic Site, 1411 W Street, SE, at 14th Street, Anacostia.

Explore

The Monumental Centre

Monuments, museums and the Mall.

EXPLORE

The Monumental Centre is the neo-classical heart of picture-postcard Washington, centred on a long swathe of green – the National Mall – which is crowned by the Capitol at its eastern end. The area's distinctive look is a result of George Washington's wish that his new nation have a suitably imposing capital – and for a man of his era, a classical style that referenced Athenian democracy was the way to achieve this. He hired Pierre-Charles L'Enfant to design the fledgling city. The L'Enfant Plan consisted of a grid system; superimposed on this were

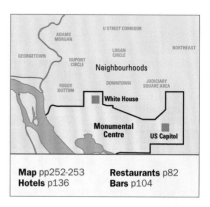

| Map pp252-253 | Restaurants p82 |
| Hotels p136 | Bars p104 |

broad diagonal avenues radiating from ceremonial squares and circles, and from the Capitol and White House. And given that the one thing a government is good at doing is producing plans, sure enough, in 1902, another scheme – the McMillan Plan – reinterpreted L'Enfant's original vision. Now, more than a century later, the National Capital Planning Commission referees continual development debates over the quasi-sacred space of the Mall and its immediate surrounds.

THE MALL & TIDAL BASIN
The Mall from west to east

The western boundary of the Mall centres on the iconic **Lincoln Memorial** (*see p32*), in front of the long Reflecting Pool. It has been the site of many demonstrations; perhaps most famously, it was the location from which Martin Luther King delivered his 'I have a dream' speech. Beyond rises the needle of the Washington Monument and, finally, at the eastern end of the Mall, the Capitol, two miles away.

Starting south-east of the Lincoln Memorial, across the Tidal Basin, the circular **Jefferson Memorial** (*see p32*) commemorates the third US president and author of the Declaration of Independence. Tucked just to the south is a monument to Thomas Jefferson's contemporary and friend, the local Revolutionary-era thinker

George Mason, portrayed relaxing on a bench with his ever-present books.

The **Franklin Delano Roosevelt Memorial** (*see p31*) enlivens West Potomac Park, across the cherry tree-rimmed Tidal Basin, which has paddleboats for rent. Nearby, a new memorial to civil rights leader **Martin Luther King** (*see p30* **A Stone of Hope**) opened to the public in August 2011. This latest monument to grace the Mall features a statue of King, and a wall of quotations from his writings and speeches.

Two war monuments flank Lincoln's. To the north-east is the V-shaped black wedge of the **Vietnam Veterans Memorial** (*see p38*); to the south-east is the evocative **Korean War Veterans Memorial** (*see p32*). Walking east past Constitution Gardens on the Mall's northern border, you first encounter the **National World War II Memorial** (*see p37*). Aligned with the Lincoln Memorial, the long Reflecting Pool lies between the two structures. Next is the starkly impressive obelisk of the **Washington Monument** (*see p39*), honouring the 'father of his country', who selected this site for its capital. The monument is currently closed for renovations following earthquake damage in 2011; it is expected to reopen in 2014.

To the north spreads the Ellipse, formally the President's Park South. It contains the **Boy Scout Memorial**, in Socialist Realist style, and the **First Division Memorial**, an 80-foot monument to the soldiers of the First Division of the US Army. Atop is a gilded bronze Victory. On the north of the Ellipse is the **Zero Milestone**, from which distances from the capital are measured.

The Washington Monument overlooks museumland. Nearest to it, on the Mall's north side, is the **National Museum of American History** (*see p37*). The turreted red fortress, guarded by a carousel, is the **Smithsonian Castle** (*see p41*), which houses an information centre and the crypt for Smithsonian benefactor, Englishman James Smithson.

Clustered about are the palazzo-like **Freer Gallery** (Asian art, *see p31*); its younger sibling, the subterranean **Arthur M Sackler Gallery** (*see p31*); the Sackler's twin, the **National Museum of African Art** (*see p35*); and the neo-Gothic **Arts & Industries Building**, currently under renovation; it's scheduled to reopen in 2014. Further along are the doughnut-shaped **Hirshhorn Museum & Sculpture Garden**; the modernist glass and marble of the **National Air & Space Museum** (*see p32*) – the world's most visited museum; and the organic, curving structure of the **National Museum of the American Indian** (*see p37*).

INSIDE TRACK
ACCESS ALL AREAS

No opening times are listed for the Franklin, Jefferson, Korean War Veterans, Lincoln, Martin Luther King, National World War II and Vietnam Veterans memorials. These can be accessed 24 hours a day. Rangers are usually on duty to assist from 9.30am to 11.30pm (or 11pm in the case of the Korean War Veterans Memorial).

On the north side of the Mall, the space between 14th and 15th Streets is designated for the **National Museum of African American History & Culture** (http://nmaahc.si.edu). Construction began in 2012 and should be completed in 2015. In the meantime, items from its collection are on show in the adjacent National Museum of American History. Next door, between 9th and 12th Streets, is the **National Museum of Natural History** (*see p37*). An adjacent sculpture garden's pool becomes an ice rink in winter. Next in line, the neo-classical West Building of the **National Gallery of Art** (*see p33*) contrasts with the angular geometry of its East Building.

On the far side of the Capitol Reflecting Pool, at the foot of Capitol Hill, stands a sprawling sculptural group that features an equestrian statue of Ulysses S Grant, the triumphant Union general, modelled after the Victor Emmanuel memorial in Rome. Crowning the hill is the **United States Capitol** (*see p45*), whose dome Lincoln insisted be finished during the Civil War as a symbol of the Union's durability.

EXPLORE

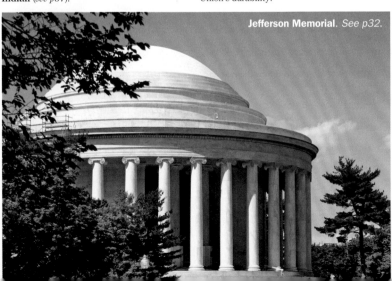

Jefferson Memorial. *See p32.*

A Stone of Hope

The new Martin Luther King Memorial.

It's been a long time coming, but African Americans have finally found their place on the National Mall. The National Museum of African American History & Culture is set to open in 2015, and the Martin Luther King Memorial was dedicated in late 2011 – the result of years of campaigning and fundraising. On the south-west of the Mall, with an official address – 1964 Independence Avenue – that references the year of the passing of the Civil Rights Act, the location was chosen to create a symbolic, visual 'line of leadership' with the Lincoln Memorial. It was here that King made his legendary 'I have a dream' speech in 1963 at the culmination of the March on Washington.

Quotes from King's various speeches and sermons are carved, in no particular order, on a 450-foot-long crescent-shaped 'inscription wall' on the memorial site. Covering four acres, the landscaped site – with plenty of seating and planted with elms and cherry trees – is dominated by a colossal statue, a 30-foot relief sculpture of King hewn from an oblong of cream granite. Behind him is another large chunk of granite, roughly carved into a mountain, split in two. The oblong 'stone' is positioned to look as if it has been pulled out from the middle of the 'mountain'. The symbolism becomes clear when visitors read the King quote on the stone, 'Out of the mountain of despair, a stone of hope.'

The inscription on the other side of the statue – 'I was a drum major for justice, peace and righteousness' – has been the cause of some controversy. It emerged that the quote was actually a paraphrase of 'If you want to say I was a drum major, say I was a drum major for justice. I was a drum major for righteousness. And all of the other shallow things won't matter.' The change didn't go down well with critics, among them writer Maya Angelou, a consultant on the project, who remarked that the paraphrase made King look like 'an arrogant twit'. It was announced first that the quote would be corrected, and then, in December 2012, that it would actually be removed, the original sculptor, Lei Yixin, having said that this was the best way to ensure the structural integrity of the memorial.

The choice of Lei as sculptor was also controversial, partly because the Chinese

artist had previously made a sculpture of Mao; the fact that the Chinese government made a $25-million contribution to meet a shortfall in donations also received critical attention. There were those (including the Commission for Fine Arts, which eventually gave its official approval to the design) who criticised the Socialist Realist feel of the piece. Some complained about the sternness of King's appearance, or the fact that an African American artist wasn't used. Others have praised the memorial.

All that is certain is that when it comes to the 'language of enshrinement', and a figure who generates so much emotion, there are a lot of competing voices.

For listings, see p32.

FREE Arthur M Sackler Gallery (S)

1050 Independence Avenue, SW, between 11th &
12th Streets (1-202 633 4880, www.asia.si.edu).
Smithsonian Metro. **Open** *July-mid Aug* 10am-
5.30pm daily. **Admission** free. **Map** p252 J7.
The Sackler contains some of the most important
holdings of Asian art in the world. It has more flexibility than its neighbour, the Freer Gallery (*see below*),
whose mandate forbids the exhibition of anything
from outside its collection. The Sackler, on the other
hand, stages international loan exhibitions of Asian
art (a recent show featured Ai Wei Wei).

Connected to the Freer by an underground pas-
sageway, the Sackler was built up around a 1,000-
piece Asian art gift from Dr Arthur M Sackler.
Visitors enter through architects Shepley Bulfinch
Richardson and Abbott's first-floor granite pavilion
(a similar pavilion, by the same firm, is at the National
Museum of African Art). You then head below ground
into a maze of overlapping bridges and long passage-
ways that give the feel of an ancient temple. Artefacts
on permanent display include a large collection of
pieces from China – among them ancient Chinese
jades and bronzes, plus paintings, objects and callig-
raphy from later eras. There's also sacred Buddhist
and Hindu sculpture from South Asia and the
Himalayas, dating from the 10th to the 18th century,
along with contemporary Asian art ranging from
Japanese ceramics to *Monkeys Grasping for the Moon*,
a sculpture designed for the museum by Chinese artist
Xu Bing and displayed in the museum's atrium.

In the galleries connecting the Freer and Sackler is
a new installation of gold and silver Iranian pieces
dating from the fourth to the seventh centuries.
▶ *For children's activities at the museum, see p156.*

FREE Franklin Delano Roosevelt Memorial

Off West Basin Drive, SW, at the Tidal Basin (1-
202 426 6841, www.nps.gov/fdrm). Smithsonian
Metro. **Map** p252 G7.
FDR, who led the country through the Great
Depression and World War II, was the only president
to be elected four times. In 1997, designer Lawrence
Halprin created an epic monument here. The four 'galleries' combine waterfalls, giant stones engraved with
memorable quotations and sculptures (including a
statue of Eleanor Roosevelt, the first First Lady to be
honoured in a national memorial). Disabled advocates
objected that the original, somewhat dyspeptic statue
of the polio-stricken president only hinted that he used
a wheelchair. A second, jauntier FDR, with wheels in
full view, joined the display in 2001.
▶ *Roosevelt himself favoured a simple desk-sized*
memorial slab. One was made and is still on
display, outside the National Archives.

FREE Freer Gallery of Art (S)

Jefferson Drive, SW, at 12th Street (1-202 633
4880, www.asia.si.edu). Smithsonian Metro. **Open**
10am-5.30pm daily. **Admission** free. **Map** p252 J7.

When Detroit business magnate Charles Lang Freer
(1854-1919) began collecting the works of American
painter James McNeill Whistler in the 1880s, the
artist encouraged him also to collect Asian art while
on his travels to the Middle and Far East. Freer did
so, and he eventually amassed Neolithic Chinese pottery, Japanese screens and Hindu temple sculpture,
along with works by 19th-century American
painters – which included over 1,300 works by
Whistler. A room interior, the *Peacock Room*,
painted by Whistler in 1876-77, is probably the
gallery's best-known piece.

In 1904, Freer offered his collection to the
Smithsonian, which commissioned this dignified,
grey granite, Renaissance palazzo-style building
from architect Charles Adam Platt to house it; it
opened in 1923. The collection's mandate precludes
any lending of its 26,500-piece holdings, which are
rotated regularly on display. Occasional special
exhibitions are small but smart. An underground
passage connects the Freer to the neighbouring
Sackler Gallery.
▶ *For more on the Peacock Room, see p63*
Treasure Rooms. For films at the Freer,
see p162.

★ FREE Hirshhorn Museum & Sculpture Garden (S)

Independence Avenue, SW, at 7th Street (1-202
633 4674, www.hirshhorn.si.edu). L'Enfant Plaza
Metro. **Open** *Museum* 10am-5.30m daily. *Plaza*
7.30am-5.30pm daily. *Sculpture Garden* 7.30am-
dusk daily. **Admission** free. **Map** p253 J7.
This spectacular, aggressively modern cylindrical
building by Skidmore, Owings and Merrill enlivens
the predominantly neoclassical architecture lining the
Mall. The purpose of the structure, which was completed in 1974, was to house self-made Wall Street
millionaire Joseph Hirshhorn's collection of 20th-
century painting and sculpture. The museum now
presents art in a range of media, including works on
paper, painting, installation, photography, sculpture,
digital and video art. SOM's chief architect, Gordon
Bunshaft, has created a three-storey hollow concrete
drum supported on four curvilinear piers. In keeping
with the modernist tradition, there is no ceremonial
entrance, only a utilitarian revolving door (strictly
speaking there are two, but usually only one is in use).

Third-level galleries house works from the permanent collection. These include a significant
Giacometti collection, the largest public collection of
works by Thomas Eakins outside the artist's native
Philadelphia, works by Arshile Gorky and Clyfford
Still and a pair of Willem de Kooning's rare 'door
paintings' (the museum has the largest public collection of his work in the world).

On the second level are rotating exhibitions.
These might explore the work of a particular artist,
or a theme. From October 2013 to February 2014,
Damage Control: Art & Destruction Since 1950
explores the use by artists of destruction as part of

EXPLORE

the creative process, beginning in the era of the atomic bomb and the fear of mutually assured destruction.

The basement galleries house large-scale installations, often recent acquisitions, and rotating moving-image artwork in the museum's 'Black Box'. The museum also offers the well-regarded Directions series, spotlighting emerging or cutting-edge artists.

The Sculpture Garden is located on the side of the gallery facing the National Mall, across Jefferson Drive. It has works by Rodin, Matisse, Koons, Calder and more, set amid green space and a reflecting pool.

► *For films at the National Gallery, see p162.*

FREE Jefferson Memorial

Southern end of 15th Street, SW, at the Tidal Basin & East Basin Drive (1-202 426 6841, www.nps.gov/thje). Smithsonian Metro. **Map** p252 H8.

FDR promoted this 1943 shrine to the founder of his Democratic Party, balancing that to the Republicans' icon, Lincoln. Roosevelt liked it so much he had trees cleared so he could see it from the Oval Office. John Russell Pope designed an adaptation (sneered at by some as 'Jefferson's muffin') of the Roman Pantheon that the architect Jefferson so admired. It echoes the president's designs for his home, Monticello, and for his rotunda at the University of Virginia. The Georgia marble walls surrounding Jefferson's 19ft likeness are inscribed with his enduring words. Alas, the 92-word quote from the Declaration of Independence contains 11 spelling mistakes and other inaccuracies. *Photo p29.*

FREE Korean War Veterans Memorial

The Mall, SW, just south of Reflecting Pool & adjacent to Lincoln Memorial, at Daniel French Drive & Independence Avenue (1-202 426 6841, www.nps.gov/kwvm). Smithsonian Metro. **Map** p252 G7.

This monument, which honours the 12 million Americans who fought in the Cold War conflict in Korea, features 19 battle-clad, seven-foot soldiers slogging across a V-shaped field towards a distant US flag. Their finely detailed faces reflect the fatigue and pain of battle, while bulky packs show beneath their ponchos. Reflected in the polished granite wall, these 19 become 38 – in reference to the 38th parallel separating North and South Korea. Unlike the wall at the Vietnam Veterans Memorial, this shows a subtle mural sandblasted into rock,

---

INSIDE TRACK EARLY BIRD

The **Smithsonian Information Center** at the Castle (*see p41*) opens at 8.30am, an hour and a half ahead of the museums, so get there early and you'll have plenty of time to plan your day's schedule.

---

a photo-montage of the support troops – drivers and medics, nurses and chaplains.

★ FREE Lincoln Memorial

The Mall, 23rd Street, NW, between Henry Bacon Drive & Daniel French Drive (1-202 426 6841, www.nps.gov/linc). Smithsonian or Foggy Bottom-GWU Metro. **Map** p252 F7.

Despite its appearance on the penny and the $5 bill, the Lincoln Memorial is perhaps most recognisable as the site of historic demonstrations. In 1939, when the Daughters of the American Revolution barred the African American contralto Marian Anderson from singing in their Constitution Hall, she performed for more than 75,000 people from these steps. It was here that Martin Luther King delivered his 'I have a dream' speech in 1963. Just a few months later, President Lyndon Johnson led candle-carrying crowds in ceremonies concluding national mourning for John F Kennedy. Half a century after followed Lincoln's assassination in 1865 before Henry Bacon's classical design was chosen in 1911 (over proposals ranging from a triumphal arch to a memorial highway from Washington to Gettysburg).

The neo-classical 'cage' surrounding Lincoln has one Doric column representing each of the 36 states in the Union at the time of his death, their names inscribed above. The 19ft marble statue of Lincoln himself, by Daniel Chester French, peers out over the Reflecting Pool, his facial expression seeming to change at different times of day. Cut into the wall to the left of the entrance is Lincoln's Gettysburg Address; to the right is his second inaugural address.

FREE Martin Luther King Memorial

The Mall, 1964 Independence Avenue, SW (1 202-426-6841, www.nps.gov/mlkm). Smithsonian Metro. **Map** 252 J7.

See p30 **A Stone of Hope**.

FREE National Air & Space Museum (S)

6th Street & Independence Avenue, SW (1-202 633 1000, www.nasm.si.edu). L'Enfant Plaza Metro. **Open** 10am-5.30pm daily; 10am-7.30pm select dates late Mar-early Sept; phone or check website for details. **Admission** *Museum* free. *IMAX & Planetarium* films $9.50; $7.50 reductions. **Credit** AmEx, MC, V. **Map** p253 J7.

Air & Space tops visitors' to-do list, year in, year out. The imposing Tennessee marble modernist block, by Hellmuth, Obata and Kassabaum, incorporates three skylit, double-height galleries, which house missiles, aircraft and space stations. In the central Milestones of Flight hall, towering US Pershing-II and Soviet SS-20 nuclear missiles stand next to the popular moon rock station, where visitors can stroke a lunar sample acquired on the 1972 Apollo 17 mission. The 1903 *Wright Flyer* – the first piloted craft to maintain controlled, sustained flight (if only for a few seconds) – and Charles Lindbergh's *Spirit of St Louis* are both suspended here.

National Air & Space Museum.

Permanent exhibitions in the museum detail the history of jet aviation, space travel and satellite communications. Updates acknowledge modern information technology, but much of the collection's presentation maintains the quaint optimism of the early space age. Apollo to the Moon explores that era, while Moving Beyond Earth deals with contemporary space exploration and examines how humans live and work in space aboard the space shuttle and International Space Station. The gallery often features live presentations with guest astronauts and space pioneers. A new exhibition for 2013, Time & Navigation, explores how revolutions in time keeping over three centuries have influenced how we find our way.

The Albert Einstein Planetarium offers half-hour multimedia presentations about stars and outer space; the Langley Theater shows IMAX films on air and space flight. An upgrade involving dual digital projection and surround-sound gives viewers the sensation of speeding through the cosmos.

The museum's annex, the Steven F Udvar-Hazy Center, named after its major donor, opened in Chantilly, Virginia, in 2003. Its hangar-like halls hold the restored *Enola Gay*, the B-29 that dropped the first atomic bomb on Japan, and the space shuttle *Enterprise*, among other large-scale air-related artefacts. A shuttle bus service makes a round trip between the two outposts several times a day (tickets cost $15 for the round trip, and you're strongly advised to book in advance by calling 1-202 633 4629).

Other locations Steven F Udvar-Hazy Center, 14390 Air & Space Museum Parkway, Chantilly, VA (1-703 572 4118, http://airandspace.si.edu/udvarhazy).
▶ *The How Things Fly gallery is a favourite with children. For other child-friendly museums, see p155.*

★ FREE National Gallery of Art
West Building *Constitution Avenue, NW, between 4th & 7th Streets.*
East Building *Constitution Avenue, & 4th Street, NW.*
Both *1-202 737 4215, www.nga.gov. Archives-Navy Memorial, Judiciary Square or Smithsonian Metro.*
Open 10am-5pm Mon-Sat; 11am-6pm Sun.
Admission free. **Map** p253 J6.

Pittsburgh investment banker and industrialist Andrew Mellon was born the son of a poor Irish immigrant but went on to serve as US Treasury secretary from 1921 to 1932. In 1941, he presented the National Gallery's West Building as a gift to the nation. Mellon's son, Paul, created the gallery's East Building in 1978. Mellon junior, who had donated over 900 artworks during his lifetime, bequeathed $75 million and 100 paintings – including works by Monet, Renoir and Cézanne – on his death in 1999.

In designing the Tennessee marble West Building, architect John Russell Pope borrowed motifs from the temple architecture of the Roman Pantheon. The white marble stairs at the Constitution Avenue entrance lead to the main-floor rotunda, with its impressive green Italian marble

EXPLORE

floors and columns around a bubbling fountain encircled by fragrant flora and greenery. On this level, galleries lead off the building's 782ft longitudinal spine. The ground level houses galleries as well as a gift shop and garden court café. An underground concourse has a cafeteria, another shop and a moving walkway that connects the West Building to the skylit, IM Pei-designed East Building.

West Building

The West Building's skylit main floor covers European and American art from the 13th to the early 20th centuries. Exhibits begin in gallery 1 with Italian Gothic works 1270-1360, among them Giotto's seminal *Madonna and Child*. Pre- to high Renaissance Italian works represent a large proportion of the collection; highlights include Leonardo da Vinci's almond-eyed portrait of *Ginevra de' Benci* (gallery 6) and Botticelli's *Adoration of the Magi*. Giovanni Bellini and Titian's *Feast of the Gods* commands Gallery 17, to the north of the West Garden Court.

Late medieval Flemish highlights include Jan Van Eyck's *Annunciation* (gallery 39). Unmistakeable among the Netherlandish works 1485-1590 in gallery 41 is Hieronymus Bosch's *Death and the Miser*.

Spanish, Dutch, Flemish, French and German works of the 17th century also have a large presence (galleries 29-34, 36, 37, 42-51). Among them are works by Vermeer (*Woman Holding a Balance*, in gallery 50A) and Rembrandt's 1659 self-portrait, with his intense gaze, in gallery 48.

On the east side of the Rotunda, there's 18th- and 19th-century Spanish painting (gallery 52), including Goya's *The Marquesa de Pontejos*. Highlights among the French paintings of a similar era in galleries 53-56 include work by Jean Simeon Chardin in gallery 53 and Jacques-Louis David's *The Emperor Napoleon in his Study at the Tuileries* (gallery 56). British landscapes by Turner and Constable are in gallery 57, among them Turner's *Keelmen Heaving Coals by Moonlight*, while gallery 58 is devoted to portraits by Gainsborough and Reynolds. Galleries 60-60B and 62-71 are the American rooms. Among the works are naive paintings in gallery 63, immense and idealised 19th-century landscapes, such as Thomas Cole's *A View of the Mountain Pass Called the Notch of the White Mountains* (gallery 64). George Catlin's distinctive American Indian portraits are in gallery 65. American Impressionism 1860-1925, in gallery 70, includes John Singer Sargent's *Repose*. Early 20th-century American painting in gallery 71 includes

Edward Hopper's *Cape Cod Evening*. Galleries 80-93 feature 19th-century French work.

Downstairs, the West Wing sculpture galleries, which occupy the entire north-west quadrant of the building's ground floor, now register 24,000sq ft divided into 22 galleries, following a major expansion in 2002. More than 900 works on view, including masterpieces from the Middle Ages to the early 20th century. Visitors entering from the museum's 6th Street entrance encounter sculpture by Auguste Rodin and Augustus Saint-Gaudens. From there, they move in reverse chronological order from the 19th century to the Middle Ages, with detours into a pair of galleries housing early modern sculpture. Highlights of the collection include Leone Battista Alberti's bronze *Self-Portrait* plaque (c1435); Honoré Daumier's entire bronze sculptural oeuvre, including all 36 of his caricatures of French government officials; and the world's largest collection of Edgar Degas original wax and mixed-media sculptures.

The Micro Gallery, just inside the West Building's main-floor Mall entrance, has 15 individual cubicles with touch-screen colour monitors where visitors can learn more about individual works, movements, artists and the precise location of each work. Conservation techniques are also explained.

The concourse tunnel to the East Building takes you on a moving walkway through what seems like a fantastic journey through the Milky Way; swathes of starry lights seem to ebb and flow above you. Called *Multiverse*, the installation is the work of American artist Leo Villareal.

East Building

The East Building's triple-height, skylit atrium is dominated by Alexander Calder's 32ft by 81ft aluminium and steel mobile. The gallery's small but strong collection of modern and contemporary art includes several must-sees on view in the concourse-level galleries. Don't miss Barnett Newman's minimalist *Stations of the Cross*, a 15-panel installation of monochromatic paintings that ring the walls of a dedicated room (gallery 29A). Salvador Dali's *Sacrament of the Last Supper* hangs in the mezzanine elevator lobby. The East Building devotes much of its space to temporary exhibitions.

Sculpture Garden

The gallery opened a sculpture garden in 1998 on a six-acre square across 7th Street from the West Building. Designed by Philadelphia landscape architect Laurie Olin, the garden's circular fountain bubbles in summer, and is transformed into an ice rink in winter. Among trees are Louise Bourgeois's 10ft

bronze cast *Spider*, whose spindly legs span 24ft, Sol LeWitt's 15ft concrete *Four-Sided Pyramid*, and Tony Smith's stout *Moondog*.

FREE National Museum of African Art (S)
950 Independence Avenue, SW, between 7th & 12th Streets (1-202 633 4600, http://africa.si.edu). *Smithsonian Metro.* **Open** 10am-5.30pm daily. **Admission** free. **Map** p252 J7.

This museum's entrance pavilion, designed by Shepley Bulfinch Richardson and Abbott, lies across the amazing Enid Haupt Garden from its twin, the Sackler (*see p31*). The primary focus of the collection, which opened in 1987, is ancient and contemporary work from sub-Saharan Africa. The museum offers a changing selection of 'highlights', drawing viewers into different aspects of African art and – by extension – culture. At the time of writing, Artful Animals, Musical Instruments and African Cosmos: Stellar Arts were among the featured topics. Temporary shows present a wide variety of visual arts, including sculptures, textiles, ceramics and photos. Contemporary art surveys are also included in the museum's roster. Earth Matters: Land as Material and Metaphor in the Arts of Africa runs until 4 January 2014. It brings

National Gallery Of Art. *See p33.*

EXPLORE

National Museum of the
American Indian.

EXPLORE

together around 100 works from the 18th to the 21st centuries that examine the relationship between artists and the land.

★ FREE National Museum of American History (S)

Constitution Avenue, NW, at 14th Street, NW (1-202 633 1000, www.americanhistory.si.edu). **Open** 10am-5.30pm daily; 10am-7.30pm many dates early May-early Sept; phone or check website for details. West Wing currently closed for renovation. **Admission** free. **Map** p252 H6.
The continuing transformation of the National Museum of American History led to the closing of the west wing for renovation in 2012 – it's scheduled to reopen in 2015. A first-stage renovation (completed 2008) created a central atrium, a grand staircase, ten-foot artefact walls on the first and second floors, as well as a dedicated Star-Spangled Banner gallery.

Floors are organised around loose themes, allowing a huge diversity of exhibits to tell American stories in a populist, entertaining and informative manner. At ground level, the theme is Transportation and Technology. Among the exhibitions, America on the Move chronicles the changing ways Americans have got around a large country and how different modes of transport have transformed the nation. Exhibits here include a Southern Railways locomotive, all 199 tons of it, along with a reconstructed 1920s railway station. Also examined is the evenutal domination of cars over public transport and how this enabled the suburbanisation of America. Also here is Food: Transforming the American Table 1950-2000. The kitchen (plus contents) of America's best-known chef, Julia Childs, forms a substantial part of the exhibition, which explores how technology, as well as social and cultural shifts, have changed the way we eat. Visitors are encouraged to sit at the large, communal table in the centre of the exhibition to share their own thoughts and experiences about food and change. Other exhibitions cover money, electricity, machinery and shipping.

The second floor is devoted to American Ideals. One gallery holds the nucleus of the collection that will find its way into the National Museum of African American History & Culture when it opens in 2015. A new signature exhibition, American Stories, allows visitors to follow a chronology of American history from the Pilgrims' arrival to the 2008 presidential election. Among the 100-plus items on display are iconic pieces of popular culture, among them Kermit from the Muppets and Dorothy's red shoes from *The Wizard of Oz*. The sole exhibition remaining open in the west wing at the time of writing, Within These Walls, contains a partially reconstructed house that stood for 200 years in Ipswich, Massachusetts, and tells the stories of five families who lived there over the years. Also here is the museum's Documents Gallery.

A highlight of the third floor, dedicated to American Wars and Politics, is the First Ladies exhibition. The exhibition is known for its collection of inaugural gowns, and its focus on the First Lady's role as hostess, but it now contains more than 1,000 objects, documenting the lives and contributions of America's first ladies, both in the White House and beyond. On the same floor, American Presidency: a Glorious Burden examines the nation's highest office and the men who have occupied it, while the Price of Freedom: America at War documents the American experience from the French and Indian Wars to the conflict in Iraq, exploring wars as defining episodes in politics, culture and personal experience.

▶ *For more on the Star-Spangled Banner, see p209* **Profile**.

★ FREE National Museum of the American Indian (S)

Independence Avenue & 4th Street, SW (1-202 633 1000, www.nmai.si.edu). L'Enfant Plaza Metro. **Open** 10am-5.30pm daily. **Admission** free. **Map** p253 J7.

Dedicated to America's colonised and historically abused indigenous people, the National Museum of the American Indian is the most recent addition to the Mall's museum ring – a status it will lose once the National Museum of African American History Culture opens. The structure was designed by a Native American team; the building is as much a part of the message as the exhibits. The details are extraordinary: dramatic, Kasota limestone-clad undulating walls resemble a wind-carved mesa; the museum's main entrance plaza plots the star configurations on 28 November 1989, the date that federal legislation was introduced to create the museum; fountains enliven outdoor walkways. Outside, landscaping and planting (more than 27,000 trees, shrubs and plants, representing 145 species) have created a natural environment that recalls that existed prior to European contact, when the Chesapeake Bay region abounded in forests, wetlands, meadows, and Algonquian peoples' croplands.

Visitors enter at the dramatic Potomac Hall rotunda, with its soaring 120ft stepped dome. The museum's permanent collection, exhibited on the third and fourth floors, orbits around thousands of works assembled at the turn of the 19th century by wealthy New Yorker George Gustav Heye, including intricate wood and stone carvings, hides and 18th-century materials from the Great Lakes region. Collections also include a substantial array of items from the Caribbean, Central and South America, including a dramatic quantity of gold, and the individual and non-stereotypical portraits of George Caitlin.

Native history from a native perspective is a theme of much of the rest of the material on show. Our Peoples looks at how contact changed the world, bringing disease, guns, Bibles and foreign governments to native peoples, and exporting corn, tobacco and chocolate. It focuses on eight tribes, from the Blackfeet of Montana to the Ka'apor of Brazil. Our Universes explores native cosmologies and traditions, including the Day of the Dead, which was eventually assimilated into Christian tradition. Our Lives

looks at life and identities in the 21st century through the experiences of eight communities, while Return to a Native Place: Algonquian Peoples of the Chesapeake focuses on tribes of the local area, telling the story through photographs and objects of how events from the 17th century to the present have impacted on lives.

A growing contemporary art collection is based around four broad themes: cultural memory and resistance; landscape and place; personal memory and identity; and history and the contemporary urban experience.

▶ *For the museum's unusual cafeteria, see below* **Inside Track**.

★ FREE National Museum of Natural History (S)

10th Street & Constitution Avenue, NW (1-202 633 1000, www.mnh.si.edu). Smithsonian Metro. **Open** 10am-5.30pm daily. **Admission** free. **Map** p252 J6.

The gem at the heart of the Museum of Natural History is a state-of-the-art IMAX cinema and an 80,000sq ft brushed steel and granite Discovery Center housing a cafeteria and exhibition space. The rotunda, too, is an impressive structure, dominated by an eight-ton African elephant. In 2003, the museum's restored west wing opened its glistening, 25,000sq ft Kenneth E Behring Hall of Mammals, featuring interactive displays alongside 274 taxidermied animals striking dramatic poses. The gem and mineral collection attracts spectators, who ring two-deep the very well-guarded 45.52-carat cut blue Hope Diamond. The David H Koch Hall of Human Origins tells the story of evolution, examining scientific evidence and providing striking representations of early humans, while the Sant Ocean Hall examines the world's oceans through items from the museum's collections, as well as research in marine science. The museum is a real magnet for children: its Dinosaur Hall has an assortment of fierce-looking dinosaur skeletons and a 3.4-billion-year-old stromatolite; tarantulas and other live arthropods ripe for petting inhabit the Insect Zoo.

FREE National World War II Memorial

The Mall, 17th Street, from Independence to Constitution Avenues, at eastern end of Reflecting Pool (1-202 426 6841, www.wwii memorial.com). Smithsonian or Farragut West Metro. **Map** p252 G6/7.

> **INSIDE TRACK**
> **AMERICAN INDIAN DISHES**
>
> The cafeteria at the **National Museum of the American Indian** (*see left*) serves traditional Native dishes from around the continent.

EXPLORE

Dedicated in 2004, the monument that honours America's 'Greatest Generation' is a grandiose affair on a 7.4-acre plot. Designed by Friedrich St Florian, it is a granite-heavy space dominated by the central Rainbow Pool, which is set between two 43ft triumphal arches, representing the Atlantic and Pacific theatres of war. Fifty-six wreath-crowned pillars represent the US states and territories (including the Philippines), while a bronze Freedom Wall displays 4,000 gold stars, each signifying 100 war dead. The ceremonial entrance, descending from 17th Street, passes bas-reliefs depicting events of the global conflict. A Circle of Remembrance garden off to the side fosters quiet reflection. A visitor kiosk and rest-rooms clutter the periphery.

The memorial attracted controversy at the time of its inauguration, partly due to its location (the land is boggy enough to require pumping and, in addition, the monument breaks the sweep of the Mall), and partly because of its heavy neo-classical design, which prompted *Der Spiegel* to quip that to look at the monument, one would think that Hitler had won. However, the memorial's apologia is engraved in granite at the 17th Street entrance, saying why those who defended freedom during World War II fully deserve their place between the heroes of the 18th (Washington) and 19th (Lincoln) centuries. To partly preserve the open vista, the memorial was sunk below street level.

FREE Vietnam Veterans Memorial

West Potomac Park, just north of the Reflecting Pool, at Henry Bacon Drive & Constitution Avenue, NW (1-202 462 6841, www.nps.gov/vive). Foggy Bottom or Smithsonian Metro.
Map p252 G6.

The sombre black granite walls of the Vietnam Veterans Memorial have become a shrine, with pilgrims coming to touch the more than 58,000 names, make pencil rubbings and leave flowers, letters and flags. In 1981, 21-year-old Yale University senior Maya Ying Lin won the nationwide competition with this striking abstract design – two walls, each just over 246ft long – angled to enfold the Washington Monument and the Lincoln Memorial in a symbolic embrace. Political pressures forced later additions: first, a flagpole, then a sculpture by Frederick Hart of three Vietnam GIs. In 1993 came the Vietnam Women's Memorial, a sculpture group inspired by Michelangelo's *Pietà*. Happily, these additions were placed harmoniously.

Names on the wall appear in the chronological order that they became casualties. To descend gradually past the thousands of names to the nadir, then slowly emerge, is to follow symbolically America's journey into an increasingly ferocious war, only to try to 'wind it down' over years. It can be a genuinely touching experience.

Fundraising is currently under way for an education centre at the memorial.

National World War II Memorial.
See p37.

Vietnam Veterans Memorial.

FREE Washington Monument

The Mall, between 15th & 17th Streets, &
Constitution & Independence Avenues (1-202 426
6841, www.nps.gov/wamo). Smithsonian Metro.
Open *June-6 Sept* 9am-10pm daily. *7 Sept-May*
9am-5pm daily. Currently closed for repairs.
Map p252 H7.

At the time of writing, the Washington Monument was closed for repairs, following earthquake damage in 2011. It's expected to reopen in 2014, when timed tickets for same-day visits will be available for free from the 15th Street kiosk, which opens at 8.30am. During summer, lines can form by 7am. You will also be able to reserve tickets at http://www.recreation.gov, or by calling 1-877 444 6777. There is a $1.50 service charge per ticket.

The Washington Monument was completed in 1884, 101 years after Congress authorised it. It rises in a straight line between the Capitol and the Lincoln Memorial, but is off-centre between the White House and the Jefferson Memorial because the original site was too marshy for its bulk. Private funding ran out in the 1850s, when only the stump of the obelisk had been erected. Building resumed in 1876, producing a slight change in the colour of the marble about a third of the way up. The 555ft monument – the tallest free-standing masonry structure in the world – was capped with solid aluminium, then a rare material.

South of the monument, a cast-iron plate near the light box conceals an underground 162in miniature of the monument, measuring the rate at which the big version is sinking into the ground: around a quarter of an inch every 30 years.

▶ *For alternative places with great views over the Mall and surrounding city, see p48 Inside Track.*

THE WHITE HOUSE & AROUND

Set above the Ellipse to the north of the Mall, the **White House** (*see p42*) opens up the rectangular dynamic of the Mall with north–south sightlines to the Washington Monument and Jefferson Memorial. Directly north of it is the park named for the Marquis de Lafayette, hero of the American Revolution. Workers and tourists fill its benches at lunchtime; a round-the-clock anti-nuclear protest has camped here continuously since 1981, and various eccentrics choose this spot to try and get their message to the American people. The stretch of Pennsylvania Avenue between the park and the White House is reserved for the use of pedestrians due to security considerations.

Though the park is named after Lafayette, its most prominent statue – the hero on the horse in the middle – is Andrew Jackson at the Battle of New Orleans in 1815. This was the first equestrian statue cast in the US at the time of its unveiling in 1853. His four companions are European luminaries of the American Revolution: Lafayette, Comte de Rochambeau, General Kosciusko and Baron von Steuben.

Every president since James Madison has attended at least one service at the mellow yellow St John's Episcopal Church north of the park at 16th and H Streets. A brass plate at pew 54 marks the place reserved for them.

TV news-watchers might recognise the green awning across Jackson Place to the west of the square: this is **Blair House** (1660 Pennsylvania Avenue, NW), where visiting heads of state bunk. Next door, at Pennsylvania

EXPLORE

and 17th Street, is the **Renwick Gallery** (*see right*) – an 1859 building in the French Second Empire mode, named after its architect, James Renwick. Part of the Smithsonian American Art Museum, it commonly features 20th-century crafts, with paintings from the American Art Museum's permanent collection hung salon style – densely, one above the other, lending a 19th-century look – in the Grand Salon. At the end of the 19th century, the original collection moved three blocks south into the purpose-built **Corcoran Museum of Art** (*see below*), the Beaux Arts building on the south-west corner of 17th and E Streets. Just west of it, toward Foggy Bottom, is the **Octagon** (*see p51*).

Decatur House (*see right*) was home to naval hero Stephen Decatur, as well as French, British and Russian diplomats, and 19th-century statesmen Henry Clay and Martin Van Buren. It has temporarily discontinued its guided tours for renovations. Across the square, at H Street and Madison Place, is the **Dolley Madison House** (closed to the public), home of the widowed but effervescent First Lady until her death.

Bookending Lafayette Square are the New Executive Office Building on the west and the US Court of Claims opposite, tucked behind historic edifices. West of the White House is the **Dwight D Eisenhower Executive Office Building**, aka the Old Executive Office Building (OEOB). With its 900 Doric columns and French Empire bombast, this was the largest office building in the world in 1888, housing the entire State, War and Navy departments.

The **Treasury**, the third-oldest federal office building in Washington, interrupts Pennsylvania Avenue because the ornery President Jackson, exasperated at endless debate, declared, 'Put it there!' Symbolically close is a cluster of solid-looking banks and former banks, vestiges of the old financial district, once known as 'Washington's Wall Street', now the 15th Street Financial Historic District.

Corcoran Museum of Art

500 17th Street, NW, between New York Avenue & E Street (1-202 639 1700, www.corcoran.org). Farragut West Metro. **Open** 10am-5pm Wed-Sun. *Corcoran Uncorked events* 5-9pm Wed. **Admission** $10; $8 reductions; free under-12s. **Credit** AmEx, MC, V. **Map** p252 G6.

When District financier William Wilson Corcoran's collection outgrew its original space (now the Renwick Gallery, *see right*), gallery trustees engaged architect Ernest Flagg to design its current Beaux Arts building, which opened in 1897. Despite significant bequests that now added the minor Renoirs and Pissarros that now grace the wood-panelled Clark Landing, the Corcoran's strength remains its 19th- and early 20th-century American paintings, featuring landscapes of the American West by Albert Bierstadt,

Frederick Church and Winslow Homer. Church's mammoth oil, *Niagara*, and Bierstadt's *Mount Corcoran* capture 19th-century Americans' awe of the western landscape, with idealised, almost fantastical portrayals of western scenery.

The museum's 6,000 pieces also include more European art (especially 17th-century Dutch landscapes, 18th- and early 19th-century British paintings, and 19th-century French paintings), contemporary art (with work from post-war artists including Willem de Kooning, Ellsworth Kelly and Cy Twombly), photography, prints, drawings and sculpture. Notable displays include the Evans-Tibbs collection of African American art and drawings by John Singer Sargent. Special exhibitions also highlight contemporary work, such as Ellen Harvey's installation, *The Alien's Guide to the Ruins of Washington, DC*, which envisages the city 10,000 years in the future, and was shown in 2013.

Corcoran Uncorked events, on Wednesday evenings (admission $15 including one drink), feature special tours, music, exhibition viewings and artist appearances, with food and drink from Todd Gray's Muse at the Corcoran.

Decatur House

748 Jackson Place, NW, at H Street (1-202 842 0920, www.decaturhouse.org). Farragut West Metro. **Open** Guided tours suspended for renovation work.
The Shop at President's Square *1610 H Street, NW, at Jackson Place (1-202 218 4337, www.whitehousehistory.org/decatur-house).* **Open** 10am-5pm Mon-Fri; usually open Sat but phone to check first.
Both Map p252 H5.

Admiral Nelson declared Stephen Decatur 'the greatest hero of the age' for his 1804 raids crippling the 'Barbary' pirates. Decatur uttered the famous toast, 'my country, right or wrong', but he died in a needless duel in 1820. The property, a square three-storey townhouse constructed with red brick in Federal style, was designed by architect Benjamin Henry Latrobe for Decatur in 1818. The permanent collection comprises furniture, textiles, art and ceramics of the period. In 2010, the National Trust for Historic Preservation and the White House Historical Association established the National Center for White House History at Decatur House, dedicated to housing artefacts and promoting research. Occasional lectures and other events are held here. Also here is the White House Historical Association gift shop, the Shop at President's Square.

FREE Renwick Gallery of the Smithsonian American Art Museum (S)

17th Street & Pennsylvania Avenue, NW (1-202 633 2850, http://americanart.si.edu/ renwick). Farragut North or Farragut West Metro. **Open** 10am-5.30pm daily. **Admission** free. **Map** p252 G5.

EXPLORE

The Smithsonian

The institution behind the city's landmark museums.

Founded by wealthy British chemist and mineralogist James Smithson (1765-1829), who – rather bizarrely, as he never visited the US – conferred his fortune on the United States government, the Smithsonian Institution was created by an act of Congress in 1846. Smithson requested that it be an institution promoting research and the dispersal of academic knowledge.

Architect James Renwick designed the first building, known as the **Castle** because its combination of late Romanesque and early Gothic styles included signature turrets, on a prime piece of national real estate on the verdant Mall. Completed in 1855, the Castle now serves as the Smithsonian Information Center and administrative hub – and should be the first port of call for any visitor. The Victorian red-brick Arts & Industries Building, designed as the Smithsonian's first hall devoted solely to exhibitions, was added in 1881 (it is currently under renovation). Over the years, collections shown here became large enough to warrant their own buildings. After the creation of the National Zoo in 1890, Congress began the steady erection of museums lining the Mall, beginning with the Museum of Natural History in 1910. From 1923 to 1993, 11 new museums entered the Smithsonian portfolio, most of them holding fine art.

Today the Smithsonian owns more than 140 million objects (plus a further 128 million in its libraries and archive collections), covering everything from ancient Chinese pottery to dinosaurs, Italian Renaissance painting to moon landings, so you're bound to find at least one collection that interests you.

INFORMATION
There is one central phone number – 1-202 357 2700 – where you can get information on all the Smithsonian's museums. The website – www.si.edu – is also useful and has links to individual museum websites.

Smithsonian Access, a brochure detailing the disabled facilities at the museums, is available at each museum – or call 1-202 786 2942. If you need to arrange special facilities you should call the museum two weeks in advance.

Smithsonian Institution museums are marked with an **(S)** in our listings.

Smithsonian Information Center
Smithsonian Institution Building (The Castle), 1000 Jefferson Drive, SW, between Seventh & 12th Streets, The Mall & Tidal Basin (1-202 357 2700, 24hr recorded information 1-202 357 2020, www.si.edu). Smithsonian Metro. **Open** 8.30am-5.30pm daily. *Information desk* 8.30am-4.30pm daily. **Map** p252 J7.

EXPLORE

EXPLORE

White House.

This mansarded building, modelled on the Louvre, was built across from the White House in 1859 by architect James Renwick to house the art collection of financier and philanthropist William Wilson Corcoran. It changed hands several times before opening in 1972 as the Smithsonian's craft museum, and it remains a branch of the Smithsonian American Art Museum (*see p55*). The exhibition of American crafts from the 19th century to the present often showcases striking work. Major works by well-established craftsmen and -women, including Wendell Castle, Dale Chihuly, Robert Ebendorf, David Ellsworth, Sheila Hicks, Karen LaMonte, Beth Lipman, Sam Maloof and Albert Paley, are featured. Jewellery, furniture, and wood art make up a significant part of the collection. In the mansion's refurbished Grand Salon picture gallery, paintings that exemplify the taste of wealthy late 19th-century collectors hang in gilt frames stacked two and three high; works on view rotate regularly. Temporary exhibitions, which are held downstairs, survey artistic movements or artists.

FREE White House

1600 Pennsylvania Avenue, NW, between 15th & 17th Streets (1-202 456 7041, www.white house.gov/about/tours-and-events). McPherson Square Metro. **Open** Tours suspended at the time of writing; see below. *Normal tour hours* 7.30-11am Tue-Thur; 7.30am-noon Fri; 7.30am-1pm Sat. Booking essential, at least 30 days in advance; see review. *Visitors' centre* (temporarily relocated to

Ellipse area south of White House between 15th & 17th Streets) 7.30am-4pm daily. **Admission** free. **Map** p252 H6.

Note: in 2012 tours were suspended for overseas visitors and, at the time of writing, all tours were suspended due to budget cuts brought about by the federal sequestration; check the website for updates or call the number listed. If tours are reinstated, US citizens should contact their member of Congress to arrange one. Tours may be scheduled up to six months in advance and must be scheduled no fewer than 21 days in advance. Citizens of other countries should check with their embassies on the status of tours for citizens of foreign countries.

Part showplace, part workplace, probably one of the world's most-recognised buildings, it's hard to imagine now that until the 20th century the public could walk in freely, and the grounds remained open until World War II. Today, visitors simply get to peek at a scant eight rooms out of the house's 132, and with little time to linger (the tour can take as little as 20 minutes). The public tour is self-guided (though highly regimented) and there's not much in the way of interpretation, but the nation proudly clings to keeping its leader's residence open to the public.

Completed in 1800, and damaged by fire when the city was torched by the British in 1814, the White House has been home to every US president except George Washington. Early presidents lived and worked above the shop. In 1902, Teddy Roosevelt added the East Gallery and the West Wing, which grew to include today's renowned Oval Office.

Each new First Lady can furnish the White House as she pleases: Jacqueline Kennedy, for example, replaced the B Altman department store furniture and frilly florals of her predecessors, the Trumans and Eisenhowers, with understated blues and whites. Her overall refurbishment of the White House restored many historic furnishings and artworks to the rooms. Her tour on national television was a triumph. Each president, meanwhile, imposes his character on the Oval Office, bringing in favourite furniture and personal selections from the White House art collection.

There are also offices for around 200 executive branch staffers, and recreational facilities, including a cinema, tennis courts, putting green, bowling alley and, courtesy of the elder George Bush, a horseshoe pitch. All told, there are 32 bathrooms, 413 doors, three elevators, seven staircases and a staff of more than 100, including florists, carpenters and cooks.

On the tour, you may get a look in the China Room, the pantry for presidential crockery. Don't miss Nancy Reagan's $952-per-setting red-rimmed china, which sparked a controversy about conspicuous consumption – as had Mrs Lincoln's previously.

Up the marble stairs, visitors enter the cavernous East Room, which holds the sole item from the original White House: the 1797 portrait of George Washington that Dolley Madison rescued just before the British burned the place down on 24 August 1814. The East Room is the ceremonial room where seven presidents have lain in state – and where Abigail Adams, wife of the second president, John, hung her laundry. At 3,200sq ft, the space could hold the average American home.

Next is the Green Room, once Jefferson's dining room, and where James Madison did his politicking after Dolley had liquored up important guests in the Red Room, the tour's next stop, decorated as an American Empire parlour of 1810-30. It was here that Mary Todd Lincoln held a seance to contact her dead sons and where President Grant and his former generals refought the Civil War on the carpet using salt shakers and nut dishes as troops.

The colour naming scheme continues in the Blue Room – although it actually has yellow walls. The furnishings here, the traditional home of the White House Christmas tree, were ordered in 1817 by President Monroe. Last stop: the cream and gold State Dining Rooms, which can seat up to 140. Then you're out the door.

The White House Visitor Center, two blocks away at 1450 Pennsylvania Avenue, NW, has exhibits related to the White House. It closed for renovations in July 2012, and is expected to reopen in autumn 2013. A temporary visitor centre, with gift shop, is open at the Ellipse Visitor Pavilion near the corner of 15th and E streets NW, just south-east of the White House.

▶ *The White House Historical Association gift shop at Decatur House (see p40) stocks books and White House-themed gifts and artefacts of all kinds.*

THE CAPITOL & AROUND

An angry senator once scolded President Lincoln that his administration was on the road to hell – in fact, just a mile from it. Lincoln shot back that that was almost exactly the distance from the White House to the Capitol. The Legislative Branch on the east end of Pennsylvania Avenue balances the Executive on the west.

Standing at the east end of the Mall is the commanding presence of the **United States Capitol**. Achieving both dignity and grace from every angle – though the walk along the Mall via the Capitol Reflecting Pool and its ducks shouldn't be missed – the Capitol rises elegantly to the occasion.

The **United States Botanic Garden** at the foot of the Capitol employs high-tech climate controls to replicate the home climate of flora from around the globe. Its highlight is the central rainforest room, equipped with a catwalk affording palm tree-top views. This glass palace houses tropical and subtropical plants, cacti, ferns, palm trees, shrubs and flowers, including its hallmark 500 varieties of orchid.

North of the Capitol, the grounds extend towards **Union Station**. Downhill is a carillon dedicated to conservative 'Mr Republican', Ohio senator Robert A Taft, son of a president and perennial aspirant himself.

Around the Capitol throbs a civic city of Congressional office buildings (the Senate's to the north, the House's to the south). In its eastern lee are the decorous **Supreme Court** and the lavish **Library of Congress**. Beside the art deco Adams Building annex is the incomparable **Folger Shakespeare Library**. Books here are available only to scholars, but the Elizabethan Garden and the museum reward public visits.

Adjoining the Senate offices is the **Sewall-Belmont House** (144 Constitution Avenue, NE, *see p219*), a three-storey Federal Period mansion, with a museum detailing women's suffrage struggles.

FREE Folger Shakespeare Library

201 East Capitol Street, SE, between 2nd & 3rd Streets (1-202 544 4600, www.folger.edu). Capitol South or Union Station Metro. **Open** 10am-5pm Mon-Sat; noon-5pm Sun. *Reading Room* researchers only 8.45am-4.45pm Mon-Fri; 9am-noon, 1-4.30pm Sat. *Guided tours* 11am, 3pm Mon-Fri; 11am, 1pm Sat; 1pm Sun. Reading room tour 1pm Sat. **Admission** free. **Map** p253 L7.

The marble façade sports bas-relief scenes from Shakespeare's plays. Inside is the world's largest collection of his works, including the 79-volume First Folio collection. Standard Oil chairman Henry Clay Folger, who fell in love with Shakespeare after hearing Ralph Waldo Emerson lecture on him, endowed the lot. Other items include books, musical instruments, costumes and films, as well as paintings, drawings, playbills and many fascinating manuscripts. Reflecting the collection, exhibitions and events, such as music recitals, focus on the West during the Renaissance and early modern age. There are special events for Shakespeare's birthday on 21 April. Note that the exhibition hall is closed until 27 September 2013 for renovations.

▶ *The intimate theatre at the Folger (see p181) is a replica of one from the Elizabethan era.*

FREE Library of Congress

Visitors' Center, Jefferson Building, First Street & Independence Avenue, SE (1-202 707 9779, www.loc.gov). Capitol South Metro. **Open** *Thomas Jefferson Building* 8.30am-4.30pm Mon-Sat. *James Madison Building* 8.30am-9.30pm Mon-Fri. *John Adams Building* 8.30am-9.30pm Mon, Wed, Thur; 8.30am-5pm Tue, Fri, Sat. *Guided tours* 10.30am, 11.30am, 1.30pm, 2.30pm, 3.30pm Mon-Fri; 10.30am, 11.30am, 1.30pm, 2.30pm Sat. **Admission** free. **Map** p252 L7.

The national library of the US, the Library of Congress is the world's largest. Its three buildings hold some 100 million items – including the papers of 23 US presidents – along 535 miles of bookshelves. Contrary to popular notion, the library does not have a copy of every book ever printed, but its heaving shelves are still spectacular.

To get to grips with the place, it's best to start with the 20-minute film in the ground-floor visitors' centre, excerpted from a TV documentary, which provides a clear picture of the place's scope and size. An even better option is to join a guided tour.

The original library was crammed into the Capitol. Ransacked by the British in 1814, it revived when president-scholar Thomas Jefferson offered his collection of 6,487 books. The Thomas Jefferson Building – the main one – was finished in 1897 and splendidly restored upon its centennial. Based on the Paris Opera House, the Library has granite walls supporting an octagonal dome, which rises to 160ft above the impressive Main Reading Room. Gloriously gaudy mosaics, frescos and statues overwhelm the visitor with a gush of 19th-century high culture.

The Main Reading Room has classical marble archways and great plaster figures of disciplines (Philosophy, Religion, Art, History – all women) flanked by bronze images of their mortal instruments (Plato, Moses, Homer, Shakespeare – all men).

The library hosts several long-term exhibitions, all with an interactive focus. Hope for America: Performers, Politics and Pop Culture draws on papers, jokes, films and TV programmes from comedian Bob Hope, and examines the careers of Hope and other entertainers who chose to involve themselves with the political issues of their day. Exploring the Early Americas uses material from the Jay I Kislak collection to look at indigenous cultures and the consequences of contact with European settlers. Also on display are the library's collection of Bibles and Thomas Jefferson's collection of books and manuscripts.

The James Madison Building, opened in 1980, encloses an area greater than 35 football fields. It houses the copyright office, manuscript room, film and TV viewing rooms and the incredible photography collections. Diagonally opposite is the 1939 John Adams Building, which contains the Science and Business reading rooms.

Anyone with photo ID can obtain a research card within about ten minutes. You can't wander all the shelves yourself: a librarian will dig out your selected text. The library catalogue is also available online at www.lcweb.loc.gov, though many of the old card-catalogue entries are found only in their original drawers.

FREE Supreme Court

1st Street & Maryland Avenue, NW (1-202 479 3211, www.supremecourtus.gov). Capitol South or Union Station Metro. **Open** 9am-4.30pm Mon-Fri. **Map** p253 L6.

The ultimate judicial and constitutional authority, the United States Supreme Court pays homage in its architecture to the rule of law. Justices are appointed for life, and their temple reflects their eminence. Designed by Cass Gilbert in the 1930s, its classical façade incorporates Corinthian columns supporting a pediment decorated with bas-reliefs representing Liberty, Law, Order and a crew of historical lawgivers. The sober style conceals whimsy in the shape of sculpted turtles lurking to express the 'deliberate pace' of judicial deliberations. There are also ferocious lions – enough said.

You can tour the building any time. Visitors enter from the plaza doors, on either side of the main steps. The ground level has a cafeteria, an introductory video show, a gift shop and changing exhibitions. The cathedral-like entrance hall daunts one into hushed tones. The courtroom, with its heavy burgundy velvet draperies and marble pillars, is where the nine judges hear around 120 of the more than 6,500 cases submitted each year. The black-robed figures appear as the court marshal announces 'Oyez! Oyez! Oyez!' and sit in seats of varying height, handcrafted to their personal preferences. Goose-quill pens still grace the lawyers' tables, for tradition's sake.

When the court is in session, generally in two-week intervals from October to April, on Mondays, Tuesdays and Wednesdays, visitors can see cases argued ('oral arguments'). There are generally two one-hour arguments a day, at 10am and 11am, with occasional afternoon sessions. The website has details of which days are 'argument days'. Two lines form in the plaza in front of the building: one for those who want to hear the whole argument (better be there by 8am), and the 'three-minute line', for those who just want a peek. Seating for whole-argument visitors is at 9.30am; three-minute visitors are admitted from 10am. In May and June, 'opinions' are handed down usually on Tuesdays and Wednesdays. Check the newspapers' Supreme Court calendars or www.supremecourt.gov/oral_arguments to see what cases are scheduled. Celebrated cases draw massive queues.

Thirty-minute courtroom lectures, by docents, are available daily. On days that the Court is not sitting, they are hourly, on the half-hour, beginning at 9.30 a.m. with a final lecture at 3.30pm. When the Court is in session, lectures take place only after Court adjourns for the day. A line forms in the Great Hall on the ground floor before each lecture, and visitors are admitted on a first-come, first-served basis.

FREE United States Botanic Garden
245 1st Street, at Maryland Avenue (1-202 225 8333, www.usbg.gov). Federal Center SW Metro. **Open** *Conservatory & National Garden* 10am-5pm daily. *Bartholdi Park* dawn to dusk. **Admission** free. **Map** p253 K7.
In 1842, the Navy's Wilkes Expedition returned from exploring Fiji and South America, showering Congress with a cornucopia of exotic flora. The present conservatory was erected in 1930 and recently modernised with state-of-the-art climate controls and a coconut-level catwalk around the central rainforest.

The conservatory displays 4,000 plants, including endangered species. Themed displays feature the desert and the oasis, plant adaptations and the primeval garden. The orchid collection is a particular delight. Across Independence Avenue, Bartholdi Park displays plants thriving in Washington's climate, ranged around an alluring fountain created by Bartholdi, sculptor of the Statue of Liberty. The new National Garden aims to be a showcase for 'unusual, useful, and ornamental plants that grow well in the mid-Atlantic region'.

★ FREE United States Capitol
Capitol Hill, between Constitution & Independence Avenues (recorded tour information 1-202 225 6827, www.visitthecapitol.gov). Capitol South or Union Station Metro. **Open** *Guided tours* 8.30am-3.20pm Mon-Sat; should be booked in advance (see below). *Visitors' centre* 8.30am-4.30pm Mon-Sat. **Admission** free. **Map** p253 K7.
French architect Major Pierre-Charles L'Enfant, hired by President Washington to plan the federal city, selected Capitol Hill – a plateau, actually – as 'a pedestal waiting for a monument'. Indeed it was. In 1793, George Washington and an entourage of local masons laid the building's long-lost cornerstone, then celebrated by barbecuing a 500-pound ox. Thirty-one years later, despite a fire, a shortage of funds and the War of 1812, the structure was complete. But as the Union grew, so did the number of legislators. By 1850, architects projected the Capitol would have to double its size. In 1857, they added wings for the Senate (north) and the House of Representatives (south). An iron dome (a 600-gallon paint job each year makes it look like marble) replaced the wooden one in 1865.

Today, as well as being a landmark of neoclassical architecture, the Capitol – which has 540 rooms, 658 windows (108 in the dome alone) and 850 doorways – is something like a small city. As well as the 535 elected lawmakers, an estimated 20,000 workers toil each day among the six buildings (not including the Capitol itself) – all connected

EXPLORE

United States Botanic Garden

United States Capitol. See p45.

by tunnels – that make up the complex. A US flag flies over the Senate and House wings when either is in session; and at night a lantern glows in the Capitol dome.

Tickets for a Capitol tour are free but should be booked online in advance; you'll be assigned a time (it's usually possible to secure a slot within a day or two). US citizens can also book through their senator or representative. A limited number of same-day passes are also available from the information desk in Emancipation Hall on the lower level of the Capitol Visitor Center. Entrance to the Capitol is also through the Emancipation Hall. Once inside you will also be able to obtain a pass for the House and Senate floors. More information is available at http://www.visitthecapitol.gov/visit/book_a_tour.

Visits begin with an orientation film, *Out of Many, One*. The highlight of the short tour is the Rotunda, its dome containing nine million tons of iron. On its ceiling is a massive fresco by Constantino Brumidi, consisting of a portrait of the nation's first president rising to the heavens flanked by allegorical figures of Liberty and Authority, Victory and Fame. They are surrounded by maidens representing the original 13 colonies. Around the walls are other paintings, with figures depicting elements in American life such as commerce and agriculture; in these scenes mythological gods and goddesses interact with historical figures. The National Statuary Hall was originally the chamber of the House of Representatives, but it outgrew the room, moving to a new chamber, and the room was devoted to statuary. Each state was invited to contribute two statues to honour individuals significant to their state; these are displayed throughout the Capitol and in the visitors' centre.

UNION STATION & AROUND

Daniel Burnham's Beaux Arts-style **Union Station** is a monument to the railroad age. The Thurgood Marshall Judiciary Building east of Union Station complements the former City Post Office – now the **National Postal Museum** – also built by Burnham, to present an elegant urban vista. In front of the trio, the flags of all the US states and territories are ranged around the central Columbus Memorial Fountain (1912).

The neighbourhood around Union Station was once a shantytown of Irish railroad labourers, who christened their marshy abode 'Swampoodle' after its swamps and puddles.

FREE **National Postal Museum (S)**

2 Massachusetts Avenue, NE, at 1st Street (1-202 633 5555, http://postalmuseum.si.edu). Union Station Metro. **Open** 10am-5.30pm daily. **Admission** free. **Map** p253 L6.

Audio-visual and interactive presentations in this family-friendly museum detail the invention and history of stamps, the postal service, the role of letters as a means of communication (including letters to and from soldiers during wartime), and stamp collecting. The frequent special exhibitions aren't likely to bowl over serious philatelists. They should head to the museum's huge library and research centre.

▶ *For children's activities at the museum, see p155.*

FREE **Union Station**

40 Massachusetts Avenue, NE, at Delaware Avenue (1-202 298-1908, www.unionstation dc.com). Metro Union Station. **Open** *Station*

EXPLORE

24hrs daily. *Shops* 10am-9pm Mon-Sat; noon-6pm Sun. **Map** p253 K/L 5/6.

Built in 1908, Union Station grandiosely reflects its inspiration – the Baths of Diocletian in Rome. Envisioning the most splendid terminal in the country, architect Daniel 'make no small plans' Burnham lavished the building with amenities, including a nursery, a swimming pool and even a mortuary for defunct out-of-towners. The Main Hall is a huge rectangular space, with a 96ft barrel-vaulted ceiling and a balcony with 36 sculptures of Roman legionnaires.

The station languished when rail travel declined. The President's Room, reserved for chief executives welcoming incoming dignitaries such as King George VI and Haile Selassie, is now a restaurant. In 1953, a decidedly non-stop express train bound for Eisenhower's inauguration smashed into the crowded concourse; incredibly, nobody was killed. Two decades later, a deliberate but also disastrous hole was sunk in the Great Hall to make way for the multi-screen video set-up of an ill-conceived (and short-lived) visitors' centre. At this stage, despite its lingering grandeur, the station seemed doomed to the wrecking ball.

But in 1988 a painstaking $165-million restoration programme was begun, during which time entertainment came into play. There are now shops, amusements and eateries of all sorts, and even a multi-screen cinema. Rents are high and some of the shops have failed, but successors always seem to come along and more sales per square foot move through the shops here than any other DC mall. It's easy to forget that the marble and gilt palace's main function is still as a railway station – with lines to New York, Chicago, Miami and New Orleans, as well as the suburbs – though the crowds at rush hour will bring you back to your senses.

▶ *For shops at Union Station, see p116.*

THE FEDERAL TRIANGLE

The nine-block-long triangle of monolithic federal buildings wedged between Pennsylvania Avenue, NW, and the Mall is known as the Federal Triangle. The government bulldozed the whole district in the 1920s, claiming 'eminent domain' (the right of compulsory purchase), and today the Federal Triangle is the ballpark for the heavy hitters of the government machine, housing some 28,000 office workers. The triangle is both a labyrinth and a fortress. Security is tight, and visitors usually end up asking about six different people before finally making it to their destination. Some call it the Bermuda Triangle.

All but three of the buildings in the Triangle were built between 1927 and 1938 as massive Beaux Arts limestone structures, complete with high-minded inscriptions, to house various federal agencies, such as the Departments of

Commerce and Justice, and the **National Archives**. The Internal Revenue Service headquarters are inscribed with the words of former justice Oliver Wendell Holmes: 'Taxes are what we pay for a civilised society'. The three exceptions are the **John Wilson (District) Building** (the city hall, on the corner of 14th and E Streets), the Ronald Reagan Building and the **Old Post Office**. Once sneered at as the 'old tooth' and slated for demolition, the latter now sports a tourist mall and a brilliant view from the top of its 315ft tower.

Built in the 1990s, the **Ronald Reagan Building & International Trade Center** (on 14th Street, opposite the Department of Commerce) is the most expensive building ever constructed in the US for federal use, at a cost of over $700 million.

In the basement of the Department of Commerce is an unexpected novelty: the **National Aquarium of Washington DC**, an old-fashioned exhibit that affords a closer look at sea creatures than many more modern aquaria.

FREE National Archives

Constitution Avenue, at 9th Street (1-866 272 6272, www.archives.gov). Archives-Navy Memorial Metro. **Open** *Rotunda & Exhibit Hall* 10am-5.30pm daily. *Research Center* 9am-5pm Mon-Sat. **Admission** free. **Map** p253 J6.

The vast collection of the National Archive & Record Administration (NARA) represents the physical record of the birth and growth of a nation in original documents, maps, photos, recordings, films and a miscellany of objects. The catalogue resonates with national iconography and historical gravitas (and pathos), and includes the Louisiana Purchase, maps of Lewis and Clark's explorations, the Japanese World War II surrender document, the gun that shot JFK, the Watergate tapes and documents of national identity (collectively known as the Charters of Freedom). Nearby is one of the original copies of the Magna Carta. The Public Vaults, where most of the documents on permanent display are housed, has over 1,000 items on display at any one time. Sections are divided into themes inspired by words in the preamble of the Consitution: We the People is records of family and citizenship; To Form a More Perfect Union deals with liberty and law; Provide for the Common Defense is war and diplomacy, and so on.

There's no doubt that the Archives' star attraction is the Rotunda, where the original Charters of Freedom – the Constitution, the Declaration of Independence and the Bill of Rights – are mounted, triptych-like, in a glass case at the centre of a roped-off horseshoe containing other key documents. A renovation completed in 2003 protecting them with high-tech gizmos proved itself in 2006 when the building flooded.

EXPLORE

INSIDE TRACK CITY VIEWS

The temporary closure of the Washington Monument means that one of the city's top spots for citywide panoramas is out of action. But there are alternatives: the **Old Post Office** clocktower (*see below*) has stupendous views (including the Washington Monument itself) as does the roof terrace at the **Newseum** (*see p61*).

The building that houses the archives was opened in 1935 and designed to harmonise with existing DC landmarks – in other words, it's neo-classical in style. In a city of monumental architecture the most distinctive features are the bronze doors at the Constitution Avenue entrance. Each weighs six and a half tons and is 38ft high and 11in thick. Though security is their main function, they also remind the visitor of the importance of the contents.

▶ *The Archives' Lawrence F O'Brien Gallery hosts imaginative temporary exhibitions using all kinds of records and documents, including photographs.*

FREE Old Post Office

1100 Pennsylvania Avenue, NW, between 11th & 12th Streets (1-202 606 8691, www.nps.gov/opot). Federal Triangle Metro. **Open** *Late May-early Sept* 9am-8pm Mon-Wed, Sat; 9am-7pm Thur; noon-6pm Sun. *Sept-late May* 9am-5pm Mon-Sat. Last tours 15mins before closing time.
Admission free. **Map** p252 J6.

With the Washington Monument temporarily closed, the Old Post Office has taken over as the city's best viewing point – and you can see the Washington Monument from here too. It's a 47-second ride to the ninth floor; you then change to another elevator bound for the 12th, and top, floor. The 270ft observation level allows visitors an awe-inspiring view of the city and surrounding area.

THE NORTHWEST RECTANGLE

The Northwest Rectangle is not an official appellation, but it's sometimes used to describe the rectangle of federal buildings west of the Ellipse and south of E Street that roughly mirrors the Federal Triangle to the east. It's really just part of Foggy Bottom (*see p50*), an industrial immigrant area in the 19th century, but any original character that the area has retained emerges only further north.

In this southern part, it's grandiose federal anonymity all the way. From west to east, the buildings of interest are the **State Department**, whose opulent reception rooms can be toured by arrangement; then, dropping down to Constitution Avenue, the American Pharmaceutical Association, the National Academy of Sciences,

with its invitingly climbable statue of Einstein, the Federal Reserve Board and the Organization of American States (OAS). Behind the OAS art gallery annex is the **Department of the Interior**, housing in its museum examples of Native American arts, with authentic goods for sale in its craft shop. Attempting to improve its PR, the **IMF Center** – scene of an annual siege by anti-globalisation protesters – offers displays explaining international finance.

FREE Department of the Interior Museum

1849 C Street, NW, between 18th & 19th Streets (1-202 208 4743, www.doi.gov/interiormuseum). Farragut West Metro. **Open** Museum closed for renovations. *Mural tour* 2pm Tue, Thur (advance reservations necessary). **Admission** free.
Map p252 G6.

Secretary of the Interior Harold Ickes believed that the Interior building, which was completed in 1936, should reflect the Department's mission to manage and conserve the nation's natural resources. So in 1941, he hired photographer Ansel Adams to create a photographic mural for the building that reflected this mission. The Interior Museum Murals Tour lasts an hour and visits 26 photographic murals by Ansel Adams and many of the over 50 mural panels painted by artists including Maynard Dixon, Allan Houser, Gifford Beal, John Steuart Curry and William Gropper. Spaces on the twice-weekly tours are filled quickly – reserve well in advance by phoning the museum.

The museum itself remains closed to the public. Its exhibits are a hotchpotch of Indian arts and crafts: Pueblo drums; Apache basketwork; Cheyenne arrows that a soldier plucked from dying buffalos at Fort Sill Indian Territory (Oklahoma) in 1868.

FREE State Department Diplomatic Reception Rooms

C & 22nd Streets, NW (1-202 647 3241, www.state.gov/www/about_state/diprooms/index. html). Foggy Bottom-GWU Metro. **Guided tours** 9.30am, 10.30am, 2.45pm Mon-Fri. **Admission** free. **Map** p252 G6.

When the State Department was finished in 1951, the wife of the secretary of state wept when confronted with the chrome, glass-and-concrete walls and tasteless furniture. Today, the diplomatic reception rooms are dubbed Washington's best-kept secret – a delight for serious art- and antiques-lovers. They contain national masterpieces from 1740 to 1825, valued at some $90 million. Among the collection are Chippendale pieces; the English Sheraton desk on which the Treaty of Paris was signed in 1783, ending the Revolutionary War; and a table-desk used by Thomas Jefferson. There are also some none-too-exciting exhibits in the lobby on the history of the State Department. Note that you can only visit by guided tour, for which reservations are required (call or book on https://receptiontours.state.gov).

SOUTH OF THE MALL

To the south of the Mall lie mostly nondescript federal buildings (Federal Aviation Administration, Transportation Department and so on). The principal exceptions are the **United States Holocaust Memorial Museum** and the **Bureau of Engraving & Printing**, where the greenback is printed. Both are to the west near the Tidal Basin.

To the east, L'Enfant Plaza is ironically named, considering that it's supposed to honour the man whose city plan made Washington so stately – it's a barren expanse of ground.

FREE Bureau of Engraving & Printing

14th Street, SW, at C Street (1-202 874 2330, www.moneyfactory.com). Smithsonian Metro. **Open** *Visitor centre* 8.30am-3.30pm Mon-Fri. *Tours* Sept-Feb every 15mins 9-10.45am; 12.30-2pm Mon-Fri. Mar-Aug every 15mins 9am-7pm Mon-Fri. **Admission** free. **Map** p252 H6.

As the sign says, 'The Buck Starts Here!'. The printing in the title refers to hard currency: this is where the dollar bill is born. The 40-minute guided tour provides a glimpse into the printing, cutting and stacking of the 37 million banknotes produced daily. It's all done behind the thickest of plate glass, with scads of security. In the off-season (September to the end of February) you should be able to go in with a minimal wait; lines form at the visitors' entrance on 14th Street. In summer, you'll need a timed same-day ticket, given out from 8am from the booth just outside in Raoul Wallenberg Place. Tickets are usually gone by 9am and queues form especially early during peak times

United States Holocaust Memorial Museum.

such as spring break and cherry blossom season. Alternatively, US citizens can contact their senator or congressman for access to special tours.

★ FREE United States Holocaust Memorial Museum

100 Raoul Wallenberg Place, SW, at 14th Street (1-202 488 0400, www.ushmm.org). Smithsonian Metro. **Open** 10am-5.20pm daily. Timed passes required for main exhibition Mar-Aug, available from 10am on day of visit or book online in advance ($1 per pass). **Admission** free, except for online or phone bookings (*see above*). **Map** p252 H7.

Since its opening in 1993, the Holocaust Museum has attracted legions of visitors to its permanent exhibition, The Holocaust. The three-floor exhibition, containing over 900 artefacts, many video screens and four theatres showing archive footage and survivor testimony, presents a chronological history of the Nazi holocaust. On the top level, Nazi Assault covers the rise of Hitler and Nazism in the mid 1930s; the incarceration of Jews in ghettos and their murder – along with gypsies and many others – in death camps in the 1940s is the focus of Final Solution on the third floor; on the second floor, Last Chapter covers Allied liberation and subsequent war-crime trials. Visitors travel to the exhibition in a steel-clad freight elevator that deposits them into an environment of unparalleled sobriety. Themes, such as murder of the disabled, Nazi eugenics, resistance, and so on, are comprehensively covered. The photo- and text-intensive accounts of events and atrocities unfold dispassionately, but objects and symbols make powerful impressions: thousands of camp victims' shoes piled in a heap personalise the losses.

While the main exhibition is suitable for children of 11 and over only, a specially designed children's exhibition, Daniel's Story, at ground level, is suitable for children of eight and over and teaches about the holocaust through the story of one boy. Other exhibitions include an examination of *The Protocols of the Elders of Zion*. The museum also attempts to highlight recent genocides and genocide prevention in From Memory to Action: Meeting the Challenge of Genocide, an installation with eyewitness testimonies and interactive displays, in the museum's Wexner Center.

The building (designed by Pei Cobb Freed) incorporates red brick and slate-grey steel girders and catwalks, echoing death camp architecture; within the permanent exhibition, skylit zones alternate with claustrophobic darkness. Notable artworks include a Richard Serra sculpture and graceful Ellsworth Kelly and Sol LeWitt canvases. The Hall of Remembrance, the national memorial to victims of the Holocaust, is a simple, windowless space with a high central skylight of translucent glass. Narrow openings in the walls also let in light and offer partial views of the Washington Monument and the Jefferson Memorial.

EXPLORE

DC Neighbourhoods

Beyond the monumental façade lies the real city.

Beyond the monumental core of the Mall is a real, rather quirky city, full of distinctive and interesting neighbourhoods, populated by people rather than institutions and made more from brick than marble. If there is a theme to this other Washington's history over the last few decades, it has been one of regeneration, as areas such as Downtown, U Street and – more recently – H Street have pulled themselves out of decline and regained the vibrancy and economic pulling power that they once had.

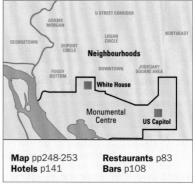

| Map pp248-253 | Restaurants p83 |
| Hotels p141 | Bars p108 |

The city is divided into quadrants, taking the Capitol – slightly east of the centre – as its nexus, and we follow these divisions below.

EXPLORE

Northwest

Northwest is the most affluent quadrant. It is roughly bisected from south to north by Rock Creek Park. The Northwest section of this chapter starts with the neighbourhoods nearest the Monumental Centre, heads north and then west to Rock Creek Park, Georgetown and further suburbs.

FOGGY BOTTOM

West and south-west of the White House down to the Potomac River, Foggy Bottom takes its name from its original, marshy riverside location. That the name is so well known in the US is due largely to the Department of State, which moved into the Truman Building (2201 C Street, NW) in 1950. The immigrant settlers who once worked in the factories wouldn't recognise the area's current hauteur. A historic district on the National Registry since 1987 because of the design of its rowhouses, these days Foggy Bottom is home to highly transient foreign service workers, federal appointees, college students and performing artists – along with older long-term residents.

Near the dock where the US government first arrived in its muddy new capital in 1800, the white marble box of the John F Kennedy Center

for the Performing Arts (known as the **Kennedy Center**, *see p51*) rises above the river. North of the Kennedy Center lie the swirling contours of the **Watergate Complex** (at 26th Street & Virginia Avenue, NW), site of the eponymous 1972 burglary that unravelled Richard Nixon's presidency. Shops and delis line its courtyard. The humble Howard Johnson motel across the street, from where Tricky Dicky's 'plumbers' monitored the break-in, is now a George Washington University dorm.

At Virginia and New Hampshire Avenues, a statue of Mexican president Benito Juarez points symbolically towards the distant monument to George Washington, who inspired him. Above Virginia Avenue, Foggy Bottom seeps from monumental into urban Washington. Although many of the neighbourhood's characteristic tiny townhouses were bulldozed to make way for the notoriously expansionist George Washington University, some neat pockets – such as the area between New Hampshire Avenue and K Street – survive.

The **Octagon** was President James Madison's refuge for seven months after the British invaders torched the executive mansion in 1814. The **Arts Club of Washington** (2017 I Street, NW) was home to his successor, James Monroe, until the charred mansion was rebuilt.

Around Pennsylvania Avenue, Foggy Bottom frequently succumbs to 'façadism', token retention of the fronts of historic buildings to satisfy preservation rules, with massive modern structures ballooning behind. The blatant Mexican Chancery (1911 Pennsylvania Avenue, NW) and slightly subtler Red Lion Row (2000 Pennsylvania Avenue, NW) are prime examples. The Spanish Chancery on Washington Circle is subtler still, and more stylish.

North of Pennsylvania Avenue, the 'New Downtown' to the west of Farragut Square is the traditional haunt of the 'K Street lawyer' lobbyists. However, these days, few lobbying firms are actually based in K Street.

FREE Kennedy Center

2700 F Street, NW, at New Hampshire Avenue & Rock Creek Parkway (1-800 444 1324, 1-202 467 4600, www.kennedy-center.org). Foggy Bottom-GWU Metro. **Open** *10am-11pm daily. Guided tours every 10mins 10am-5pm Mon-Fri; 10am-1pm Sat, Sun.* **Map** *p252 F6.*

Festooned with decorative gifts from many nations and some wonderful 20th-century works of art, 'Ken Cen' is as much a spectacle as the shows it presents, with its flag-filled Hall of States and Hall of Nations, six theatres and concert halls, three rooftop restaurants and great views from the open-air terrace. Free concerts (6pm daily) liven up the Millennium Stage, and there are free 45-minute guided tours (call

Watergate Complex.

1-202 416 8340 or walk-ins welcome; visit the Tour Desk on Level A). Parking is inadequate when several shows are playing at once – better to walk or take the free shuttle bus from the Foggy Bottom-GWU Metro stop.

▶ *For the Kennedy Center as a performance venue, see p176 and p179.*

Octagon Museum

1799 New York Avenue, NW, at 18th Street (1-202 638 3221, www.theoctagon.org). Farragut West or Farragut North Metro. **Open** *1-4pm Thur, Fri.* **Map** *p252 G6.*

Designed for its odd-shaped lot by Dr William Thornton, first architect of the Capitol, this elegant brick mansion was completed in 1800. The aristocratic Tayloes offered it to a fellow Virginian, President Madison, when he was made homeless by the 1814 White House fire. More like a pregnant hexagon than an octagon, the house – reputedly haunted – is a gem of light and proportion. The related American Institute of Architects headquarters are next door; hence the Octagon hosts topical architectural exhibitions as well as Madison-era furnishings – including the desk where Madison signed the Treaty of Ghent in 1815, ending the war between the US and Britain.

DOWNTOWN

Once a bustling city hub, synonymous with F Street's theatres, restaurants and department stores, the Downtown area slumped in the 1960s as shoppers began to prefer suburban malls; and it virtually keeled over after the 1968 riots tarnished it as unsafe. In 1985, the Hecht Company – whose original Downtown store at 7th Street had been vandalised during the riots – reopened at 12th and G Streets, the first freestanding department store built in an American downtown in four decades. It was later bought out by **Macy's** (*see p115*), which still trades on the site. In 1997, the **Verizon Center** (*see p57*) opened, pushing a revival that has totally transformed the area into a safe restaurant, entertainment and retail district.

An influx of law firms spawned such power-lunch hangouts as DC Coast at K and 14th Streets (*see p85*) and Oceanaire Seafood Room (*see p86*) at F and 12th. At Franklin Square (14th & I Streets, NW), strip clubs long ago gave way to offices, which chip in to maintain the park. Even the statue facing 14th Street – of Irishman John Barry, Father of the US Navy – got its purloined sword restored.

National Theatre (1321 Pennsylvania Avenue, NW, *see p180*) just about gets by as an independent theatre, while the **Warner Theatre** (at 13th & E Streets, NW, *see p178*) reflects a thorough restoration. At 511 10th

EXPLORE

Profile National Portrait Gallery/ Smithsonian American Art Museum

A dilapidated landmark building reborn.

By the late 1990s, the former Patent Office building in Downtown was in a sad state of disrepair. One of the finest examples of Greek Revival architecture in the city, the original, Robert Mills-designed south wing opened in 1840 and was the site of President Lincoln's inaugural ball in 1865. Three other wings were added later, each facing a central courtyard. Two museums – American Art and Portraiture – were housed here from 1968. But in 2000, beset with problems, the once-magnificent building was closed for careful renovation. Gifts allowed for the building of an auditorium, constructed beneath the courtyard. Two large elms there suffered from Dutch elm disease and had to be removed, and what had been a grassy area was paved over. Another gift allowed for the covering of the courtyard with a glass canopy designed by Norman Foster. This created the Kogod Courtyard, a pleasantly airy space rendered slightly dour by the grey stone of its surrounding walls. The buildings that surround the courtyard are once again home to the two museums, each accessible from the other, each telling the story of America from a different perspective.

The **National Portrait Gallery** features people who played a role in the shaping of the nation and its culture, with figures as diverse as Pocahontas and Juliette Gordon Low, founder of the US Girl Scouts. Presidents are gathered in the America's Presidents section on the second floor. Among the portraits is Gilbert Stuart's seminal 'Lansdowne' portrait of George Washington. Other paintings feature the Bushes, father and son, in separate portraits side by side. A TV plays excerpts from epoch-making presidential speeches, Kennedy's 'ask not what your country can do for you', and Reagan's 'Mr Gorbachev, tear down that wall' among them.

Alongside the magnificently re-created grand hall on the third floor is 20th-Century Americans. Andy Warhol's iconic *Marilyn* is

MORE PORTRAITS Other examples of George Catlin's portraits of Native Americans can be seen in the **National Museum of the American Indian** (*see p37*).

here, alongside a striking kitsch-classical *Elvis* by Ralph W Cowan, looming huge over a rural scene with Gracelands in the background, as well as serious figures such as Hillary Clinton.

The theme of art as a window on America continues in the **American Art Museum**. On the second floor is American Art Through 1940, a chronological collection that reflects America's changing self-image. In the 19th and early 20th centuries, the West was a distant and intriguing place and the frontier a big concept in the national mindset, so artists sought to bring them to the viewing public. Huge, idealised and stylised visions of an almost supernatural landscape were the speciality of Albert Bierstadt, and nothing came bigger or more idealised than his *Among the Sierra Nevada, California*, which was actually painted in Rome. George Catlin, meanwhile, had a very different mission: to record disappearing tribal cultures. Contrary to his own prevailing culture, he sought to portray native people not as savages but as individuals and his moving portraits are a testament to this.

Contemporary art and art since 1945 is on the third floor, with work from leading artists, such as Frank Kline's *Merce C*, a dynamic representation in black and white of dancer Merce Cunningham. Perhaps the most striking exhibit here is Nam June Paik's huge neon map, *Electronic Superhighway: Continental US, Alaska, Hawaii (see above)*. This floor is also home to the Lunder Conservation Center, which allows the public to see the work of conservation staff, and the Luce Foundation Center for American Art, the first public study and art storage centre in Washington, wtih more than 3,300 works from the permanent collection on display. Interactive kiosks provide detailed information.

Back down on the first (ground) floor, American Experience explores themes of land, frontier, cities, monuments and ideals. Here, Edward Hopper's *Cape Cod Morning (see left)* shows a woman looking out of a window; she seems to have spotted something we can't see, and the picture hints at anxiety and isolation. And Georgia O'Keefe's *Manhattan (see above)* is a series of dynamic geometrical shapes reaching skywards, their sharp lines contrasting with flowers floating in the sky.

For listings, *see p55*.

EXPLORE

Street, NW, is **Ford's Theatre** (*see p55*). Still a functioning theatre, its main claim to fame is as the site of Lincoln's assassination. Across the street is **Ford's Theatre Center**.

The National Press Club (14th & F Streets, NW), opened in 1924, still draws reporters, and sponsors speeches by newsmakers, foreign and domestic. The *Washington Post* is at 1150 15th Street, NW. One block west is the home of the National Geographic Society.

The **Russian Embassy** (1125 16th Street, NW, between L & M Streets) was a wedding gift for the daughter of sleeping-car tycoon George Pullman; the grandiose building became the embassy of Tsarist Russia in 1917. With US recognition in 1934, the USSR moved in, planting hammer-and-sickle motifs amid the gilt cherubs adorning the walls. The red flag finally came down in 1991. This Russian Embassy is now only the ceremonial appendage of the working compound on Wisconsin Avenue at Calvert Street. In 2001, it came to light that US spies had burrowed a surveillance tunnel under the latter building.

Sixteenth Street is also notable for its procession of handsome houses of worship, which line it all the way to Maryland, and its Renaissance-style **Meridian Hill Park** (aka Malcolm X Park), adorned with cascading waterfalls and a statue of Joan of Arc. The former Greyhound bus terminal at 12th Street and New York Avenue used to be a wino magnet. Now its streamlined façade, treasured by Washington's ardent art deco devotees, fronts an office building complementing its lines. Street-level tenants include restaurants and bars. In 1987, the **National Museum of Women in the Arts** redeemed a dignified 80-year-old Renaissance Revival Masonic lodge that had become a cinema.

The gigantic **Convention Center** north of Mount Vernon Square replaced a drab, punier predecessor at 9th Street and New York Avenue. On the square itself, the old wedding-cake Carnegie Library housed the failed City Museum of Washington, DC. The successor **Martin Luther King Jr Memorial Library** is a late design of Bauhaus guru Mies van der Rohe.

The **Smithsonian American Art Museum** and the **National Portrait Gallery** (*see p52* **Profile**), which split the historic Patent Office building at 7th and F Streets, reopened in 2006 to acclaim after six years' restoration – the building has been renamed the Donald W Reynolds Center for American Art and Portraiture. Across 7th Street looms the **Verizon Center**, the huge venue for basketball, hockey, concerts and horse shows that did so much to revive the neighbourhood. The explosive revival it triggered along 7th Street, and the accompanying escalating rents, blew some old Chinese businesses out of Chinatown. Chinoiserie still obscures some quite old house façades; Wok-'n'-Roll restaurant (604 H Street, NW, 1-202 347 4656) occupies Mary Surratt's boarding house, where in 1865 John Wilkes Booth's co-conspirators plotted Abe Lincoln's doom. Texan barbecues and Irish bars now thrive within sight of the world's largest **Chinese arch** (over H Street, at 7th Street), given by the People's Republic of China.

Chinatown.

DC's Chinese population has largely dispersed to the suburbs, but Chinatown remains the community's spiritual centre and site of celebrations at Chinese New Year.

Nearby houses of worship testify to Washington's immigrant past, particularly **St Mary's Mother of God** (727 5th Street, NW), a downsized copy of Germany's Ulm Cathedral, ministering to German immigrants, now drawing nostalgic Catholics to its Tridentine Latin masses. **St Patrick's Catholic Church** (619 10th Street, NW) was established in 1794 to serve the Irish immigrants who came to build the White House; the present building rose a century later. **Holy Rosary Church** (595 3rd Street, NW) has masses in Italian, plus cultural events at its Casa Italiana next door. In 2004, a cluster of Jewish congregations bought back the historic synagogue at 6th and I Streets from the black Baptist congregation that had long occupied – then outgrown – it. In 2005, the revived congregation of Adolf Cluss's **Calvary Baptist Church** (8th & I Streets) regained its innovative steeple (*see p69* **Adolf Cluss's Capital**).

The District's long-frustrated goal of a 'living downtown' is finally real, as recent urban deserts bloomed with costly condos. The hottest coming property is north-east of Mount Vernon Square, in an area known as NoMa, named (after Manhattan's SoHo) for NOrth of MAssachusetts Avenue).

★ FREE Smithsonian American Art Museum/National Portrait Gallery (S)

Reynolds Center, 8th & F Street, NW (1-202 633 1000, http://americanart.si.edu, www.npg.si.edu). Gallery Place-Chinatown Metro. **Open** 11.30am-7pm daily. **Admission** free. **Map** p285 J6.
See p52 **Profile**.

Ford's Theatre, Museum, Theatre Center & Petersen House

511 10th Street, NW, between E & F Streets (box office 1-202 347 4833, www.fords.org). Metro Center or Gallery Place-Chinatown Metro. **Open** Hours can vary with theatre peformances & events. *Theatre Center* 9am-4pm daily. *Theatre* 9am-4.30pm daily. *Petersen House* 9am-5pm daily. **Admission** $2.50 in advance, booked online at website. Some free same-day tickets available from box office from 8.30am daily. **Map** p252 J6.
On Good Friday 1865, President Lincoln was enjoying a comedy in Ford's Theatre when actor John Wilkes Booth entered the presidential box and shot him. Wounded in his dramatic leap to the stage, Booth escaped painfully on horseback, only to be killed by US troops 12 days later. Today, the still-working theatre, which underwent major restoration in 2009, looks as it did that day. Also the subject of

a recent revamp, Ford's Theatre Museum tells the story of the Lincoln presidency, from his arrival in Washington to his assassination, through tableaux, artefacts and videos. Exhibits explore life in the Lincoln White House, his cabinet and, of course, the Civil War, highlighting key events and Lincoln's role, and including his speeches. Artefacts include the clothing Lincoln was wearing on the night of his assassination and the gun that was used to fatally wound him.

Across the street, at 516 10th Street, the Petersen House is where the wounded Lincoln was carried after the shooting, and nursed until his death hours later. The red-brick three-storey townhouse has been maintained as a museum, recreating the scene at the time of Lincoln's death.

At 504 10th Street, across the street from the theatre and adjacent to the Petersen House, the new Theatre Center explores Lincoln's legacy, including the impact of his ideas on the civil rights movement and his emergence as a pop culture icon. A video installation remixes his famous speeches – and shows how his words still resonate. The Lincoln Book Tower is an installation featuring a winding staircase and a 34ft tower of books – all of them about Abraham Lincoln. The 'books' are actually made of aluminium, with cover art printed on to them. The tower features 205 real titles, most of which are currently in print. Titles appear several times, and the tower totals approximately 6,800 books.

Madame Tussauds

1001 F Street, NW, between 10th & 11th Streets (1-202 942-7300, www.madametussauds.com/ washington). **Open** 10am-4pm Mon-Thur; 10am-6pm Fri-Sun. **Admission** *In person* $22.79; $18.02 reductions; free under-3s. *Online* $19.37; $16.32 reductions; free under-3s. Further reductions for weekday visits booked online; see website for details. **Credit** AmEx, MC, V. **Map** p252 H6.
Whoopi Goldberg waits to greet you outside Washington's version of Madame Tussauds. And isn't that Penélope Cruz over there by the counter? Inside you'll find all kinds of distinguished personages,

EXPLORE

INSIDE TRACK CITY TRAILS

Cultural Tourism DC's **neighbourhood heritage trails** are a great way to get the best out of exploring the city's diverse neighbourhoods. You'll spot the trails' information boards as you walk around town. Each combines stories, historic photos, and maps. In addition, Audio Journeys are available for the Downtown Heritage Trail and the Greater U Street Heritage Trail. See www.culturaltourismdc.org.

EXPLORE

beginning with historical figures such as King George III (this is where the labels come in handy) and the authors of the Declaration of Independence. You can sit next to Rosa Parks in the civil rights room and meet the likes of Martin Luther King and Malcolm X. There are little nuggets of information throughout, too, such as the fact that the FBI began wiretapping King in 1961, using information gained to try and blackmail him. This being DC, it's not surprising that the nation's presidents are immortalised here – among them President Obama in the Oval Office. You have to wait until the end to find the celebrities: Beyoncé, George Clooney and Oprah among them.

FREE Martin Luther King Jr Memorial Library

901 G Street, NW, between 9th & 10th Streets (general information 1-202 727 0321, www.dc library.org/mlk). Gallery Place-Chinatown Metro. **Open** noon-9pm Mon, Tue; 9.30am-5.30pm Wed-Sat; 1-5pm Sun. **Map** p253 J6.

The main premises of DC's public library system contains the third-floor Washingtoniana Room, where extraordinary reference librarians help researchers sort through books, historical directories, photographs, maps, archival collections from 150 individuals and organisations, and more than 13 million newspaper clippings concerning the District of Columbia and vicinity. Designed by Mies van der Rohe in steel, brick and glass, and built in 1972, the library is one of DC's few modernist buildings. It was listed on the National Register of Historic Places in 2007.

National Museum of Women in the Arts

1250 New York Avenue, NW, at 13th Street (1-202 783 5000, www.nmwa.org). Metro Center Metro. **Open** 10am-5pm Mon-Sat; noon-5pm Sun. **Admission** $10; $8 reductions; free under-18s; free to all 1st Sun of mth. **Credit** AmEx, MC, V. **Map** p252 H5.

With a mission to redefine traditional art history, and the world's only museum devoted entirely to the art of women, the NMWA has a collection of more than 4,500 works by more than 1,000 artists from the 16th century to the present. Highlights include Renaissance artist Lavinia Fontana's dynamic *Holy Family with St John* and Frida Kahlo's defiant 1937 self-portrait *Between the Curtains*. Other artists represented include Elisabetta Sirani, Alma Thomas, Barbara Hepworth and Louise Bourgeois. There are also special collections of 17th-century botanical prints by Sibylla Merian and works by British and Irish women silversmiths from the 17th to 19th centuries. Though it was founded in 1981 by Wallace and Wilhelmina Holladay, the museum didn't occupy its current 70,000sq ft Renaissance Revival building (by Waddy Butler Wood) until six years later. Special exhibitions feature women's work from around the world.

National Geographic Museum

1145 17th Street, NW, at M Street (1-202 857 7588, http://events.nationalgeographic.com/events/ national-geographic-museum/). Farragut North Metro. **Open** 9am-5pm daily. **Admission** varies according to exhibition. **Map** p252 H5.

Founded in 1890 by local patricians, the Geographic has funded nearly 6,000 exploration and research projects to destinations from China to Peru and pole to pole. The National Geographic Museum hosts changing exhibitions on subjects as diverse as Real Pirates: the Untold Story of the *Whydah* from Slave Ship to Pirate Ship, and Birds of Paradise: Amazing Avian Evolution. The adjacent Grosvenor Auditorium hosts traditional illustrated lectures by explorers, but also presents international concerts and videos, and even beer tastings.

National Museum of Crime & Punishment

575 7th Street, NW, between E & F Streets (1-202 393 1099, www.crimemuseum.org). Gallery Place-Chinatown Metro. **Open** *Sept-mid Mar* 10am-7pm Mon-Thur, Sun; 10am-8pm Fri, Sat. *Mid Mar-Aug* 9am-7pm Mon-Sat; 10am-7pm Sun. **Admission** $21.95; $14.95-$19.95 reductions; free under-5s. *Online* $17; $14-$16 reductions. **Credit** AmEx, Disc, MC, V. **Map** p253 J6.

This rather grandly named attraction has crime – real and fictional – covered. Reality bites in the lobby, where serial killer Ted Bundy's VW Bug (Beetle), which he used to pick up the women he later killed, is on display. Visitors head up a black stairwell to the first gallery, a romp through gruesome medieval tortures, gunslingers of the old Wild West, and so on, along with props from some of the big moments of Hollywood crime (Bonnie and Clyde's 1934 Ford, a machine gun used in *Scarface*). Elsewhere, there's lots of interactive stuff: you can take part in a line-up or try and beat a lie detector in the Consequences of Crime section, which also has a line-up of judicial killing machines – a lethal

INSIDE TRACK
CATALYST OF CHANGE

The first time business magnate Abe Pollin visited the site where he would later build the **Verizon Center** (*see right*), the area was so infested with crime and drugs that he was warned not to get out of his car. But he and his wife, Irene, were determined to move their suburban arena to Downtown, in the hope of encouraging urban renewal. The Center opened in 1997, and kick-started a dramatic revival of the area.

US Navy Memorial. *See p60.*

injection machine, gas chamber and Tennessee's electric chair, Old Smokey. The sections on crime fighting allow you to have a go on an FBI firing range, and take part in a simulated police motorcycle chase. The exploration of the work of CSIs and forensic scientists includes a 'body' on a slab showing different injuries and how to interpret them. There's also a section on *America's Most Wanted*.

Verizon Center

601 F Street, NW, at 7th Street (1-202 628 3200, www.verizoncenter.com). Gallery Place-Chinatown Metro. **Open** events only. **Map** p253 J6.

This huge arena hosts some 200 public events every year, including concerts, family entertainment, horse shows and college athletics, as well as professional games by the Washington Capitals NHL hockey team and the Washington Wizards NBA basketball team, along with college basketball. It involves all the economic excesses now de rigueur in American professional sport: startling admission prices, 110 exorbitant sky-boxes for corporate entertaining, restaurants restricting admission to top-end ticketholders, and so on. Still, it's well designed and conveniently situated on top of a Metro station.

PENN QUARTER

North of Federal Triangle, this area is known simply as 'Downtown' to residents. Older people remember it as the city's main shopping district. Then came years of decline – followed by revival. From the late 1990s, the area blossomed, with a host of new restaurants, developments, displays and theatres.

District residents in the 19th century shopped along Pennsylvania Avenue and 7th Street. But then the success of the fixed-price Woodward & Lothrop department store after 1882 made F Street the principal shopping mecca, while business on the Avenue declined. Distressed by the tawdriness of Pennsylvania Avenue as he rode in his 1961 inaugural procession, President Kennedy charged a commission to revamp 'America's Main Street'. The Pennsylvania Avenue Development Corporation rose to the occasion.

The sinuous water crane perched on the quirky Temperance Fountain at 7th Street and Pennsylvania Avenue punctuates the 7th Street arts corridor of galleries and studios behind Victorian storefronts. The former Lansburgh's department store now houses posh apartments above the **Shakespeare Theatre** (450 7th Street, NW, *see p180*). The **US Navy Memorial** plaza nicely frames the 8th Street axis between the **National Portrait Gallery/Smithsonian American Art Museum** (*see p55*) and the **National Archives** (*see p47*). The **International Spy Museum** at 9th and F is a smash hit. Nearby, the **Marian Koshland Science Museum** beckons more soberly.

In the vicinity of the White House, hotels like the **W** (*see p136*), with its famous rooftop bar, and the lavish and historic **Willard InterContinental** (*see p138*) prove that the area has recovered all its lustre. JFK would have been pleased.

The **J Edgar Hoover FBI Building** (935 Pennsylvania Avenue, NW, between 9th & 10th Streets) presents a sterile streetscape because Hoover vetoed planned street-level shops and restaurants as potential security threats.

A locally popular pastime is the Tuesday auction conducted at **Weschler's** (909 E Street, NW, 1-202 628 1281, www.weschlers.com). Treasures, trash and grab bags keep the bidders lively.

EXPLORE

Profile Newseum

All the news about the news.

The line of stands by the Pennsylvania Avenue entrance, filled with copies of today's front pages from newspapers around the world, draws passers-by to this museum dedicated to journalism and free speech, which opened in 2008. The museum's mission is further clarified by a huge marble tablet stretching most of the height of the striking, blue-grey rectilinear building, engraved with the words of the First Amendment, guaranteeing free speech.

Visitors first take an escalator down to **concourse level**, where they are drawn to eight large, graffitied sections of the Berlin Wall, displayed along with an East German watchtower. Photos and words tell the story of the Wall, while screens focus on the media: news reporting from East and West Germany, and, in particular, coverage of the Wall and its fall.

One of the world's largest glass hydraulic lifts speeds visitors straight to **Level 6**, and one of the city's most magnificent panoramas (there's a clear view of the Capitol from the terrace), as well as a display of more than 80 front pages from around the world.

Level 5 contains a theatre with a 90ft screen, showing multiple images of unforgettable news moments. It is also home to the News History exhibition, built around the museum's collection of over 30,000 newspapers, and tracing more than 500 years of news and covering any number of issues – slavery, the Scopes trial and women's suffrage among them. Also explored here are issues of media bias and credibility, modern phenomena of blogging and 'citizen journalists' and the environment of 24-hour rolling news. The Great Books gallery, meanwhile, features books and documents influential to ideas of press freedom. Touch screens allow visitors to see digital images of pages.

The First Amendment is explored on **Level 4**, through current issues such as prayer in schools as well as historic milestones. Also on this level, the 9/11 Gallery has as its centrepiece the upper section of the antenna mast from the World Trade Center's North Tower. There are 9/12 front pages from all 50 states and many other countries, along with first-person accounts from journalists who covered the story. Also included

are pictures by photojournalist William Biggart, taken moments before he was killed when the second tower collapsed.

News in an electronic age is the theme of the Internet, TV & Radio Timeline exhibit on **Level 3**. The timeline traces media milestones, with examples of technology and photographs from the different eras. Touch screens allow visitors to view and listen to important media moments, such as the 1960 Nixon-Kennedy presidential debates and the election of Obama. Coming up to the present, the exhibition looks at the decline of print publications and the role of new media.

The World News Gallery, meanwhile, covers press freedom around the world and highlights hazards faced by journalists. One startling photo depicts photojournalists in the midst of a battle, lying prone on the ground shooting pictures of gunmen, who are shooting their weapons, also lying prone. The Journalists Memorial is a two-storey glass structure that includes the names of thousands of journalists who have died reporting the news. More are added every year. Also

on this level are two TV control rooms, sometimes used for broadcasts by major networks, when visitors may have the opportunity to join the audience. At other times there are guided tours.

Things get interactive on **Level Two**, a popular spot for younger visitors. Here you can try reading the news or weather in front of a live camera, and watch your TV performance later (videos can be downloaded at www. newsmuseum.org). Be A Reporter is an animated game that puts the player in the role of a reporter trying to file a story before deadline. Touch screens in the Ethics Center deal with real ethical questions faced by real journalists, and asks viewers to decide what they would do in similar circumstances.

On **Level 1**, the Pulitzer Prize Photographs Gallery includes every prize-winning entry from 1942 onwards. Over 1,000 images can be viewed through interactive screens. The 535-seat Walter and Leonore Annenberg Theater is the museum's largest, currently showing *I-Witness*, a 4D interactive film that gives viewers an in-the-thick-of-it experience of news events: Isaiah Thomas reporting on the Battle of Lexington and Edward R Murrow broadcasting from London during World War II. Viewers wear 3D glasses; the extra dimension comes from the movement of seats to create motion effects.

At the museum's core is the **Great Hall of News**, a 90-foot atrium that houses some of the biggest artefacts, including the first satellite to send and receive signals simultaneously, thus allowing the first global TV broadcast, as well as a giant media screen, playing reports of historic events, documentaries and breaking news.

For listings, *see p61*.

EXPLORE

TAKE A BREAK
Tucked under the Newseum, Wolfgang Puck's **Source** has a ground-floor lounge (*see p107*) that's ideal for an upscale post-museum drink.

International Spy Museum

800 F Street, NW, between 8th & 9th Streets (1-202 393 7798, www.spymuseum.org). Gallery Place-Chinatown Metro. **Open** daily. Hours vary; check website for details. *Last admission* 2hrs before closing. **Admission** $19.95; $14.95-$15.95 reductions; free under-6s. **Credit** AmEx, Disc, MC, V. **Map** p253 J6.

If your idea of a fun museum experience includes adopting a cover and memorising your alias's vitals – age, provenance, travel plans and itinerary (you'll be asked questions later) – you've come to the right spot. Testing your sleuthing abilities, along with gawking at an array of spy gadgets, including KGB-issued poison pellet shooting umbrellas and Germany's Steineck ABC wristwatch camera, adds up to fun for some folks – many of them under 20. James Bond junkies will be in heaven – the groovy silver Aston Martin from 1964's *Goldfinger* assumes a central spot on the circuit. And in 2013, Exquisitely Evil: 50 Years of Bond Villains, with over 100 film artefacts, marked the anniversary of the Bond films. There's interesting stuff, too, about the part played by codes and codebreaking in World War II, about the spying heyday of the Cold War, and the modern world of cyber attacks and cyber forensics. Not surprisingly, the museum has proved a huge hit since it opened in 2002; consider booking tickets in advance.

Marian Koshland Science Museum of the National Academy of Sciences

6th Street & E Streets, NW (1-202 334 1201, www.koshland-science-museum.org). Gallery Place-Chinatown Metro. **Open** 10am-6pm Mon, Wed-Sun (last admission 5pm). **Admission** $7; $4 reductions. **Credit** MC, V. **Map** p253 J6.

Though modestly sized and featuring only five exhibitions at a time, this museum, named after immunologist and molecular biologist Marian Koshland, proves something of an eye-opener. State-of-the-art, interactive displays teach visitors by doing, not just showing. At the time of writing, exhibitions covered global warming with Earth Lab: Degrees of Change; images of earth at night with Lights at Night; the ageing process with Life Lab, along with the self-explanatory Safe Drinking Water. In addition, Wonders of Science examines recent research aiming to unravel some of the greatest mysteries of the universe.

[FREE] US Navy Memorial & Naval Heritage Center

701 Pennsylvania Avenue, NW, between 7th & 9th Streets (1-202 737 2300, www.navy memorial.org). Archives-Navy Memorial Metro. **Open** *Heritage Center* 9.30am-5.30pm daily. **Admission** free. **Map** p253 J6.

Dedicated on the Navy's 212th birthday in 1987, this memorial features the world's biggest map of itself – a flat granite circular map measuring 100ft across, with this very spot at its centre – compassed by an apron with 22 bas-reliefs depicting naval highlights like Teddy Roosevelt's globe-circling Great White Fleet of 1907, Commodore Perry's 1854 expedition to Japan and the 'Silent Service' of submarines. Off-centre stands a statue of the Lone Sailor, stolid in his pea jacket. Just off the Memorial plaza, the Heritage Center has exhibits on the Gallery Deck and screens several movies daily on a 52ft screen. *Photo p57.*

JUDICIARY SQUARE

Judiciary Square is the hub of the city's courts. The **National Building Museum** occupies the 1883 Pension Building, a Renaissance palace sporting an extraordinary frieze of Civil War troops perpetually patrolling the premises. Its atrium is spectacular and its gift shop imaginative. Across F Street, bronze lions flank the **National Law Enforcement Officers Memorial** to the nearly 19,000 cops killed in the line of duty since 1792 with an explanatory visitors' centre (605 E Street, NW, 1-202 737 3213).

The Court of Appeals building (5th & D Streets) was once Washington's city hall, a chaste 1820 Greek Revival design by British architect George Hadfield. Lincoln's statue at the front is significant as the first public memorial to the murdered president, sculpted by his acquaintance, Lot Flannery, who knew how he looked while orating, and dedicated in 1868 on the third anniversary of his death.

Down the stairs that constitute 4th Street, beside the statue of Chief Justice John Marshall that once graced the Capitol grounds, the **Canadian Embassy** (501 Pennsylvania Avenue, NW) – awarded its prominent site in honour of close bi-national relations – houses a gallery spotlighting Canadian artists. The distinctive and strikingly rectangular **Newseum** rises adjacent on its west side.

Protected by statues of General Meade, victor at Gettysburg, and legal commentator Sir William Blackstone, the US Court House opposite the embassy has gradually lost its 'Watergate Courthouse' identity over the years, as subsequent scandals unfold before interminable grand juries. A new wing to the east has enlivened its appearance.

The **Japanese-American Memorial** at Louisiana and D, NW, honours Americans of Japanese descent interned during World War II, and the Nisei regiments of their sons who fought for the US. An eloquent sculpture depicts traditional Japanese cranes trapped in barbed wire.

Dating from 1876, Washington's first synagogue now houses the **Jewish Historical Society** and its museum.

Jewish Historical Society of Greater Washington

701 3rd Street, NW, at G Street (1-202 789 0900, www.jhsgw.org). Judiciary Square Metro. **Open** 1-4pm Mon, Tue, Thur or by appointment; for admission, call or ring bell at office, 701 4th Street, Suite 200. **Admission** suggested donation $5. **Credit** MC, V. **Map** p253 K6.

Exhibits of local Jewish history organised by the Jewish Historical Society occupy the ground floor of this now-landmarked former synagogue – the oldest in Washington. Built in 1876 of red brick, the structure was adopted by the society in 1960; its sanctuary was restored in the 1970s, preserving the original ark, pine benches, and slender columns that support the women's balcony.

National Building Museum

401 F Street, NW, between 4th & 5th Streets (1-202 272 2448, www.nbm.org). Judiciary Square Metro. **Open** 10am-5pm Mon-Sat; 11am-5pm Sun. **Admission** suggested donation $5. **Credit** AmEx, MC, V. **Map** p253 J6.

A privately run collection, the National Building Museum produces smart, noteworthy exhibits focusing on architects and the built environment, both contemporary and historical. However, the main attraction is without doubt the building's Italian Renaissance-style Great Hall, with its central fountain and eight colossal 75ft Corinthian columns: visitors crane their necks for a vertiginous look at the ceiling 15 storeys above. Among the exhibitions, House & Home discovers the history and many meanings of 'home', both physical and cultural, with an array of all things household, from household goods and decorations (including a poster of Farrah Fawcett and a fondue set), to building materials to mortgage papers. The red-brick building, designed as the US Pension Building, was completed in 1887. Note that the Building Zone, a hands-on introduction for visitors aged two to six, closes at 4pm.

★ Newseum

555 Pennsylvania Avenue, at 6th Street, NW (1-888 639 7386, www.newseum.org). Archives-Navy Memorial Metro. **Open** 9am-5pm daily. **Admission** $21.95; $12.95-$17.95 reductions; free under-6s. **Map** p253 J6.
See p59 **Profile.**

DUPONT CIRCLE

Dupont Circle is perhaps one of the most cosmopolitan DC neighbourhoods, its bars and restaurants drawing a diverse public. The circle itself is a popular green space, with a collection of chess tables in constant use. A central marble fountain sprays into the air in honour of Civil War admiral Samuel Francis Dupont. In the late 19th century, mansions began sprouting in what had been a backwater to accommodate arriviste millionaires, in time morphing into Embassy Row. The area was a countercultural hotbed in the 1960s, when anti-Vietnam War and Black Power activists claimed the circle for demonstrations.

Today, though, the neighbourhood has hit the mainstream. Chain stores have infiltrated Connecticut Avenue, but enough idiosyncratic bookstores and bistros and galleries (sporting open-house receptions every first Friday evening) survive to reward a wander.

Large hotels and apartment buildings start to dominate the landscape about four blocks north, heading towards Adams Morgan (*see p64*). The pavement outside the Washington Hilton on the corner of Connecticut Avenue and T Street was the site of John Hinckley's attempted assassination of President Reagan in 1981.

Off Connecticut Avenue, the blocks north of the circle consist largely of well-kept Edwardian rowhouses, art galleries and gorgeous mansions now occupied by embassies or non-profit associations. If the weather is fine, amble northwards through the blocks west of Connecticut Avenue – known as Kalorama – to check out the impressive architecture and exhibitions. The galleries display contemporary, experimental and traditional art, from painting

Marian Koshland Science Museum of the National Academy of Sciences

EXPLORE

to sculpture to photography. At the heart of them all is the **Phillips Collection**, opened in 1921 as the first permanent museum of modern art in America. For more information on other galleries, *see pp128-129*.

Massachusetts Avenue, from Scott Circle, east of Dupont Circle, through to Upper Northwest (*see p80*) is known as 'Embassy Row'. For a cheap tour, catch any westbound 'N' Metrobus at Dupont Circle and cruise past the mosque established for diplomats in the 1950s (No.2551, at Belmont Road, Kalorama), the embassies of Turkey, the Netherlands, Brazil, the Vatican, and others. Further on, into Upper Northwest, the British Embassy (No.3100) sports a statue of Churchill, with one foot on British soil (all embassies are deemed their nations' territory) and the other on American, reflecting his ancestry. The US confiscated the former Iranian Embassy across the way following the seizure of the American Embassy in Tehran and the holding of its staff hostage in 1979, only to rent it out for extremely expensive parties and wedding receptions. Lots of embassies open their doors for concerts, art displays and charity events (see www.embassyseries.org).

Foreign heroes patrol this strand: there's a statue of Gandhi at 21st Street, near the Indian Embassy; Czechoslovakian leader Masaryk adorns 22nd Street; and, further north, political martyr Robert Emmet gazes toward the Irish Embassy from the 2200 block. At the Norwegian Embassy (2720 34th Street, NW), in 2005, King Harald V dedicated a statue of his mother, Crown Princess Märtha, who stayed at the White House with the Roosevelts after the Nazis overran her country in 1940.

★ Phillips Collection

1600 21st Street, NW, at Q Street (1-202 387 2151, www.phillipscollection.org). Dupont Circle Metro. **Open** 10am-5pm Tue, Wed, Fri, Sat; 10am-8.30pm Thur; 11am-6pm Sun. **Admission** *Special exhibitions & museum collection* $12; $10 reductions; free under-18s. *Museum collection only (when no special exhibition in progress)* Sat, Sun $10; $8 reductions; free under-18s. Tue-Fri admission by donation. **Credit** AmEx, MC, V. **Map** p282 G4.

This mansion was opened as a gallery in the 1920s by Marjorie and Duncan Phillips as a memorial to his father. The building was remodelled in the 1960s and underwent further renovation in the '80s, when an extension increased its space by almost 20,000sq ft. In 2006, the museum unveiled its Sant Building, another expansion project that added airy galleries for modern art, an outdoor sculpture terrace and café, an art and technology laboratory and an auditorium. The museum's signature painting, Renoir's *Luncheon of the Boating Party*, enjoys pride of place in the permanent collection galleries. There, significant Van

Gogh oils rub shoulders with Steiglitz prints and a solid selection of works by Picasso, Paul Klee, Bacon, Vuillard and Rothko – that is, if a travelling show hasn't deposed them temporarily. Special exhibitions cover subjects as diverse as Italian contemporary photography and cross-cultural artistic dialogue as revealed in work by Americans Jackson Pollock and Alfonso Ossorio, and French painter Jean Dubuffet.

FREE Society of the Cincinnati, Anderson House Museum

2118 Massachusetts Avenue, NW, at 21st Street (1-202 785 2040, www.societyofthecincinnati.org). Dupont Circle Metro. **Open** 1-4pm Tue-Sat. *Guided tours* 1.15pm, 2.15pm, 3.15pm Tue-Sat. **Admission** free. **Map** p282 G4.

This museum, the former residence of American diplomat Larz Anderson III and his wife Isabel, contains works acquired on the couple's many trips to Asia and Europe. Anderson, a direct descendant of a founding member of the Society of the Cincinnati, bequeathed his house to that organisation, which was formed just after the American Revolution with the aim of sharing wealth among bereft army veterans who had fought for independence (the group included Founding Father George Washington). In 1902, the Andersons hired Boston architectural firm Arthur Little and Herbert Browne to construct the limestone Beaux Arts mansion, and imported Italian artisans to carve and inlay wood and gilt floors and ceilings. Downstairs, one room is devoted to an exhibition about the American Revolution; another is devoted to the history of the Cincinnati Society. Rooms on the first and second floors house the Anderson Collection, whose treasures include numerous bejewelled Chinese semi-precious stone and jade trees, and Flemish Renaissance tapestries dating from the late 16th and early 17th centuries.

▶ *Tapestries depicting the biblical battle of David and Goliath that once hung in the ballroom at the Anderson House were donated to Washington National Cathedral (see p70). They can be seen today in St Mary's Chapel.*

Textile Museum

2320 S Street, NW, between 23rd & 24th Streets (1-202 667 0441, www.textilemuseum.org). Dupont Circle Metro. **Open** 10am-5pm Mon-Sat; 1-5pm Sun. **Admission** suggested donation $5. **Credit** AmEx, MC, V. **Map** p282 F4.

A modest collection nestled amid regal townhouses, the Textile Museum has two permanent exhibitions: the Textile Learning Center describes the history and procedures of textile production, while the Collections Gallery rotates selections of historic rugs and textiles. Temporary exhibitions also feature. In 2013, Out of Southeast Asia: Art that Sustains revealed how textiles in the region originally served as markers of ethnicity, and how their various patterns have been developed and interpreted by contemporary artists.

EXPLORE

Treasure Rooms

Some rooms in the city's art museums are as extraordinary as the paintings.

SALON DORÉ AT THE CORCORAN MUSEUM OF ART

The 18th-century neo-classical Salon Doré – transported from the Hôtel de Clermont in Paris, complete with gilded and mirrored panelling decorated with garlands, Corinthian pilasters and trophy panels – is a feast for the eyes. Given to the museum by industrialist and US senator William A Clark (1839-1925), the room was removed from its original location in aristocratic Faubourg Saint-Germain and brought to New York, where it was installed in Clark's Fifth Avenue mansion. For the Corcoran, *see p40*.

MUSIC ROOM AT THE PHILLIPS COLLECTION

Duncan Phillips' luxuriant 1897 mansion holds a special treat: a dark, enveloping Music Room with spectacular oak wainscoting and ceiling coffers. The room originally functioned as Duncan and his brother James' recreation room – and a very sophisticated rec room indeed. Later, it was converted to a recital space, playing host to Sunday afternoon concerts, beginning in 1941. Today, the room continues to host Sunday concerts from October to May. For the Phillips Collection, *see p62*.

PEACOCK ROOM AT THE FREER GALLERY OF ART

Whistler's deep green and gilt Peacock Room was purchased by Detroit business magnate Charles Lang Freer in 1904. The 1876-77 dining room was transported wholesale from British shipowner Frederick R Leyland's London townhouse. Whistler covered the ceiling with a gold leaf and peacock feather pattern, and added gilded shelving and painted wooden shutters with immense plumed peacocks. His Japanese-influenced canvas, *The Princess from the Land of Porcelain*, presides over the room. For the Freer Gallery of Art, *see p31*.

DINING ROOM AT HILLWOOD MUSEUM AND GARDENS

This sumptuous room, covered in 18th-century French oak panels, hosted some of Washington's most lavish dinner parties. Though today the dining table is set with spectacular displays of porcelain, silver and glassware, once a year these are removed and the gorgeous table uncovered. Spanning 28 feet, the piece features around 70 types of minerals and marbles set into its surface in glorious stylised floral motifs. For Hillwood Museum and Gardens, *see p70*.

EXPLORE

Peacock Room.

**INSIDE TRACK
PHILLIPS AFTER FIVE**

Phillips after Five, at the **Phillips
Collection** (*see p62*) from 5pm to
8.30pm on the first Thursday of every
month, offers evening visitors jazz, food
and drink, lectures, films, and more.

ADAMS MORGAN

To the east of Dupont Circle, 18th Street becomes
the main strip of lively Adams Morgan some
nine walkable blocks north, known for its ethnic
restaurants and diversity. Streetlife started out
as Latino, with Africans and others livening the
mix today. The pace picks up at night, when
18th Street (up to and including the spots along
Columbia Road, which intersects 18th Street at
the top of the hill) morphs into a big bar and
dining scene. The bars range from flat-out frat-
boy hangouts to salsa and reggae clubs, and on
warm summer evenings outdoor cafés pack in
customers while the streets pack automobiles in
futile late-night quests for parking spaces. The
area is also particularly known for its Ethiopian
restaurants (*see p99* **Ethiopian Eats**).

Adams Morgan got its name in the 1950s,
when progressive-minded residents opted to
integrate the white Adams school with the black
Morgan school. One place in Adams Morgan that
is always lively during the day is **Malcolm X
Park** – officially Meridian Hill Park (bordered
by 16th, Euclid, 15th and W Streets, NW).

SHAW

Bounded by North Capitol Street and 16th Street
on the east and west, and by Irving Street and
M Street to the north and south, Shaw embraces
historic neighbourhoods, including Howard
University, the U Street Corridor and Logan
Circle – all the latter two are more often called
by their own names, and we have treated them
as separate areas in this guide. All were bastions
of African American DC, fostering black
businesses, churches and scholarship – with the
historically black **Howard University** – during
the decades of racial segregation. Today, Shaw
has bounced back from long decline, exacerbated
by the disastrous 1968 riots following the
assassination of Martin Luther King.

Howard University

*2400 6th Street, NW, at Howard Place (1-202
806 6100, www.howard.edu). Shaw-Howard
University Metro then 70, 71 bus.* **Map** p283 J2.
With a hall of fame that includes former mayors and
Supreme Court justices, Howard University has a

legacy to brag about. It was chartered in 1867 as a
theological seminary to train black ministers to
teach slaves emancipated by the Civil War. By 1940,
half of African Americans in college studied here,
including much of the leadership that planned the
legal assault on Jim Crow segregation. Howard holds
some of the best collections on African history and
art in the country at the Howard University Museum
on the first floor of the Founders Library.

U STREET CORRIDOR

Known during the Jazz Age as America's
'Black Broadway', the neighbourhood around
U Street became an African American cultural
powerhouse during the 1920s and '30s. Poet
Langston Hughes and jazz great Duke Ellington
matured here. Along with Ella Fitzgerald, Nat
King Cole and Redd Fo, they made 'You' Street
world-famous.

Like most of the surrounding area, the
neighbourhood was trashed during the 1968
riots, which began at the corner of 14th and
U Streets when the news reached Washington
that Martin Luther King had been shot dead.
The riots hastened the decline of the old
U Street, and the area languished for many
years, with empty storefronts and high crime.
Thankfully, it has since come back to life as

Georgetown.

a shopping and nightlife corridor for a diverse group of consumers, diners, drinkers and partyers. These days, it seems a new business opens along the stretch between 9th Street and 16th Street nearly every week.

Restaurant, café and art space **Busboys & Poets** (1390 V Street, NW, *see p98*) was a pioneer of the 'new' U Street corridor; its well-known old-school neighbour is **Ben's Chili Bowl** (*see p98*), on U Street between 12th and 13th Streets, a restaurant frequented by celebs such as Bill Cosby. Meanwhile, the stretch of U Street between 15th and 16th Streets has become the centre for thriving vintage clothes shops (*see p122* **Vintage on U Street**). The **Lincoln Theatre** (*see p178*), next door to Ben's, was once a grand stage for black performances in the age of segregation. In 2012, the historic **Howard Theatre** (620 T Street, NW, at 7th Street, *see p172*) – where so many jazz greats performed before it closed in 1980 – reopened after a major renovation. This restored the façade to its original glory and revamped the interior with walnut panelling and giant portraits of the legends that once graced its stage. Its reopening cements the area's reputation as the best part of the city for music. The **9:30 Club** (*see p170*) is Washington's top rock venue, with concerts that sell out nearly every night. And smaller clubs such as **Twins Jazz** (*see p174*), **Velvet Lounge** (*see p174*), and the **U Street Music Hall** (*see p169*) bring in good performers too. And it's not unusual to find a jazz trio playing at one of the low-key bars along this stretch.

At the U Street-Cardozo Metro station is an **African American Civil War Memorial**.

LOGAN CIRCLE

On the edge of downtown DC, the Logan Circle neighbourhood – with housing stock composed largely of solid Victorian rowhouses – has experienced similar ups and downs to U Street. Predominantly an African American residential district in the early 20th century, with 14th Street a shopping street for both black and white, it suffered from decline and crime in the 1980s and '90s, followed by regeneration and gentrification in the 2000s. On Vermont Avenue the **Mary McLeod Bethune Council House** (no.1318, www.nps.go/mamc, open 9am-5pm Mon-Sat) was bought by Bethune and the National Council of Negro Women, which she founded, as its headquarters. Bethune was also a special advisor on race to FDR and a member of his cabinet and this was her last home in DC. On display are photos, manuscripts and other artefacts related to her life.

Today, in addition to restaurants, bars and a lively gay scene, Logan Circle is home to the

INSIDE TRACK
1515 14TH STREET

Developer Giorgio Furioso cemented the status of Logan Circle as DC's art hub when he opened **1515 14th Street**, a building that collects some of the city's strongest dealers under a single roof. Furioso found elegant proportions, generous spaces and period details in a former car dealership built in the 1920s; his team then refurbished the interior plasterwork and preserved exterior details, including the original rosettes and Greek motifs occupying the structure's cornice and lintels. Furioso and his gallery tenants were doing what gentrifiers usually do: following the pioneers. As chain stores and high-end furniture outlets moved in and condominiums mushroomed in Logan Circle in the noughties, Furioso and the galleries recognised an opportunity. To some, though, the institutionalisation of the Logan Circle gallery neighbourhood was more death knell than jubilee, with some galleries already decamping to the Atlas District around H Street, where cheaper rents beckon.

Studio Theatre (*see p181*), and is also the centre of the city's art scene. Some of Washington's strongest dealers are collected under a single roof at **1515 14th Street** (*see above* **Inside Track**), with others throughout the neighbourhood.

MOUNT PLEASANT/COLUMBIA HEIGHTS

Columbia Heights has become a hot neighbourhood in recent years. It's home to the **GALA Hispanic Theatre** (*see p184*), which moved into what had been the old Tivoli Theatre in 2005, along with bars, restaurants and a young population of gentrifiers who have made their mark on an area that has traditionally had a large Latino population.

GEORGETOWN

George, Maryland, was laid out in 1751 and variously tried to unite with Washington City (1857) and secede from the District (often). Losing its separate government in 1871, Georgetown drew the line at its proposed designation as 'West Washington'. Today's Georgetown is unlike the rest of the city, with tranquil residential streets lined with historic homes and haughty boutiques. Its physical

Walk Georgetown

Affluent and distinctive, Georgetown is a different Washington.

Starting the walk where Rock Creek flows into the Potomac, note the new House of Sweden, a unique embassy/trade office/condo at 2900 K Street, NW. A detour north on 30th Street leads to the C&O Canal visitor centre, embarkation point for leisurely mule-drawn barge-rides evoking early trade. An inviting towpath parallels the Potomac, although beware how far you go: it runs 186 miles west to Cumberland, Maryland.

Back on K Street, a turn north on Thomas Jefferson Street leads to the **Old Stone House** (*see left*), Georgetown's earliest, a modest home that dates from 1768. A right turn down M Street leads past historically plaqued buildings to the Thomas Sim Lee corner, which was Georgetown's original boundary.

A block north is the 3000 block of N Street, NW. Jacqueline Kennedy lived in the 1794 mansion at 3017 for a year after her husband's assassination.

Crossing Georgetown's shopping and bar-hopping thoroughfare, Wisconsin Avenue, at N Street, one finds Martin's Tavern thriving as it did when Jack Kennedy (by some accounts) proposed to Jackie in Booth #3. They lived down the street at 3307 when he was elected president. (JFK junkies can download a self-guided tour called 'The Kennedys' Georgetown' at www.georgetowndc.com.)

Ascending to O Street in search of other glam couples, one encounters antiquated cobblestones and streetcar tracks as well as the **Bodisco House** (3322 O Street, NW), home of the fiftysomething Russian ambassador who in 1840 married a local 16-year-old, the lovebirds being dubbed Beauty and the Beast. Now it is the home of sometime Democratic presidential candidate John Kerry, the wealthiest member of the US Senate through his ketchup-heiress spouse, Teresa Heinz Kerry.

Straight ahead looms **Georgetown University** (*see p67*), dominated by the distinctive neo-Gothic Healy Hall (1877). Founded in 1789, Georgetown is the nation's oldest Catholic and Jesuit college and one of America's hottest universities.

If the gatehouse information booth isn't open, any student can point you to Loyola Hall, where Bill Clinton '68 once bunked.

A turn down 37th Street passes **Holy Trinity Church**, where JFK last attended mass before his assassination. A left turn down N Street passes the renowned Georgetown School of Foreign Service, its building betraying its origins as the original university hospital. Nearby you'll find Georgetown's most iconic image: a turn down 36th Street dead-ends at Prospect Street, where a turn to the left in the 3500 block leads past the homes and the steep stairs immortalised on film in *The Exorcist*. Descend them if you dare. Note that the houses are considerably further from the steps than Hollywood magic placed them.

Passing the massive car-barn building, cross M Street at 34th Street to Francis Scott Key Park, flying a 15-star flag to honour the author of America's national anthem, 'The Star-Spangled Banner' (1814). Plaques here display Key's history, and that of the neighbourhood. Key's home was torn down to build the western access loop to the bridge named for him, which at least affords splendid views of the river.

A stroll east down M Street – Georgetown's other commercial corridor – approaches the area's heart, the intersection of Wisconsin and M Streets, NW. Dean & Deluca gourmet grocery (3276 M Street, NW) occupies the old **Georgetown Market House** (1865), which spanned the Canal until raised 15 feet to its present site by mule power in 1871. Nearby, Georgetown Park has imaginatively transformed a sprawling transit facility into an inviting shopping mall.

division from the rest of the District by Rock Creek – and lack of Metro coverage – enhances its insularity.

At the upriver limit of navigation for ocean vessels, the town started life as a colonial tobacco port. Oxen pulled huge cylinders of 'sot weed' down its 'rolling road', now Wisconsin Avenue. Construction on the **C&O Canal**, running 185 miles from the Potomac to Cumberland, Maryland, began in 1828. From the mid 1800s, black Georgetown thrived south of P Street between Rock Creek and 31st Street. Some 1,000 African American families slept here at night, working by day as cooks, domestics and stable boys. Although it's hard to fathom now, Georgetown was dwindling into slumishness by the 1930s. Then, a 'colonial revival' made old homes fashionable again. Many of FDR's New Dealers moved in amid the multi-generation 'cave dwellers', turning Georgetown into a chic address; JFK's 'New Frontiersmen' finished the transformation. **Georgetown University** is an academically rigorous institution; its students populate the nightlife throngs.

The intersecting shopping strips are M Street and Wisconsin Avenue. The sidewalks are crowded at weekends with people throwing money around at the chic clothing stores. Built by cabinet-maker Christopher Layman in 1765, the **Old Stone House** (3051 M Street, NW, 1-202 426 6851, www.nps.gov/olst/index.htm, open noon-5pm daily) is the oldest home in DC, its garden offering repose to the weary consumer. The garden is open during daylight hours and is accessible through the gate on M Street.

Stately **Tudor Place** (1644 31st Street, NW) rests serenely isolated on extensive grounds, while **Dumbarton Oaks** is home to a first-class collection of Byzantine and pre-Columbian art. Landscape architect Beatrix Farrand designed its celebrated formal gardens.

At night Georgetown jumps with dozens of bars and restaurants filled with suburban twentysomethings and international glitterati. In the summer, **Washington Harbour**, on the Potomac River, is overrun with revellers. The restaurants are forgettable and the drinks overpriced, but breezes off the Potomac make the promenade a nice stroll. To the west, ten acres of previously derelict land, between K Street and the river, have been transformed into **Georgetown Waterfront Park**.

Georgetown University

37th & O Streets, NW (1-202 687 0100, www.georgetown.edu). Dupont Circle Metro then G2 bus, Foggy Bottom-GWU Metro then 30, 32, 34, 35, 36, 38B bus or Circulator bus. **Map** p281 D4.

This Jesuit institution was founded in 1789 by John Carroll, first Catholic bishop in the United States. Alumni fought on both sides in the Civil War, inspiring the school colours, blue and grey. Equally polarising alumni of more recent vintage include Bill Clinton and pundit Pat Buchanan.

FREE Georgetown Waterfront Park

Wisconsin Avenue & Whitehurst Freeway (K Street), NW (www.georgetownwaterfrontpark.org). **Open** 24hrs daily. **Map** p249 E5.

After decades of lobbying and fundraising, the once-derelict land on the Georgetown bank of the Potomac south of K Street has been transformed into a ten-acre landscaped park at the water's edge. The once-thriving commercial waterfront had long lain derelict. By the 1960s, the land had been condemned, earmarked for an interstate highway that was never built. Part of the area was occupied by a parking lot, with the removal of many tons of concrete and other debris necessary before the vision of the park could be realised. The final completed section opened in 2011, linking 225 miles of parkland along the Potomac, from Cumberland, Maryland, to Mount Vernon, Virginia.

Geography – the park spans a curve on the river – contributes to the organic, fluid landscaping, with gently sloping grassy hills, flowering trees, shady seating and winding paths. At the water's edge runs a bio-engineered rain garden – a line of plants that not only helps keep the shoreline in place but also filters run-off before it enters the river. The western part of the park, from Wisconsin Avenue to the Key Bridge, is less ordered and a little wilder. It's here that you'll find the wide green spaces, with panoramic river overlooks in the form of granite slabs etched with historical scenes, allowing visitors to get close to the water. Also here is a labyrinth. The eastern side of the park, between Wisconsin Avenue and Washington Harbor at 31st Street, is more heavily used and formal. The city meets the park at the southern end of Wisconsin Avenue at Wisconsin Plaza, with a line of arching, interactive fountains and benches alongside. Also here are wide river stairs down to the water's edge, which form a kind of ampitheatre for watching rowing races, with a pergola above.

EXPLORE

INSIDE TRACK WATER TAXIS

Get another view of the city from the river. Water taxis ply the Potomac from Washington Harbor in Georgetown to the Wharf on the Southwest waterfront (690 Water Street, SW) to the Yards, near the new Nationals Park in SE (*see p189*) and RFK Landing, for RFK Stadium (*see p189*). See www.americanrivertaxi.com or call 1-240 547 9493 for schedules and prices.

Upper Northwest

The affluent sector north of Georgetown is often referred to as 'West of the Park', the park being the extensive, leafy landscape of **Rock Creek Park**. It is home to some of the city's wealthiest residents. Massive homes and posh boutiques stack up, one after another, on streets such as Foxhall Road and upper Wisconsin Avenue.

    Washington National Cathedral is the second-largest place of worship in the US. On the cathedral grounds are two selective prep schools favored by the children of the elite: St Alban's and National Cathedral School. Beyond lies another, Sidwell Friends, where current students include Sasha and Malia Obama. Nearby are the **Khalil Gibran Peace Garden** and the **US Naval Observatory** (3450 Massachusetts Avenue, NW, 1-202 762 1467), housing the official residence of the vice-president. Its first occupant, multimillionaire Nelson Rockefeller, reportedly found the mansion too small.

Dumbarton Oaks Research Library & Collections

1703 32nd Street, NW, between R & S Streets, Georgetown (1-202 339 6401, www.doaks.org). Bus 30, 32, 34, 36. **Open** *Museum 2-5pm Tue-Sun. Gardens mid Mar-Oct 2-6pm Tue-Sun. Nov-mid Mar 2-5pm Tue-Sun.* **Admission** *Museum free. Gardens $8; $5 reductions; free in winter.* **No credit cards. Map** p249 E4.

Wealthy art connoisseurs Mildred and Robert Woods Bliss purchased the 19th-century Federal-style brick mansion Dumbarton Oaks in 1920. In 1940, they commissioned architects McKim, Mead and White to build an extension, which they filled with their modest-sized collection of Byzantine art. The array of portable, sumptuous Byzantine objects, including rare sixth-century ecclesiastical silver, is one of the world's finest. That same year the Blisses gave the property, collections and a newly endowed research library to Harvard University.

    In 1963, the octagonal Philip Johnson-designed wing was completed; today it houses the pre-Columbian collection in galleries encircling a central fountain. Unmissable exhibits here include a miraculously preserved Peruvian burial mantle from 400 BC and the grotesque 'Head of a Maize God', originally crafted in AD 775 for a Honduran temple. The House Collection, principally in the Music Room, has tapestries, sculpture and paintings dating from the 15th to 19th centuries, with highlights including El Greco's *Visitation*. The 16 acres of flora-filled formal gardens skirting the mansion, the creation of Beatrix Farrand, are also open to the public and worth a wander.

Katzen Arts Center at American University

4400 Massachusetts Avenue, NW, at Nebraska Avenue (1-202 885 1300, www.american.edu/museum). Tenleytown-AU Metro then N2, M4 bus or Friendship Heights Metro then N3, N4, N6, N8 bus. **Open** *Museum 11am-4pm Tue-Sun.* **Admission** free.

This 36,000sq ft public museum and sculpture garden is devoted to special exhibitions of contemporary art and student shows from the university's art department. Check the museum website for up-to-date listings.

Kreeger Museum

2401 Foxhall Road, NW, between Dexter & W Streets (1-202 337 3050, reservations 1-202 338 3552, www.kreegermuseum.org). D6 bus. **Open** *10am-4pm Fri, Sat. Guided tours 10.30am, 1.30pm Fri; 10.30am, noon, 2pm Sat. Open for guided tours only (must be booked in advance) 10.30am, 1.30pm Tue-Thur.* **Admission** $10; $7 reductions. **Credit** AmEx, MC, V. **Map** p248 C3.

This intimate museum, housed in a spectacular 1967 Philip Johnson-designed travertine home nestled in woods, is best visited on one of its small, 90-minute guided tours. Alternatively, visitors may stop in during the day on Saturday. Either way, it's worth it: the late insurance magnate David Lloyd Kreeger and his wife Carmen amassed a small but striking collection of 180 works by 19th- and 20th-century heavyweights. The museum's scale allows visitors to savour the details of works by Kandinsky, Chagall, Stella and Braque; two rooms showcase Monet's cliffside landscapes. The Kreegers also collected African ceremonial art, and their outdoor sculpture terrace overlooking verdant woodland has bronzes by Henry Moore, Jean Arp and Aristide Maillol. Public transport doesn't take you very close to the museum; it's probably easier to take a cab. See the website for details of Open House events.

FREE Rock Creek Park

1-202 895 6070, www.nps.gov/rocr. **Open** *Park dawn-dusk daily. Nature Center & Planetarium 9am-5pm Wed-Sun.* **Map** p249 F3.

Nestled between sprawling condo corridors and busy commercial strips lie 1,750 acres of forest called Rock Creek Park, following that stream all the way to the city line to join an extension into Maryland. One of the largest such preserves in the nation, its 29 miles of hiking trails and ten miles of bridle paths intersect a net of bicycle paths. At weekends, several park roads close to motor vehicles. Its central thoroughfare, Beach Drive, a major commuter cut during weekday rush hour, is a quiet route to picnic groves (some with barbecue facilities) and playing fields at other times. The park is a magnet for wildlife, its deer population swollen to nuisance levels. The

Adolf Cluss's Capital

The architect who added red brick to Washington's palette.

Architect Adolf Cluss (1825-1905) emerged from obscurity as a draughtsman at the Navy Yard to become the prime mover in redesigning the city in the wake of the Civil War. With a background in engineering, Cluss was able to move into architecture, favouring brick made from the city's clay soil and obsessing over light, ventilation and fire safety. His great opportunity came in 1871, when the Territory of the District of Columbia was formed under Alexander 'Boss' Shepherd, with a programme to turn the tawdry town into 'a capital worthy of a republic'. As the city's chief engineer, Cluss plunged into giving Washington what would become its characteristic look, planning 'tree boxes' of greenery between the streets and the sidewalks, ceding homeowners tax-free front yards, with freedom to extend bay windows into that space, and designing public and private buildings on a human scale.

Few would have realised that the makeover of the post-Civil War capital was actually in the hands of a communist. Born in Heilbrunn, Wurrtemberg, Cluss had led the Communist League of Mainz during the 1848 revolution, coming as Marx's personal agent to Washington, where he ran the Communist League, USA from his Navy Yard office. He prospered and married, experiencing social mobility unlikely in Europe, finally telling Marx that communism

wouldn't work here. But his early social philosophy remained a major influence on his urban planning.

Even after the spendthrift Shepherd regime collapsed in scandal in 1874, Cluss continued to leave his mark through many churches, private homes, public buildings, and Washington's first apartment house. Most are gone, because they centred on old Downtown, where office blocks claimed the sites of Cluss's winsome, eclectic Rundbogenstil works. We list those that remain below.

● **Sumner School** (1872) 17th & M Streets, NW. The first public high school for African Americans, now the DC Public School Museum and Archives.

● **Masonic Temple** (1869) 910 F Street, NW. The building has thrived as a restaurant and offices. Across the street, the National Portrait Gallery reopened in 2006 drawing acclaim for its interiors, which Cluss had redesigned after a fire. (He also restored the Smithsonian's Castle Building interiors after another conflagration.)

● **Calvary Baptist Church** (1864, 1869) 777 Eighth Street, NW. In 2004 Cluss's unique steeple, which had been blown down by a 1913 hurricane, was replaced with a replica.

● **Eastern Market** (1873) 7th and C Streets, SE. Now meticulously restored to its former glory, following a fire in 2007.

● **Alexandria, Virginia City Hall** (1873) 301 King Street. It retains the original Cluss look on the Cameron Street side only.

● **Franklin School** (1869) 13th and K Streets, NW. The building won international contemporary design acclaim.

● **Arts & Industries Building** (1881) 900 Jefferson Drive, SW. Regarded as Cluss's mid-Mall masterpiece, it became the centre of controversy when the Smithsonian Institution left the premises, pleading that the handsome but deteriorating roof it had long neglected was too costly to fix. The building is now on the National Trust for Historic Preservation's list of top ten endangered buildings.

Nature Center just off Military Road details its history and ecology, offering daily nature walks and similar events. The planetarium offers free stargazing sessions from April to November. Staff also provide directions to the attractions concealed in the foliage, including a golf course, walking and biking trails, even the remains of Civil War fortifications. Birders flock to Picnic Groves 17 and 18 just south, prime perches from which to observe the warblers migrating during the spring and autumn, DC being fortuitously situated on the 'Eastern Flyway' migration route. The District's only public riding stable, sharing the Nature Center parking lot, offers guided trail rides through the hilly terrain. East lies Carter Barron Amphitheatre, which stages low-cost summertime shows, from free Shakespeare in the Park productions to R&B and gospel concerts. Nearby FitzGerald centre hosts major tennis competitions.
▶ *For more on Rock Creek's sporting facilities, see p186 and p187.*

ᴳᴿᴱᴱ Washington National Cathedral

Massachusetts & Wisconsin Avenues, NW (1-202 537 6200, www.cathedral.org/cathedral). Bus 30, 32, 34, 35, 36, 90, 92, 93, N2, N3, N4, N6 bus. **Open** 10am-5.30pm Mon-Fri; 10am-4.30pm Sat; 1-4pm Sun (opens for worship 8am). **Admission** requested contribution $10. **Credit** AmEx, Disc, MC, V. **Map** p249 E2.

Washington National Cathedral was built in 14th-century Gothic style, stone upon stone, without structural steel, an exercise that took most of the 20th century and was only finished in 1990. Its medievalism has been somewhat updated: there's a gargoyle of Darth Vader in the north-west corner, while the much-admired stained-glass Space Window contains a piece of lunar rock. The top of the tower is the highest point in DC; there are great views from the observation gallery.

The cathedral offers self-paced CD-based audio tours ($10); alternatively, join one of various guided tours, which are held at regular intervals. Special events can often mean that certain parts of the cathedral are closed at short notice, so it's best to phone first to check (the same applies if you have a specific tour in mind).

The Episcopalian cathedral holds some 1,200 services a year, yet has no congregation of its own. It is meant to be a church for all. Every president since Theodore Roosevelt has visited, as have Martin Luther King Jr and the Dalai Lama. Funeral services of various distinguished national figures have been held here. Medieval gardens adorn the cathedral's spacious grounds, supporting a popular herb shop.

WOODLEY PARK

East towards Connecticut Avenue before Rock Creek Park, Woodley Park is a small but bustling neighbourhood featuring upscale homes, varied restaurants and the **National Zoo**.

★ ᴳᴿᴱᴱ National Zoo

3001 block of Connecticut Avenue, NW, at Rock Creek Park (1-202 673 4800, www.nationalzoo. si.edu). Woodley Park-Zoo/Adams Morgan Metro. **Open** *Apr-Oct* 10am-6pm daily. Grounds 6am-8pm. *Nov-Mar* 10am-4.30pm daily. Grounds 6am-6pm. **Admission** free. **Map** p249 F2.

The free-admission National Zoo offers a diverting escape. Particularly during the off-season, when the paths are not cluttered by pushchairs, the zoo offers a perfect (albeit hilly) stroll, away from the bustle of Connecticut Avenue. Tree-shaded paths wind through the margins past the various animals. The stars are two pandas, Mei Xiang and Tian Tian, brought on ten-year loan from China in 2001; their cub Tai Shan was returned to China in 2010. The panda habitat is part of the Asia Trail, which links the habitats of sloth bears, fishing cats, red pandas, clouded leopards, Asian small-clawed otters and a Japanese giant salamander. The zoo has built a new environment for Asian elephants as part of its effort to preserve these endangered animals. The Elephant Trails are large enough to house between eight and ten adults along with their young; they have indoor and outdoor facilities, with features such as pools and sand piles that stimulate natural elephant behaviour.

CLEVELAND PARK

Further north is Cleveland Park, an affluent enclave sited on the farm where in 1886 President Cleveland and his gorgeous 21-year-old bride preferred to live rather than in the White House. It boasts a mix of restaurants and the AMC Loews Uptown (*see p161*), a premier venue with a gigantic screen and comfy seats.

North of Cleveland Park is **Hillwood Museum & Gardens**, with late socialite Marjorie Merriweather Post's remarkable collection of Russian objets d'art and serene Japanese landscaping.

Hillwood Museum & Gardens

4155 Linnean Avenue, NW, between Tilden & Upton Streets (1-202 686 8500, reservations 1-202 686 5807, www.hillwoodmuseum.org). Van Ness-UDC Metro. **Open** 10am-5pm Tue-Sat (reservations required). Also occasional Sun, check website for details. Closed Jan. *Guided tours* 11.30am, 1.30pm Tue-Sat. **Admission** suggested donation $15; $10-$12 reductions; $5 under-18s; free under-6s. **Credit** AmEx, MC, V.

It's not for nothing that it's known as a museum and a garden: the grounds are as much a reason as the collection of Russian art for making the trek from Downtown to this quiet, residential neighbourhood. The house and garden were purchased by cereal heiress Marjorie Merriweather Post in 1955 to house her collection of French and Russian decorative art.

Seduced by Russian culture after living there for 18 months in the 1930s, Post amassed the largest collection of imperial Russian art objects outside that country. Portraits of tsars and tsarinas, palace furnishings and a porcelain service commissioned by Catherine the Great are displayed in Hillwood's gilt and wood-panelled rooms. The French collection includes Sèvres porcelain, 18th-century furniture and Beauvais tapestries.

Visitors can also roam the 12-acre manicured grounds, including a Japanese-style garden with plunging waterfall. Guided evening tours, when offered, are not to be missed: the waning light makes for romantic strolls in the gardens.

Northeast

Washington was never known for industry. Today, its minimal manufacturing and warehouse area, mostly along New York Avenue, NE, is sprouting high-tech businesses.

A couple of blocks east of the Supreme Court is the **Frederick Douglass Museum** (316 A Street, NE, 1-202 547 4273), early residence of the famous abolitionist, now housing the Caring Foundation, celebrating worthy philanthropists but maintaining one room as it was in Douglass's time. It is open for guided tours by arrangement. Constantino Brumidi, the artist who painted the frescos in the Capitol, lived nearby, at 326 A Street.

To the north, the **Catholic University of America** (620 Michigan Avenue, NE) is a pontifical institution known for its drama department (its members perform at the university's **Hartke Theatre**). Adjoining the university is the **National Shrine of the Immaculate Conception** (400 Michigan Avenue, NE, 1-202 526 8300, www.national shrine.com). Begun in 1914 in a Byzantine style rarely seen in US Catholic churches, it was only completed in 1959. Across Harewood Road at No.4250 gleam the traditional golden domes of the **Ukrainian Catholic National Shrine of the Holy Family** (1-202 526 3737, www.ucns-holyfamily.org).

Across North Capitol Street is the leafy campus of the **Armed Forces Retirement Home**, founded as the Soldiers' Home with Mexican War tribute. On its grounds, **President Lincoln's Cottage**, the 34-room Gothic Revival house that Lincoln used as his retreat, is open to the public for guided tours (1-202 829 0436, www.lincolncottage.org, Visitor Center open 9.30am-4.30pm Mon-Sat, 11.30am-5.30pm Sun, tours on the hour, 10am-3pm Mon-Sat, noon-4pm Sun). Access to the house is from the Eagle Gate entrance on the corner of Rock Creek Church Road, NW, and Upshur Street, NW.

INSIDE TRACK HIGH TEA

The Pilgrim Observation Gallery at **Washington National Cathedral** has superb views over the city and beyond. A tour followed by tea in the Gallery, with sandwiches, scones and a scenic view can be taken here on Tuesdays and Wednesdays at 1.30pm (reservations are required).

The **Franciscan Monastery** (1400 Quincy Street, NE, 1-202 526 6800, www.myfranciscan. org) has a glorious mixture of influences: the church is modelled on Hagia Sophia in Istanbul, while beneath is a replica of the catacombs of Rome; the splendid garden's meandering paths connect replicas of religious sites.

Along the west bank of the Anacostia, DC's previously neglected river now enjoying ecological restoration, is the **United States National Arboretum**, a 440-acre enclave containing both local and exotic foliage. Near the arboretum is **Mount Olivet Cemetery** (1300 Bladensburg Road, NE, between Montana Avenue & Mount Olivet Road, 1-202 399 3000), final resting place of White House architect James Hoban and of Mary Suratt, who was hanged for her alleged role in Lincoln's assassination. On the New York Avenue side of the arboretum, one brick kiln stands as a reminder of the brickyards that constituted Northeast's first major industry. Anacostia Park follows the river's east bank and contains **Kenilworth Aquatic Gardens**. Although located near a highway that shares its name, the gardens are a quiet retreat full of aquatic plants, including lilies and lotuses. Now that the Anacostia is getting cleaner, this area attracts all sorts of reptiles, amphibians and water-loving mammals.

FREE **Kenilworth Aquatic Gardens**
Anacostia Avenue & Douglas Street, NE, at Quarles Street (1-202 426 6905, www.nps.gov/ keaq/index.htm). Deanwood Metro. **Open** 7am-5pm daily. **Admission** free.
Kenilworth Aquatic Gardens is a 12-acre garden with a network of ponds displaying a variety of aquatic plants, including water lilies and lotus. A one-armed Civil War veteran started water gardening here as a hobby in 1880; then, in the 1920s, the public – and President Coolidge – began to visit for a stroll. On the northern boundary, a path leads to the Anacostia River. On the southern boundary, a boardwalk leads to vistas of the reviving wetlands. During the week you may have the place to yourself. It's off the beaten track, and shunned by some who assume the low-income neighbourhood at the approach is dangerous.

EXPLORE

FREE United States National Arboretum

3501 New York Avenue, NE, entrance at Bladensburg Road & R Street (1-202 245 2726, www.usna.usda.gov). Stadium-Armory Metro then B2 bus. **Open** *Grounds* 8am-5pm daily. *National Bonsai & Penjing Collection* 10am-3.30pm daily. **Admission** free.

Technically a research division of the Agriculture Department, this 446-acre haven always has many more trees than people, even on its busiest days during the spring azalea season. Highlights include a boxwood collection, dwarf conifers, an Asian collection, a herb garden and 'herbarium' of dried plants, as well as the National Bonsai Collection, which contains more than 200 trees donated by Japan and is said to be worth something in the order of $5 million. Also on display, somewhat incongruously, are 22 columns removed from the Capitol's East Front during its 1958 expansion. See the website for details of tram tours, talks and other events such as garden fairs.

H STREET CORRIDOR

In the south of the area, bordering on Capitol Hill, H Street, NE, has undergone a radical revival following decades of decline in the wake of destruction in the 1968 riots that followed the assassination of Martin Luther King. Heading east from **Union Station**, H Street is now a cutting-edge shopping and entertainment zone, home to bars, restaurants and performance spaces, including the **Atlas Performing Arts Center** (*see p177*) and the **H Street Playhouse** (*see p184*). Nearby, Florida Avenue, NE, has become a new hub for the DC art scene, home to several galleries (*see pp128-129*). The long-awaited DC streetcar (*see p229*) is due to run along H Street and should make access to the further reaches of the street much easier.

For more on H Street's foodie attractions, *see p96* **A Taste of H Street**.

Southeast

There's Southeast and then there's 'Southeast'. The latter usually refers not to the whole quadrant but to some of the city's rougher neighbourhoods, across the Anacostia River and far from the centre of town.

CAPITOL HILL

Bounded to the west by the Capitol building (*see p45*) and South and North Capitol Streets, to the south by the Southeast Freeway, to the north by H Street, NE, and to the east by 11th Street, this genteel neighbourhood overlays two quadrants – Southeast and Northeast. Since more of it falls into the former, most of it is dealt with here.

Eastern Market.

East of the Capitol building, a working-class town developed around the Navy Yard, separated from the rest of the city by a 'desert', as a Swiss visitor noted in 1825. Today, its parochial small-town origins afford it a distinctively strollable ambience, although million-dollar home sales are no longer news. Businesses along Pennsylvania Avenue, SE, include bars and restaurants luring a youthful, politics-obsessed crowd. There are still vintage hangouts like the fabled Tune Inn (331 Pennsylvania Avenue, SE, *see p107*), little changed since VJ Day. The neighbourhood's heart is **Eastern Market**, restored after being damaged by fire, now complemented by the revived Barracks Row on 8th Street between Pennsylvania Avenue and M Street, SE. Its growing restaurant roster dishes out a wide variety of cuisines.

Aside from Pennsylvania Avenue itself, the Hill's principal shopping streets are the 7th–8th Street dogleg from Eastern Market, featuring food stores, galleries and craft shops, supplemented by the market's weekend flea and craft marts.

The **US Marine Barracks** (8th & I Streets, SE) has been on this site since 1801 and its commandant's house is the second oldest federal residence after the White House. On Friday nights from May to September, an impressive Marine parade drill is held (reservations required; call 1-202 433 6060).

Capitol Hill's largest open space is **Lincoln Park**, which interrupts East Capitol Street between 11th and 13th Streets. Grateful freedmen chipped in for its Emancipation

EXPLORE

Monument (1876), depicting Abraham Lincoln and a newly freed slave, though the monument was criticised when it was unveiled because the bondsman seemed to be kneeling before the president. Nearby is a sculpture of African American educator Mary McLeod Bethune, flanked by festive children.

Congressional Cemetery (1801 E Street, SE) is the resting place of such eminent Washingtonians as photographer Matthew Brady, Choctaw chief Pushmataha and 'March King' John Philip Sousa. Look for free guide pamphlets at the gatehouse. Plots are available if you care to stay permanently.

Eastern Market

225 7th Street, SE, between C Street & North Carolina Avenue (1-202 544 0083, www.eastern market.net). Eastern Market Metro. **Open** *dawn-late afternoon Sat, Sun. Permanent inside stalls* 7am-6pm Tue-Sat; 9am-4pm Sat. **Map** p253 L7.
Built in 1873 on plans by Adolf Cluss, Washington's last remaining public food market has become the heart of the Capitol Hill community; its weekend flea and craft markets are a popular draw. The market building was badly damaged by fire in 2007. It reopened in 2009 after reconstruction work, including restoration of the roof, allowing the previously hidden historic skylight to be reintroduced as a prominent architectural feature of the South Hall.
▶ *For more about shopping at Eastern Market, see p127.*

SOUTHEAST

South of Capitol Hill, the once-dodgy tract by the Washington Navy Yard is the site of DC's new ballpark, **Nationals Park**, constructed after Washington regained a major league baseball team after three dark decades (*see p188* **Inside Track**). The new ballpark has brought some revival to the surrounding area – it still has a way to go, though.

Anacostia

FREE Anacostia Community Museum (S)
1901 Fort Place, SE, at Martin Luther King Jr Avenue (1-202 633 4820, http://anacostia.si.edu). Anacostia Metro then W2, W3 bus. **Open** 10am-5pm daily. **Admission** free.
Housed in an unprepossessing red-brick building at the top of a hill in the District's historically black Anacostia neighbourhood, this modest museum hosts changing thematic exhibitions spotlighting history, culture and creative expression from an African-American perspective. Exhibits include the 19th-century diary of one-time slave Adam Francis Plummer, who wrote of his foiled plan to escape on the Underground Railroad, and a section on black baseball in segregated DC.

Frederick Douglass National Historic Site (Cedar Hill)

1411 W Street, SE, at 14th Street (1-877 444 6777, www.nps.gov/frdo). Anacostia Metro then B2 bus. **Open** *Park* mid Oct-mid Apr 9am-4.30pm daily. Mid Apr-mid Oct 9am-5pm daily. *Tours* mid Oct-mid Apr 9am-4.30pm daily. Mid Apr-mid Oct 9am-5pm daily. Tour times vary, phone or »check website for details. **Admission** $1.50. **Credit** MC, V.
Built in 1854, this Victorian country house was the home of black leader Frederick Douglass from 1877 until his death in 1895. Born a slave in Maryland, Douglass escaped to found an abolitionist newspaper, eventually advising Lincoln and other presidents. The museum's visitor centre shows *Fighter For Freedom*, a 17-minute film on Douglass's life. There's a sweeping view of downtown Washington from the grounds.

Southwest

There's not much of Southwest DC, the reason being that Virginia took back its quadrangle in 1846. The sliver of territory east of the Potomac that remained was not helped by a massive 1950s 'urban renewal' project that obliterated neighbourhoods in favour of office space. Its primary draws are the museums and federal buildings to the south of the Mall, and the Tidal Basin, which are covered – down to the Eisenhower Freeway – in the Monumental Centre chapter (*see pp28-49*). Development of the Southwest waterfront is under way, however, with the **Wharf**, slated to be up and running in 2015. Plans include building new restaurants, shops, housing, a hotel, marinas, a waterfront park, and a riverfront promenade with access to the water.

Fishing boats have hawked their catch near the Tidal Basin inlet since 1790, before there was a city. You can still get seafood at the **Fish & Seafood Market** on Maine Avenue, just south of the Case Memorial Bridge; some vendors will even cook it up for you.

Inland, **Wheat Row** (1315-21 4th Street, SW) is a curiosity of the 1950s urban renewal programme. Built in 1794, these distinguished residences were incorporated into a modern apartment complex. The area's theoretical juxtaposition of rich and poor populations did not uniformly foster the envisioned social harmony. Law House (1252 6th Street), dubbed 'Honeymoon House' in 1796 when its prominent owners moved in, kept the tag, despite their messy celebrity divorce a while later. Nearby, the pioneering theatre company **Arena Stage** (1101 6th Street, SW) continues its vital dramatic presence in a gleaming new landmark building (*see p182* **Crystal Palaces**). The **Mandarin Hotel** (*see p140*) is another area pioneer.

Arlington & Alexandria

Virginia highlights.

Northern Virginia is a comparatively liberal pocket of a famously conservative state. As well as being a dormitory suburb, Northern Virginia (or NOVA to some) is home to some of the capital's important institutions, among them the Pentagon, the CIA's headquarters at Langley and Arlington Cemetery.

Arlington and part of Alexandria were part of the original District of Columbia diamond from 1800 to 1846, when they retroceded to Virginia, claiming federal neglect but covertly fearing that Congress might ban slavery in the capital.

Map p75   **Hotels** p153

EXPLORE

Beyond its military precinct along the river – with Arlington Cemetery and the Pentagon – Arlington is a lively suburb, popular with young professionals, with a restaurant and entertainment strip sprouting above Metro stations along Wilson Boulevard. Its Fashion Center mall at Pentagon City draws throngs of visitors. Self-consciously quaint but vigorous 'Old Town' Alexandria, a restored riverport with a history that pre-dates the capital by half a century, can make a welcome break from all that federal seriousness.

ALEXANDRIA

Downstream on the Potomac River, the town of Alexandria was established in 1749 by Scottish traders and laid out by a young surveyor named George Washington. Old Town's 18th-century charm started drawing crowds of sightseers and shoppers back in the 1960s. The cobbled streets, which had survived more from lethargy than historical sensibility, were re-stoned at vast expense, and once-neglected houses meticulously restored; the vacant warehouses along King Street sprouted bars, boutiques and antiques shops. Commerce now extends 19 blocks from the river to King Street Metro station, with an atmosphere that is vibrant yet leisurely.

Old Town rewards random wanderings. For background and orientation arm yourself with

some maps and pamphlets from the visitors' center in historic **Ramsay House** (221 King Street, 1-703 746 3301) before setting out to discover the flounder houses, dwellings with half-gable roofs descending asymmetrically, that are characteristic of 18th- and early 19th-century Alexandria dwellings. Forty originals survive, with dozens of neo-flounders marking recent developments.

The Civil War indelibly marked the town; some reminders include the Confederate Statue (1888), glowering in the middle of the intersection of South Washington and Prince Streets, its back defiantly turned on the nation's capital. A free map of significant local war sites is available at the nearby **Lyceum, Alexandria's History Museum**.

A few blocks east, at 121 N Fairfax Street, is the 18th-century **Carlyle House**. Next door, the old Bank of Virginia has been restored for use – as a bank, surprise, surprise. Across the street is **Gadsby's Tavern Museum**.

George Washington prayed as well as played in Alexandria, attending **Christ Church**. He was also a patron of the voluntary fire company that built the original **Friendship Firehouse**, west on King Street.

From 1792 until 1933, Quaker druggist Edward Stabler's family made medicines for patrons including Washington and Lee. Today the **Stabler-Leadbeater Apothecary Shop** on Fairfax Street appears just as it did for generations. Further north is the **Alexandria Black History Museum**.

Alexandria is not only a heritage town; at the **Torpedo Factory Art Center** local artists create new sculpture and painting, although the past can't be escaped even here: the site is a renovated factory that produced munitions for World War I.

Back towards King Street Metro station, Dulany Street is the home of the **National Inventors Hall of Fame & Museum**. To the west, on Callahan Drive, you'll find the **George Washington Masonic National Memorial**.

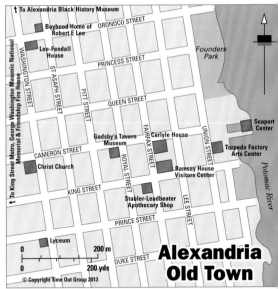

Alexandria Old Town

Alexandria Black History Museum

902 Wythe Street, at Alfred Street (1-703 746 4356, http://alexandria va.gov/blackhistory). Braddock Road Metro. **Open** 10am-4pm Tue-Sat. **Admission** $2.

Paintings, photographs, books and other artefacts document the African American experience in Virginia from 1749 to the present. The museum occupies a former Jim Crow library built in 1940 to escape racially integrating the Alexandria Public Library.

Carlyle House Historic Park

121 N Fairfax Street, between King & Cameron Streets (1-703 549 2997, www.nvrpa.org/park/ carlyle_house_historic_park). King Street Metro then 15min walk. **Open** 10am-4pm Tue-Sat; noon-4pm Sun. Guided tours every 30mins. **Admission** $5; $3 reductions; free under-11s.

John Carlyle built his Scottish-Palladian stone palace here in 1753 and it was then used as the meeting place for British colonial governors to plan their campaign against the French forces squeezing the Crown's claims to the Ohio river valley. General Edward Braddock then marched down the eponymous road west, towards Pennsylvania – and disaster.

Christ Church

Cameron & N Washington Streets (1-703 549 1450, www.historicchristchurch.org). King Street Metro then 15min walk. **Open** 10am-4pm Mon-Sat; 8.45am-1pm Sun. **Admission** free.

Dubbed 'the Church in the Woods' in 1773, this Episcopal house of worship has been in continuous service since. It was designed by James Wren in the colonial Georgian style, and George Washington and Robert E Lee were regular worshippers here. The pew assigned to Washington, No.15, is preserved in its original high-backed eminence.

Friendship Firehouse

107 S Alfred Street, between King & Prince Streets (1-703 746 3891, http://alexandriava. gov/friendship). King Street Metro then 15min walk. **Open** 1-4pm Sat, Sun. **Admission** $2.

The volunteer fire brigade, formed in 1774, built this snug station in 1855. The museum has a display of antique firefighting apparatus.

Gadsby's Tavern Museum

134 N Royal Street, between King & Cameron Streets (1-703 746 4242, http://alexandriava. gov/gadsbystavern). King Street Metro then 29K bus or Dash bus AT2, AT3, AT5, AT7. **Open** Nov-Mar 11am-4pm Wed-Sat; 1-4pm Sun. Apr-Oct 10am-5pm Tue-Sat; 1-5pm Mon, Sun. Guided tours every 30mins. **Admission** $5; $3 reductions; free under-11s. **Credit** MC, V.

These buildings comprise a tavern dating from 1785 and a hotel built in 1792. Towards the end of the 18th century they were joined together by Englishman John Gadsby and quickly became a local meeting place for many significant 18th-century figures. In 1798, George Washington graced a ball here, the first of two occasions on which he attended the celebrations in honour of his birthday. The 18th-century hostelry is well preserved in the older building. The tavern next door serves colonial-style food and drink.

George Washington Masonic National Memorial

101 Callahan Drive, between King & Duke Streets (1-703 683 2007, www.gwmemorial.org).

King Street Metro. **Open** *Oct-Mar* 10am-4pm Mon-Sat; noon-4pm Sun. *Apr-Sept* 9am-4pm daily. *Guided tours* 10am, 11.30am, 1.30pm, 3pm. **Admission** *1st & 2nd floor* free; *tower exhibits & observation desk* $8.

Sitting on a hill above Alexandria, in the imagined style of the ancient Pharos of Alexandria, the George Washington Masonic National Memorial is in striking contrast to the general's more famous tower across the river in DC. Masonic memorabilia related to US presidents who were also Freemasons includes a reconstruction of the lodge hall Washington attended. The view from the top of the monument (only accessible as part of a guided tour) is impressive.

Lyceum, Alexandria's History Museum

201 S Washington Street, at Prince Street (1-703 746 4994, http://alexandriava.gov/lyceum). King Street Metro then 15min walk. **Open** 10am-5pm Mon-Sat; 1-5pm Sun. **Admission** $2.

In 1839, local notables with intellectual interests built a Greek Revival library-auditorium for debates, concerts and literary soirées. Today, the building celebrates Alexandria's unique heritage with changing displays on local history – from the town's founding and growth as a port, through its role as a Civil War railroad centre, to its contemporary place as part of the DC metropolitan area.

National Inventors Hall of Fame & Museum

400 Dulany Street (1-571 272 0095, www.uspto. gov/web/offices/ac/ahrpa/opa/museum/welcome. html). Eisenhower Avenue Metro. **Open** 11am-5pm Tue-Fri. **Admission** free.

In 2009, the National Inventors Hall of Fame moved from Akron, Ohio, to become part of the United States Patent & Trademark Museum. The new museum features interactive exhibits and a portrait gallery, along with a video theatre, to tell tales of inventors and their inventions.

Stabler-Leadbeater Apothecary Shop

105-107 Fairfax Street, at King Street (1-703 746 3852, http://alexandriava.gov/apothecary). King Street Metro then 29K bus or Dash bus AT2, AT3, AT5, AT7. **Open** *Apr-Oct* 10am-4pm Tue-Sat; 1-5pm Mon, Sun. *Nov-Mar* 11am-4pm Wed-Sat; 1-4pm Sun. **Admission** $5; $3 reductions; free under-5s. **Credit** AmEx, Disc, MC, V.

When the original apothecary on this premises was forced to close during the Depression, in 1933, the doors were locked but the contents in the Gothic Revival interior were left intact: over 8,000 objects, including pill rollers, mortars and pestles and hand-blown medicine bottles with gold-leaf labels, remained. It reopened as a museum in 1939. There is also a collection of archive materials, with journals, letters, and prescription and formula books.

Torpedo Factory Art Center

105 N Union Street, at King Street (1-703 838 4565, www.torpedofactory.org). King Street Metro then 15min walk. **Open** *Building hours* (individual galleries vary) 10am-6pm Mon-Wed, Fri-Sun; 10am-9pm Thur. *Archaeology Museum* (1-703-746-4399, www.alexandriaarchaelogy.org) 10am-3pm Tue-Fri; 10am-5pm Sat; 1-5pm Sun. **Admission** free.

Originally a World War I munitions plant, the Torpedo Factory now spawns arts rather than arms, with three storeys containing 82 studios, six galleries – among them spaces dedicated to enamelling, ceramics and photography – and two workshops, one devoted to fibrework, the other to printmaking. Also on site is the Alexandria Archaeology Museum.

ARLINGTON

Stately **Memorial Bridge** (1932) formally connects Lincoln's memorial to the home of his Civil War nemesis, Robert E Lee, symbolically linking North and South. The bridge makes landfall at Lady Bird Johnson Park, which

Memorial Bridge.

includes the discreet **Lyndon B Johnson Memorial Grove** (www.nps.gov/lyba). At the adjacent **Pentagon** is the **Pentagon Memorial**, opened in September 2008. The open-air memorial features a 1.93-acre maple grove (it's going to take a few years for the trees to mature), sheltering 184 cantilevered benches in marble, one for each person killed on 9/11 when terrorists flew a hijacked jet into the building. The days of public tours around the Pentagon, the world's largest public building, are long gone, but the memorial is open to all. The monument is on the Pentagon's west side. To reach it, travel to the Pentagon Metro station and follow the signs for the Memorial Gateway.

Another feature in this martial terrain is the **Air Force Memorial** (1-703 247 5808, www.airforcememorial.org), three stainless steel spikes soaring 270 feet from a promontory south of **Arlington National Cemetery**.

Arlington National Cemetery

Across the Memorial Bridge from DC, Virginia side of the Potomac River (1-877 907 8585, 1-703 607 8000, www.arlingtoncemetery.org). Arlington Cemetery Metro. **Open** *Apr-Sept* 8am-7pm daily. *Oct-Mar* 8am-5pm daily. **Admission** free.

It is the right of anyone killed in action in any branch of military service, or who served for 20 years, to be buried at Arlington, along with their spouse. It's ironic, then, that the cemetery started almost as an act of Civil War vengeance: in 1861 Union forces seized the estate of Confederate General Robert E Lee and in 1864 they began burying soldiers close enough to Arlington House to make sure that Mr and Mrs Lee could never take up residence again. However, time has worked its healing magic and transformed Arlington into a place of honour and memory.

Built in 1802-16, Arlington House is now a museum (open 9.30am-4.30pm daily) and appears as it did in Lee's time. Entranced by the view, President Kennedy was said to have murmured, 'I could stay here forever.' And shortly afterwards he took up residence in the cemetery, to be joined later by Robert F Kennedy and Jacqueline Kennedy Onassis.

By an imposing marble amphitheatre is the Tomb of the Unknowns, including unidentified casualties of US conflicts up to Vietnam. Today, the Pentagon keeps DNA samples of all military personnel, making it unlikely that future remains will be unidentifiable. The changing of the guard on the hour (every hour between October and March, every half an hour from April to September) remains moving in its reverent precision. Horse-drawn caissons still bear the remains of troops qualified for burial, from the dwindling veterans of World War II to those killed in Afghanistan.

Tombs range from unadorned white headstones, such as that of actor Lee Marvin, to sculpted personal memorials, like the one to the former world heavyweight boxing champion Joe Louis (both men were veterans of World War II) that sits next to it. The

Arlington National Cemetery.

Tourmobile route naturally features celebrity sites, but strollers can discover more obscure, but often just as interesting, memorials and tombs. Memorials include the mast of the battleship *Maine* (whose explosion in Havana harbour sparked the Spanish-American War), the monument to the Navajo Code Talkers (whose language baffled Japanese codebreakers during World War II), and commemorations of the Space Shuttle *Columbia* casualties.

At the north end is the Netherlands Carillon, a Dutch thank you for their liberation from the Nazis. Beyond is the US Marines' **Iwo Jima Memorial**, a giant re-creation of the celebrated photo of the raising of the flag during the 1942 battle.

The Women in Military Service to America Memorial is inset behind the original Main Gate wall to create a light-flooded arch with 16 display niches. Three photo displays survey women at war from the earliest days to the present.

Arlington Cemetery's visitors' centre is just past the entrance on Memorial Avenue, close to the Metro station. Here you can locate particular graves or pick up maps to wander the cemetery on foot (note that some significant graves are a mile or more uphill).
▶ *The Iwo Jima Memorial is slightly closer to Rosslyn Metro station.*

Drug Enforcement Agency Museum

700 Army Navy Drive, across from Pentagon City Mall (1-202 307 3463, www.deamuseum.org). Pentagon City Metro. **Open** 10am-4pm Tue-Fri. **Admission** free.

The exhibits trace the history of drugs and the law in America, primarily through relics of 20th-century drug culture that have been collected by DEA agents.

EXPLORE

Washington in 48 Hours

Day 1 Museums and Monuments

8.30AM Start your day by roaming the halls of power at the **US Capitol** (*see p45*). The underground visitor centre features exhibits on the history of US lawmakers and the building itself. To arrange a free hour-long tour of the rest of the Capitol building, book online in advance.

10.30AM Stroll along the National Mall to the **National Gallery of Art** (*see p33*), which has one of the best art collections in the US. You'll find works by da Vinci, Rembrandt, Vermeer and others in the West Building and contemporary artists such as Lichtenstein and Pollock in the East Building. The gift shop is great for unusual souvenirs.

1.30PM Next, head outside to the National Gallery's Sculpture Garden, where you can grab a bite to eat at the Pavillion Cafe and sit near the huge fountain – its pool doubles as a skating rink in winter – and enjoy some of DC's best people-watching.

3PM Time for a trip through the **National Portrait Gallery** (*see p55*). Stop to admire the undulating steel-and-glass roof of the enclosed courtyard, a great place for an afternoon pick-me-up. Then take a quick walk through the collections – the special exhibits often offer an interesting perspective on American history and culture.

6.30PM Penn Quarter – the neighbourhood surrounding the Portrait Gallery – happens to be Washington's best restaurant district. **Central** (*see p88*) is a modern French bistro, with upscale takes on traditional staples like fried chicken. For something slightly less expensive, try the Mediterranean small plates at **Zaytinya** (*see p88*).

8.30PM Take in one of the best views in Washington from the roof terrace at **POV** (*see p105*) at the W Hotel, where you can look out on the White House (and see the snipers on the roof) while sipping a cocktail. Just make sure to call ahead – reservations are required.

NAVIGATING THE CITY

Washington is great for walking, with a wealth of attractions packed close together. The Metro system is efficient, but it doesn't go everywhere. Buses can fill in the gaps, particularly the Circulator service. Its six colourcoded routes run frequently to parts of town that draw lots of tourists, including those not covered by Metro, like Georgetown. The Capital Bikeshare programme lets you pick up a bike at any of the 110 stations around town and drop it off at any other. One-day memberships cost $5, plus hourly rates for bike usage.

The streets are laid out on a grid, with numbered streets running north–south and lettered streets going east–west in alphabetical order. Beyond W Street, the roads have two-syllable names in alphabetical order (Belmont, Chapin), then threesyllable names (Albemarle, Buchanan). Avenues named after states cut through the city on diagonals. Washington is divided into four quadrants

EXPLORE

Day 2 From Antiques to Half-Smokes

9AM Start your morning with coffee and a croissant at **Patisserie Poupon** (*see p103*), a tiny French bakery popular with wealthy Georgetowners. From here, shop your way down Wisconsin Avenue – lined with interesting antiques shops and boutiques – to M Street, Georgetown's other main drag, where you'll find name-brand stores like Coach and Kate Spade.

1PM There's no shortage of good lunch spots in Georgetown. Try the crusty wood-fired pizzas at Pizzeria Paradiso (*see p93*), or, if the weather's nice, grab something at **Dean and Deluca** (*see p127*), a gourmet market, and sit outside.

2.30PM Take a short afternoon stroll along the **C&O Canal** (*see p67*), which once ran from Georgetown all the way to Cumberland, Maryland – 185 miles to the west. Then head up to the grounds of **Dumbarton Oaks** (*see p68*), a mansion with 53 acres of gorgeous gardens.

6PM Visit the **Kennedy Center** (*see p51*), the city's premiere performing arts venue, for a free performance at the Millennium Stage. While some of the concerts are good, the real draw is the lovely view of the Potomac River from the Kennedy Center's terrace.

7.30PM For dinner, take a taxi to the fashionable Logan Circle/U Street area, where scores of new restaurants have opened in recent years. Try **Estadio** (*see p98*) for authentic Spanish tapas or **Cork** (*see p97*), a cosy wine bar that serves excellent small plates. Or for a downscale, yet quintesssential, DC experience, try **Ben's Chili Bowl** (*see p98*), a long-established landmark known for its half-smokes – thick, spicy sausages.

9.30PM After dinner, there's time to catch some music at one of the many nearby clubs such as **Twins Jazz** (*see p174*), **U Street Music Hall** (*see p169*), the **9:30 Club** (*see p170*) or the **Black Cat** (*see p171*).

EXPLORE

(Northwest, Northeast, Southwest, and Southeast, with Northwest being by far the largest). The numbered streets count up from the US Capitol Building on both the east and west sides. The letter streets do the same from the north and south. That means, for example, that there are two 1st Streets – one to the east of the Capitol and one to the west. To get to the right place, you often have to specify the quadrant. H Street, NW is very different from H Street, NE.

SEEING THE SIGHTS
Most of Washington's attractions are free for visitors and open seven days a week.

PACKAGE DEALS
One of Washington's most appealing features is that most of its major museums are free, and therefore city package deals are not needed. For Metro travel, you may find it worth your while to buy one of various passes that are available (*see pp227-228*).

Consume

Restaurants

Old-school power dining, fashionable eating and ethnic enclaves.

As the DC dining scene finally shakes off its inferiority complex with relation to the country's other dining powerhouses, the options for eating out have never been more diverse. From ethnic enclaves of Ethiopian and Vietnamese fare to modern hotspots with month-long waiting lists, the culinary landscape in the nation's capital is rapidly maturing.

One noteworthy trend is that celebrity chefs are flocking to DC to capitalise on a savvy dining public. Ask a local and they may bristle at the notion of absentee chefs, but their presence has raised the bar around town.

EATING IN WASHINGTON

Diversity in the city's restaurant world is reflected in recent openings, which range from upmarket, authentic Thai (**Little Serow**, *see p92*), through late-night dining and music spot the **Hamilton** (*see p87*), to the seriously foodie, kitchen-as-laboratory vibe of **Rogue 24** (*see p88*) and the bistro style and American comfort food of **Mintwood Place** (*see p97*).

Another fun prevailing force on the culinary scene: the new wave of food trucks rolling around town serving portable fare ranging from lobster rolls to cupcakes (*see p89* **Food on the Move**). At the time of writing, their presence in Downtown was threatened by possible new parking restrictions that could limit the numbers of trucks in the area.

Intimate wine bars serving cheese, charcuterie and dozens of choices by the glass have helped fill what used to be a void in neighbourhood restaurants. And as in many big cities, DC diners are becoming more relaxed about eating out. Restaurants are responding by ditching the white tablecloths, relaxing dress codes and crafting menus made for sharing. Fine dining chefs are branching out with more casual options, such as Michel Richard's bustling bistro **Central** (*see p88*). Meanwhile, Bryan Voltaggio has brought

> ❶ Blue numbers in this chapter correspond to the location of each restaurant as marked on the street maps. *See pp248-253.*

his Italian-inflected food with seasonal mid-Atlantic ingredients in from Maryland (VOLT in Frederick) to DC, with **Range** (*see p104*).

As the city continues to regenerate, so the area with a notable restaurant presence widens. There's now a variety of tastes to be found, from bargain bowls of ramen at **Toki Underground** (*see p105*) to bistro-style cooking at the **Atlas Room** (*see p105*) on the newly revivified H Street, NE, (*see p96* **A Taste of H Street**).

TIPPING

Whatever your food tastes and budget, keep in mind that Washington is an expensive city and servers make a high proportion of their pay from gratuities. As elsewhere in the States, diners tend to tip 20 per cent or even higher; 15 per cent on the pre-tax bill is expected, even at the most humble of restaurants.

MONUMENTAL CENTRE

White House & around

$ Breadline

1751 Pennsylvania Avenue, NW, between 17th & 18th Streets (1-202 822 8900, www.breadline. com). Farragut West Metro. **Open** 7am-5.30pm Mon-Fri. **Main courses** $5.50-$11. **Credit** AmEx, MC, V. **Map** p252 G5 ❶   Sandwich bar
On a Downtown block with plenty of other quick breakfast and lunch options available in the area, Breadline is always packed. This counter-order sandwich bar has earned cult status among

Washingtonians for its soups, salads and gargantuan sandwiches, made with artisanal loaves, which are baked on the premises, and quality fillings. The food isn't cheap, but the portions are large enough to keep the average person going all day. The turkey sandwich, for example, comes with so much meat that it is physically impossible to keep more than half between the slabs of fresh bread. If you've got room, add some boutique soda and Route 11 chips – Virginia-made potato crisps that come in a variety of novelty flavours.

Capitol & around

Johnny's Half Shell
400 North Capitol Street, NW, at Louisiana Avenue (1-202 737 0400, www.johnnyshalf shell.net). Union Station Metro. **Open** 11.30am-2.30pm (lunch), 4.30-7.30pm (happy hour), 5-10pm (dinner) Mon-Fri; 5-10pm Sat. **Main courses** $18.25-$40. **Credit** AmEx, MC, V. **Map** p253 K6 ❷ Fish

Owned and run by renowned culinary pair Ann Cashion (chef) and John Fulchino, Johnny's relocated to North Capitol Street a few years ago. The restaurant has stayed the same, though: it's famous for its super high-grade seafood ingredients, from oysters on the half shell to grilled sea scallops, prepared to simple perfection. Jazz and blues – and strong drinks – create a vibrant atmosphere and the restaurant hums with its own success.

DC NEIGHBOURHOODS
Foggy Bottom

★ Equinox
818 Connecticut Avenue, NW, between H & I Streets (1-202 331 8118, www.equinoxrestaurant. com). Farragut West Metro. **Open** 11.30am-2pm, 5.30-10pm Mon-Thur; 11.30am-2pm, 5.30-10.30pm Fri; 5.30-10.30pm Sat; 5.30-9pm Sun. **Main courses** $28-$35. **Credit** AmEx, MC, V. **Map** p252 H5 ❸ Contemporary American

Chef Todd Gray is known for his emphasis on the seasonal and regional; Equinox's three- to six-course tasting menu generally includes such delicacies as Chesapeake Bay crab, Carolina grouper and locally grown organic vegetables. The suited power brokers who frequent the place may or may not appreciate Gray's efforts to acquire sustainably farmed fish and humanely raised meat, but they surely appreciate the deceptively simple preparations in which such ingredients shine. Service is deft and friendly. Call well in advance for reservations.

Kaz Sushi Bistro
1915 I Street, NW, between 19th & 20th Streets (1-202 530 5500, www.kazsushibistro.com). Farragut West Metro. **Open** 11.30am-2pm, 6-10pm Mon-Fri; 6-10pm Sat. **Main courses** $10-$16 lunch; $12-$25 dinner; $14-$15 bento boxes. **Credit** AmEx, MC, V. **Map** p252 G5 ❹ Japanese

Bibiana. *See p85.*

CONSUME

Sushi king Kazuhiro Okochi made his mark at Sushi-Ko (*see p104*), successfully melding Asian and Western ingredients, before bringing the winning formula here. The sushi itself is top-notch, featuring fish that is gorgeous and glistening, while the rice has a touch of sweetness unlike any you'll find elsewhere. But should your tastes not include raw fish, there's also a bounty of wonderfully cooked items on offer, including grilled baby octopus, coriander-crusted calamari and Asian-style short ribs.

★ Marcel's
2401 Pennsylvania Avenue, NW, between 24th & 25th Streets (1-202 296 1166, www.marcels dc.com). Foggy Bottom-GWU Metro. **Open** 5.30-10pm Mon-Thur; 5.30-11pm Fri, Sat; 5.30-9.30pm Sun. **Set meals** (3-5 courses) $65-$130. **Credit** AmEx, MC, V. **Map** p252 F5 ❺ French
Marcel's is the kind of restaurant that you'd expect to find on Pennsylvania Avenue: exquisite food, beautifully served in a sumptuous dining room by adept professionals. Chef Robert Wiedmaier's Flemish-inflected French fare manages the classical balance of taste and textures: subtle versus sharp-flavoured, savoury versus sweet, generous versus leaving you wanting more. Boudin blanc with black mushroom truffle purée and truffle madeira sauce is exemplary, and a gratin of mussels with Chimay, salsify and bacon is a blast of intense flavours. The servers get extra points for friendliness: even if you're not one of the place's traditional, old-money clients, they'll still treat you as if you were.

★ Ris
2275 L Street, NW, at 23rd Street (1-202 730 2500, www.risdc.com). Foggy Bottom-GWU Metro. **Open** 11.30am-11pm Mon-Fri; 5-11pm Sat; 10am-3pm (brunch), 3-9pm Sun. **Main courses** $22-$36. **Map** p252 F5 ❻
Contemporary American
Ris Lacoste, who earned her stellar reputation as former executive chef of Georgetown's classic 1789 (*see p101*), struck out on her own with this comfortable West End restaurant. (Pronunciation hint: Ris is short for Doris.) Neighbours, power players and the chef's devotees fill the 200-some seats, spread over a bar, café, patio and segmented dining areas with plush banquettes. The American menu taps into international influences, with dishes like monkfish osso bucco, braised lamb shank with chickpeas and yoghurt, and sesame crusted salmon with red curry broth. Regular daily specials include meatloaf on Mondays.

Vidalia
1990 M Street, NW, between 19th & 20th Streets (1-202 659 1990, www.vidaliadc.com). Dupont Circle Metro. **Open** 11.30am-2.30pm, 5.30-9.30pm Mon-Thur; 11.30am-2.30pm, 5.30-10pm Fri; 5.30-10pm Sat; 5-9pm Sun. **Main courses** $16-$26 lunch; $30-$36 dinner. **Credit** AmEx, Disc, MC, V. **Map** p250 G5 ❼ Southern

Onions are much in evidence in the hushed, golden dining room of Vidalia, which itself is named after the Southern sweet variety. You'll find them in a spread for the complimentary bread, in a rich hot soup and in the discreet artwork adorning the walls. But the restaurant's raison d'être is neither single-ingredient schtick nor even strictly Southern cooking; it proudly proclaims its cuisine to be 'American regional'. There are many dishes in which pork is the star player, and grits and oysters are likely suspects on winter menus.

Downtown

Austin Grill
750 E Street, NW, at 8th Street (1-202 393 3776, www.austingrill.com). Gallery Place-Chinatown or Archives Navy-Memorial Metro. **Open** 11.30am-11pm Mon-Thur; 11.30am-midnight Fri; 11am-midnight Sat; 11am-10pm Sun. **Main courses** $9-$18.50. **Credit** AmEx, Disc, MC, V. **Map** p253 J6 ❽ Tex-Mex

The Hamilton. See p87.

The Tex-Mex cousin of Jaleo (see p88), Austin Grill fills the gap between upscale dining and fast-food munching. It's popular with a variety of diners – families who don't want to deal with high-maintenance restaurants and singles who are looking for chow that doesn't interrupt meeting potential suitors. It also offers a gluten-free menu. There are plenty of tequilas to sample and everything comes with chips and salsa.
Other locations throughout the city.

★ Bibiana

1100 New York Avenue, NW, between 11th & 12th Streets (1-202 216 9550, http://bibiana dc.com). Metro Center Metro. **Open** 11.30am-2.30pm (lunch), 5.30-10.30pm Mon-Wed; 11.30am-2.30pm (lunch), 5.30-11pm Thur, Fri; 5.30-11pm Sat. **Main courses** $7-$29. **Credit** AmEx, MC, V. **Map** p250 J5 ❾ **Italian**
A sleek and sophisticated downtown spot, Bibiana is a member of restaurateur Ashok Bajaj's empire, which also includes the Oval Room, Rasika (see p88), Bombay Club (see below), 701 and Ardeo+Bardeo. Chef Nick Stefanelli's well-executed Italian menu features exceptional pastas such as black spaghetti with Maryland lump crab as well as fish and meat entrées. The dining room, often packed with a diverse mix of stylish Washingtonians, is done up with dark wood, warm orange tones and sculptural silver pendant lights hanging overhead. A seat at the bar, with its black and white photos of Italian scooters and a small window that looks in on the kitchen action, is a great perch for cocktails, such as the signature Bibiana (Prosecco and fresh peach purée) or one of the house-made liqueurs. *Photo p83.*

Bombay Club

815 Connecticut Avenue, NW, between H & I Streets (1-202 659 3727, www.bombayclub dc.com). Farragut West or Farragut North Metro. **Open** 11.30am-2.30pm, 5.30-10.30pm Mon-Thur; 11.30am-2.30pm, 5.30-11pm Fri; 5.30-11pm Sat; 11.30am-2.30pm, 5.30-9pm Sun. **Main courses** $16-$32. **Set brunch** $18.50. **Credit** AmEx, MC, V. **Map** p252 H5 ❿ **Indian**
Bombay Club evokes not the multihued Mumbai of today but India in the time of the Raj, when English gentlemen could sit in restrained, masculine dining rooms and, presumably, cherry-pick the best of the subcontinent's cuisine. Decorous waiters in penguin suits warn against the supposed heat of a non-threatening lamb vindaloo (thali platters, tandoori meats and Goan curries are also on offer); the menu offers discreet explanations of the various regional styles.

Ceiba

701 14th Street, NW, at G Street (1-202 393 3983, www.ceibarestaurant.com). Metro Center Metro. **Open** 11.30am-2.30pm, 5.30-10.30pm Mon-Thur; 5.30-11pm Fri, Sat; 11am-4pm Sun.

INSIDE TRACK QUICK TIPS

A quick way to figure the standard 20 per cent tip: simply double the sales tax on your bill.

Main courses $16-$32. **Credit** AmEx, Disc, MC, V. **Map** p252 H5 ⓫ **Latin/Caribbean**
Brightly coloured murals, discreetly placed, are about the only whimsical touches in Ceiba's majestic space, much frequented by expense-account diners. Otherwise, the look is sleek, modern neutrals, with furniture from Brazil and stone and tiles from Yucatán. The cuisine, though, is an abundance of invention, with Latin American and Caribbean food as inspiration. There's a lot of seafood – conch chowder, crab fritters, several variants on ceviche – as well as Cuban pork sandwiches and black bean soup. It's hearty rather than homey food, as studied as its slick presentation.

DC Coast

Tower Building, 1401 K Street, NW, at 14th Street (1-202 216 5988, www.dccoast.com). McPherson Square Metro. **Open** 11.30am-2.30pm, 5.30-10.30pm Mon-Thur; 11.30am-2.30pm, 5.30-11pm Fri; 5.30-11pm Sat; 5.30-9.30pm Sun. **Main courses** $13-$28 lunch; $23-$29 dinner. **Credit** AmEx, MC, V. **Map** p252 H5 ⓬ **Contemporary American**
The 'coast' of the name refers not just to the Atlantic but also the West and Gulf Coasts. It's a pretty wide net to cast, but the brains behind DC Coast – and they are brains, the creators of several of Washington's hottest dining spots – have found a way to integrate Southern, Southwestern and even Pacific Rim influences on the menu in their cavernous, well-appointed dining room. Soy sauce and tabasco share space in the kitchen; bok choy and bacon both grace the tables. The busy, businessy crowd eats it all up with gusto. Reservations recommended.

Georgia Brown's

950 15th Street, NW, between I & K Streets (1-202 393 4499, www.gbrowns.com). McPherson Square Metro. **Open** 11.30am-10pm Mon-Thur; 11.30am-11pm Fri; noon-11pm Sat; 10am-2.30pm, 5.30-10pm Sun. **Main courses** $18-$30. **Set brunch** $41, $21.95 under-12s. **Credit** AmEx, Disc, MC, V. **Map** p252 H5 ⓭ **Southern**
One of DC's earliest and best attempts to upscale Low Country cooking, Georgia Brown's makes the case for saying that Washington is, in fact, a Southern city. Soul music plays softly in the warm-wood dining room; cornbread and dense, creamy biscuits, served with sweet butter, accompany the entrées. Fried green tomatoes, a showpiece of the restaurant, involve thin slices of the vegetable layered with herbed cream cheese, breaded, and laced

CONSUME

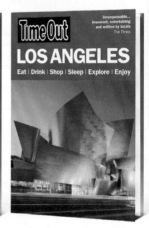

with a spicy remoulade. In another twist on tradition, there are even a few decent vegetarian options. Beloved of local politicos, the restaurant serves power lunches, dinners and a Sunday jazz brunch.

★ The Hamilton

600 14th Street, NW, at F Street, Downtown (1-202 787 1000, http://thehamiltondc.com). Metro Center Metro. **Open** 11am-1am Mon-Thur; 11am-2am Fri; 11.30am-2am Sat; 8.30am-1am Sun **Main courses** $10-$30. **Credit** AmEx, Disc, MC, V. **Map** p252 H6  **American**

This newcomer filled a serious gap in the late-night dining scene in DC, with a kitchen that stays open until 2am at weekends. It's the latest outpost from the Clyde's Group, which is known for simple-but-good American food. That reputation holds true at this combination restaurant/concert venue – the dining room is on the first floor, live music is downstairs – which serves easy-to-love classics like crab cakes, BBQ brisket, mac and cheese, and nine different varieties of milkshakes. There are more ambitious entrées, too, but – with the exception of the reliably good sushi – these can be hit-or-miss. And anyway, when it comes to late-night dining, what could beat a burger, fries and a chocolate-and-peanut butter shake? *Photo p84.*

► *For more music venues, see pp170-174.*

Matchbox

713 H Street, NW, at 7th Street (1-202 289 4441, www.matchboxdc.com). Gallery Place-Chinatown Metro. **Open** 11am-10.30pm (last seating) Mon-Fri; 10am-11.30pm Sat, Sun. **Main courses** $14-$28. **Credit** AmEx, Disc, MC, V. **Map** p253 J5 **Pizza/American**

Aptly named, this narrow, three-storey restaurant is always packed. Why? Three reasons: the thin-crust pizzas that come out of Matchbox's brick oven; the platters of mini hamburgers, and the casual, fun

atmosphere. In the mood for something a little fancier? Matchbox also serves traditional bistro dishes like pork tenderloin and rockfish.

Other locations 521 8th Street, SE, between E & G Streets, Capitol Hill (1-202 548 0369); 1901 14th Street, NW, at T Street, U Street Corridor (1-202 328-0369).

Oceanaire Seafood Room

1201 F Street, NW, at 12th Street (1-202 347 2277, www.oceanaireseafoodroom.com). Metro Center Metro. **Open** 11.30am-10pm Mon-Thur; 11.30am-11pm Fri; 5-11pm Sat; 5-9pm Sun. **Main courses** $14-$43 lunch, $23-$52 dinner. **Credit** AmEx, Disc, MC, V. **Map** p252 H6 **Fish**

Don't be surprised if you spot senators and lobbyists making back-room deals at this see-and-be-seen spot for Washington's power set. Seafood is given steakhouse treatment – in other words, served in huge portions – in this art deco-styled dining room that feels like an ocean liner. The menu, of sustainably caught seafood, changes daily, reflecting availability and seasonality of the goods. Ever tried Arctic char? Now's your chance. Or sample oysters, clams, crab and lobster at the raw bar. And for dessert? Go for the baked Alaska.

★ Proof

775 G Street, NW, between 7th & 8th Streets (1-202 737 7663, www.proofdc.com). Gallery Place-Chinatown Metro. **Open** 5.30-10pm Mon; 11.30am-2pm, 5.30-10pm Tue-Thur; 11.30am-2pm, 5.30-11pm Fri; 5.30-11pm Sat; 5-9.30pm Sun. *Bar* 5.30pm-1am Mon; 11.30am-2pm, 5.30pm-1am Tue-Thur; 11.30am-2pm, 5.30pm-2am Fri; 5.30pm-2am Sat; 5pm-midnight Sun. **Main courses** $24-$29. **Credit** AmEx, MC, V. **Map** p253 J6 **Fusion/wine bar**

Former tax attorney Mark Kuller turned his passion for great food and wine (his home cellar boasts some

—Rogue 24. *See p88.*

CONSUME

7,000 bottles) into his first foray into the restaurant business: the wine-focused Proof. (He followed up with Estadio, *see p98*, in 2010.) This hotspot is a tough table to snag at the last minute, so plan ahead to get a taste of chef Haidar Karoum's excellent cooking. His ahi tuna tartare with wasabi soy emulsion makes the cliché dish fresh again, and his veal sweetbreads are some of the best around. The wine director is Joe Quinn, who was part of Proof's opening waitstaff and became its sommelier in 2010. A seat at the bar in front of the shiny Enomatic wine dispenser comes with a side of culture – the flat screens overhead display a mesmerising rotation of artwork from the neighbouring National Portrait Gallery.

★ Rogue 24
922 N Street, NW, between 9th & 10th Streets (1-202 408 9724, http://rogue24.com). Mount Vernon Square Metro. **Open** 6-11pm Tue-Sat. **Set meals** from $75. **Credit** AmEx, Disc, MC, V. **Map** p251 J4 ⓭ Eclectic
This is dinner as performance art: an open kitchen in the centre of the dining room; 16-course 'progression' or 24-course 'journey' tasting menus that unfold over three or more hours. Courses might consist of a single, artfully constructed bite – a sliver of iberico lomo over a chunk of watermelon, say, or a small ball of dough filled with 'liquid chicken'. The kitchen staff assemble some dishes using tweezers and medicine droppers. It's a meal full of surprises, and for serious foodies, an entertaining show. *Photo p87.*

Zaytinya
Pepco Building, 701 9th Street, NW, at G Street (1-202 638 0800, www.zaytinya.com). Gallery Place-Chinatown Metro. **Open** 11.30am-10pm Mon, Sun; 11.30am-11pm Tue-Thur; 11.30am-midnight Fri, Sat. **Main courses** (small plates) $6-$14.50. **Credit** AmEx, Disc, MC, V. **Map** p253 J5 ⓭ Mediterranean
With a stunning white and blue interior, this place finds inspiration in Greece, Turkey and Lebanon. Trendy Zaytinya, created by famed chef José Andrés, is one of DC's most popular restaurants. Once parties are seated, cones of piping hot bread arrive, and the fun begins. The menu of 60-plus meze dishes is kind to both vegetarians and carnivores. Our tips? grape leaves dolmades or *piyuz* (warm giant beans with oven roasted tomato, garlic and kale) to start, followed by braised lamb shank with eggplant purée.

Penn Quarter

Central Michel Richard
1001 Pennsylvania Avenue, NW, between 10th & 11th Streets (1-202 625 0015, www.centralmichel richard.com). Federal Triangle Metro. **Open** 11.30am-2.30pm, 5-10.30pm Mon-Thur; 11.30am-2.30pm, 5-11pm Fri; 5-11pm Sat; 5-9.30pm Sun. **Main courses** $18-$32. **Credit** AmEx, MC, V. **Map** p252 J6 ⓴ French/American

You can see why Michel Richard's effusive Pennsylvania Avenue brasserie wins raves. The playful menu fuses American and French classics with Richard's signature whimsy. There's 'faux' gras (made from chicken liver not foie gras), a towering lobster burger, a spin on fried chicken, and a monstrous banana split sure to attract any nearby spoon.

★ Fiola
601 Pennsylvania Avenue, NW, between 6th & 7th streets, Penn Quarter (1-202 628 2888, http://fioladc.com). Archives Metro. **Open** 11.30am-2.30pm, 5.30-10.30pm Mon-Thur; 11.30am-2.30pm, 5.30-11.30pm Fri; 5-11.30pm Sat. **Main courses** $24-$36. **Set dinners** $105, $115. **Credit** AmEx, Disc, MC, V. **Map** p253 J6 ㉑ Italian
When chef Fabio Trabocchi opened Fiola in 2011, he quickly established his new trattoria as the place to go in Washington for exquisite, sumptuous Italian. Pastas, naturally, are the stars of the menu, especially the tender pappardelle with bolognese ragu. But seafood plays a strong supporting role, and the bar offers a serious cocktail menu, including six different variations on the negroni. An order of bomboloni – Sardinian-style ricotta doughnuts – is a fitting end to a decadent evening. *Photo p90.*

Jaleo
480 7th Street, NW, at E Street (1-202 628 7949, www.jaleo.com). Gallery Place-Chinatown or Archives Navy-Memorial Metro. **Open** 11.30am-10pm Mon, Sun; 11.30am-11.30pm Tue-Thur; 11.30am-midnight Fri, Sat. **Tapas** $5-$22. **Main courses** $32-$48. **Credit** AmEx, Disc, MC, V. **Map** p253 J6 ㉒ Spanish
Created by Jose Andres (Zaytinya, *see left*), Jaleo focuses on tapas: garlic shrimp, chorizo with garlic mash, salads of apple and manchego cheese and marinated mushrooms – to name just a few. Don't miss the date and bacon fritters or the patatas bravas, a steaming hot bowl of potatoes with a spicy sauce.
Other locations 7271 Woodmont Avenue, Bethesda, MD (1-301 913 0003); 2250A Crystal Drive, Arlington, VA (1-703 413 8181).

Rasika
633 D Street, NW, between 6th & 7th Streets (1-202 637 1222, www.rasikarestaurant.com). Archives-Navy Memorial Metro. **Open** 11.30am-2.30pm, 5.30-10.30pm Mon-Thur; 11.30am-2.30pm, 5.30-11pm Fri; 5-11pm Sat. **Main courses** $12-$28. **Credit** AmEx, Disc, MC, V. **Map** p253 J6 ㉓ Indian
Rasika brings the delicacy of upmarket Indian cooking to Washington. One of restaurateur Ashok Bajaj's empire, which also includes the Oval Room, Bombay Club (*see p85*), 701, Ardeo+Bardeo and Bibiana (*see p85*), Rasika is under the creative eye of Vikram Sunderam, who ran the kitchen at London's Bombay Brasserie for 14 years. Grouped into categories

CONSUME

including 'chaat', 'tawa' and 'tandoor', the menu covers much ground, with ample choices for both vegetarians and carnivores. Whatever you do, try the palak chaat, a signature dish of crispy baby spinach leaves dressed with yoghurt that melts on the tongue. **Other location** Rasika West End, 1190 New Hampshire Avenue, NW, at M Street, Foggy Bottom (1-202 466 2500).

Judiciary Square area

Bistro Bis
Hotel George, 15 E Street, NW, between North Capitol Street & New Jersey Avenue

(1-202 661 2700, www.bistrobis.com). Union Station or Judiciary Square Metro. **Open** 7-10am, 11.30am-2.30pm, 5.30-10.30pm daily. **Main courses** $14.50-$21 brunch; $15.75-$23.50 lunch; $26-$33 dinner. **Credit** AmEx, Disc, MC, V. **Map** p253 K6 **❷ French**
A soigné restaurant in the George hotel (*see p138*), within walking distance of the Capitol and Union Station, Bistro Bis serves the gamut of French food, from mussels and pommes frites to complicated preparations and composed plates. Of-the-moment design firm Adamstein & Demetriou created the decor, a riff on the classic brasserie: the dining room features warm woods, tile floors and frosted glass;

Food on the Move

Lunches that get around town.

Once upon a time, thanks to a moratorium on food truck licences, DC's street food landscape was limited to mediocre half smoke hot dogs and stale pretzels. You'd be lucky to find a burrito cart or anything that broke the monotonous mould. But no longer. The moratorium was lifted a few years ago, ushering in a new age of creativity for the city's street food scene. It seems like a new truck gets rolling each week, and no visit to Washington would be complete without stopping by one for a meal on the go. At the time of writing, however, another black cloud hung over the world of happy food truck dining: proposed parking restrictions would restrict the number of trucks in Downtown at any time. These are being strongly contested.

Short of happening on to a truck on a corner, Twitter is the best way to track their movements; or there's a helpful website, www.foodtruckfiesta.com, that tracks the trucks in real time. At lunchtime at the time of writing, many congregate in office-heavy Downtown, including Franklin Park and Metro Center. A few trawl around nightlife spots such as Adams Morgan to feed hungry bargoers. And many spend time running from parking meter attendants. In spring and summer, monthly Truckeroo festivals are held in the Bullpen area in front of the Nationals Park (*see p188*), gathering a slew of local food truck options in one place.

Some of the longest lines form at the Red **Hook Lobster Pound** (@LobsterTruckDC), which serves amazing lobster rolls and shrimp rolls with buttery buns. Then there's the irreverent culinary carnival that is the **Fojol Bros of Merlindia** (@fojolbros), where chicken masala, curry and mango lassi pops

are dished up by a bunch of guys in fake mustaches and turbans. They make lunch feel like a party, with loud music blaring from the bright truck. They often throw colourful patchwork quilts out for customers to sit on on the lawns in the city's squares.

TaKorean (@takorean) peddles an Asian spin on tacos, like bulgogi steak with spicy *kimchi* slaw. Pasta-lovers will want to hunt down **CapMac DC** (@capmacdc), which serves an incredible macaroni and cheese as well as chicken parm meatballs and 20-layer lasagne. José Andrés's **Pepe Food Truck** (@pepefoodtruck), specialises in Spanish *flauta* sandwiches, with the likes of fried chicken, and a butifarra 'burger' (with fresh pork, roasted peppers and alioli), served in long, flute-like baguettes.

Dessert is well represented curbside too. Find a slice of apple, blueberry or pecan pie at **Dangerously Delicious Pies'** truck (@thepietruckdc), or popsicles made with local fruits from **Pleasant Pops** (@pleasantpops). Cupcake shops have popped up all over the city, so naturally there are cupcake trucks: **Curbside Cupcakes** (@curbsidecupcake) and **Sweetbites** (@sweetbitestruck).

Fiola. *See p88.*

and the front room, which opens on to a patio with more tables, popular for summing dining, has a zinc-topped bar. Weekend brunch, which adds egg dishes and beef-based bloody marys to the brasserie mix, is justly popular.

Full Kee

509 H Street, NW, between 5th & 6th Streets (1-202 371 2233, www.fullkeedc.com). Gallery Place-Chinatown Metro. **Open** 11am-2am daily. **Main courses** $8-$22. **Credit** MC, V. **Map** p253 J5 Asian

One of several old-school joints still hanging on in gentrified Chinatown, Full Kee meets all the criteria for a Chinese-food snob: poultry hanging in the window, menu additions posted on the walls on brightly coloured paper, a largely Asian clientele. Short on luxury, the place is long on food options. DC foodies rave about Full Kee's noodle soups. The place now serves beer and wine by the glass.

Kushi

465 K Street, NW, between 4th & 5th Streets (1-202 682 3123, http://eatkushi.tumblr.com). Mount Vernon Square/7th Street Convention Center Metro. **Open** 11.30am-2.30pm Mon; 11.30am-2.30pm, 5.30-11pm Tue-Thur; 11.30am-2.30pm, 5.30pm-1am Fri; noon-2.30pm, 5.30-11pm Sat, Sun. **Main courses** $12-$28. **Credit** AmEx, MC, V. **Map** p251 J5 Japanese

In the up-and-coming neighbourhood just north of Penn Quarter, this Japanese Izakaya-style restaurant draws a young and hip crowd with its pristine sushi and excellent small plates. The spare space centres around a lively robata grill, where diners at the bar can watch as the flames lick skewers loaded with pork belly, cubes of beef and whole fish. Across the restaurant is the sushi bar, another prime seat, where the chefs masterfully slice fish. The huge menu can be daunting, but if you're looking for a little bit of what of the restaurant does best, go for the omakase tasting menu, available Wednesday to Saturday.

★ The Source

575 Pennsylvania Avenue, between 6th Street & Constitution Avenue (1-202 637 6100, www. wolfgangpuck.com/restaurants/fine-dining/3941). Archives-Navy Memorial or Penn Quarter Metro. **Open** 11.30am-2pm, 5.30-10pm Mon-Thur; 11.30am-2pm, 5.30-11pm Fri; 11.30am-3pm (brunch), 5.30-11pm Sat. **Main courses** $30-$45. **Credit** AmEx, MC, V. **Map** p253 K6 Modern Asian

Plenty of celebrity chefs have staked a claim in Washington in recent years, but few have done it as well as Wolfgang Puck. The Source, located adjacent to the Newseum, feels less like an absentee-chef outpost and more like a vibrant part of the city, thanks to executive chef Scott Drewno and an eclectic mix of diners, from city-dwelling twentysomethings to tourists to famous TV talking heads. If fine dining is on the agenda, book a table in the elegant and sleek upstairs dining room for Drewno's well-executed menu of modern Asian fare. Or stick to the more casual downstairs bar and lounge for delicious dumplings, udon noodles and mini banh mi. *Photo p93.*

Capitol Hill

$ ★ DC-3

423 8th Street, between D & E Streets (1-202 546 1935, www.eatdc3.com). Eastern Market Metro. **Open** 11am-10.30pm daily. **Main courses** $3.99-$6.99. **Credit** MC, V. **Map** p253 M7 American

The team behind Matchbox (*see p87*) and Ted's Bulletin have another crowd-pleaser in DC-3, their hot dog joint on Capitol Hill. Named for the Douglas DC-3 air plane from the 1930s – which explains the giant vintage propeller on one wall – the counter-service restaurant dishes up a roster of regional hot dogs from around the US, from the famous DC half smoke to the New Jersey bacon-wrapped ripper, the Chicago 7 with pickles and tomatoes, and even a version of the standard New York dirty water dog. And then there's the not so classic. The Bay Bridge pretzel dog nods to the mid-Atlantic with crab dip heaped on the hot dog. Fried pickles, cotton candy and soft-serve ice-cream round out the playful menu.

$ ★ Good Stuff Eatery

*303 Pennsylvania Avenue, between 3rd &
4th Streets (1-202 543 8222, www.goodstuff
eatery.com). Capitol South Metro.* **Open** 11.30am-
11pm Mon-Sat. **Main courses** $5.50-$10.
Map p253 L7 ㉙ American
DC claims several stars from the popular *Top Chef*
tv cooking competition, and one of the most recog-
nisable is Spike Mendelsohn. His fun, laid-back
burger joint on Capitol Hill (right next to his We, The
Pizza restaurant) is a favourite of Hill staffers and
First Lady Michelle Obama. The Michelle Melt, a
free-range turkey burger with Swiss cheese and a
wholewheat bun, is named after her. Grab your order
at the counter and don't miss the dipping bar where
you can doctor up your handcut fries with flavoured
mayonnaises and sauces. The delicious toasted
marshmallow milkshake is the stuff of legend.

$ Market Lunch

*Eastern Market, 225 7th Street, between
Pennsylvania & North Carolina Avenues (1-202
547 8444, www.easternmarket.net). Eastern
Market Metro.* **Open** 7.30am-2.30pm Tue-Fri;
8am-3pm Sat; 11am-3pm Sun. **Main courses** $3-
$5. **No credit cards. Map** p253 L7 ㉚ American
On weekends, the crab-cake sandwiches at this
counter-service-only restaurant vie with outdoor
craft vendors as Eastern Market's main draw. But
Market Lunch is perhaps best visited on weekdays:
the line is shorter then and you're more likely to get
a seat at the communal table in the centre aisle of
the historic food hall. It's also a popular spot for
breakfast, with locals waiting in line for the famous
'blue bucks' (blueberry buckwheat pancakes).

Montmartre

*327 7th Street, between C Street & Pennsylvania
Avenue (1-202 544 1244, www.montmartredc.
com). Eastern Market Metro.* **Open** 11.30am-
2.30pm, 5.30-10pm Tue-Thur; 11.30am-2.30pm,
5.30-10.30pm Fri; 5.30-10.30pm Sat; 5.30-9pm Sun.
Brunch 10.30am-3pm Sat, Sun. **Main courses** $16-
$22. **Credit** AmEx, Disc, MC, V. **Map** p253 L7 ㉛
French

THE BEST FOR FUN

With wine
Cork Wine Bar. See p97.

With burgers
Good Stuff Eatery. See above.

With sushi
Sushi Taro. See p94.

With table tennis
Comet Ping Pong. See p103.

Its dining room bustling even when it's not full, its
patio seats constantly occupied, Montmartre is much
beloved of Capitol Hill residents, who stop by for
weekend brunch and people-watching (Eastern
Market is just steps away) as well as reliable daily
dinners. The walls bear the inevitable Moulin Rouge
poster, but the vibe is sophisticated, and the elegantly presented food is more than just café fare: in
addition to hanger steak and duck confit, the menu
includes such dishes as braised rabbit leg, or lighter
fare such as endive salad with blue cheese, roasted
walnuts and apples or home-made country pâté.

$ Ugly Mug

*723 8th Street, at G Street (1-202 547 8459,
www.uglymugdc.com). Eastern Market Metro.*
Open 11.30am-1.30am Mon-Thur; 11.30am-
2.30am Fri; 11am-2.30am Sat; 11am-1.30am
Sun. **Main courses** $8-$14. **No credit cards**.
Map p253 M8 ㉜ American
At first glance, the Ugly Mug is a neighbourhood
pub with plenty of beer (20-plus on tap) and sports
TV (five flat-screens). Attracting both old timers and
new college grads, the Mug is undoubtedly a popular
local watering hole, but it's not the beer alone that's
roping them in – it's the food. Offering brunch, pizza
and sandwiches it departs from standard bar grub,
offering a twist on some of the classics: an elegant
eggs benedict and egg Chesapeake – poached egg,
crab meat and hollandaise sauce. For a really healthy
option the *huevos rancheros* have diced tomatoes,
green pepper, onions and so on, and are followed
with fresh fruit.

Dupont Circle

Afterwords Café

*1517 Connecticut Avenue, NW, at Q Street (1-
202 387 3825, www.kramers.com). Dupont Circle
Metro.* **Open** 7.30am-1am Mon-Thur; 7.30am Fri-
1am Mon continuously. **Main courses** $9-$15.
Credit AmEx, Disc, MC, V. **Map** p250 G4 ㉝
Contemporary American
The best place in DC for a first date – you meet in
the adjoining Kramerbooks and rejoice or despair at
your new friend's taste in literature – Afterwords
Café tries to be all things to all people. Bustling and
capacious, the glass-enclosed dining room serves
food from morning until late night, including
'sharezies' – make-your-own appetiser platters,
ambitious New American dinners with suggested
wine or beer pairings, and decadent desserts. You
and your date are sure to find common ground somewhere on the menu. And when you've got to know
each other better, you can return for Afterwords'
hearty weekend brunch.

Hank's Oyster Bar

*1624 Q Street, NW, between 16th & 17th Streets
(1-202 462 4265, www.hanksdc.com). Dupont
Circle Metro.* **Open** 5.30-10pm Mon, Tue;

CONSUME

5.30-11pm Wed, Thur; 11.30am-3pm, 5.30-11pm Fri, Sat; 11am-3pm (brunch), 5.30-10pm Sun. **Main courses** $15-$23. **Credit** AmEx, Disc, MC, V. **Map** p250 H4 ❹ Fish
Offering a daily rotation of oysters on the half shell, Hank's has become a serious contender among Washington raw bar destinations. For this reason alone, a visit is worthwhile. But there are lots of other reasons to hit this popular neighbourhood spot with a café feel. Here, you can make a meal of small plates (garlic steamed mussels, popcorn shrimp and calamari, peel 'n' eat shrimp) or dive right into a larger plate of lobster roll with fries. There are also daily 'Meat and Two' specials, where the 'two' means side dishes (including seasonal veg, macaroni and cheese and buttermilk onion rings). The only thing that's missing is dessert, the reason for the parting gift of dark chocolate chunks delivered with the bill.
Other locations 633 Pennsylvania Avenue, SE, between 6th & 7th Streets, Capitol Hill (1-202 733 1971); 1026 King Street, Old Town Alexandria (1-703 739 4265).

Heritage India
1337 Connecticut Avenue, NW, between N Street & Dupont Circle (1-202 331 1414, www.heritage indiausa.biz). Dupont Circle Metro. **Open** 11.30am-2.30pm, 5.30-10.30pm daily. **Main courses** $12-$25. **Credit** AmEx, Disc, MC, V. **Map** p250 G4 ❺ Indian
Top-quality, complex-flavoured Indian food (the chef once plied his trade at Bombay Club, *see p85*) and an interesting wine list, without the worry of getting overly dressed up. Vegetarians love this place, where meatless dishes make up about a third of the menu – including the fabulous *begumi khazana*, a feast served on a silver platter.
Other locations 2400 Wisconsin Avenue, NW, at Calvert Street, Glover Park (1-202 333 3120).

★ Komi
1509 17th Street, NW, between P & Q Streets (1-202 332 9200, www.komirestaurant.com). Dupont Circle Metro. **Open** 5.30-9.30pm Tue-Sat. **Set menu** $135. **Credit** AmEx, MC, V. **Map** p250 H4 ❻ Contemporary American
Johnny Monis is gathering quite a following for himself in his tiny Dupont Circle restaurant. Komi's low-key dining room, a straight shot from front window to kitchen window, is home to some of the most adventurous eating in the city; the youthful chef is

essaying New American cuisine with nods to his Mediterranean heritage and whatever else strikes his fancy. But neither he nor his staff of personable, fashionable servers is lacking in discipline; just as his talent is for showcasing unusual ingredients without showboating, theirs is for putting guests at ease with the ever-changing menu. Foodies will be talking about Monis's suckling pig for years. *See also p92* **Power Points**.

$ Lauriol Plaza
1835 18th Street, NW, at T Street (1-202 387 0035, www.lauriolplaza.com). Dupont Circle Metro. **Open** 11.30am-11pm Mon-Thur; 11.30am-midnight Fri, Sat; 11am-11pm (11am-3pm brunch) Sun. **Main courses** $7.50-$19. **Credit** AmEx, Disc, MC, V. **Map** p250 G3 ❼ Tex-Mex
This has to be DC's most popular restaurant: even with a capacity for up to 350 diners in its two-tiered dining area (plus rooftop), the line for a table often spills over on to the sidewalk. Food is reasonably priced Tex-Mex fare. From margaritas and salsa, to Mexican staples such as enchiladas and fajitas, to specialities from Peru, Cuba and elsewhere, there's a little of everything for the Latin food fan, and the scene is always jumping.

★ Little Serow
1511 17th Street, NW, at Church Street (no phone, http://littleserow.com). Dupont Circle Metro. **Open** 5.30-10pm Mon-Thur; 5.30-10.30pm Fri, Sat. **Set meal** $45. **Credit** AmEx, Disc, MC, V. **Map** p250 H4 ❽ Thai
Johnny Monis was just 24 when he opened Komi (*see above*), the Greek-inspired restaurant that vaulted him to culinary stardom. For his second place, Little Serow, he took inspiration from northern Thailand. As at Komi, there is no menu; $45 gets you a family-style meal of about seven dishes. Flavours are bright and bold, and the heat can be intense. The menu changes weekly, but dishes might include snakehead fish with bamboo shoots and rice powder or pork ribs with whiskey and dill. The restaurant can only accommodate groups of up to four and doesn't take reservations, but the staff will text you when a table frees up.

Obelisk
2029 P Street, NW, between 20th & 21st Streets (1-202 872 1180). Dupont Circle Metro. **Open** 6-10pm Tue-Sat. **Set dinner** $75 5 courses. **Credit** MC, V. **Map** p250 G4 ❾ Italian
The menu changes constantly at Peter Pastan's prix-fixe-only, reservations-required townhouse, depending on what's fresh and what catches the chef's fancy. But you can always count on an array of antipasti; pasta, meat, cheese and dessert courses; and exemplary service. Squab makes regular appearances – it's worth the awkwardness of dealing with the tiny bones – as do seasonal vegetables and fish. Nominally Italian, the cooking is both catholic and

---

INSIDE TRACK HALF-SMOKES

So what exactly is a half-smoke? Not even natives can definitively define it. DC's signature speciality is a plump sausage, sometimes smoked, sometimes split, and usually a treat.

The Source. *See p90*.

classical. The wine list is extensive, the breads baked in-house, the atmosphere unpretentious.

$ Pizzeria Paradiso
2003 P Street, NW, between 20th & 21st Streets (1-202 223 1245, www.eatyourpizza.com). Dupont Circle Metro. **Open** 11.30am-11pm Mon-Thur; 11.30am-midnight Fri, Sat; noon-10pm Sun. **Main courses** $6-$19. **Credit** MC, V. **Map** p250 G4 **40** Pizza/Italian

Good quality, wood-oven pizza that keeps locals coming back for more. Expect to wait for a table, even at the larger Georgetown location. The salad of white beans and tuna, plus the antipasti plate of salami and Italian cheeses, are worth considering if pizza is not your thing. But do try the effervescent lemonade. All in all, a fun excursion.
Other locations 3282 M Street, NW, 33rd & Potomac Streets, Georgetown (1-202 337 1245).

Raku
1900 Q Street, NW, at 19th Street (1-202 265 7258, www.rakuasiandining.com). Dupont Circle Metro. **Open** 11.30am-9.30pm Mon-Thur; 11.30am-10.30pm Fri; noon-11pm Sat; noon-10pm Sun. **Main courses** $15.50-$24.50. **Credit** AmEx, MC, V. **Map** p250 G4 **41** Asian

Choosing between Thai, Japanese, Korean or Chinese restaurants can be a bit difficult. But at Raku, you don't have to. The menu includes staples from all four national cuisines, including fried egg rolls, sushi (try the tuna tartare sushi roll with

peanuts, lemon and basil) and pad Thai. If you feel like trying something new, go for the sea urchin or eel. Raku bills itself as an 'Asian diner'. The atmosphere inside is appropriately frenetic, while the food is simple and satisfying.
Other locations 7240 Woodmont Avenue, at Elm Street, Bethesda, MD (1-301 718 8680).

Regent
1910 18th Street, NW, between Florida Avenue & T Street (1-202 232 1781, www.regentthai.com). Dupont Circle Metro. **Open** 11.30am-3pm, 5-10pm Mon-Thur; 11.30am-3pm, 5-11pm Fri; noon-3pm, 5-11pm Sat; 5-10pm Sun. **Main courses** $9-$20. **Credit** AmEx, Disc, MC, V. **Map** p250 G3 **42** Thai

Regent is slightly dressier and more refined (and also somewhat more expensive) than most of DC's other Thai restaurants. The flavours – lots of coconut milk, green and red curry, lemongrass and chilli paste – are perfectly balanced, and the setting is serene, with large wood carvings and quiet fountains. Try the panang chicken, green curry and pad eggplant, which comes in a spicy black bean sauce. For dessert, the mango sticky rice is unbeatable.

Sette Osteria
1666 Connecticut Avenue, NW, at R Street (1-202 483 3070, www.setteosteria.com). Dupont Circle Metro. **Open** 11.30am- 11pm Mon-Thur, Sun; 11.30am-midnight Fri; 11am-midnight Sat. **Main courses** $9-$19. **Credit** AmEx, Disc, MC, V. **Map** p250 G4 **43** Italian

From wood-fired pizzas to veal scaloppine with lemon and caper sauce, this stylish Dupont Circle restaurant serves excellent (and affordable) Neapolitan fare. The pastas are especially good; try gnocchi alla Sorrentina (with tomato, mozzarella and basil) or baked lasagne. In warm weather, Sette's large outdoor seating area comes into its own as an arena for people-watching, while in winter, the indoors is cosy.

Sushi Taro

1503 17th Street, NW, at P Street (1-202 462 8999, www.sushitaro.com). Dupont Circle Metro. **Open** 11.30am-2pm, 5.30-10pm Mon-Fri; 5.30-10.30pm Sat. **Set meals** $80-$180 (without pairings). **Credit** AmEx, Disc, MC, V. **Map** p250 H4 **④** **Japanese**

Sushi Taro underwent a major renovation in 2009 and has been reborn as an upmarket Kaiseki-style traditional Japanese restaurant, under owner Nobu Yamazaki. In a kaiseki-style meal, diners don't order off a menu. Instead the chef presents a succession of complementary dishes. The Suppon Kaiseki Tasting focuses on the very traditional soft-shell snapping turtle. There is also an excellent saké selection.

Tabard Inn

1739 N Street, NW, between 17th & 18th Streets (1-202 331 8528, www.tabardinn.com). Dupont Circle Metro. **Open** 7-10am, 11.30am-2.30pm, 6-9.30pm Mon-Thur; 7-10am, 11.30am-2.30pm, 6-10pm Fri; 8-9.45am, 11am-2.30pm, 6-10pm

Power Points

Political haunts and presidential favourites.

Good Stuff Eatery

Washington is the kind of place where the person at the next table may be discussing state secrets and the president himself could very well walk into the neighbourhood burger joint. (Of course, the massive motorcade would probably tip you off.)

While it's possible to visit DC and opt out of the well-trodden political sights, it's hard to ignore that the city is crawling with the world's most powerful people. People who get hungry just like the rest of us.

Unlike the Bushes, who rarely dined out, the Obamas moved into the White House and made it very clear they were savvy diners and passionate foodies. Date nights for the president and first lady have taken them to the tiny foodie

mecca **Komi** (*see p92*), where Johnny Monis's multi-course tasting menu is a revelation, the stylish **Blue Duck Tavern** in the Park Hyatt (*see p141*) and, just a few blocks from the White House, **Equinox** (*see 83*), where chef Todd Gray celebrates the food of the mid-Atlantic – and Michelle Obama celebrated her birthday.

The couple nearly sparked a burger war when Michelle pledged allegiance to Capitol Hill's **Good Stuff Eatery** (*see p91*), where a free-range turkey burger is now named for her, while her husband chose to hit Arlington's **Ray's Hell Burger** (1725 Wilson Boulevard, Arlington, VA, 1-703 841 0001), with Vice-President Joe Biden for the massive prime beef patties. The pair have found

CONSUME

Sat; 8-9.15am, 10.30am-2.30pm Sun. **Main courses** $11-$17 lunch; $23-$33 dinner. **Credit** AmEx, MC, V. **Map** p250 G4 ⑮ Contemporary American

Tucked at the back of a 19th-century brownstone, home to a family-run hotel, the Tabard is an eclectic and shamelessly romantic destination. Dine in the lounge in front of the fireplace, in the garden under the shade of a silk parachute, or in the private dining room. The menu favours local, seasonal ingredients. House-smoked salmon, served with hard-boiled egg, red onion and horseradish crème fraîche is always good. Sunday's crowds (seriously, make reservations far in advance) brunch on just-made doughnuts and eggs benedict.

▶ *For a review of the hotel, see p148.*

$ Teaism

2009 R Street, NW, at Connecticut Avenue (1-202 667 3827, www.teaism.com). Dupont Circle Metro. **Open** 8am-10pm Mon-Thur; 8am-11pm Fri; 9am-11pm Sat; 9am-10pm Sun. **Main courses** $7.75-$12. **Credit** AmEx, MC, V. **Map** p250 G4 ⑯ Café/Asian

Freshly baked naan and Thai chicken curry are on offer at this café-style oasis from the bustle of urban living. Whether you stop off for a cup of chai or a bento box, you'll feel ready to pound the pavement again. Afternoon tea with ginger scones and lime curd tartlets can be quite reviving in winter, or in warm weather, try the iced Moroccan mint tea; there's nothing more refreshing. The spacious 8th Street branch, with its downstairs hideout, has a calmer vibe.

common ground with an affinity for Five Guys, the locally based burger chain.

Visiting dignitaries know whose lead to follow when they come to town. French president Nicolas Sarkozy took supermodel wife Carla Bruni to one of Barack Obama's favourites, the legendary **Ben's Chili Bowl** (*see p98*), for the famous half smokes.

Of course, the current power players certainly weren't the first to hit the town for a meal. The historic **Martin's Tavern** (1264 Wisconsin Avenue, NW, 1-202 333 7370, www.martins-tavern.com) in Georgetown claims to have hosted every president from Harry Truman to George W Bush. You can request a seat in the proposal booth (that's booth #3) where John F Kennedy supposedly popped the question to Jackie. Despite questions of historical accuracy, it's a story the family that has owned the restaurant for 75 years stands by.

A great spot for oysters and late-night wings, the **Old Ebbitt Grill** (*see p106*) was reportedly favoured by Teddy Roosevelt and is still frequented by political big-wigs.

These days, thanks to the young Obama administration, the power centre has moved away from stuffy steakhouses to more urbane locales. The hip 14th Street Corridor, including **Cork Wine Bar** (*see p97*), **Marvin** (*see p101*) and **Estadio** (*see p98*), has been a favourite of the president's team.

And if you're not rubbing elbows with Barack over burgers, you can get a bird's eye view of his backyard from **POV** (*see p106*), the chic rooftop lounge at the W hotel. That is, if you can get past the velvet rope. See, it's all about access in this town.

Ben's Chili Bowl.

CONSUME

A Taste of H Street

Eastern promise.

Until recently, Washington's H Street, NE, corridor was a run-down stretch of road still scarred by the 1968 riots. But H Street is gentrifying rapidly and the area towards the intersection with Florida and Maryland Avenues now vies for the title of DC's most vibrant nightlife strip. Revellers here tend to be more casual than those on U Street, and they're generally a bit older than the early-twentysomethings who flock to 18th Street in Adams Morgan.

Some good restaurants have settled into the street, too, including **Granville Moore's** (*see p105*), a snug Belgain place known for its mussels and frites – and Belgian beers, of course – the bar is open until 3am on Friday and Saturday; and **Sticky Rice** (*see p105*), a hip Asian bar and restaurant. Mention should also be given to **Ethiopic** (*see p105*), slightly off the main drag at the Union Station end of H Street, between 4th and 5th Streets, thought by many to be DC's best Ethiopian restaurant.

The chef/owner of one of H Street's best restaurants, the **Atlas Room** (*see p105*), spent time at Vidalia downtown. His own place serves food majoring on local ingredients, with French and Italian influences in the cooking style – the likes of lamb meatballs with a white bean garlic

purée, basil, yoghurt and an olive coulis, or roast chicken with roast potato, spring onions, oyster mushrooms, green beans and a herbed jus.

For dessert, there's **Dangerously Delicious Pies** (*see p105*). The owner used to play in a rock band, and along with tasty pies (there are savoury pies and quiches too), the place has that little touch of edge that defines this neighbourhood.

Ready for fun after dinner? The **Rock & Roll Hotel** (*see p172*) – which is a bar and music venue, not an actual hotel – has live bands and DJs. Next door **Biergarten Haus** (*see p114*) is a Bavarian-style beer hall with one-litre pours and robust German food (plus trivia on Tuesday night). A couple of blocks west, **Little Miss Whiskey's Golden Dollar** (*see p114*) has a long beers list and is popular for its dance parties. The **H Street Country Club** (*see p114*), meanwhile, is a bar with a difference: it has an indoor miniature-golf course where drinkers can putt around tiny versions of Washington landmarks.

When the long-awaited streetcar begins operation (expected late 2013), the H Street strip will be easier to reach. In the meantime, it's accessible by the X2 bus from Gallery Place-Chinatown Metro.

Other locations 800 Connecticut Avenue, NW, at H Street, Downtown (1-202 835 2233); 400 8th Street, NW, at D Street, Penn Quarter (1-202 638 6010).

$ Thaiphoon
2011 S Street, NW, between 20th Street & Connecticut Avenue (1-202 667 3505, www. thaiphoon.com). Dupont Circle Metro. **Open** 11.30am-10.30pm Mon-Thur, Sun; 11.30am-11pm Fri, Sat. **Main courses** $8-$14. **Credit** MC, V. **Map** p250 G4 ⑰ Thai

Shiny stainless steel and a striking front window invite you to be part of the buzz at this bright, bustling place. The menu is lengthy, covering many Thai classics, from papaya salad to lemongrass chicken; the presentation is pretty and the flavours freshly assertive. Try the crispy bananas with berry sauce. Vegetarians are well fed here.

Adams Morgan

$ Amsterdam Falafelshop
2425 18th Street, NW, at Belmont Road (1-202 234 1969, http://falafelshop.com). Dupont Circle

Metro then 42 bus or Woodley Park-Zoo/Adams Morgan Metro. **Open** 11am-midnight Mon, Sun; 11am-2.30am Tue, Wed; 11am-3am Thur; 11am-4am Fri, Sat. **Main courses** $5.50-$9.50. **Credit** Disc, MC, V. **Map** p250 G3 ⑱ Middle Eastern

This is the perfect place for a quick bite, whether it's two in the afternoon or two in the morning (although beware the long, hungry lines that form in the early hours). The choices at the counter are simplicity itself: small or large? Wholewheat pitta or white? Fries with that? (Say yes – they're the best in town.) You'll face tougher decisions at the extensive toppings bar, which includes houmous, grilled eggplant, marinated cucumber, and more – much more, sadly, than can fit in one pitta. This might be the best deal in town.

$ Diner
2453 18th Street, NW, between Kalorama & Columbia Roads (1-202 232 8800, www.diner dc.com). Dupont Circle Metro then 42 bus or Woodley Park-Zoo/Adams Morgan Metro. **Open** 24hrs daily. **Main courses** $9-$18. **Credit** MC, V. **Map** p250 G3 ⑲ American

CONSUME

One of DC's few 24-hour joints, the Diner is brought to you by the same folks who own coffee lounge Tryst (*see right*) just two doors away. True to its name, there's home-style chow such as home-made meatloaf with gravy and mash for lunch and buttermilk pancakes for 4am. The Diner is constantly packed with neighbourhood hipsters and night owls, but we don't think it's the food that keeps people going back for more. It's those long counters, great for flirting, sipping coffee and playing with your food behind the Sunday paper.

★ Mintwood Place
1813 Columbia Road, NW, at Biltmore Street (1-202 234 6732, http://mintwoodplace.com). Woodley Park/Adams Morgan/Zoo Metro. **Open** 5.30-10.30pm Tue-Thur; 5.30-11.30pm Fri; 10.30am-2.30pm, 5.30-11.30pm Sat; 10.30am-2.30pm, 5.30-9.30pm Sun. **Main courses** $17-$35. **Credit** AmEx, Disc, MC, V. **Map** p250 G3 ⑤⓪ French/American

Everything about this bistro is inviting – the relaxed, almost rustic decor that evokes an upscale farmhouse, the welcoming service and, most of all, the satisfying French-American comfort food, often presented with an inventive twist. You could easily make a meal of starters such as escargot hushpuppies and bacon-and-onion flammekuche, or dig into a wood-grilled bacon cheeseburger, President Obama's pick when he dined here. But it would be a shame to miss out on entrées like the tagliatelle bolognese or roasted pork for two. For dessert, try the dreamy brownie sundae or the apple tart à la mode.

Perry's
1811 Columbia Road, NW, at Biltmore Street (1-202 234 6218, www.perrysadamsmorgan.com). Dupont Circle Metro then 42 bus or Woodley Park-Zoo/Adams Morgan Metro then 90, 92, 93, L2 bus. **Open** 5.30-10.30pm Mon-Thur; 5.30-11.30pm Fri; 11am-3pm, 5.30-11.30pm Sat; 10am-2.30pm (brunch), 5.30-10.30pm Sun. **Main courses** $14-$26. **Credit** AmEx, Disc, MC, V. **Map** p250 G2/3 ⑤① Fusion

Stand smack in the middle of Adams Morgan Party Central, the intersection of 18th Street and Columbia Road, NW (the traffic is so gridlocked on weekend nights that you can often do so without any significant risk to either life or limb), and you'll see the illuminated rooftop of Perry's, hangout of beautiful people and their attendant wannabes. The largely twentysomething crowd is attracted not just to the lights – and the lively scene under them – but to the array of well-executed sushi prepared downstairs, where a classic wood-panelled dining room offers a more sedate setting for unwinding. Along with sushi, the menu features a short list of New American starters and entrées, with such favourites as seasonal heirloom tomato salad, grilled swordfish steak with lemon chutney and the chef's veg platter. Perry's drag queen brunch is offered every Sunday.

The fixed price includes all you can eat and dancers to entertain you. Arrive early for the show.

$ Tryst
2459 18th Street, NW, between Belmont & Columbia Roads (1-202 232 5500, www.tryst dc.com). Dupont Circle Metro then 42 bus or Woodley Park-Zoo/Adams Morgan Metro. **Open** 6.30am-midnight Mon-Thur; 6.30am-3am Fri, Sat; 7am-midnight Sun. **Credit** AmEx, Disc, MC, V. **Map** p250 G2/3 ⑤② Café

Not quite a club, a bar, or even a coffeehouse for that matter, Tryst makes a great community living room. Overstuffed chairs, comfy sofas and country-style kitchen tables – not to mention the free Wi-Fi access – create a hip, relaxed vibe without feeling collegiate. If you want to drink alcohol, fine. If not, the coffee, served in enormous mugs, is very good. There is also a range of sandwiches (half of which are vegetarian). Alternatively, you could create your own salad or order several small plates for nibbling.

Logan Circle

★ Birch & Barley
1337 14th Street, NW, between N Street & Rhode Island Avenue (1-202 567 2576, http://birchand barley.com). Dupont Circle, U Street/African-American Civil War Memorial/Cardozo Metro Metro. **Open** 5.30-10pm Tue-Thur; 5.30-11pm Fri, Sat; 11am-8pm Sun (all-day brunch). **Main courses** $14-$29. **Credit** AmEx, MC, V. **Map** p250 H4 ⑤③ Contemporary American

Look for the line on the sidewalk in front of the glass garage door and you've found Birch & Barley and its raucous upstairs beer bar Churchkey (*see p110*). (The line is for the latter, though you'll need a reservation for the dining room many nights.) Inside, a massive copper beer 'organ' funnels some 500 choices, all served at the proper temperature and in the correct glassware, to thirsty patrons. The kitchen here turns out rustic yet elegant dishes such as risotto with cuttlefish, marinated white asparagus, tarragon and squid ink, and flatbreads topped with figs and prosciutto. Do not skip dessert – you'll find clever renditions of all-American sweets like peanut butter cheesecake and an updated hostess cupcake. Then head upstairs to the casual Churchkey, with low lighting and its own beer-friendly menu (think grilled cheese, wings and poutine).

★ Cork Wine Bar
1720 14th Street, NW, between R & S Streets (1-202 265 2675, http://corkdc.com). U Street/African-American Civil War Memorial/Cardozo Metro. **Open** 5pm-midnight Tue, Wed, Sun; 5pm-1am Thur-Sat. **Main courses** plates to share $8-$15. **Credit** AmEx, MC, V. **Map** p250 H4 ⑤④ Wine bar

One of the best of the new wave of convivial neighbourhood wine bars that have popped up in the city,

CONSUME

Estadio.

Cork offers about 160 wines by the bottle, 50 wines by the glass and thoughtful wine tasting flights. The bar area of the historic 14th Street building is regularly packed, so come early for the best chance of scoring a seat. Dark wood floors, exposed brick walls and bare bulbs that give off a soft glow make the wine bar feel older than its actual age. The menu includes shareable plates, such as a pan-crisped brioche sandwich of prosciutto, fontina and a soft-cooked egg, rosemary chicken liver bruschetta and braised pork cheeks with creamy polenta. Husband and wife owners Khalid Pitts and Diane Gross also have a terrific wine shop and gourmet market just up the street.

★ **Estadio**

1520 14th Street, NW, at Church Street (1-202 319 1404, www.estadio-dc.com). U Street/African-American Civil War Memorial/Cardozo Metro. **Open** 5-10pm Mon-Thur; 11.30am-2pm, 5-11pm Sat; 11am-2pm, 5-9pm Sun. **Main courses** tapas $4-$14. **Credit** AmEx, V. **Map** p250 H4 ⑮ Tapas

This 14th Street tapas joint is regularly packed to the brim and for good reason. The menu reads like a grazer's dream with a host of traditional Spanish snacks perfect for sharing – cheeses and meats, toothpicks called pintxos stacked with anchovies, olives and chorizo, fresh figs stuffed with cheese and wrapped in jamon, and croquetas in mushroom or jamon. Vintage World Cup soccer games play on TVs over the bar. Don't miss the 'slushitos', boozy frozen slushies that change flavours to suit the season. Feeling daring? Order wine out of a glass porron. The traditional Spanish wine spouts will have you dribble wine down your shirt at least once, depending on your learning curve, but they make for great fun.

Rice

1608 14th Street, NW, between Q & Corcoran Streets (1-202 234 2400, www.ricerestaurant.com). Dupont Circle or U Street/African-American Civil War Memorial/Cardozo Metro. **Open** 11am-2.30pm, 5-10.30pm Mon-Thur; 11am-11pm Fri, Sat; 11am-10.30pm Sun. **Main courses** $14-$18. **Credit** Disc, MC, V. **Map** p250 H4 ⑯ Thai

The chicest of urban-chic Thai places, Rice takes minimalism to the max. The expanse of its cool and neutral-toned walls contrasted with exposed brick is interrupted only by a small fountain; its coconut-milk-scented rice arrives artistically mounded in the center of the plate. Appetisers and entrées are divided into categories of authentic Thai food, healthy options and house specialities; stick with the latter two for originality and assurance of execution. Vegetarians have plenty of choice here. There's no reason not to order a saké Martini or other fancy drink from your young, black-clad server.

U Street Corridor

★ **$ Ben's Chili Bowl**

1213 U Street, NW, between 12th & 13th Streets (1-202 667 0909, www.benschilibowl.com). U Street/African-American Civil War Memorial/Cardozo Metro. **Open** 6am-2am Mon-Thur; 6am-4am Fri, 7am-4am Sat; 11am-11pm (no breakfast) Sun. **Main courses** $4-$9. **No credit cards**. **Map** p250 H3 ⑰ American

Looking like a museum piece on the yuppified, buppified stretch of U Street once known as Black Broadway, Ben's Chili Bowl, opened in 1958, is in no danger of mouldering away, thankfully. In fact, its claim to be a 100% wind-powered business makes it very contemporary. This family-owned institution's appeal rests on three legs: nostalgia (past customers include Duke Ellington, Miles Davis, Bill Cosby and, more recently, Barack Obama), the insatiable late-night hunger of young partiers, and, of course, the great bang for the buck afforded by burgers, fries and chilli. In-the-know customers order chilli on a dog or half smoke (arguably Washington's signature speciality) and cheesefries, but you can also get a turkey sub or a veggie burger. These days, in fact, you can even order Ben's over the internet.
▶ *For more on Ben's appeal as a place to be seen, see p94 Power Points.*

Busboys & Poets

2021 14th Street, NW, between U & V Streets (1-202 387 7638, www.busboysandpoets.com). U Street/African-American Civil War Memorial/Cardozo Metro. **Open** 8am-midnight Mon-Thur; 8am-2am Fri; 9am-2am Sat; 9am-midnight Sun. **Main courses** $8.50-$22. **Credit** MC, V. **Map** p250 H3 ⑱ Café

It may not have the most exciting food (burgers, salads, sandwiches, pizza), but no matter. Busboys & Poets is an exciting space in and of itself. Located at

Ethiopia in DC

Ethiopian food is a Washington staple.

Washington is home to the US's largest population of Ethiopians and Eritreans, and one result of this influx has been a blossoming of Ethiopian restaurants in the city. Ethiopian food is a mainstay in the diet of many young Washingtonians. Diners sit around a communal platter of injera – a spongy, pleasantly sour giant pancake of bread. Stews are served on the top – and diners scoop up bites of food with more injera, torn into bite-sized pieces. Meat tends to come in conveniently sized chunks; vegetables, in properly textured piles. It's great fun, it's economical, and it's a good base for a night on the town.

For many years, Adams Morgan was the epicentre of Ethiopian cuisine, with senior statesman **Meskerem** (2434 18th Street, NW, between Columbia & Belmont Roads,

Zenebech Injera.

(1-202 462 4100, www.meskerem ethiopianrestaurantdc.com) holding its own over competitors with its decor: authentic low tables and a rustic look. The vegetarian sampler here is a great way to go; the spicy red-lentil purée is a favourite.

A block south is **Awash** (No.2218, 1-202 588 8181), less of a looker but easily Meskerem's match for cuisine; the tables outdoors are a draw in the warmer months.

These days, however, the locus of Ethiopian activity has shifted down on to U Street, NW, and 9th Street, a strip now informally dubbed Little Ethiopia. Some are large venues with bars and established nightlife, others mere townhouses with tables. **Dukem**, an old-timer at the corner of 11th and U (1114-1118 U Street, 1-202 667 8735, www.dukemrestaurant.com), is one of the former, beloved for its outdoor seating and its multiple versions of kitfo, spiced raw minced beef. At **Axum** (1934 Ninth Street, 1-202 387 0765) a sociable dining room serves not only such dishes as crispy, pleasantly chewy derek tibs – lamb cubes cooked with onions and jalapeños, accompanied by a pool of fiery sauce – but also Italian-style cotoletta sandwiches. **Etete** (1942 9th Street, 1-202 232 7600, www.eteterestaurant.com), another small wonder, is a critics' darling – especially for its spicy beef and lamb dishes.

Meanwhile, over on T Street, the very modest **Zenebech Injera** (No.608, 1-202 667 4700) has made a great name for itself for superb food, with dishes like a finely but strongly spiced kitfo and big, comforting stews. Much of its business is takeaway – it's a grocery, too, and there are just two tables – and it is also a major supplier of injera bread to the city's bigger restaurants.

Last, but certainly not least, the new restaurant area of H Street, NE, is home to **Ethiopic** (*see p105*), one of the city's most notable Ethiopian restaurants. The welcoming interior, with bare bricks, wooden floors and columns decorated with Amharic letters, is the setting for some of the most pungent Ethiopian tastes in town, with vegetarian and meat samplers being a great way to experience the cooking. Pavement table dining in warm weather is another plus.

CONSUME

Union Market

DC moves into the big league as a food town with this new market.

When people talk about DC's emergence as a serious food town, they invariably mention Union Market. And rightfully so; it's this city's equivalent of San Francisco's famed Ferry Terminal, a marketplace showcasing some of the region's best food.

The development company EDENS built the sleek, modern market, which opened in 2012, with the intention of making it the centrepiece of a vibrant new community in what was a derelict warehouse district. For now, many of the ageing industrial buildings remain, but from Wednesday to Saturday the market bustles with singles and families who would never have visited this part of town just a few years back.

What brings them are around two dozen vendors selling gourmet wares, from speciality salts and teas to cupcakes and crusty baguettes. It's a mini taste of DC, with many of the city's best venues represented here.

Perhaps the biggest draw is the **Rappahannock Oyster Bar**, where you can sample fresh oysters, clams and shrimp while sipping a cocktail or glass of wine. The company that runs the bar is known for supplying some of the finest restaurants in the region.

If seafood isn't your thing, head to the nearby **Righteous Cheese** counter for a course of three or four cheeses paired with wines, craft beers, or even sodas.

For an old-fashioned soda fountain experience, head across the way to **Buffalo & Bergen**, which serves up retro house-made concotions like blueberry floats and egg creams, along with bagels and knishes.

Other favourite stops include **Takorean** – the first bricks-and-mortar outpost of one of DC's most popular food trucks – for Korean-style tacos (think chicken, beef or tofu marinated in sweet/spicy sauce; toppings include kimchi and sesame seeds), and **DC Empanadas**, which puts a new spin on the traditional fried pastry with fillings such as chiken tikka or aubergine and mozzarella.

At the **Red Apron** butcher stand, you can pick out a beautifully marbled steak to take home, or grab a seat and chow down on one of its hearty, meat-laden sandwiches on fresh-baked bread.

The expert baristas at **Peregrine Espresso** prepare some of the city's best coffee and serve up tasty pastries to go with it, such as almond croissants and cranberry scones.

Another good bet for a treat is **Tickling Springs Creamery**, an all-natural dairy that makes its own thick, creamy ice-cream in about a dozen flavours.

If you don't feel like eating in – or if you arrived mid-afternoon on a weekend and can't find a seat – the to-go options are plentiful and enticing. Look for **Lyon Bakery** for fresh breads, **Cordial** for wines and craft beers, **Coco Sala** for artisinal chocolates, the **DC Mediterreanean Corner** for fresh houmous and spinach pies, and the **Neopol Savory Smokery** for smoked fish and meats – all perfect for a picnic on the National Mall.

Union Market

1309 5th Street, NE, at Florida Avenue (http://unionmarketdc.com). NoMA-Gallaudet Metro. **Open** *11am-8pm Wed-Fri; 8am-8pm Sat, Sun.*

the corner of 14th and U Streets, NW, it was established by Andy Shallal, an Iraqi American artist, restaurateur and activist in 2005 in an area with a history of 1960s civil rights activism. With its communal tables, sofas and cushy chairs, Busboys is the ultimate urban living room, where people meet for coffee or drinks or a snack in between meals. Open mic poetry readings, live music and book discussions are also on the menu.

Other locations 1025 5th Street, NW (1-202 789 2227); 4251 South Campbell Avenue, Arlington, VA (1-202 379 9757).

★ Marvin

2007 14th Street, NW, between U & V Streets (1-202 797 7171, www.marvindc.com). U Street/ African-American Civil War Memorial/Cardozo Metro. **Open** 5.30pm-2am Mon-Thur; 5.30pm-3am Fri, Sat; 10.30am-2.30pm, 5.30-10pm Sun. **Main courses** $14-$27. **Credit** AmEx, MC, V. **Map** p250 H3 ⑩ Belgian/soul food

From the owners of the ever-hip Eighteenth Street Lounge (*see p109*), Marvin turned a former Subway fast-food shop into one of the 14th and U Street neighbourhood's coolest hangouts. The name is a nod to Marvin Gaye, one of owner (and half of DC's music duo Thievery Corporation) Eric Hilton's musical role models. The dimly lit space is two floors – a bistro on the ground level serves a hipster crowd a clever mix of Belgian dishes and soul food, like moules frites, shrimp and grits, and fried chicken with waffles. A lounge with a regular line-up of talented DJs resides on the second floor. Also up top: a spacious outdoor deck complete with heaters for chilly nights.

Tabaq Bistro

1336 U Street, NW, at 13th Street (1-202 265 0965, www.tabaqdc.com). U Street/Cardozo Metro. **Open** 5-11pm Mon-Thur; 5pm-midnight Fri; 5pm-midnight Sat; 5-11pm Sun. *Brunch* 10am-4pm Sat, Sun. **Main courses** $14-$23. **Credit** AmEx, Disc, MC, V. **Map** p250 H3 ⑩ Mediterranean

The attraction here lies more in the setting than in the menu. Diners enjoy a dramatic rooftop view year-round in the glass-enclosed terrace, which opens up in summer for fresh air. (Be prepared to climb several flights of stairs to reach it, though.) Not that the food – kebabs, roast chicken and lamb, plus small plates from Turkey, Morocco and elsewhere – is poor. Far from it. It's hard to live up to the spectacular location, though. But what a view to aspire to.

Georgetown

1789

1226 36th Street, NW, at Prospect Street (1-202 965 1789, www.1789restaurant.com). Foggy Bottom-GWU Metro then 31, 32, 36, 38B busor Circulator bus. **Open** 6-10pm

CONSUME

Mon-Thur, Sun; 6-11pm Fri; 5.30-11pm Sat;
5.30-10pm Sun. **Main courses** $18-$35.
Credit AmEx, Disc, MC, V. **Map** p249 E5 ⑤
American

Georgetown's 1789, site of countless graduation fêtes
and anniversary dinners, is evocative of a
Washington of old, when men wore ties and women
smiled and nodded. These things still happen, of
course, and the main dining room, with its antique-
style china and gold-framed historical prints, is an
appropriate setting for them. The menu stresses
local provenance – rockfish from Kent Island,
Maryland, say, with celery root purée, braised esca-
role with citrus and black trumpet mushrooms, or
Shenandoah Valley lamb with arugula, potatoes and
roast garlic. The food is exceptional; the service, as
might be expected, impeccable.

Bangkok Joe's

*3000 K Street, NW, at Thomas Jefferson Street
(1-202 333 4422, www.bangkokjoes.com). Foggy
Bottom-GWU Metro then 31, 32, 36, 38B bus or
Circulator bus.* **Open** 11.30am-10.30pm Mon-Thur;
11.30am-11.30pm Fri; noon-11.30pm Sat; noon-
10.30pm Sun. **Main courses** $10-$18. **Credit**
AmEx, Disc, MC, V. **Map** p249 F5 ㉒ Thai

Vibrant colours and sleek design set the tone at this
stylish Thai establishment, definitely the best bet
for food among the restaurants in Washington
Harbour, along the Georgetown waterfront. While
the cooking lacks some of the complex flavours
you'll find at somewhere like the Regent (*see p93*),
Bangkok Joe's features a dumpling bar (try the
mushroom and ginger dumplings), plus lots of delicious noodle dishes.

Bourbon Steak

*Four Seasons, 2800 Pennsylvania Avenue, NW,
at 28th Street (1-202 944 2026, www.bourbon
steakdc.com). Foggy Bottom-GWU Metro.* **Open**
11.30am-2.30pm Mon; 11.30am-2.30pm, 6-10pm
Tue-Thur; 11.30am-2.30pm, 5.30-10.30pm Fri;
5.30-10.30pm Sat. **Main courses** $29-$69.
Credit AmEx, MC, V. **Map** p250 F5 ㉓
American

If you're looking for a decadent splurge and a high
probability of a celebrity sighting, head to this modern restaurant inside Georgetown's Four Seasons
hotel, where steaks are poached in butter and movie
stars and power players rub shoulders. California-
based chef Michael Mina opened a branch of his contemporary steakhouse as part of a very posh
makeover of the Four Seasons. Steakhouse classics
such as an aged porterhouse, creamed spinach and
wagyu beef are joined by locally sourced fare such
as Virginia swordfish, plus a shellfish and caviar
selection. The complimentary fries that land on the
table are crisped in duck fat and very addictive. The
swank bar is a regular hangout for VIP guests and,
true to its name, offers a nice selection of rare bour-
bons and Scotches.

Café Milano

*3251 Prospect Street, NW, at Wisconsin Avenue
(1-202 333 6183, www.cafemilanodc.com). Foggy
Bottom-GWU Metro then 31, 32, 36 bus or
Circulator bus.* **Open** 11.30am-midnight Mon, Tue,
Sun; 11.30am-1am Wed-Sat; 11.30am-11pm Sun.
Main courses $29-$44. **Credit** AmEx, MC, V.
Map p249 E5 ㉔ Italian

The crowd here is as much of an attraction as the
food; you might spot Michael Jordan or a visiting
movie star in this multi-room complex. Even the
non-famous clientele are for the most part young,
rich and glamorous. The menu – and the atmosphere
– ranges from casual to chic; you can choose from a
selection of pizzas and pastas, or opt for duck breast
in Marsala wine or spaghetti with fresh clams.

Café La Ruche

*1039 31st Street, NW, between K & M Streets
(1-202 965 2684, www.cafelaruche.com). Foggy
Bottom-GWU Metro then 31, 32, 36, 38B bus
or Circulator bus.* **Open** 11am-10.30pm Mon-Thur;
10am-12.30pm Fri, Sat; 10am-11pm Sun. **Main
courses** $11.95-$23.95. **Credit** AmEx, MC, V.
Map p249 E5 ㉕ French

Quaint from the outside, a little more hip on the inside,
La Ruche is a comfort zone for Francophiles who don't
want to drop a big wad of cash on their cuisine of
choice. They gather here in swarms, making a buzz
of conversation while waiting for chef Jean-Claude
Cauderlier's cooking. The food comes café-style, with
a wide range of choices in the quiche/sandwich/salad
range, plus a smattering of daily entrée specials such
as mussels and duck à l'orange. Desserts, which
include a range of traditional tarts, are made in-house.
Brunch (10am-3pm weekends) is popular, especially
in the garden when the weather's good.

Clyde's of Georgetown

*3236 M Street, NW, between Wisconsin Avenue
& Potomac Street (1-202 333 9180, www.
clydes.com). Foggy Bottom-GWU Metro then
31, 32, 36, 38B bus, or Circulator bus.* **Open**
11.30am-midnight Mon-Thur; 11.30am-1am
Fri; 10am-1am Sat; 9am-midnight Sun. **Main
courses** $11-$19. **Credit** AmEx, Disc, MC, V.
Map p249 E5 ㉖ American

No visit to Georgetown's see-and-be-scene M Street
promenade is complete without a stop at one of the
neighbourhood's many watering holes, and Clyde's
of Georgetown is first among the local equals. High-
volume in both senses of the phrase, the place easily
absorbs busfuls of tourists yet somehow still manages
to attract regulars to its brass-railed bar. Perhaps it's
the food. In addition to serving tavern staples – herb-
roasted half chicken, for example – Clyde's has some
local and southern twists, with the likes of jumbo
lump crab cakes, sliders and collard greens. Well-cho-
sen wines and craft-brewed beers complete your meal,
served by efficient, preternaturally cheery youngsters.
Other locations throughout the city.

$ Moby Dick House of Kabob

1070 31st Street, NW, at M Street (1-202 333 4400, www.mobysonline.com). Foggy Bottom-GWU Metro then 31, 32, 36, 38B bus, or Circulator bus. **Open** 11am-10pm Mon-Thur; 11am-11pm Fri, Sat; noon-11pm Sun. **Main courses** $7-$15. **No credit cards. Map** p249 E5 ⑰ Middle Eastern

This tiny establishment, like its many cousins throughout the metro area, serves simple, traditional Middle Eastern dishes – felafel, houmous, kebabs of chicken or lamb – with little fanfare and to many fans. You order at the counter, get a number, and then take your place at one of only two small communal tables – sit even if you're getting takeout, because this fast food isn't necessarily fast. The houmous is exceptionally creamy; the pitta bread, made fresh throughout the day, manages to be simultaneously lighter and more substantial than the ordinary. **Other locations** throughout the city.

Pâtisserie Poupon

1645 Wisconsin Avenue, NW, between Q Street & Reservoir Road (1-202 342 3248, www.patisseriepoupon.net). Foggy Bottom-GWU

Range. *See p104.*

Metro then 31, 32, 36 bus, or Circulator bus. **Open** 8.30am-6pm Tue-Fri; 8-5.30pm Sat; 8am-4pm Sun. **Credit** AmEx, MC, V. **Map** p249 E4 ⑱ Café

Light and airy in a modern European sort of way, Pâtisserie Poupon gets points for presentation and attitude. The tarts and cakes are just like you'd find in Paris, and the menu is short but oh-so-French: salade niçoise, crudités, quiches, baguettes and brioche sandwiches. All coffee drinks are made in the back at the espresso bar and delivered by the barista himself.

Upper Northwest

$ Comet Ping Pong

5037 Connecticut Avenue, NW, at Nebraska Avenue (1-202 364 0404, www.cometpingpong. com). Van Ness-UDC Metro then L1, L2 bus. **Open** 5-9pm Mon; 5-9.30pm Tue-Thur; 5-10.30pm Fri; 11.30am-10.30pm Sat; 11.30am-9pm Sun. **Credit** AmEx, MC, V. Pizza

A little off the beaten path for downtown visitors, Comet's blistery thin-crust pizzas and warehouse chic vibe are worth the trip to upper Connecticut Avenue. A rousing game of table tennis is also a draw – the restaurant's back room is home to several tables for ping pong. A kid-heavy crowd (watch out for flying ping pong balls) early in the evenings gives way to hipsters, artists and musicians (your server is probably at least one of those) as the night progresses. They all come for the wood-fired pizzaz, with toppings like soft shell crab, smoked mozzarella and tangy sauce made from locally farmed tomatoes.
▶ *Politics & Prose bookstore is nearby (see p117).*

Lebanese Taverna

2641 Connecticut Avenue, NW, at Woodley Road, Woodley Park (1-202 265 8681, www.lebanese taverna.com). Woodley Park-Zoo/Adams Morgan Metro. **Open** 11.30am-10pm Mon-Thur; 11.30am-11pm Fri, Sat; 11.30am-10pm Sun. **Main courses** $12-$23. **Credit** AmEx, Disc, MC, V. **Map** p249 F2 ⑲ Lebanese

This family-owned operation, part of a local mini chain, starts filling up early for dinner. The friendly crowd is a mix of families, couples and more formal business groups. Make a meal of appetisers, which are quite substantial, fun to share and a bit more of a bargain. There's the familiar tabouleh and falafel as well as more interesting variations, such as houmous bel shawarma (houmous with pieces of lamb) and shankleesh (herbed and spiced feta with a tomato salad). Save room for baklava, and round things off with an Arabic coffee scented with cardamom.

Palena

3529 Connecticut Avenue, NW, between Ordway & Porter Streets (1-202 537 9250, www.palena restaurant.com). Cleveland Park Metro. **Open** 5.30-10pm Tue-Sat. **Set menus** $50-$68. **Credit** AmEx, Disc, MC, V. **Map** p249 F1 ⑳ Italian/pizza

A terracotta Minerva presides over the elegant formal dining room at the back, where chef Frank Ruta's tasting menu offers seasonal and fashionable delicacies; a bar menu of American favourites is served in the casual and equally elegant café at the front. The former might feature monkfish Milanese with Seville orange-scented tomato sauce and clams; the latter, an impossibly upscale cheeseburger with seasonal pickles, hot-dog and fries (including not only potatoes but also onions and, yes, those are lemon slices). You can order from the tasting menu in the café; whatever your choice, consider leaving room for Ann Amernick's much-loved caramels, cookies or pastries.

★ Range

Chevy Chase Pavilion, 5335 Wisconsin Avenue, at Military Road, NW, Friendship Heights (1-202 803 8020, http://voltrange.com). Friendship Heights Metro. **Open** 5.30-11pm daily. **Main courses** $13-$45. **Credit** AmEx, Disc, MC, V. **American**
In recent years, Washingtonians seeking culinary thrills have happily trekked 50 miles out to Frederick, Maryland, to dine at Bryan Voltaggio's restaurant Volt. They don't have to any more, now that Voltaggio has opened Range, his new restaurant inside an upmarket shopping mall in DC's Friendship Heights neighbourhood. It's a massive space with 300 seats, and the equally sprawling menu spans simple dishes like pan-roasted chicken with lemon, garlic and rosemary, to more adventurous fare such as kimchee linguine with scallops and grilled beaf heart with chimichurri. Don't miss the excellent fresh-baked bread and the candy cart. *Photo p103.*

Sushi-Ko

2309 Wisconsin Avenue, NW, at Observatory Lane, Glover Park (1-202 333 4187, www. sushiko.us). Foggy Bottom-GWU Metro then 31, 32, 36 bus. **Open** 5.30-10pm Sun-Thur; 530-1030pm Fri, Sat. **Main courses** $16-$27. **Credit** AmEx, MC, V. **Map** p249 D3 ⓻ Asian
Behind a mock-industrial façade is a sleek little dining room containing one of the city's best sushi bars. The decor is simple, the menu compact, venturing beyond sushi and sashimi but not detracting from their star power. Tuna Six Ways, a frequent special, accentuates variations of texture and flavour; simple preparations showcase unusual fish nightly. The vibe here is casual: neighbours stop by for carryout, club kids come in to start their nights, and solo diners make friends at the sushi bar.

Columbia Heights, Mount Pleasant & Petworth

Domku

821 Upshur Street, NW, between 8th & 9th Streets, Petworth (1-202 722 7475, www.domkucafe.com). Georgia Avenue/Petworth Metro. **Open** 6-11pm Tue-Thur; noon-midnight Fri; 10am-midnight

Toki Underground.

Sat; 10am-10.30pm Sun. **Main courses** $17-$22. **Credit** Disc, MC, V. **Slavic/Scandinavian**
A bit off the beaten track, but worth seeking out, Domku brings a fresh blast of Slavic and Scandinavian tastes to Petworth. Mains range hearty Polish bigos, a bacon and cabbage stew to Scandie favourite meatballs with lingonberries. There's borscht, pickled herrings and gravadlax, too, along with salads and sandwiches at lunchtime. Brunch has a Scandinavian twist, too, with scrambled eggs with smoked herring and Norwegian pancakes. The barebricked room is inviting and the service friendly.

$ Red Rocks

1036 Park Road, NW, at 11th Street, Columbia Heights (1-202 506 1402, www.redrocksdc.com). Columbia Heights Metro. **Open** 11am-midnight Mon-Thur, Sun; 11am-1am Fri, Sat. **Main courses** $9-$14. **Credit** AmEx, Disc, MC, V. **Map** p250 H1 ⓻ **Pizza**
In a converted Columbia Heights rowhouse, lively Red Rocks is all about pizzas – the traditional Neapolitan thin-crust variety, with authentic ingredients, such as buffalo mozzarella and prosciutto, baked in a wood-burning oven. They're joined by rustic Italian plates such as meatballs al forno.

Sticky Fingers

1370 Park Road, NW, between 13th & 14th streets, Columbia Heights (1-202 299 9700, http://stickyfingersbakery.com). Columbia Heights Metro. **Open** 7am-8pm Mon-Thur; 7am-10pm Fri; 9am-10pm Sat; 9am-8pm Sun. **Main courses** $5-$9.50. **Credit** AmEx, Disc, MC, V. **Map** p250 H2 ⓻ **Bakery/café**

CONSUME

Best known as a bakery, with a well-loved range of top-quality cakes (cupcakes a speciality), pastries and cookies, Sticky Fingers also serves vegetarian sandwiches and other savouries, among them a whole range of veggie burgers and a veggie chilli dog.

Tonic

3155 Mount Pleasant Street, NW, between 16th & 17th Streets, Mount Pleasant (1-202 986 7661, www.tonicrestaurant.com). Columbia Heights Metro. **Open** 5-10.30pm Mon-Thur; 5-11pm Fri; 10am-3pm (brunch); 5-10.30pm Sat, Sun. **Main courses** $10-$17. **Credit** AmEx, Disc, MC, V. **Map** p250 H2 ❼ American

Depending on your mood, you've got a choice of dining experiences at Tonic: upstairs is for a quieter, sit-down, tablecloth vibe; downstairs is a cavernous bar, with dark wood, television and plenty of beer on tap. No matter where you choose, the menu is the same, a shout-out to comfort food with regional American touches. Think macaroni and cheese, meatloaf sandwiches, pulled pork, a lox plate for brunch or roasted tomato salad with goat's cheese.

H Street Corridor

New places to eat and drink are opening all the time on this newly popular strip.

Atlas Room

1015 H Street, NE, between 10th & 11th Streets (1-202 388 4020, www.theatlasroom.com). Gallery Place-Chinatown Metro then X2 bus. **Open** 5.30-9.30pm Mon; 5.30-10pm Tue-Thur; 5.30-10.30 Fri, Sat; 5-9pm Sun. **Main courses** $19-$25. **Credit** AmEx, Disc, MC, V. **Map** p248 M5 ❼ **Modern European**
See p96 **A Taste of H Street**.

$ Dangerously Delicious Pies

1339 H Street, NE, between 13th & 14th Streets (1-202 398 7437, www.dangerouspiesdc.com). Gallery Place-Chinatown Metro then X2 bus. **Open** 11am-midnight Mon-Thur; 11am-3.30pm Fri; 9am-3.30pm Sat; 9am-10pm Sun. **Slice of pie** $6.50-$7.50. **Credit** Disc, MC, V. **Map** p248 M5 ❼ **Pies**
See p96 **A Taste of H Street**.
Other locations 675 I Street, NW, between 6th & 7th streets, Downtown (1-202 450 1292); Union Station, 50 50 Massachusetts Avenue, NE (1-202 289 1600).

$ Ethiopic

401 H Street, between 4th & 5th Streets (1-202 675 2066, www.ethiopicrestaurant.com). Union Station Metro. **Open** 5-10pm Tue-Thur; noon-10pm Fri-Sun. **Main courses** $10-$18. **Credit** Disc, MC, V. **Map** p248 L5 ❼ **Ethiopian**
See p96 **A Taste of H Street**.
▶ *For more on DC's many Ethiopian restaurants, see p99 Ethiopian Eats.*

Granville Moore's

1238 H Street, NE, between 12th & 13th Streets (1-202 399 2546, www.granvillemoores.com). Gallery Place-Chinatown Metro then X2 bus. **Open** *Meals served* 5-10pm Mon-Thur; 11am-3pm, 5-11.30pm Fri, Sat; 11am-3pm, 5-10pm Sun. *Bar* 5pm-midnight Mon-Thur; 11am-3am Fri, Sat; 11am-midnight Sun. **Main courses** $12-$17. **Credit** AmEx, Disc, MC, V. **Map** p248 M5 ❼ **Belgian**
See p96 **A Taste of H Street**.

$ Sticky Rice

1224 H Street, NE, between 12th & 13th Streets (1-202 397 7655, www.stickyrice dc.com). Gallery Place-Chinatown Metro then X2 bus. **Open** 11.30am-10..30pm Mon-Wed, Sun; 11.30am-11.30pm Thur-Sat. **Main courses** $10-$12. **Credit** MC, V. **Map** p248 M5 ❼ **Asian**
See p96 **A Taste of H Street**.

$ Taylor Gourmet

1116 H Street, NE, between 11th & 12th Streets (1-202 684 7001, http://taylorgourmet.com). Gallery Place-Chinatown Metro then X2 bus. **Open** 11am-9pm Mon-Thur; 11am-3.30am Fri; 8am-3.30am Sat; 8am-9pm Sun. **Credit** AmEx, Disc, MC, V. **Map** p248 M5 ❼ **Deli**
This mini chain of delis was started by two guys from Philadelphia, and it shows: the hoagies – high quality Italian-style ingredients piled high on thick, chewy rolls – are all named for streets in Philadelphia. There's the Lombard Street, stacked with soppresata, salami, red peppers, pesto and mozzarella, for example, or the Lancaster Avenue – breaded eggplant topped with marinara sauce and sharp provolone. A side of fried risotto balls make a great – if heavy – accompaniment. If you're less hungry, the arugula and pastina salads make a nice light lunch.
Other locations throughout the city.

$ Toki Underground

1234 H Street, NE, between 12th & 13th Streets (1-202 388 3086, http://tokiunderground.com). Gallery Place-Chinatown Metro then X2 bus. **Open** 5-10pm Mon-Wed; 5-11pm Thur; 5pm-midnight Fri, Sat. **Main courses** $5-$12. **Credit** MC, V. **Map** p248 M5 ❼ **Japanese**
Hip twentysomethings squeeze into this tiny spot to slurp big bowls of ramen in rich, house-made broth. The dumplings are great, too – we especially like the grilled pork ones – and there are more than 20 kinds of saké available. The space is decorated with graffiti, skateboards and comic books, and for dessert, you can dunk warm chocolate-chip cookies in a glass of milk. What's not to like? Just one thing: the wait for seats can take a couple of hours. There are no reservations, but you can hang out at the bar downstairs until the staff text you.

CONSUME

Bars

Cocktails and lobbying, or beer and pool.

Washington might be all about politics, but that's all the more reason why bars are such an integral part of the capital's scene. After all, where else can you rub shoulders with some of the world's most powerful lawmakers while nursing a martini, imagining the deals being done in those quiet corners. Washington's conservative reputation allows for plenty of hallowed joints – such as the famous Round Robin (*see p107*) at the Willard InterContinental. But the city's bar scene is surprisingly diverse, especially in the thriving Logan Circle and U Street areas, along the newly regenerated H Street Corridor, and – latest of all – on 11th Street in Columbia Heights. Look out for a particular resurgence in speakeasies and craft cocktails.

INFORMATION

The Metro runs until 3am on Friday and Saturday nights, although the last train from your station may be earlier. If you're planning to party late into the night, it's probably easier to get a cab home.

Be aware that the drinking age is strictly enforced in Washington. See *p114* **Inside Track**. Smoking is banned in bars.

For gay-oriented bars and clubs, *see pp163-167*.

THE WHITE HOUSE & AROUND

Old Ebbitt Grill

675 15th Street, NW, between F & G Streets (1-202 347 4800, www.ebbitt.com). Metro Center Metro. **Open** 7.30am-2am Mon-Thur; 7.30am-3am Fri; 8.30am-3am Sat; 8.30am-2am Sun. **Credit** AmEx, Disc, MC, V. **Map** p252 H6 ❶
The Old Ebbitt first opened in 1856 as a boarding house, and over the years its more illustrious guests have included Presidents Grant, Johnson, Cleveland and Teddy Roosevelt. Just a block from the White House, it's a popular place for the power lunch (in the main dining room, that is, not in the atrium). The two bars – one at the back, one at the front – are

---

❶ Green numbers given in this chapter correspond to the location of each bar on the street maps. *See pp248-253.*

---

always packed, usually with men who ensure that no nubile young thing has to pay for her own drinks.

★ POV

W Hotel, 515 15th Street, NW, at F Street (1-202 661 2400, www.pointofviewdc.com). Metro Center Metro. **Open** 11am-3am Fri, Sat; 11am-midnight Thur, Sun. *Rooftop terrace* 11am-2am Mon-Fri; noon-2am Sun. **Credit** AmEx, Disc, MC, V. **Map** p252 H6 ❷
See p112 **Hotel Havens**.

CAPITOL HILL & AROUND

★ Hank's Oyster Bar

633 Pennsylvania Avenue, SE, between 6th & 7th Streets (1-202 733 1971, www.hanks oysterbar.com). Eastern Market Metro. **Open** 5pm-midnight Mon-Thur; 11.30am-midnight Fri; 11am-midnight Sat, Sun. **Map** p253 L7 ❸
A recent addition to the neighbourhood, this stylish, all-white Capitol Hill outpost of the Dupont Circle and Alexandria seafood chain boasts ownership of the Eddy Bar, a long stretch of marble offering house-made sodas in flavours such as 'citrus sage' and punny cocktails (the Oh Rickey You're So Fine features bourbon, Gewürtzraminer, and lemongrass). The beer menu is esoteric, consisting mostly of brews you've never heard of, from the 21st Amendment Dub Step IPA on draft to the local Port City Tartan. Come for happy hour (Monday to Friday, 5-7pm), stay for the cocktails and bowls of Goldfish crackers.

Sonoma

223 Pennsylvania Avenue, SE, between 2nd & 3rd Streets (1-202 544 8088, www.sonomadc.com). **Capitol South or Eastern Market Metro. Open** 11.30am-2.30pm, 5-10pm Mon-Thur; 11.30am-2.30pm, 5-11pm Fri; 5-11pm Sat; 5-9pm Sun. **Credit** Disc, MC, V. **Map** p253 L7 ❹

Sonoma offers a welcome grown-up respite from all the other dives and sports bars stretching down Pennsylvania Avenue. The long granite bar, exposed brick and extensive wine list make for a stylish, urban feel, and the upstairs lounge has plenty of comfortable alcoves to settle in to (although it's often closed for political functions and events). Sonoma's proximity to the House office buildings also allows for great eavesdropping while you're savouring that Russian River Valley pinot gris – as long as you're not put off by the ping of a thousand BlackBerrys.

Tune Inn

331 Pennsylvania Avenue, SE, at 4th Street (1-202 543 2725). **Capitol South Metro. Open** 8am-2am Mon-Thur, Sun; 8am-3am Fri, Sat. **Credit** AmEx, MC, V. **Map** p253 L7 ❺

The Tune Inn is one of the few places in DC that starts serving beer at 10am – and you'll probably need a pint to deal with the rowdy blue-collar crowd and the sometimes surly staff. There are no fancy artisan brewed beers on offer here – this place regularly wins awards for being Washington's best dive bar, with prices to match.

THE FEDERAL TRIANGLE

★ Round Robin Bar

Willard InterContinental Hotel, 1401 Pennsylvania Avenue, NW, at 14th Street (1-202 637 7348, www.washington.intercontinental.com). **Metro Center Metro. Open** noon-1am Mon-Thur; 3pm-1am Fri; noon-1am Sat; noon-midnight Sun. **Credit** AmEx, Disc, MC, V. **Map** p252 H6 ❻ *See p112* **Hotel Havens**.

★ The Source

575 Pennsylvania Avenue, NW, at 6th Street (1-202 637 6100, www.wolfgangpuck.com/ restaurants/fine-dining/3941). **Archives or Judiciary Square Metro. Open** 11.30am-2pm, 5.30-10pm Mon-Thur; 11.30am-2pm, 5.30-11pm Fri; 11.30am-3pm (brunch), 5.30pm-midnight Sat. **Credit** AmEx, MC, V. **Map** p253 J6 ❼

Wolfgang Puck's dramatic Asian-Fusion restaurant tucked under the Newseum also has a ground-floor lounge ideally located for an upscale post-museum fortifier. The minimalist/contemporary scene attracts a diverse crowd, with power players joining the tourists to watch sports on the three flatscreen TVs. Try the extensive (and inventive) cocktail list (sample: Asian Pear Drop with saké and pear purée); or one of the hundreds of bottles of wine lining the walls. And if you're in the area between 4pm and 6pm, stop by for happy hour and sample some of the city's best small plates for a fraction of the usual price.

▶ *For a tour of the Newseum, see p58* **Profile**.

UNION STATION & AROUND

Union Pub

201 Massachusetts Avenue, NE, at 2nd Street (1-202 546 7200, www.unionpubdc.com). **Union Station Metro. Open** 11.30am-2am Mon; 11.30am-3am Tue-Fri; noon-3am Sat; noon-midnight Sun. **Credit** AmEx, MC, V. **Map** p253 L6 ❽

Not all outdoor patios are created equal. At Union Pub a giant awning covering the 80 or so seats elevates the al fresco concept to greatness. Happy hour is also bumped up a few notches, with an extraordinary array of cut-price drinks available seven nights a week. On Tuesdays local draught beers are $5; Thursdays craft gin is $4 and pitchers of Bud Light are $12.

POV.

CONSUME

DOWNTOWN

★ Donovan House Rooftop Pool Bar

Donovan House Hotel, 1155 14th Street, NW, at Thomas Circle (1-202 737 1200, www.donovan househotel.com). McPherson Square Metro. **Open** 5pm-1am Mon-Thur; 7pm-1am Sat, Sun. **Credit** AmEx, Disc, MC, V. **Map** p250/p252 H5 ❾
See p112 **Hotel Havens**.

★ Hill Country

410 7th Street, NW, at D Street (1-202 556 2050, www.hillcountrywdc.com). Archives or Gallery Place Metro. **Open** 11.30am-2am daily. **Credit** AmEx, MC, V. **Map** p253 J6 ❿
The scent of molasses and ribs might be enough to draw you into this Downtown Texan barbecue spot, but it's the downstairs Boot Bar, where live country music alternates nights with rock-band karaoke, that really brings in the crowds. The bare-brick space is sizeable but cosy, with home-style wooden tables and chairs and tributes to the Lone Star state everywhere you look. Cocktails also have a Southern twang, with ingredients ranging from tequila to jalapeños – but don't miss the $20 pitchers of Shiner beer, a beloved Texas staple with a malty, delicate flavour.

★ Passenger/Columbia Room

1021 7th Street, NW, between L Street & New York Avenue (1-202 393 0220, www. passengerdc.com). Mount Vernon Square Metro. **Open** 5pm-1.30am Mon-Thur; 5pm-2.30am Fri, Sat; 2pm-midnight Sun. **Credit** AmEx, MC, V. **Map** p251/p253 J5 ⓫
GQ once declared that mixologist Derek Brown makes the best martini in America. Judge for yourself at the Passenger, the former Gibson bartender's venture in the gentrifying Mount Vernon Square area. The bar is named after the Iggy Pop song; inside you'll find an informal drinking den with bespoke cocktails (there's no list, but tell the bartender what drinks you like and he'll cater one to your preferences) and gourmet bar snacks. Behind an unmarked door at the back of the bar lies the Columbia Room, a 12-seat, reservations-only speakeasy with some of the most inventive cocktails in the city. For a flat rate (around $50), Brown will mix you three craft cocktails with some nibbles on the side, and lecture you at length on the art of drinking.

★ Poste

Hotel Monaco, 555 8th Street, NW, between E & F Streets (1-202 783 6060, www.poste brasserie.com). Gallery Place-Chinatown Metro. **Open** 11.30am-1am daily. **Credit** AmEx, Disc, MC, V. **Map** p253 J6 ⓬
See p112 **Hotel Havens**.

Rosa Mexicano

575 7th Street, NW, at F Street (1-202 783 5522,www.rosamexicano.com). Gallery Place-Chinatown Metro. **Open** 11.30am-10.30pm Mon-Thur; 11.30am-11.30pm Fri, Sat; 11.30am-10pm Sun. **Credit** AmEx, DC, MC, V. **Map** p253 6J ⓭
Sip a pomegranate margarita and watch the beautiful people – made even more gorgeous by a backdrop of glittering blue tiles and rose petals embedded in clear Lucite – eye each other's press credentials under the pink-hued lights. Then order some guacamole, which comes in strengths from mild to medium to wowee. It's whipped up table-side in a volcanic stone mortar and pestle. And remember, things really do look better through rose-coloured sangria glasses.

St Regis Bar

St Regis Hotel, 923 16th Street, NW, at K Street (1-202 638 2626, www.starwoodhotels.com/ stregis). McPherson Square, Farragut North or Farragut West Metro. **Open** 11.30am-midnight Mon-Thur, Sun; 11.30am-1am Fri, Sat. *Lunch served* 11am-2pm daily. **Credit** AmEx, Disc, MC, V. **Map** p250/p252 H5 ⓮
See p112 **Hotel Havens**.

Hill Country.

Bar Rouge.

FOGGY BOTTOM

Science Club
*1136 19th Street, NW, between L & M Streets
(1-202 775 0747, www.scienceclubdc.com).
Farragut North Metro.* **Open** 3pm-2am Mon,
Tue; 11.30am-2am Wed, Thur; 11.30am-3am Fri;
7pm-3am Sat. **Credit** MC, V. **Map** p252 G5
Rest assured, you don't need to know the difference
between the second law of thermodynamics and the
third law of motion to get in here. In fact, the name
comes from the decor: bargoers in this four-level
space sit on round metal stools salvaged from a high-
school chemistry lab. Apart from that, Science Club
sticks with tried and trusted new bar practice. The
$5 bottles of Yuengling are mixed with DJs who spin
dub and funk, plus there's a basement bar that looks
like a Prohibition speakeasy.

DUPONT CIRCLE

Bar Rouge
*Rouge Hotel, 1315 16th Street, NW, at Scott
Circle (1-202 232 8000, www.rougehotel.com).
Dupont Circle Metro.* **Open** 5-10.30pm daily.
Credit AmEx, Disc, MC, V. **Map** p250 H4
See p112 **Hotel Havens**.

Eighteenth Street Lounge
*1212 19th Street, NW, by Jefferson Place
(1-202 466-3922, www.eighteenthstreetlounge.
com) Dupont Circle or Farragut North Metro.*
Open 5.30pm-2am Tue-Thur; 5.30pm-3am Fri;
9.30pm-3am Sat; 9pm-2am Sun. **Cover charge** $5
after 10pm Wed; $10 after midnight Sat. **Credit**
AmEx, Disc, MC, V. **Map** p250 G5
Before it metamorphoses into an achingly hip club
around 10pm each night, this sprawling former
townhouse offers up one of DC's best secret gardens
(or patios, anyway). If you can find your way
through the unmarked door (it's the mirrored one
next to the mattress store), up the stairs, and out to
the back, a sunny, wood-panelled outdoor drinking

space awaits. The crowd has a distinctly Euro feel
(the World Bank and the BBC headquarters are
nearby), but the music curated by co-owner (and one-
half of Thievery Corporation) Eric Hilton is chill dis-
tilled, and staff even lay out spreads of free mezze
around happy hour (5.30-8pm Tue-Fri; 9-11pm Sun).
▶ *For more on music at Eighteenth Street, see p168.*

★ Firefly
*Hotel Madera, 1310 New Hampshire Avenue,
NW, between N Street & Sunderland Place
(1-202 861 1310, www.firefly-dc.com). Dupont
Circle Metro.* **Open** 5.30-10pm Mon-Thur, Sun;
5.30-10.30pm Fri, Sat. **Credit** AmEx, Disc, MC,
V. **Map** p250 G4
See p112 **Hotel Havens**. *Photo p110.*

Fox & Hounds
*1533 17th Street, NW, between Church & Q
Streets (1-202 232 6307). Dupont Circle Metro.*
Open 4pm-2am Mon-Thur; 11am-3am Fri, Sun;
10am-3am Sat. **Credit** AmEx, Disc, MC, V.
Map p250 G4
A local pub that's dim and cave-like, with hardcore
drinkers hunched over the bar. It becomes a real
biergarten in warm weather, when crowds pack
the patio and swarm around the jukebox. This is a
place for lingering.

THE BEST BARS WITH A VIEW

With sunloungers and an
outdoor fireplace
Donovan House Rooftop Pool Bar.
See p108.

Overlooking the White House
POV. *See p106.*

Looking out over to Potomac
Sequoia. *See p115.*

CONSUME

Russia House Restaurant & Lounge

1800 Connecticut Avenue, NW, at Florida Avenue (1-202 234 9433, www.russiahouselounge.com). Dupont Circle Metro. **Open** 5pm-midnight Mon-Thur, Sun; 5pm-2.30am Fri, Sat. **Credit** AmEx, MC, V. **Map** p250 G3 ⑳

Once a private restaurant and lounge, Russia House retains something of the mystery of the Kremlin, despite the fact that any Tom, Dick or Vladimir can now down vodka here. The walls are covered in bordello-red silk and serious Russian oil paintings, with cushy sofas and low coffee tables adding to the room's intimacy. A selection of more than 160 vodkas – a mix of Russian favourites, East European brands and American blends – further aids foreign affairs, as do the hordes of homesick hockey players. There's also a downstairs restaurant, serving the likes of chicken kiev and beef stroganoff.

Tabard Inn

1739 N Street, NW, between 17th & 18th Streets (1-202 785 1277, www.tabardinn.com). Dupont Circle Metro. **Open** 11.30am-12.30am Mon-Fri; 11am-12.30am Sat; 10.30am-11pm Sun. **Credit** AmEx, DC, MC, V. **Map** p250 G4 ㉑ *See p112* **Hotel Havens**.

ADAMS MORGAN

Jack Rose Dining Saloon

2007 18th Street, NW, between California & Vernon Streets (1-202 588 7388, www.jackrose diningsaloon.com). Woodley Park-Zoo/Adams Morgan Metro then Circulator bus, or 90, 92, 96 bus. **Open** 5pm-2am Mon, Thur-Sun; 5pm-3am Fri, Sat. **Credit** AmEx, Disc, MC, V. **Map** p250 G3 ㉒

Firefly. *See p109.*

ChurchKey.

Were Jim Morrison ever to be reincarnated and transported to Washington, the response to his immortal request, 'Show me the way to the next whisky bar' would inevitably lead him to Jack Rose. This is, quite simply, the only place to drink whisky in Washington, with a remarkable selection of more than 1,500 different varieties. The tall, clubby space feels like a library, with leather seats and ladders to help bartenders reach the highest bottles; if you don't know much (or anything) about whisky, don't be afraid to ask, since the staff are happy to impart their wisdom. On sunnier days, there's also an outdoor terrace and tiki bar.

Reef

2446 18th Street, NW, between Belmont & Columbia Roads (1-202 518 3800, www.the reefdc.com). Woodley Park-Zoo/Adams Morgan Metro then Circulator bus, or 90, 92, 96 bus. **Open** 5pm-2am Mon-Thur; 5pm-3am Fri, Sat; 5pm-2am Sun. **Credit** AmEx, MC, V. **Map** p250 G3 ㉓

Fish tanks as decorations, trippy fluorescent lighting, long lines to get in: all are hallmarks of the Reef. The second-storey floor-to-ceiling windows – and, in warm months, the spectacular roof deck – offer a good vantage point for watching the foot traffic on 18th Street. The bar showcases a wide selection of beers – nothing in bottles – and is spacious enough to facilitate the requisite hook-up mingling.

LOGAN CIRCLE

★ ChurchKey

1337 14th Street, NW, at Rhode Island Avenue (1-202 567 2576, www.churchkeydc.com). U Street/African-American Civil War Memorial/ Cardozo Metro or McPherson Square Metro. **Open** 4pm-1am Mon-Fri; noon-2am Sat; noon-1am Sun. **Credit** AmEx, Disc, MC, V. **Map** p250 H4 ㉔

CONSUME

The upstairs bar above sister restaurant Birch & Barley has one thing on its mind: beer. More than 500 varieties, to be precise. But this isn't your average brewhouse – the shiny wood floors, sculptural light fixtures and bustling crowd should tell you that. ChurchKey opened in late 2009 and has barely had time to breathe since, drawing crowds nightly for its gourmet lagers and ales (housed in state-of-the-art, temperature-controlled vaults), upscale comfort food (tater tots and grilled cheese), and energetic scene. Wednesday through Saturday, expect long waits and don't bank on a table.

▶ For restaurant Birch & Barley, see p97.

U STREET CORRIDOR

Another popular fixture in this vibrant area is **Nellie's** (see p165), a gay-friendly sports bar that is also big on bingo and other games.

Bar Pilar

1833 14th Street, NW, between S & T Streets (1-202 265 1751, www.barpilar.com). U Street/ African-American Civil War Memorial/Cardozo Metro. **Open** 5pm-1.30am Mon-Thur, Sun; 5pm-2.30am Fri, Sat. **Credit** AmEx, MC, V. **Map** p250 H3 ㉕

The younger and less popular sister of Café Saint-Ex (see right), Bar Pilar is affectionately referred to as a dive bar, dressed up. The vibe is intimate, with just 38 seats, and the low-key attractions include bacon bloody marys at brunch (sort of a liquefied BLT, hold the lettuce) and a kitschy photo booth.

★ Brixton

901 U Street, NW, at 9th Street (1-202 560 5045, www.brixtondc.com). U Street/African-American

Civil War Memorial/Cardozo Metro or Shaw-Howard University Metro. **Open** 5pm-2am Mon-Thur; 5pm-3am Fri, Sat; 11am-2am Sun. **Credit** AmEx, Disc, MC. V. **Map** p251 J3 ㉖

Yes, the second floor of this three-level bar looks more like a Downton-era hunting lodge than a real Brixton tavern. And no, the menu offerings of Thai chicken salad and miso-glazed black cod aren't really authentic either (although, to be fair, rotis and samosas are available too). But don't let that bother you, because the Brixton's vibe is charming, with leather stools and wood panelling inside and a spectacular roof terrace. It gets packed to the rafters with college kids late at night so come early for surprisingly good Pimm's cups, Boddingtons and Newcastle on draft, and Fuller's London Pride in bottles.

Café Saint-Ex

1847 14th Street, NW, at T Street (1-202 265 7839, www.saint-ex.com). U Street/African-American Civil War Memorial/Cardozo Metro. **Open** 5pm-1.30am Mon; 11am-1.30am Tue-Thur; 11am-2.30am Fri, Sat; 11am-1.30am Sun. **Credit** AmEx, MC, V. **Map** p250 H3 ㉗

CONSUME

Bar Pilar.

Named for Antoine de Saint-Exupéry, the French aviator and author of *The Little Prince*, this brasserie aims to evoke the watering holes of Paris's Latin Quarter and, in the basement-level lounge, the heroic days of aviation. And if pressed-tin ceilings, tobacco-stained walls and borderline service are your thing, then *voilà*! DJs spin ironically hip new wave nightly.

★ Gibson

2009 14th Street, NW, between U & V Streets (1-202 232 2156, www.thegibsondc.com). U Street/African-American Civil War Memorial/ Cardozo Metro. **Open** 6pm-late daily. **Credit** AmEx, MC, V. **Map** p250 H3 ❷⓿

If you're in a bar in Washington drinking a cocktail, listening to dub bossa nova and watching hipsters at play, chances are that the bar is owned by Eric Hilton. Hilton, who makes up one-half of DJ duo Thievery Corporation, has been slowly taking over DC's bar scene in his spare time (Eighteenth Street Lounge, *see p109*, Marvin, Dickson Wine Bar). The Gibson is Hilton's take on the New York speakeasy. First, you'll need to find the entrance, an unobtrusive doorbell next to Marvin. Once inside you'll find some of the best cocktails in the city, with drinks updated on a chalkboard daily, and ingredients from celery-infused Pisco to burnt cinnamon. Reservations recommended.
► *For neighbouring Marvin, see p98.*

Hotel Havens

Check into DC's finest hotel bars.

Come on, you're in Washington, spook central, surely you want to have a secret assignation in a hotel bar? The trouble is, it's much harder these days to find somewhere quiet where you and your personal Deep Throat can plot the downfall of governments and decide what to do after dinner: those pesky locals have commandeered all the best bars. Still, on the basis that if you can't beat them you might as well drink with them, we offer here some hotel bars suitable for meeting a generous lobbyist.

Where better to start than the bar where, it's said, the term 'lobbying' was first coined. Those wanting a quiet word in President Grant's ear used to hang around in the lobby of the Willard InterContinental Hotel hoping perhaps to stand the president or one of his advisors a drink in the **Round Robin Bar** (*see p107*). The lobbyists may have moved on but you'll find that the bar is still reminiscent of an old-fashioned gentlemen's club. Take a seat in the dark green, round space and see how many of the portraits of previous guests you can recognise: Walt Whitman, Mark Twain, Nathaniel Hawthorne and President Abraham Lincoln, who lived at the hotel for two weeks before his inauguration, are among the distinguished subjects.

If you're looking for proximity to the White House, the W Hotel's **POV** (*see p106*) is hard to beat: the rooftop terrace has such great views of 1600 Pennsylvania Avenue that you can see the snipers lurking on the roof. The bar gets packed in good weather so reservations are recommended. Just a few blocks away, the **St Regis** (*see p108*), the bar next to Alain Ducasse's

Adour restaurant, makes for a stylish and discreet assignation. Former Obama chief of staff Rahm Emanuel was a regular before he moved back to Chicago.

A generous lobbyist would be an ideal drinking companion at **Degrees Bar & Lounge** (*see p113*) in the Ritz-Carlton Georgetown: if you have to buy your own classic-with-a-twist cocktails be prepared to hand over $10-$15 a go. Degrees aims to capture the clubby feel of a 1940s supper club, and patrons can pose to their heart's content at the sleek 25-seat bar.

A different kind of chic dominates **Bar Rouge** (*see p109*) at the Hotel Rouge. The bar is comfortable, with throne-like armchairs, long couches and white leather seats. Cocktails are pricey ($8-$14) and a little too syrupy, but strangely addictive, especially in combination with the hypnotic acid jazz oozing out of the sound system.

The Madera, meanwhile, goes for a 'contemporary rustic' aesthetic with its **Firefly** bar (*see p109*), which features a lot of wood, including a huge tree trunk with minuscule copper lanterns hanging from its branches. Seating is comfy, with intimate nooks and low, expansive tables for cocktails and small plates.

East of Dupont Circle, the Donovan House Hotel has a snazzy rooftop pool complete with bar, **Donovan House Rooftop Pool Bar** (*see p108*), and glittering views of the city. The gay-friendly location has reasonably priced drinks, sun loungers, and even an outdoor fireplace, making for a relaxed vibe and an ideal spot after dinner at Zentan restaurant downstairs.

Heading downtown, **Poste** (*see p108*), part of the Monaco Hotel, is set in the

Velvet Lounge
915 U Street, NW, between Vermont Avenue
& 9th Street (1-202 462 3213, www.velvetlounge
dc.com). U Street/African-American Civil War
Memorial/Cardozo Metro. **Open** 8pm-2am Mon-
Thur, Sun; 8pm-3am Fri, Sat. **Credit** MC, V.
Map p251 J3 ㉙
Comfy, funky and groovy, the Velvet Lounge is a
popular, divey kind of place to stop off for a drink.
It's like a neighbourhood bar that just happens to
have live music: many come to enjoy martinis and
beers with friends, while others are here for the band.
▶ *For a review of Velvet Lounge as a music venue,*
see p174.

restored sorting office of the 1841
General Post Office, which explains the
high ceilings and skylights: they made
it easier for the letter sorters to read
addresses. The courtyard – reached
through a long arcade that was designed
for horse-drawn mail wagons – is one
of the loveliest outdoor spots in DC.
Cocktails are full of fresh herbs and
vegetables – like the Basil Lemontini,
courtesy of the hotel's herb garden.

Finally, the **Tabard Inn** (*see p110*)
makes for a most relaxing place to start,
end or break a day of sightseeing. The bar
is set in a shabby-chic, living-room-like
front room, where patrons can relax on
Victorian sofas in front of a log fireplace
that might have come straight from the
pages of *Wuthering Heights*, while sipping
a fortifying glass of wine or brandy.

Round Robin Bar.

GEORGETOWN

New Georgetown hotels the **Capella** (*see p150*)
and the **Graham** (*see p152*) both have rooftop
bars with great views.

Birreria Paradiso
3282 M Street, NW, between Potomac Street &
Georgetown Park (1-202 337 1245, www.eatyour
pizza.com). Farragut West Metro then 35 bus or
Foggy Bottom-GWU Metro then 32 bus. **Open**
11.30am-11pm Mon-Thur; 11.30am-midnight Fri,
Sat; noon-10pm Sun. **Credit** AmEx, MC, V.
Map p249 E5 ㉚
Pizza paradise above, beer heaven below, what
more could you want? Birreria Paradiso is in the
basement of the hugely popular Pizzeria Paradiso
(*see p93*) and the English-style hand pumps behind
the bar serve up cask-conditioned ales that will
soon produce heavenly visions in imbibers. The
brews on offer include Britain's Old Speckled Hen,
Belgium's Chimay Cinq Cents and a blood-coloured
Flemish beer named the Duchesse de Bourgogne.
There are three- and four-taste flights ($9 and $11),
so sensation seekers can sample a cross-section
of Birreria's extensive offerings – culled from a six-
page menu.

Degrees Bar & Lounge
Ritz-Carlton Georgetown, 3100 South Street,
NW, at 31st Street (1-202 912 4100/www.ritz
carlton.com/hotels/georgetown). Foggy Bottom/
GWU Metro then 34 bus. **Open** 2.30-10pm Mon-
Thur, Sun; 2.30pm-1am Fri, Sat. **Credit** AmEx,
DC, MC, V. **Map** p249 E5 ㉛
See p112 **Hotel Havens**.

J Paul's
3218 M Street, NW, at Wisconsin Avenue (1-202
333 3450, www.j-pauls.capitalrestaurants.com).
Foggy Bottom-GWU Metro then 30, 32, 34, 35,
36, Georgetown Metro Connection bus. **Open**
11.30am-2am Mon-Thur; 11.30am-3am Fri, Sat;
10.30am-2am Sun. **Credit** AmEx, Disc, MC, V.
Map p249 E5 ㉜
In good weather, young DC professionals fight for
the seats of choice along the open windows facing
M Street. They're also drawn to the good raw shellfish and the 30 varieties of Scotch. Like almost every
other drinking hole in Georgetown, this bar gets its
fair share of student drinkers.

Sequoia
3000 K Street, NW, at Wisconsin Avenue,
Washington Harbour (1-202 944 4200, www.
arkrestaurants.com/sequoia_dc.html). Foggy
Bottom-GWU Metro then 30, 32, 34, 35, 36,
Georgetown Metro Connection bus. **Open**
11.30am-11pm Mon-Thur; 11.30am-midnight
Fri, Sat; 10.30am-3pm, 4-11pm Sun. **Credit**
AmEx, Disc, MC, V. **Map** p249 E5 ㉝

CONSUME

Argonaut

This enormous bar and restaurant is people-watching central. The interiors are spacious, with high ceilings and tall windows. The outside bar, which looks out over the Potomac River and has views of Georgetown University and the Kennedy Center, is a popular nightspot-cum-pickup joint in the summer.

CLEVELAND PARK

Nanny O'Brien's
3319 Connecticut Avenue, NW, between Macomb & Newark Streets (1-202 686 9189, www.nanny obriens.com). Cleveland Park Metro. **Open** noon-2am Mon-Thur; noon-3am Fri. Sat; noon-1.30am Sun. **Credit** AmEx, DC, Disc, MC, V. **Map** p249 F1 ❸
Nanny's is closer to an 'authentic' Irish pub than most DC bars. The traditional music sessions, held on Monday nights at 9pm, are legendary. Three dartboards in the back attract many locals and some of the city's sharpest shooters.

H STREET CORRIDOR

Other swingin' bars on this newly popular strip include the **Rock & Roll Hotel** (*see p172*), which is as much a music venue as a bar, with live bands and DJs, and the **Star and Shamrock** (1341 H Street, 1-202 388 3833, http://starandshamrock.com), which does a good job of combining pints of Guinness with a hot beef brisket sandwich.

Argonaut
1433 H Street, NE, at Florida Avenue (1-202 250 3660, www.argonautdc.com). Metro Center or Gallery Place/Chinatown Metro, then X2 bus. **Open** 5pm-2am Mon-Thur; 11.30am-3am Fri; 10am-3am Sat; 10am-2am Sun. **Map** p248 M5 ❸
Gentrified H Street has gone from sketchy to super-cool over the last few years, boasting a fleet of hipster bars offering cut-price cans of PBR and adult entertainment (no, not that kind – think arcade games and pinball). Perched on the end of the H Street strip, the Argonaut is one of its better bar options, with a pretty, spacious terrace outside and regular themed nights (trivia's on Wednesday, live bluegrass on Thursday). There are 12 draft beers on tap, including the excellent DC Brau, and sample flights of four are available. Thanks to its Metro-unfriendly location, the bar also tends to get less crowded and raucous than other H Street nightlife spots.

Biergarten Haus
1355 H Street, between 13th & 14th Streets (1-202 388-4053, http://biergartenhaus.com). Metro Center or Gallery Place/Chinatown Metro, then X2 bus. **Open** 4pm-midnight Mon-Thur; 4pm-2.30am Fri; 11am-2.30am Sat; 11am-midnight Sun. **Credit** AmEx, Disc, MC, V. **Map** p248 M5 ❸
See p96 **A Taste of H Street**.

H Street Country Club
1335 H Street, between 13th & 14th Streets (1-202 399 4722, www.thehstreetcountryclub.com). Metro Center or Gallery Place/Chinatown Metro, then X2 bus. **Open** 5pm-1am (kitchen until 10pm) Mon-Thur; 4pm-3am (kitchen until midnight) Fri, Sat; 4pm-1am (kitchen until 10pm) Sun. **Credit** AmEx, Disc, MC, V. **Map** p248 M5 ❸
See p96 **A Taste of H Street**.

Little Miss Whiskey's Golden Dollar
1104 H Street, between 11th & 12th Streets (1-202 555 1212, www.littlemisswhiskeys.com). Metro Center or Gallery Place/Chinatown Metro, then X2 bus. **Open** 5pm-1.30am Mon-Thur, Sun; 5pm-2.30am Fri, Sat. **No credit cards.** **Map** p248 M5 ❸
See p96 **A Taste of H Street**.

INSIDE TRACK
SHOW YOUR AGE

The drinking age in the US is 21, and it's strictly enforced, especially in venues popular with young people and areas like Georgetown and Adams Morgan, which get a lot of college-age traffic. So bring a photo ID with you, even if you reckon you look well over 40.

CONSUME

Shops & Services

Had enough of museums and monuments? Time to go shopping.

DC has a hard-to-kick reputation for being the capital of less-than-creative personal style. However, one visit to the capital city and you'll notice that it has progressed by leaps and bounds in the last few years, led by artists and creative leaders who advocate not just for a more vibrant fashion culture, but for a fashion industry. Walk the streets of Georgetown, the U Street Corridor or Chinatown, and you'll see DC locals stepping up their style game; you'll also find new independent boutiques and local designers popping up around every corner. Go to Georgetown for the retail staples and chain stores, but venture out to 14th Street and U Street for top-notch vintage clothing and housewares, locally designed accessories and edgy international brands. Here's our guide to shopping Washington like a local.

GENERAL

Department stores

Don't forget **Nordstrom** and **Bloomingdale's** at **Tysons Corner Center** (*see p117*) and **Macy's** at the **Fashion Centre at Pentagon City** (*see p116*).

Lord & Taylor
5255 Western Avenue, NW, at Wisconsin Avenue, Chevy Chase, Upper Northwest (1-202 362 9600, www.lordandtaylor.com). Friendship Heights Metro. **Open** 10am-9.30pm Mon-Thur; 10am-10pm Fri; 10am-9.30pm Sat; 11am-7pm Sun. **Credit** AmEx, Disc, MC, V.
Grown-ups' and children's dresses and sportswear with broad, basic appeal by the likes of Calvin Klein and Perry Ellis, with the requisite cosmetics and jewellery departments. There are plus sizes for women too.

Macy's
1201 G Street, NW, at 12th Street, Downtown (1-202 628 6661, www.macys.com). Metro Center Metro. **Open** 10am-8pm Mon-Sat; noon-6pm Sun. **Credit** AmEx, Disc, MC, V. **Map** p252 H6.
What was Hecht's now belongs to Macy, so you know what to expect: reasonably priced, mid-range fashions by famous makers, and an outstanding source of undies, socks, ties, shades and cologne. If you see a cool cake mixer at Williams-Sonoma, you can probably buy it slightly cheaper here.

Other locations 5400 Wisconsin Avenue, at Western Avenue, Chevy Chase (1-301 654 7600).

Neiman Marcus
5300 Wisconsin Avenue, NW, at Western Avenue, Upper Northwest (1-202 966 9700, www.neimanmarcus.com). Friendship Heights Metro. **Open** 10am-8pm Mon-Fri; 10am-5pm Sat; noon-6pm Sun. **Credit** AmEx, DC, Disc, MC, V.
With Corneliani men's suits, Ugg handbags, flirty Anna Sui dresses, Prada shoes, Wedgwood dinner services and Acqua di Parma beauty products, you can smell the money when you walk in.

Saks Fifth Avenue
5555 Wisconsin Avenue, NW, at South Park Avenue, Chevy Chase, MD (1-301 657 9000). Friendship Heights Metro. **Open** 10am-7pm Mon-Wed, Fri; 10am-7pm Thur; 10am-8pm Sat; noon-6pm Sun. **Credit** AmEx, DC, Disc, MC, V.
Luxury a go-go from casual to couture, with designers such as Marc Jacobs, Michael Kors and John Varvatos, and cosmetics by La Prairie, Chanel and Kiehl's. Guys would rue missing the Saks men's shop at 5300 Wisconsin Avenue.

INSIDE TRACK SALES TAX

In DC and Maryland, sales tax is six per cent, which is added to the ticket price. In Viriginia, sales tax is four per cent.

Where to Shop

The city's top retail locations.

GEORGETOWN
Assuming you're the owner of a well-endowed bank balance, this gracious district is a great place to shop. You'll find a veritable outdoor mall of global retail chains – from Armani Exchange to Zara – around lower Wisconsin Avenue and along M Street, NW.

DUPONT CIRCLE
You can walk from Georgetown to Dupont Circle, home to several of DC's favourite local merchants selling books, records, clothes, jewellery and household wares.

14TH STREET/U STREET CORRIDOR & LOGAN CIRCLE
After years of decline, U Street and 14th Street have now firmly re-established themselves as bona fide retail rows. Vintage clothes and edgier boutiques are in the ascendant here.

ADAMS MORGAN
Just north of Dupont Circle, the 18th Street strip in Adams Morgan has more food and beverage (especially beverage) purveyors than anything, but if you go there to eat, you'll come across plenty of good finds in its clothing, music and home stores.

CONNECTICUT AVENUE, NW
South of Dupont, lower Connecticut Avenue, NW, on the way to the White House, irr has an array of excellent if businesslike clothiers (Brooks Brothers, Burberry, et al).

CHINATOWN
More or less everything authentically Chinese has disappeared from the area around the MCI Center, with popular brand stores moving in instead.

CAPITOL HILL
Away from everything else is Capitol Hill – perhaps you've heard of it. But influence is not all that gets peddled here. There are fresh foods galore and, at weekends, arts and crafts at Eastern Market, a creditable remnant of a more agrarian age, and an expanding row of shops along 8th Street, SE.

FRIENDSHIP HEIGHTS
For the fancy stuff, follow the money to upper Wisconsin Avenue, NW, at DC's border with Maryland, where you can stare into a firmament that includes Neiman Marcus, Saks Fifth Avenue, Louis Vuitton and Jimmy Choo.

Other locations Tysons Galleria, 2051 International Drive, McLean, VA (1-703 761 0700).

Malls

Chevy Chase Pavilion
5335 Wisconsin Avenue, NW, at Western Avenue, Friendship Heights, Upper Northwest (1-202 686 5335, www.ccpavilion.com). Friendship Heights Metro. **Open** 9am-11pm Mon-Sat; 7am-11pm Sun. Hours of specific stores vary. **Credit** varies.
Feeding mainly off the better stores across the street at Mazza Gallerie (*see p117*) this minor mall offers clothing and home stuff, plus a food court. Highlights include Pottery Barn and an H&M scheduled to open spring 2013.

Collection at Chevy Chase
5471-5481 Wisconsin Avenue, Chevy Chase, MD (1-301 654 2292, www.thecollectionatchevychase.com). Friendship Heights Metro. **Open** 10am-9pm Mon-Sat; 11am-6pm Sun. Hours of specific stores vary. **Credit** varies.

Quite near Mazza Gallerie (*see p117*), this shopping centre combines a line-up of magnetic retail names under one roof, including Jimmy Choo, Louis Vuitton, Tiffany & Co, Ralph Lauren, Christian Dior, Cartier and Gucci.

Fashion Centre at Pentagon City
1100 South Hayes Street, between Army Navy Drive & 15th Street, Arlington, VA (1-703 415 2400, www.simon.com/mall/the-fashion-centre-at-pentagon-city). Pentagon City Metro. **Open** 10am-9.30pm Mon-Sat; 11am-6pm Sun. **Credit** varies.
Not bad for an old-school mall, with copious daylight and royal palms in its deep, plunging atria; its levels are accessible by glass elevator. Anchored by department stores Macy's and Nordstrom, Fashion City offers better (but maybe not the best) apparel, gifts and speciality goods from 160-odd national franchises such as Gap, Limited and Kenneth Cole, and is surrounded by big-box discount stores to its east and a flank of decent shops in a too-cute outdoor mall (with a winter outdoor skating rink) to its west.

CONSUME

Mazza Gallerie

5300 Wisconsin Avenue, NW, between Western Avenue & Jenifer Street, Friendship Heights, Upper Northwest (1-202 966 6114, www.mazza gallerie.net). Friendship Heights Metro. **Open** 10am-8pm Mon-Fri; noon-6pm Sun. **Credit** varies. Stores here run from snooty (Neiman Marcus) to congenially high-end (Saks Fifth Avenue's Men's Store) to over-a-barrel discount (Filene's Basement). Also houses a multi-screen cinema.

Shops at Georgetown Park

3222 M Street, NW, at Wisconsin Avenue, Georgetown (1-202 298 5577, www.shopsat georgetownpark.com). Foggy Bottom-GWU Metro then 32, 36 bus or Georgetown Circulator bus. **Open** 10am-8pm Mon-Fri; 10am-7pm Sat; noon-6pm Sun. **Credit** varies. **Map** p249 E5. Tucked between M Street and the C&O Canal, this skylit, air-conditioned escape from Georgetown's hectic streets has major clothing chains such as J Crew and Sisley, jewllery craft at the Joy of Beading, and presents for pets at Phat Dog. But if you get peckish, skip the meagre food court and pay a visit to Dean & Deluca (*see p127*) next door on M Street, NW.

Shops at Union Station

50 Massachusetts Avenue, NE, at North Capitol Street, Union Station & Around (1-202 289 1908, www.unionstationdc.com/shopping). Union Station Metro. **Open** 10am-9pm Mon-Sat; noon-6pm Sun. **Credit** varies. **Map** p253 L6. In the 1980s, before all the airports became malls, the refurbished Union Station assembled a lively range of boutiques and cafés beneath its soaring, coffered vaults. Thus the future of this magnificent building, under threat of demolition due to the long-term decline in the numbers of rail passengers, was ensured. Before travelling you can shop at several gift shops, bookshops and chocolatiers as well as an eclectic mix of stores such as Rosetta Stone for language learning packs or Appalachian Spring (*see also p130*) for handmade crafts and ceramics. You can also get your shoes polished, your eyebrows done or your jewellery and watches fixed.

Tysons Corner Center

1961 Chain Bridge Road, McLean, VA (1-888 289 7667, 1-703 893 9400, www.shop tysons.com). West Falls Church-VT/UVA Metro then 28A, 28B or 3T bus. By car: Route 66 west to Route 7 west to Tysons Corner. **Open** 10am-9.30pm Mon-Sat; 11am-7pm Sun. **Credit** varies. You could spend an entire weekend inside TCC, grounded at one end by Bloomingdale's and at the other by Nordstrom, with over a hundred shops such as Benetton, Banana Republic and West Elm elsewhere on two levels. It also hosts higher-end retailers like Armani Exchange. Nearby is its smaller, more upscale counterpart, Tysons Galleria, at 2001

International Drive, anchored by Neiman Marcus, Macy's and Saks Fifth Avenue. (1-703 827 7730, www.tysonsgalleria.com)

BOOKS & MAGAZINES

Following the nationwide trend, Washington has lost many of its bookstores in recent years. What was once the best-known local chain, Olsson's Books & Records, is now sadly closed; two remaining Borders locations suffered the same fate recently. Chapters Literary Art Center & Bookstore, once on 11th Street downtown, is reportedly looking for a new home and keeps fans updated on Facebook. Listed below are DC's remaining independent and speciality booksellers.

★ Kramerbooks

1517 Connecticut Avenue, NW, at Q Street, Dupont Circle (1-202 387 1400, www.kramers. com). Dupont Circle Metro. **Open** 7.30am-1am Mon-Thur, Sun; 24hrs Fri, Sat. **Credit** AmEx, Disc, MC, V. **Map** p250 G4. Not just a bookshop, but an episode of *Blind Date*, Kramerbooks is an oft-used venue for a first assignation. First, meet in the bookshop, then repair to the attached café (Afterwords, *see p91*), which serves meals and snacks throughout the day. Possibilities of romance aside, the book selection is good.

★ Politics & Prose

5015 Connecticut Avenue, NW, between Fessenden Street & Nebraska Avenue, Upper Northwest (1-800 722 0790, 1-202 364 1919, www.politics-prose.com). Van Ness-UDC Metro then northbound L1, L2, L4 bus. **Open** 9am-10pm Mon-Sat; 10am-8pm Sun. **Credit** AmEx, Disc, MC, V. As you might guess, Politics & Prose carries a lot of both, plus a large section that is set aside for children and teenagers, and there's a coffee shop downstairs too. The store is much more than just a thriving independent bookshop, it's a much-loved institution and a must-stop for prominent authors who are on the reading-tour circuit. Carla Cohen, the shop's well-known founder and co-owner, died in late 2010; two former *Washington Post* journalists, married couple Bradley Graham and Lissa Muscatine, took over the following year.

Specialist

Big Planet Comics

1520 U Street, NW, between 15th & 16th Streets, U Street Corridor (1-202 342 1961, www.big planetcomics.com). Dupont Circle or U Street, African-American Civil War Memorial/Cardozo Metro. **Open** 11am-7pm Mon, Tue, Thur, Fri; 11am-8pm Wed; 11am-6pm Sat; noon-5pm Sun. **Credit** AmEx, MC, V. **Map** p250 H3.

Bags packed, milk cancelled, house raised on stilts.

You've packed the suntan lotion, the snorkel set, the stay-pressed shirts. Just one more thing left to do – your bit for climate change. In some of the world's poorest countries, changing weather patterns are destroying lives.

You can help people to deal with the extreme effects of climate change. Raising houses in flood-prone regions is just one life-saving solution.

**Climate change costs lives.
Give £5 and let's sort it *Here & Now***

www.oxfam.org.uk/climate-change

Be Humankind Oxfam

This purveyor of underground comics and graphic novels moved out of its Georgetown store in 2011 and set up shop on the U Street Corridor.

Used & antiquarian

Capitol Hill Books
657 C Street, SE, at 7th Street, Capitol Hill (1-202 544 1621, www.capitolhillbooks-dc.com). Eastern Market Metro. **Open** 11.30am-6pm Mon-Fri; 10am-6pm Sat, Sun. **Credit** AmEx, MC, V. **Map** p253 L7.
Two packed and dusty floors of second-hand books – fiction, mysteries, politics, cooking and more – plus rare and first editions. Navigate the maze of narrow aisles to browse shelves packed floor to ceiling with hardbacks and paperbacks.

Second Story Books
2000 P Street, NW, at 20th Street, Dupont Circle (1-202 659 8884, www.secondstorybooks.com). Dupont Circle Metro. **Open** 10am-10pm daily. **Credit** AmEx, Disc, MC, V. **Map** p250 G4.
A venerated, musty space, chock-a-block with all kinds of curious used titles, plus second-hand music and prints. Check the sidewalk bins for bargains. This shop, along with its counterpart in Rockville, stocks over a million rare and used books.

CHILDREN

You can find clothes and shoes for youngsters at **H&M** (*see p121*), **Macy's** (*see p115*) and **Lord & Taylor** (*see p115*). There's a **Gap Kids** in Georgetown (1267 Wisconsin Avenue, NW, 1-202 333 2411) and in Chevy Chase. Any CVS drug store has baby and child sundries galore. And check the museum shops for one-of-a-kind toys.

Dawn Price Baby
3112 M Street, NW, between 31st Street & Wisconsin Avenue, Georgetown (1-202 333 3939, www.dawnpricebaby.com). Foggy Bottom-GWU Metro then 32, 36 bus or Georgetown Circulator bus. **Open** 11am-7pm Mon-Sat; noon-5pm Sun. **Credit** AmEx, MC, V. **Map** p249 E5.
A handy place to pick up gifts for newborns or young children. In keeping with the DC location, you might find 'Tiny Democrat' and 'Tiny Republican' emblazoned T shirts. Also in stock are knitted animal backpacks and personalised first plates and christening mugs.
Other locations 325 7th Street, SE, Capitol Hill (1-202 543 2920).

Monkey's Uncle
321 7th Street, SE, between Pennsylvania Avenue & C Street, Capitol Hill (1-202 543 6471, www.monkeysuncleonthehill.com). Eastern Market Metro. **Open** 10.30am-6pm Tue, Wed,

Fri; 11am-7pm Thur; 9am-6pm Sat; 11am-5pm Sun. **Credit** AmEx, Disc, MC, V. **Map** p253 L7.
Recycled clothes for babies up to pre-teens, with the usual chances for sartorial serendipity and a high baseline of quality. Discerning Hill mothers come here for cheap party clothes and seasonal wear for their children and maternity clothes for themselves. The owners have started a useful and popular sideline business of renting baby gear: there's travel equipment for local parents flying out, highchairs and play yards for local grandparents hosting in.

Toys

Fairy Godmother
319 7th Street, SE, between Pennsylvania Avenue & C Street, Capitol Hill (1-202 547 5474). Eastern Market Metro. **Open** 10.30am-6pm Mon-Fri; 10am-5pm Sat; 10.30am-3.30pm Sun. **Credit** AmEx, MC, V. **Map** p253 L7.
This tiny shop holds a remarkable range of children's books and toys. The emphasis is on parent favourites: Haba and Plan wooden toys, Corolle and Madame Alexander dolls. There is a good selection of fiction for second-graders up to teens, plus French and Spanish books for babies and toddlers. New picture books get prominent placement, and staff are friendly and knowledgeable.

Sullivan's Toy Store & Art Supplies
4200 Wisconsin Avenue, NW, between Chesapeake & Brandywine Streets, Tenleytown, Upper Northwest (1-202 362 1343,). Tenleytown-AU Metro. **Open** 10am-6pm Mon, Tue; 10am-7pm Wed-Fri; 9am-6pm Sat; noon-5pm Sun. **Credit** AmEx, Disc, MC, V.
Before the onslaught of Toys 'R' Us, the world was full of toy stores like this one, which stocks craft kits, kites and puzzles, dolls and action figures and a separate section for proper art supplies. There are claims that this is the oldest toy store in DC. It recently relocated to digs in Tenleytown due to development on its old Cleveland Park spot.

ELECTRONICS & PHOTOGRAPHY

CVS drugstores, with branches all over the city, offer a one-hour photo developing service. Radio Shack has stores throughout the area.

Best Buy
4500 Wisconsin Avenue, NW, at Albemarle Street, Tenleytown, Upper Northwest (1-202 895 1580, www.bestbuy.com). Tenleytown-AU Metro. **Open** 10am-9pm Mon-Sat; 11am-7pm Sun. **Credit** AmEx, Disc, MC, V.
A carnival of mass-media gizmos that offers just about anything you want – if it's in stock.
Other locations 3100 14th Street, between Irving Street & Park Road, Columbia Heights.

CONSUME

CONSUME

Meeps. *See p123.*

Graffiti Audio-Video

4914 Wisconsin Avenue, NW, Upper Northwest (1-202 244 9643, www.graffitiaudio.com). Friendship Heights Metro. **Open** 10am-7pm Mon-Sat; noon-6pm Sun. **Credit** AmEx, Disc, MC, V. **Map** p250 G4.
Graffiti sells TV and audio equipment of the better kind. Home cinemas and discreet audio systems.

Penn Camera

840 E Street, NW, between 8th & 9th Streets, Penn Quarter (1-202 347 5777, www.calumet photo.com). Gallery Place-Chinatown Metro. **Open** 8.30am-6pm Mon-Fri; 10am-5pm Sat, Sun. **Credit** AmEx, Disc, MC, V. **Map** p253 J6.
All the equipment a pro could need, but the smart staff will help novices too. Camera equipment also available to rent.
Other locations Tyson's Corner (*see p117*).

FASHION

Designer

The greatest concentration of clothing from well-known designers is to be found in Washington's better department stores, such as **Neiman Marcus** and **Saks Fifth Avenue**
(for both, *see p115*). **Betsey Johnson** keeps her stylish pieces at 3029 N Street, NW (1-202 338 4090). If you're feeling especially thin, you can take a trip to visit the **Chanel** boutique in Tysons Galleria (2001 International Drive, McLean, VA, 1-703 874 0555). Women of a certain quiet sophistication have shopped at **Claire Dratch** for 65 years (7615 Wisconsin Avenue, Bethesda, MD, 1-301 656 8000). Or they visit **Rizik's** (1100 Connecticut Avenue, NW, Downtown, 1-202 223 4050), across the street from which is a convenient **Burberry** store (No.1155, 1-202 463 3000).

Betsy Fisher

1224 Connecticut Avenue, NW, between N Street & Jefferson Place, Dupont Circle (1-202 785 1975, www.betsyfisher.com). Dupont Circle Metro. **Open** 10am-7pm Mon-Wed; 10am-8pm Thur, Fri; 10am-6pm Sat; noon-4pm Sun. **Credit** AmEx, DC, Disc, MC, V. **Map** p250 G4.
Approachable chic, from the tailored to the saucy. Ensembles, dresses and the rest by the likes of Caractère, Gazebo and Three Dots.

★ Ginger Root Design

1530 U Street, NW, between 15th & 16th streets, U Street Corridor (1-202 567 7668, www.ginger rootdesign.com). U Street, African-American Civil War Memorial/Cardozo Metro. **Open** 2-7pm Mon; noon-7pm Thur-Sat; 1-6pm Sun. **Credit** MC, V. **Map** p250 H3.
Founded by two Midwestern redheads with a reputation for being the nicest ladies on the block, you'll find a great selection of jewellery and accessories by local designers for men and women at Ginger Root, as well as gifts, stationery, and other environmentally friendly and stylish wares. The upper floor recently expanded to a full-service tailoring operation. Don't leave without trying on one of the famous lady ties, made from repurposed vintage fabrics and sewn by hand by the owners themselves.

Nana

3068 Mount Pleasant Street, NW, between Irving & Hobart Streets, Mount Pleasant (1-202 667 6955, www.nanadc.com). Columbia Heights Metro. **Open** noon-7pm Tue-Sat; noon-6pm Sun. **Credit** MC, V. **Map** p250 H2.
Wearing escapism on its sleeveless little dress, Nana sells her own line of fun, funky vintage-inspired dresses, blouses, skirts and more, using eco-friendly materials and ethical practices. Fresh!

★ Redeem

1810 14th Street, NW, between S Street & Swan Street, Logan Circle (1-202 332 7447, www. redeemus.com). U Street, African-American Civil War Memorial/Cardozo Metro. **Open** noon-8pm Mon Wed-Sat; noon-6pm Sun. **Credit** MC, V. **Map** p250 H4.

Known as one of DC's most cutting-edge boutiques, Redeem carries pieces by international designers with a modern slant, in dark colours: black is definitely the new black here. You'll also find a selection of independent magazines, high-end men's shoes, and a section of the store devoted to Mutiny, a DC-based menswear accessories company that carries vintage pieces, stationery and accessories.

Relish
3312 Cady's Alley, NW, M Street between 33rd & 34th Streets, Georgetown (1-202 333 5343, http://relishdc.com). Foggy Bottom Metro then 32, 36 bus, or Georgetown Circulator bus. **Open** 10am-6pm Mon- Sat; evenings by appointment. **Credit** AmEx, MC, V. **Map** p249 E5.
Relish is in an airy loft on Georgetown's design-oriented Cady's Alley, and its designer lines are similarly rarefied, with pieces by Marni, Dries van Noten, Marc Jacobs, Jil Sander and more. Plus shoes by Balenciaga and Pedro Garcia.

Treasury. *See p123.*

Discount

Filene's Basement
1133 Connecticut Avenue, NW, Downtown (1-202 872 8430, www.filenesbasement.com). Farragut North Metro. **Open** 9.30am-8pm Mon-Sat; noon-5pm Sun. **Credit** AmEx, Disc, MC, V. **Map** p250 G5.
Massive markdowns on every category of clothing and accessories by familiar names.
Other locations National Press Building, 529 14th Street, NW, Downtown (1-202 638 4110); Mazza Gallerie, 5300 Wisconsin Avenue, NW, Chevy Chase (1-202 966 0208).

General

Most of the mainstream clothiers – the likes of American Apparel, Banana Republic, J Crew, Gap – make appearances in the District. Georgetown has one of nearly all of the above, plus choicer chains like Club Monaco, French Connection, Diesel and Armani Exchange. You will also find them in most of the city's malls (*see pp116-117*).

H&M
1025 F Street, NW, between 10th & 11th Streets, Downtown (1-202 347 3306, www.hm.com). Metro Center Metro. **Open** 10am-9pm Mon-Sat; 11am-8pm Sun. **Credit** AmEx, DC, Disc, MC, V. **Map** p252 J6.
The Swedish retailer has taken DC by storm, selling sportswear and dresswear (including plus sizes) for men, women and children under its own label.
Other locations Shops at Georgetown Park, 3222 M Street, NW (1-202 298 6792); Chevy Chase Pavilion, 5335 Wisconsin Avenue, NW (1-202 256 7896).

Urban Outfitters
3111 M Street, NW, between 31st & 32nd Streets, Georgetown (1-202 342 1012). Foggy Bottom-GWU Metro then 32, 36 bus or Georgetown Circulator bus. **Open** 10am-10pm Mon-Thur; 10am-11pm Fri, Sat; 10am-9pm Sun. **Credit** AmEx, Disc, MC, V. **Map** p249 E5.
Young neo-bohemians trawl the creaky floors of this bazaar for geek fashions and groovy housewares with a folkloric theme.
Other locations: 737 7th Street, NW, between G & H Streets, Chinatown (1-202 737 0259).

Second-hand & vintage

Ginger Root (*see p120*) also stocks vintage.

★ Blues Hard Goods
1803A 14th Street, NW, at S Street, U Street Corridor (1-202 462 6200, http://blueshard goods.com). U Street/African-American Civil

CONSUME

Vintage on U Street

Old clothes get a new life.

Over the past five years, the U Street Corridor, particularly the stretch between 15th and 16th Streets, has become the go-to destination for vintage in DC. Four of the top vintage stores in the city live nearly next door to each other, where they've built a supportive community and a band of loyal customers. From repurposed vintage pieces to Levi's from the 1940s – if it's not new you'll find it on U Street. Here's where to go and who to talk to when you crave something special.

Ginger Root.

To satisfy the eccentric vintage-lover with a wild side, the owners of **Junction** (No.1510, *see p123*) scour estate sales and fill the store with eclectic accessories and colourful styles. From cigarette holders, tiny earrings, vintage ties and bowties barely ever worn to an entire rack of high-end designer threads – you can find it here. Even that 1960s jumpsuit, if you're brave enough to wear it.

Nearby, **Ginger Root** (No.1530, *see p123*) is a haven for local designers as well as vintage-lovers. The two-storey shop, with a recent extension at the back, hosts a revolving selection of vintage finds from various independent vintage collectives in DC without brick and mortar locations of their own. Ginger Root also produces its own in-house clothing lines from repurposed and vintage fabrics.

You'll find plenty of women's vintage in town, but **Dr. K** (No.1534; *see p123*) is the epicentre of men's vintage, with owner Somkiat becoming a quiet advocate for upping men's style game in DC, one customer at a time. Open at odd hours (and often not at all), Dr. K is the best-kept sartorial secret in DC. Don't be surprised to find vintage Levi's from the 1940s, letterman jackets, denim shirts, hats and bags that would easily sell for double in other more style-obsessed cities. Make friends with Somkiat (aka Dr. K) and he might pull out something special for you from the back. And there's more. For the dandy within every man, **Rock it Again** (No.1528, *see p123*) is filled to the brim with tweed blazers, shiny oxfords, plaid vests and vintage fedoras. Visit in winter and you'll snag fur-lined London Fog coats, leather gloves and warm scarves at great prices.

Rock It Again.

War Memorial/Cardozo Metro. **Open** noon-7pm Tue-Fri; 11am-7pm Sat; noon-6pm Sun. **Credit** AmEx, Disc, MC, V. **Map** p250 H4.

A hidden second floor gem on 14th Street, owner Andrew Nguyen is a master at effortless cool style, which shows in the vintage denim, hand-sewn bandana scarves and bolo ties in his store. Blues Hard Goods is also home to Las Gitanas pop-up boutique in the back room, for delicate vintage gowns, gloves, and hats.

Buffalo Exchange

1318 14th Street, NW, between N Street & Rhode Island Avenue, Logan Circle (1-202 299 9148, www.buffaloexchange.com). McPherson Square Metro. **Open** 11am-7pm Mon-Sat; noon-6pm Sun. **Credit** Disc, MC, V. **Map** p250 H4.

Recently opening two locations in Washington, this one on 14th Street and another in Georgetown, this second-hand clothing shop buys and sells your pieces from last season that are taking up room in your closet but could easily be someone else's ultimate steal. Look carefully through the racks and you could find a pair of Diesel jeans for $20, or barely worn designer shoes for less than the price of lunch. We recommend going early on a Monday when new merchandise gets put out.

Other locations 279 M Street, NW, at Potomac Street, Georgetown (1-202 333 2829).

Current Boutique

1809 14th Street, NW, between S & T Streets, U Street Corridor (1-202 588 7311, www.current boutique.com). U Street, African-American Civil War Memorial/Cardozo Metro. **Open** 11am-8pm Mon-Fri; 11am-8pm Sat; 11am-6pm Sun. **Credit** AmEx, Disc, MC, V. **Map** p250 H3.

Ladies looking for the latest trends but not willing to pay full price flock to Current to dig through the racks of second-hand clothing. Fast fashion is a reality at this store, where if you found it first, you shouldn't put it down. Popular brands on the racks include Zara, H&M, and the occasional designer shoes and accessories.

★ Dr. K Vintage

1534 U Street, NW, between 15th & 16th streets, U Street Corridor (1-202 506-1817). U Street/ African-American Civil War Memorial/Cardozo Metro. **Open** usually 10am-10pm daily; call to check. **Credit** AmEx, Disc, MC, V. **Map** p250 H3. *See p122* **Vintage on U Street**.

Ginger Root Design

1530 U Street, NW, between 15th & 16th Streets, U Street Corridor (1-202 567 7668, gingerrootdesign.com). U Street/African-American Civil War Memorial/Cardozo Metro. **Open** 2-7pm Mon; noon-7pm Thur-Sat; 1-6pm Sun. **Credit** MC, V. **Map** p250 H3. *See p122* **Vintage on U Street**.

★ Junction

1510 U Street, NW, between 15th & 16th Streets, U Street Corridor (1-202 483 0260, www.junctionwdc.com). Dupont Circle or U Street, African-American Civil War Memorial/ Cardozo Metro. **Open** 3-7pm Wed; noon-7pm Thur-Sat; noon-5pm Sun. **Credit** AmEx, MC, V. **Map** p250 H3. *See p122* **Vintage on U Street**.

Meeps

2104 18th Street, NW, between California Street & Wyoming Avenue, Adams Morgan (1-202 265 6546, www.meepsdc.com). Woodley Park-Zoo/Adams Morgan Metro then 96 bus. **Open** noon-8pm Mon, Tue; noon-9pm Wed-Sat; noon-6pm Sun. **Credit** MC, V. **Map** p250 G3.

Recently taken over by the owners of 14th Street's Treasury boutique (*see below*), Meeps is Treasury's younger, edgier sister, who loves vintage rock and roll tees, combat boots and big sunglasses. Meeps also has a great selection of local magazines and costumes, should you be in town for Halloween. *Photo p120.*

★ Rock it Again

1528 U Street, NW, between 15th & 16th Streets, U Street Corridor (1-202 643 0717, www.rockit again.com). U Street/African-American Civil War Memorial/Cardozo Metro. **Open** noon-7pm Mon, Thur; noon-6.30pm Fri; noon-5.30pm Sun. **Map** p250 H3. *See p122* **U Street Vintage**.

Treasury

1843 14th Street, NW, at T Street, U Street Corridor (1-202 332 9499, www.shoptreasury. com). U Street/African-American Civil War Memorial/Cardozo Metro. **Open** noon-7pm Mon-Sat; noon-6pm Sun. **Credit** AmEx, Disc, MC, V. **Map** p250 H3.

If you ask a stylish local on U Street where they got that incredible hat or handbag they'll undoubtedly say 'Treasury'. Known by locals as a treasure trove of designer and classic vintage finds, the secondfloor rowhouse boutique is the place to go for recast vintage jewellery, a vintage slip silk dress, or a chic hat that gives an outfit that extra je ne sais quoi. *Photo p121.*

Menswear

Alton Lane

3rd floor, 1506 19th Street, NW, at Dupont Circle (1-646 896 1212, www.altonlane.com). Metro Dupont Circle. **Open** 9am-9pm Mon; 10am-7pm Tue, Wed, Fri, Sun; 10am-9pm Thur; 10am-8pm Sat. **Credit** AmEx, Disc, MC, V. **Map** p250 G4. *See p125* **Man Style**.

BOSS Hugo Boss

1517 Wisconsin Avenue, NW, between P & Q Streets, Georgetown (1-202 625 2677,

CONSUME

www.hugoboss.com). Foggy Bottom-GWU Metro then 32, 36 bus or Georgetown Circulator bus.
Open 11am-7.30pm Mon-Sat; noon-6pm Sun.
Credit AmEx, Disc, MC, V. **Map** p249 E4.
A range of smart city clothing: suits, coats, shirts and trousers. All are made in good-quality fabrics and prices aren't unreasonable for this standard of gentlemen's clothing.

Brooks Brothers

1201 Connecticut Avenue, NW, at M Street, Dupont Circle (1-202 659 4650, www.brooks brothers.com). Farragut North or Dupont Circle Metro. **Open** 9.30am-7pm Mon-Fri; 9.30am-6pm Sat; noon-6pm Sun. **Credit** AmEx, Disc, MC, V. **Map** p250 G5.
Ever the classicists, Brooks Brothers has elegant and sober men's and women's clothes ideal for politicking on Capitol Hill.
Other locations 3077 M Street, NW, Georgetown (1-202 298 8797); 5504 Wisconsin Avenue, Chevy Chase, MD (1-301 654 8202).

Everard's Clothing

1802 Wisconsin Avenue, NW, at S Street, Georgetown (1-202 298 7464, www.everards clothing.com). Foggy Bottom-GWU Metro then 32, 36 bus or Georgetown Circulator bus. **Open** 10am-6pm Mon-Sat, or by appointment. **Credit** AmEx, DC, Disc, MC, V. **Map** p249 E3.
The well-dressed Washington man knows Louis Everard, and Mr Everard knows the well-dressed Washington man – or at least his measurements. This is the place to come for suits beautifully made to customer specifications. An added bonus is that you never know which of the rich and powerful you might see within, or upstairs browsing through the fine women's collections.

Hugh & Crye

N0.5, 3212 O Street, NW, at Wisconsin Avenue, NW, Georgetown (1-202 250 3807, www.hughand crye.com). Foggy Bottom-GWU Metro then 32, 36 bus or Georgetown Circulator bus. **Open** 10am-7pm Mon-Fri; noon-4pm Sat, Sun. **Credit** AmEx, Disc, MC, V. **Map** p249 E4.
See p125 **Man Style**.

★ Lost Boys

1033 31st Street, NW, between K & M Streets, Georgetown (1-202 333 0093, www.lostboys.com). Foggy Bottom-GWU Metro then 32, 36 bus or Georgetown Circulator bus. **Open** 11am-7pm Wed-Sat; noon-6pm Sun. **Credit** AmEx, Disc, MC, V. **Map** p249 F5.
If there's one independent boutique in DC that knows menswear, it's Lost Boys. Owner Kelly Muccio will personally walk you through the selection of designer brands, including Rage & Bone, Band of Outsiders and Theory, to create a look tailored to your individual style. If you thought you couldn't pull off that

jacket, one look in the mirror after her styling says you can. Be prepared to drop some serious cash, as great style here doesn't come cheap.

FASHION ACCESSORIES & SERVICES
Cleaning, laundry & repairs

Imperial Valet

1331 Connecticut Avenue, NW, between Dupont Circle & N Street, Dupont Circle (1-202 785 1444, www.sterlingcleaner.com). Dupont Circle Metro. **Open** 7.30am-6.30pm Mon-Fri; 9am-3pm Sat. **Credit** AmEx, MC, V. **Map** p250 G4.
In an hour, you can have a hat dry-cleaned. In a day, laundry done. Imperial Valet also undertakes reasonably fast alterations and repairs and will also fix your shoes so you can walk comfortably back down Connecticut Avenue.

Jewellery

Jewelerswerk Galerie

3319 Cady's Alley, Georgetown (1-202 337 3319, www.jewelerswerk.com). Foggy Bottom-GWU Metro then 32, 36 bus or Georgetown Circulator bus. **Open** 11am-6pm Mon-Sat; noon-5pm Sun. **Credit** AmEx, Disc, MC, V. **Map** p252 G5.
This cool little gallery, now relocated to Cady's Alley, near the Francis Scott Key Bridge, sells unique jewellery made by over 50 international artists in a variety of media.

★ Tabandeh

5300 Wisconsin Avenue, NW (Mazza Gallerie), Friendship Heights (1-202 244 0777, www. tabandehjewelry.com). Friendship Heights Metro. **Open** 11am-6pm Mon-Sat; noon-5pm Sun. **Credit** AmEx, MC, V.
The glittering window displays of Tabandeh stop passers-by in their tracks. This jewellery boutique features pieces from high-end designers scarcely available elsewhere in the city. Giant grey and white Tahitian pearls from Samira 13, stunning chunky gemstone pieces from Iradj Moini, and case after case of precious gems tempt the buyer of means. More-affordable pieces include those from Hollywood-popular Gas Bijoux and angular pieces from Alexi Bittar. Accessories, such as bags, belts and scarves, are also in store. *Photo p126*.

Tiny Jewel Box

1147 Connecticut Avenue, NW, between L & M Streets, Downtown (1-202 393 2747, www.tiny jewelbox.com). Farragut North or Farragut West Metro. **Open** 10am-5.30pm Mon-Sat. **Credit** AmEx, MC, V. **Map** p252 G5.
A vast range of pieces, from classic to contemporary and from antique to modern one-off designer pieces,

Man Style

An end to corporate drone dressing.

Hugh & Crye.

Take a walk Downtown at 9am and you'll find yourself surrounded by a purposeful, marching swarm of the very same black suit and blue button-down shirt. The culprit? We blame the vast array of government office jobs for the lack of colour among the male cohort in DC's business circles. So what is the professional yet stylish man to do if he wants to dress better but still fit in? Thankfully, a couple of local menswear companies have stepped in to solve this very problem.

'Shirts that fit' is the motto of **Hugh & Crye** (*see p124*), which designs shirts in 12 sizes to fit every man from the short and skinny to the tall and broad. Primarily an online company, Hugh & Crye now runs a showroom in the heart of Georgetown, where customers can try on their shirts in person before buying.

Meanwhile, over in Dupont Circle, the custom suit company **Alton Lane** (*see p123*) dresses you a notch above your pay grade by taking a 3D scan of your body to guarantee that your tailor-made suit will fit perfectly. Make an appointment to visit the showroom and sip a whisky sour while picking out silk ties to go with your new suit.

Alton Lane.

are to be found in this long-established, well-respected three-storey Downtown favourite. Other products for sale here include scarves, bags, gloves and gifts.

Shoes

Georgetown has several good shoe stores, including **Steve Madden** (3109 M Street, NW, 1-202 342 6194) and the **Walking Company** (3101 M Street, NW, 1-202 625 9255).

★ Palace 5ive

2220 14th Street, NW, between Florida Avenue & W Street, U Street Corridor (1-202 299 9008, www.palace5ive.com). U Street, African-American Civil War Memorial/Cardozo Metro. **Open** 11am-9pm Mon-Sat; noon-6pm Sun. **Credit** AmEx, Disc, MC, V. **Map** p250 H3.

If you're a sneaker head, this is your paradise. Carrying the very latest in skateboarding shoes and designer sneakers, Palace 5ive is where you'll find all the latest designer collaborations and limited edition sneaks, as well as the classic Nikes, Vans, Converse and Adidas. If you're a skater, it's got the decks and wheels to go with the shoes.

Soulier

1434 Wisconsin Avenue, NW, between O & P Streets, Georgetown (1-202 342 7160). Foggy Bottom-GWU Metro then 32, 36 bus or Georgetown Circulator bus. **Open** 10.30am-8pm Mon-Thur; 10.30am-8.30pm Fri, Sat; 12.30-6.30pm Sun. **Credit** AmEx, Disc, MC, V. **Map** p249 E4.

In a stretch of Wisconsin Avenue dominated by stores for gentlemen, Soulier stands out for its excellent selection of sleek European-style men's shoes. Look for Bally, Bruno Magli and Magnanni, as well as the more widely available Cole Haan. Other makers include Cesare Paciotti, Moreschi and Aldo Bruè. Pointy toes abound; there's nary a clunker in sight.

FOOD & DRINK

Bakeries

La Madeleine

3000 M Street, NW, at 30th Street, Georgetown (1-202 337 6975, www.lamadeleine.com). Foggy Bottom-GWU Metro then 32, 36 bus or Georgetown Circulator bus. **Open** 7am-10pm Mon-Thur, Sun; 7am-11pm Fri, Sat. **Credit** AmEx, Disc, MC, V. **Map** p249 F5.

A decent chain French bakery with all the classics, such as chocolate almond croissants, crème brûlée and decadent mini parfaits. Baguettes and other breads are baked on the premises.

Marvelous Market

3217 P Street, NW, at Wisconsin Avenue, Georgetown (1-202 333 2591, www.marvelous market.com). Foggy Bottom-GWU Metro then

Tabandeh. See p124.

32, 36 bus or Georgetown Circulator bus. **Open** 6.30am-9pm Mon-Sat; 7am-10pm Sun. **Credit** AmEx, MC, V. **Map** p249 E4.

Delicious breads, rolls, scones and pastries can be paired with ready supplies of cheeses, salami and olives. Home deliveries of deli fare also available. **Other locations** throughout the city.

★ Pâtisserie Poupon

1645 Wisconsin Avenue, NW, between Q Street & Reservoir Road, Georgetown (1-202 342 3248, www.patisseriepoupon.net. Foggy Bottom-GWU Metro then 32, 36 bus or Georgetown Circulator bus. **Open** 8.30am-6pm Tue-Fri; 8am-5.30pm Sat; 8am-4pm Sun. **Credit** AmEx, Disc, MC, V. **Map** p249 E4.

All the calorific authentic French pastries and breads are here. Opera cake is a favourite. *Poupon is also a café, see p102.*

Drink

Best Cellars

1643 Connecticut Avenue, NW, between Q & R Streets, Dupont Circle (1-202 387 3146, www.bestcellars.com). Dupont Circle Metro. **Open** 10am-9pm Mon-Thur; 10am-10pm Fri, Sat. **Credit** AmEx, MC, V. **Map** p250 G4.

With stores in several US cities, these wine realists take you beyond the freemasonry of wine snobs and their secret codes and boil it down to a simple glossary of 'luscious' (an Alsatian pinot gris, for example), 'big' (Californian zinfandel or syrah from

CONSUME

France), 'smooth' (Chilean merlot), and so on. Also 'handcrafted' beers and some small-batch spirits.

Calvert Woodley Wine & Spirits

4339 Connecticut Avenue, NW, at Windom Place, Upper Northwest (1-202 966 4400, www.calvert woodley.com). Van Ness-UDC Metro. **Open** 10am-8.30pm Mon-Sat. **Credit** Disc, MC, V.

The old hands here have mounted a large yet well-focused selection of voluptuary treats. The extensive wine shop is especially strong in Burgundy and Bordeaux and always has affordable specials. At the deli, the prodigious selection includes prosciutto, Serrano and pâtés, and a world of cheeses from cotswold to mimolette.

Rodman's

5100 Wisconsin Avenue, NW, at Garrison Street, Friendship Heights, Upper Northwest (1-202 363 3466, www.rodmans.com). Friendship Heights Metro. **Open** 9am-9.30pm Mon-Sat; 10am-7pm Sun. **Credit** AmEx, Disc, MC, V.

Open since 1955, this family-owned discount drug-store has expanded greatly and now offers one of the best selections of wine in Washington. Plus gourmet cheeses, exotic snacks, coffees and teas to round out the repast.

Markets

The growing season in the DC region is quite long, hence an ever-flowing bounty of fruits and vegetables, not to mention artisanal cheeses, baked goods and cut flowers.

Vendors at **FreshFarm Markets** (1-202 362 8889, www.freshfarmmarkets.org) at venues throughout the city sell food that has been grown or raised on their own land or made on their own premises. The longest-running and most popular is the Dupont Circle market, in the parking lot of the PNC bank (20th Street, between Massachusetts & Connecticut Avenues, open 8.30am-1pm Sun Apr-Dec, with hours shifting at winter). Other FreshFarm markets take place in Foggy Bottom, Penn Quarter, by the White House, and on H Street, NE. Personally produced, local food is also sold at **Takoma Park Farmers' Market**, on Laurel Avenue, between Eastern & Carroll Avenues, Takoma Park, MD (www.takomapark market.com, open 10am-2pm Sun).

Union Market (*see above* **Inside Track**) sells a wide variety of foodie products.

Eastern Market

225 7th Street, SE, between C Street & North Carolina Avenue, Capitol Hill (1-202 698-5253, www.easternmarket-dc.org) Eastern Market Metro. **Open** *South Hall (indoor market)* 7am-7pm Tue-Fri; 7am-6pm Sat; 9am-5pm Sun. *Farmers' Line & Outdoor Market* 7am-6pm Sat; 9am-5pm Sun.

> ### INSIDE TRACK
> ### MARKET FORCES
>
> Washington has two permanent markets. The historic 19th-century building that houses Eastern Market (*see below*) was gutted by fire in 2007. It was beautifully restored and reopened for business in 2009. **Union Market** (*see p100*) is a food market that recently opened in old warehouse premises north of Gallaudet University and H Street, NE.

Originally built in 1873, this market became the 'town centre' of the Capitol Hill neighbourhood and continues to be one of the liveliest spots in DC. The South Hall market, open throughout the week, hosts indoor merchants selling meats, baked goods, cheeses and flowers. On weekends the area around the market building hosts arts and crafts vendors and furniture sellers, flea-market style, along with farmers' stands and food vendors.

Specialist

Some of the shops listed under **Drink** (*see p126*) also stock delicatessen-style food.

★ Cowgirl Creamery

919 F Street, NW, between 9th & 10th Streets, Penn Quarter (1-202 393 6880, www.cowgirl creamery.com). Gallery Place-Chinatown or Metro Center Metro. **Open** 10am-7pm Mon-Sat. **Credit** MC, V. **Map** p253 J6.

From their original creamery in Point Reyes, California, the owners, who are daughters of the Washington DC area, are now back in the city, offering their celebrated cheeses here. Among the choices are the triple-cream Mount Tam, earthy Alpine Shepherd, buttery Constant Bliss, as well as cottage cheese and crème fraîche.

Dean & Deluca

3276 M Street, NW, at Potomac Street, Georgetown (1-202 342 2500, www.dean deluca.com). Foggy Bottom-GWU Metro then 32, 36 bus or Georgetown Circulator bus. **Open** *Shop* 9am-8pm daily. *Café* 7am-8pm daily. **Credit** AmEx, MC, V. **Map** p249 E5.

Fresh regional produce, salads, pastries, meats and more, all of exceptional quality and for prices higher than you ever thought you'd pay.

★ Vace

3315 Connecticut Avenue, NW, at Macomb Street, Cleveland Park (1-202 363 1999, www.vaceitalian deli.com). Cleveland Park Metro. **Open** 9am-9pm Mon-Fri; 9am-8pm Sat; 10am-5pm Sun. **Credit** MC, V. **Map** p249 F1.

CONSUME

There's not that much fresh Italian produce in DC, but most of what there is can be found at Vace. The aroma of freshly rolled and baked pizzas (their speciality, in slices or pies) will draw you inside, where you'll find freezers of ready-to-heat pastas, and coolers of soft, delicious linguines plus awesome imported parmesan and other cheeses, all across from a deli case of carpaccio, salamis, hams and, last but certainly not least, olives. And don't overlook the wine selection.

Whole Foods

1440 P Street, NW, between 14th & 15th Streets, Logan Circle (1-202 332 4300, www.wholefoods market.com). Dupont Circle Metro. **Open** 8am-10.30pm daily. **Credit** AmEx, Disc, MC, V. **Map** p250 H4.

Besides its piles of organic produce, mountains of granola and organically raised meats, this wonderful store has an excellent stock of wines, cheeses, antipasti and other grown-up finger foods. Though the store as a whole can be expensive, the wines are available in all price ranges. And if you buy a case there's 10% off.

Other locations 4530 Tenley Circle, ` NW, Tenleytown (1-202 237 5800); George Washington University, 2201 I Street, Foggy Bottom (1-202 296 1660).

GALLERIES

Logan Circle, the heart of the city's commercial gallery scene, shows the most refreshing art the city has to offer and should be the first stop on any aficionado's tour. **H Street, NE**, sometimes known as the Atlas District, plays host to just a handful of galleries, but they're very good ones, taking advantage of the larger, cheaper spaces available. **Dupont Circle** once boasted a dense gallery concentration but the few galleries that remain tend toward local artists of middling repute. Like Dupont, the Downtown 7th Street Corridor in **Penn Quarter** was once home to both galleries and artists, but the area's soaring property prices meant the area became prohibitively expensive for most resident artists. Still, several art spaces here should not be missed.

Civilian Art Projects

1019 7th Street, NW, between L Street & New York Avenue, Downtown (1-202 607 3804, www.civilianartprojects.com). Mount Vernon Square/7th Street-Convention Center Metro. **Open** 1-6pm Wed, Thur, Sat; 4-8pm Fri. **No credit cards. Map** p251/p253 J5.

Civilian is run by a young, smart curator with ties to the city's DIY music scene. Exhibits here won't ever bore, and they sometimes spotlight younger artists still finding their way.

★ Conner Contemporary Art

1358 Florida Avenue, NE, between Orren & Staples Streets, H Street Corridor (1-202 588 8750, www.connercontemporary.com). Gallery Place-Chinatown Metro then X2 bus. **Open** 10am-5pm Tue-Sat. **Credit** AmEx, DC, MC, V. **Map** p248 M5.

Since Leigh Conner and Jamie Smith opened their gallery in 1999, they have been showing prints, photographs, paintings and sculptures by the kind of cutting-edge artists Washingtonians usually travel to New York to see. The pair's expansive gallery on Florida Avenue, NE, is unrivalled in DC – the massive, flexible space has played host to Leo Villareal (whose LED-based light sculpture *Multiverse* is in the National Gallery of Art's collection) and video artist Federico Solmi. Strong shows by DC's younger artists have been well received.

Curator's Office

Suite 201, 1515 14th Street, NW, at Church Street, Logan Circle (1-202 387 1008, www.curatorsoffice.com). Dupont Circle or Shaw-Howard University Metro. **Open** noon-6pm Wed-Sat, and by appointment. **No credit cards. Map** p250 H4.

This tiny gallery might only be the size of most people's closets but it has an impact many times its dimensions. The curator is Andrea Pollan and this is indeed her office. It's also where sharp Washington artists such as Jason Horowitz and Victoria Gaitan exhibit. In recent years Pollan has stepped up her roster of rising international artists.

★ David Adamson Gallery

Suite 202, 1515 14th Street, NW, at P Street, Logan Circle (1-202 232 0707, http://adamson gallery.jimdo.com/gallery). Dupont Circle or Shaw-Howard University Metro. **Open** 11.30am-5pm Tue-Fri; noon-5pm Sat. **Credit** MC, V. **Map** p250 H4.

A longtime Downtown favourite, David Adamson Gallery decamped to Logan during the great gallery exodus of 2004. Now a stand-alone exhibition space that's separate from its internationally recognised printmaking studio, the gallery continues to exhibit the fruits of its printmaking collaborations with contemporary art heavyweights such as Renate Aller and Chuck Close. One of Washington's blue chip spaces.

G Fine Art

1250 Florida Avenue, NE, between Montello & Trinidad Avenues, H Street Corridor (1-202 462 1601, www.gfineartdc.com). Gallery Place-Chinatown Metro then X2 bus. **Open** noon-6pm Wed-Sat. **Credit** AmEx, MC, V. **Map** p248 M5.

Annie Gawlak left her impressive Logan Circle space for a hole-in-the-wall space near power dealer Leigh Conner. G's programme is international but also features Washington-based stars Dan Steinhilber and Iona Rozeal Brown.

CONSUME

Gallery 10 Ltd

*1519 Connecticut Avenue, NW, at Q Street,
Dupont Circle (1-202 232 3326, www.gallery
10dc.com). Dupont Circle Metro.* **Open** 11am-
5pm Wed-Sat. **Credit** MC, V. **Map** p250 G4.
Many of the District's most respected artists jump-
started careers with shows at Gallery 10. Now the
place shows an older generation of Washington
artists whose exhibitions vary from undisciplined
to cohesive – you never know what you'll get.

Gallery at Flashpoint

*916 G Street, NW, between 9th & 10th Streets,
Downtown (1-202 315 1305, www.culturaldc.org).
Gallery Place-Chinatown Metro.* **Open** noon-6pm
Tue-Sat, and by appointment. **Credit** MC, V.
Map p253 J6.
Gallery at Flashpoint occupies a multi-arts complex
sponsored by the city's Cultural Development
Corporation. Though the exhibitions vary widely,
the programming is getting better with age and
can be relied upon to favour young up-and-comers.
The complex also houses a blackbox theatre and
dance studio.

Hemphill Fine Arts

*1515 14th Street, NW, Suite 300, at Church
Street, Logan Circle (1-202 234 5601, www.
hemphillfinearts.com). Dupont Circle or Shaw-
Howard University Metro.* **Open** 10am-5pm
Tue-Sat, and by appointment. **Credit** MC, V.
Map p250 H4.
George Hemphill's contemporary art gallery plays
host to many of Washington's strongest, and safest,
artists. Occasional group shows add depty to the
regular parade of solo exhibitions.

Hillyer Art Space at International Art & Artists

*2nd floor, 9 Hillyer Court, NW, off 21st Street,
between Q & R Streets, Dupont Circle (1-202
338 0680, www.artsandartists.org). Dupont
Circle Metro.* **Open** noon-6pm Tue-Fri; noon-
5pm Sat, and by appointment. **No credit cards**.
Map p250 G4.
A handsome gallery space inside the headquarters
of a company that organises travelling art exhibitions. The programme juxtaposes Washington-
based and international artists.

★ Industry Gallery

*Suite 200, 2nd floor, 1358 Florida Avenue,
NE, between Orren & Staples Streets, H Street
Corridor (1-202 399 1730, www.industrygallery
dc.com). Gallery Place-Chinatown Metro then X2
bus.* **Open** noon-6pm Wed-Sat; by appointment
Tue-Sun. **Credit** AmEx, MC, V. **Map** p248 M5x.
Industry is Washington, DC's only avant-garde
design gallery. International artists creating func-
tional art out of industrial materials are a speciality
here. Among the names who've shown here are

Italian designer Antonio Pio Saracino and Dutch
artists Tejo Remy and Rene Veenhuizen.

Marsha Mateyka Gallery

*2012 R Street, NW, between Connecticut Avenue
& 21st Street, Dupont Circle (1-202 328 0088,
www.marshamateykagallery.com). Dupont Circle
Metro.* **Open** 11am-5pm Wed-Sat, and by
appointment. Closed Aug. **Credit** MC, V.
Map p250 G4.
Marsha Mateyka Gallery exhibits painting, sculpture and works on paper by established contemporary American and European artists. Past
highlights have included museum-quality paintings by Sam Gilliam and Nathan Oliveira. The late
19th-century brownstone's interior features spectacular cherrywood fireplaces, wainscoting and
carved wood transoms.

Project 4

*3rd floor, 1353 U Street, NW, at 14th Street,
Logan Circle (1-202 232 4340, www.project4
gallery.com). U-Street/African-American Civil
War Memorial/Cardozo Metro.* **Open** noon-6pm
Wed-Sat, and by appointment. **No credit cards**.
Map p251 J3.
Four friends, two of them architects, founded Project
4, at a time when the U Street restaurant and shopping scene was just beginning to take hold. Their
current, third-floor location feels more like a shiny
new condominium than a gallery. Selections may
vary in quality, and they tend to feature young
up-and-comers.

GIFTS, STATIONERY & SOUVENIRS

A Little Shop of Flowers

*2421 18th Street, NW, between Belmont
& Columbia Roads, Adams Morgan (1-202
387 7255, www.alittleshopofflowers-dc.com).
Woodley Park-Zoo/Adams Morgan Metro
then 96 bus.* **Open** 9am-7pm Mon-Sat; noon-5pm
Sun. Closed Aug. **Credit** AmEx, Disc, MC, V.
Map p250 G3.
Stop in for sunflowers or alstromeria to freshen
your room, or order an arrangement of any size for
a friend. Little Shop of Flowers is a florist of the
more traditional and formal kind.

A Mano

*1677 Wisconsin Avenue, NW, at Reservoir Road,
Georgetown (1-202 298 7200, www.amano.bz).
Foggy Bottom-GWU Metro then 32, 36 bus or
Georgetown Circulator bus.* **Open** 10am-6pm
Mon-Sat; noon-5pm Sun. **Credit** AmEx, MC, V.
Map p249 E4.
Welcome to a world of handmade (hence the name)
quality gifts, especially tableware, and corporate
gifts too. Sourced from all over the world but defi-
nitely not 'ethnic'.

Allan Woods Florist

2645 Connecticut Avenue, NW, at 26th Street, Woodley Park (1-202 332 3334, www.allan woods.com). Woodley Park-Zoo/Adams Morgan Metro. **Open** 9am-7pm Mon-Fri; 9am-6pm Sat. **Credit** AmEx, Disc, MC, V.

Fresh, seasonal favourites abound at this shop – hydrangeas, peonies, lilies and lilacs in spring and summer and a parade of poinsettias at Christmas – alongside a deluge of cut flowers.

Appalachian Spring

1415 Wisconsin Avenue, NW, at P Street, Georgetown (1-202 337 5780, www.appalachian spring.com). Foggy Bottom-GWU Metro then 32, 36 bus or Georgetown Circulator bus. **Open** 10am-6pm Mon-Sat; noon-6pm Sun. **Credit** AmEx, MC, V. **Map** p249 E4.

Why buy household gifts at the national chains when you can find wonderful handmade ceramics, carved-wood items, blankets and jewellery at this North American crafts boutique? Lead-free pewter ware harks back to the Founding Fathers, while iridescent 'fire and light' glass bowls in exquisite colours have a very contemporary look. The master glass blowers whose work is found here have helped define the contemporary American art glass movement. A range of handbags and other is accessories is also in store.

Other location East Hall, Union Station, 50 Massachusetts Avenue, NE (1-202 682 0505).

★ Copenhaver

1301 Connecticut Avenue, NW, between Dupont Circle & N Street, Dupont Circle (1-202 232 1200). Dupont Circle Metro. **Open** 9.30am-5.30pm Mon-Fri; 10am-4pm Sat. **Credit** AmEx, Disc, MC, V. **Map** p250 G4.

The decorous wooden shelves of Copenhaver hold what many would call the city's finest selection of stationery: there's Crane paper of all descriptions, Vera Wang and Martha Stewart invitations, and insanely expensive letterpress notecards. If you're looking for sombre double-folds for condolence letters or suitable cotton paper on which to print your dissertation, this is your place. Come December, there's a lovely selection of holiday cards, along with proper red-bordered foldovers with lined envelopes for your Christmas letters. Staff will engrave your wedding invitations too. Service is personal and exceptional.

Ginza

1721 Connecticut Avenue, NW, between R & S Streets, Dupont Circle (1-202 332 7000, www.ginzaonline.com). Dupont Circle Metro. **Open** 11am-7pm Mon-Sat; noon-6pm Sun. **Credit** AmEx, Disc, MC, V. **Map** p250 G4.

Did you leave your heart in Tokyo? This intimate but comprehensive shop sells Japanese household items such as elegant saké sets, dinnerware and ikebana vases plus specialities such as origami paper, kimonos and Japanese snacks.

Copenhaver.

Phoenix.

People drop in to Pulp for an ironic-chic greeting card and find themselves picking up things they didn't know they needed: the place has candles, masks, toys, and all manner of gag gifts for the hipsters and sophisticates who frequent the store's lively neighbourhood. The paper goods are excellent: not just occasion cards but boxes of fine-quality cotton notes, plus gorgeous wrapping paper by the sheet – and fancy ribbons to go with them. Friends having a baby? No problem. Need a present for more mature sensibilities? Pulp's got you covered.

HEALTH & BEAUTY
Spas & salons

Aveda
1325 Wisconsin Avenue, NW, between N & Dumbarton Streets, Georgetown (1-202 965 1325, www.avedageorgetown.com). Foggy Bottom-GWU Metro then 32, 36 bus or Georgetown Circulator bus. **Open** 10am-7pm Mon, Sun; 9am-8pm Tue; 9am-9pm Wed; 9am-8pm Thur; 8.30am-7pm Fri, Sat. **Credit** AmEx, MC, V. **Map** p249 E4.
Disappear into this well-regarded salon and spa to treat your scalp, wax your brows, have a massage (hot stones optional), or reward your tired feet. **Other locations** throughout the city.

Blue Mercury
3059 M Street, NW, between 30th & 31st Streets, Georgetown (1-202 965 1300, www. bluemercury.com). Foggy Bottom-GWU Metro then 32, 36 bus or Georgetown Circulator bus. **Open** 10am-8pm Mon-Sat; 11am-6pm Sun. **Credit** AmEx, Disc, MC, V. **Map** p249 E5.
Try the wide range of body treatments, then browse through the fine selection of cosmetics, fragrances and moisturisers, including Acqua di Parma and Bumble & Bumble, and take some nirvana home. **Other locations** throughout the city.

Celadon
1180 F Street, NW, between 11th & 12th Streets, Downtown (1-202 347 3333, http://shop.celadon spa.com/store). Metro Center Metro. **Open** 8.30am-6pm Mon, Wed, Fri; 8.30am-7pm Tue, Thur; 8.30am-4.30pm Sat. **Credit** AmEx, Disc, MC, V. **Map** p252 J6.
Downtown's workaholics defuse their tensions at this subdued salon and spa, and often leave with a bag of beauty and skincare products for carrying on the good work at home.

Grooming Lounge
1745 L Street, NW, between Connecticut Avenue & 18th Street, Downtown (1-202 466 8900, www.groominglounge.com). Farragut North Metro. **Open** 9am-7pm Mon-Fri; 9am-6pm Sat; 10am-5pm Sun. **Credit** AmEx, MC, V. **Map** p252 G5.

★ Phoenix
1514 Wisconsin Avenue, NW, between P Street & Volta Place, Georgetown (1-202 338 4404, www.thephoenixdc.com). Foggy Bottom-GWU Metro then 32, 36 bus or Georgetown Circulator bus. **Open** 10am-6pm Mon-Sat; 1-6pm Sun. **Credit** AmEx, Disc, MC, V. **Map** p249 E4.
This family-owned Georgetown institution offers affordable designer jewellery and comfortable clothes for women, as well as sought-after Mexican imports – Day of the Dead figurines, *alebrijes* (colourful, fanciful animals) and antique silver. There is a wide selection of separates from the likes of Eileen Fisher, Cut Loose and White + Warren. Semi-precious-bead necklaces and earrings dominate the numerous trinket cases, culled from the collections of local and international jewellery artists. Latico, Ellington and Carla Mancini bags and versatile knit dresses round out the wardrobe offerings.

★ Pulp
1803 14th Street, NW, between S & Swann Streets, U Street Corridor (1-202 462 7857, www.pulpdc.com). U Street/African-American Civil War Memorial/Cardozo Metro. **Open** 11am-7pm Mon-Sat; 11am-5pm Sun. **Credit** AmEx, Disc, MC, V. **Map** p250 H3.

CONSUME

Men finally have a place to call their own in DC. This modern retreat with an old barber shop mood offers haircuts, hot shaves, facials and nail care, plus product lines by Anthony, Dermalogica and Jack Black.

Ilo

1637 Wisconsin Avenue, NW, between Q Street & Reservoir Road, Georgetown (1-202 342 0350, www.salonilo.com). Foggy Bottom-GWU Metro then 32, 36 bus or Georgetown Circulator bus. **Open** 10am-6pm Mon, Tue, Wed, Fri; 10am-7pm Thur; 9am-5pm Sat. **Credit** AmEx, MC, V. **Map** p249 E4.

In town to accept an award and – gasp! – not looking your best after the red-eye flight? Don't panic. This spa offers traditional services, plus laser hair removal, microdermabrasion and botox to prepare you for your close-up. And it works just as well if you need to make a presentation in front of important new clients.

Splash at the Sports Club/LA

Ritz Carlton Hotel, 1170 22nd Street, NW, at M Street, Foggy Bottom (1-202 974 6600, www.mpsportsclub.com/clubs/washington-dc). Foggy Bottom-GWU or Dupont Circle Metro. **Open** 5.30am-10.30pm Mon-Thur; 5.30am-10pm Fri; 8am-8pm Sat, Sun. **Credit** AmEx, Disc, MC, V. **Map** p250 G5.

Athletes and actors have been spotted at this plush spa, checking in for facials, massages, body treatments, waxing and the like. No doubt their wallets are lighter upon leaving.

Hairdressers & barbers

Axis

1509 Connecticut Avenue, NW, between Dupont Circle & Q Street, Dupont Circle (1-202 234 1166, www.axissalon.com). Dupont Circle Metro. **Open** 9am-7.30pm Tue-Fri; 9am-5pm Sat; 11am-5pm Sun. **Credit** AmEx, MC, V. **Map** p250 G4.

Prices may rise, but those in need of a cut or a trim or eyebrow expertise keep coming, attracted in part by the cheeky window displays and funky storefront.

Christophe

1125 18th Street, NW, between L & M Streets, Foggy Bottom (1-202 785 2222, www.christophe. com). Farragut North Metro. **Open** 8am-7pm Tue-Sat. **Credit** AmEx, MC, V. **Map** p252 G4. The Washington branch of the Beverly Hills salon. You know what to expect: good haircuts, at a price.

Evolve

2905 M Street, NW, between 29th & 30th Streets, Georgetown (1-202 333 9872). Foggy Bottom-GWU Metro then 32, 36 bus or Georgetown Circulator bus. **Open** 10am-6pm Wed-Sat. **Credit** AmEx, Disc, MC, V. **Map** p249 F5.

Two decades of keeping DC's ladies beautiful attests to the excellent standards of this salon, which also offers hair treatments and facials.

Ipsa

1629 Wisconsin Avenue, NW, between Q & R Streets, Georgetown (1-202 338 4100, www. ipsaforhair.com). Foggy Bottom-GWU Metro then 32, 36 bus or Georgetown Circulator bus. **Open** 8am-6pm Mon-Fri; 9am-5.30pm Sat. **Credit** Disc, MC, V. **Map** p249 E4.

A chilled atmosphere makes for a pleasant visit and a satisfying hair-do.

Roche

3000 K Street, NW, at Thomas Jefferson Street, Georgetown (1-202 775 0775, www.rochesalon. com). Foggy Bottom-GWU Metro then 32, 36 bus or Georgetown Circulator bus. **Open** 10am-7pm Tue-Fri; 8.30am-5pm Sat. **Credit** AmEx, MC, V. **Map** p249 F5.

Fashionistas know Roche because they see it written up in the glossies. With its poppy interior and cool attitude, it will send you out a changed person – and for the better, at least in externals.

Other location 1624 I Street, NW, at 17th Street, Downtown (1-202 887-8150).

Pharmacies

CVS

6-7 Dupont Circle, NW, between Massachusetts & New Hampshire Avenues, Dupont Circle (1-202 833 5704, www.cvs.com). Dupont Circle Metro. **Open** 24hrs daily. **Credit** AmEx, Disc, MC, V. **Map** p250 G4.

Locals have a love-hate affair with this chain drugstore. It carries just about anything you'd need at 2am, but some of the staff can be a bit clueless. **Other locations** throughout the city.

Shops

Sephora

3065 M Street, NW, between 30th & 31st Streets, Georgetown (1-202 338 5644, www.sephora.com). Foggy Bottom-GWU Metro then 32, 36 bus or Georgetown Circulator bus. **Open** 10am-9pm Mon-Sat; noon-6pm Sun. **Credit** AmEx, Disc, MC, V. **Map** p249 E5.

The celebrated French chain is a beauty junkie's paradise, with skincare, cosmetics and designer scents for both men and women.

HOUSE & HOME
Antiques

Most of the fancier antiques stores are in Georgetown; they're ideal for browsing, though pieces are inevitably pricey.

Goodwood

1428 U Street, NW, U Street Corridor (1-202 986 3640, www.goodwooddc.com). U Street/African-American Civil War Memorial/Cardozo Metro. **Open** noon-7pm Mon-Fri; noon-5pm Sun. **Credit** AmEx, MC, V. **Map** p250 H3.

Scouting the best auctions in the mid-Atlantic, Goodwood brings in amazing wood tables, armoires, bookcases and mirrors, plus ornamental follies you won't find elsewhere for the prices. Go Thursday evening for the picks of the week.

Miss Pixie's

1626 14th Street, NW, between R & Corcoran Streets, Logan Circle (1-202 232 8171, www. misspixies.com). U Street/African-American Civil War Memorial/Cardozo Metro. **Open** 11am-7pm daily. **Credit** AmEx, Disc, MC, V. **Map** p250 H4.

Miss Pixie's brings in country and vintage furnishings at very reasonable prices. Take home a porch rocker, a 1950s sofa or cool garden ornaments.

General

Contemporaria

3303 Cady's Alley, NW, M Street, between 33rd & 34th Streets, Georgetown (1-202 338 0193, www.contemporaria.com). Foggy Bottom-GWU Metro then 32, 36 bus, or Georgetown Circulator bus. **Open** 10am-6pm Mon-Fri; 11am-6pm Sat; noon-5pm Sun. **Credit** AmEx, MC, V. **Map** p249 E5.

Cruise down the curved concrete ramp to enter a minimalist world of Kartell chairs, Cappellini wall systems and Minotti sofas. The owner is a Peruvian architect but most of the furniture design is Italian. Less is more, particularly when you come to paying the bill.

Home Rule

1807 14th Street, NW, at S Street, U Street Corridor (1-202 797 5544, www.homerule.com). U Street/African-American Civil War Memorial/Cardozo Metro. **Open** 11am-7pm Mon-Sat; noon-5.30pm Sun. **Credit** AmEx, Disc, MC, V. **Map** p250 H4.

In this arresting little shop the walls are lined with the latest kitchen utensils, desk supplies, incredible soaps and lotions, and tons of stocking fillers. It also has a 'made in the USA' selection, doing its bit to support the economy.

Homebody

715 8th Street, SE, between G & I Streets, Capitol Hill (1-202 544 8445, www.homebodydc.com). Eastern Market Metro. **Open** 11am-7pm Mon-Sat; noon-6pm Sun. **Credit** AmEx, Disc, MC, V. **Map** p253 M8.

Housewares, barware and gifts, with an emphasis on the modern and the green. Saloom and Bontempi

Casa furniture, Bodum and Bialetti coffee makers, and Chilewich table and floor mats are among the well-designed domestic pieces on offer. Recycled materials are everywhere: a local artist's Calder-like mobiles with found-glass pendants share space with Italian regenerated-leather wallets and bags. Smaller souvenirs include house-brand scented candles and reasonably priced jewellery.

Illuminations

415 8th Street, NW, between D & E Streets, Penn Quarter (1-202 783 4888, www.illuminc.com). Archives-Navy Memorial Metro. **Open** 10am-6pm Mon-Fri; 11am-5pm Sat. **Credit** AmEx, MC, V. **Map** p253 J6.

Two showrooms display lighting from Artemide, Ingo Maurer, Flos and Neidhardt, among others. Illumination of the cleverest kind, hence much of it is concealed.

Other locations 3323 Cady's Alley, NW, Georgetown (1-202 965 4888).

★ Millennium Decorative Arts

1528 U Street, NW, between 15th & 16th Streets, U Street Corridor (1-202 483 1218, www.millenniumdecorativearts.com). U Street/African-American Civil War Memorial/Cardozo Metro. **Open** Mon-Thur by appointment; noon-6pm Fri-Sun. **Credit** AmEx, MC, V. **Map** p250 H3.

Stylish 1940s- to '60s-vintage European furniture is stocked at this two-level store, and you'll find graphic glassware, vases and coaster sets too.

Sur La Table

5211 Wisconsin Avenue, NW, between Ingomar & Harrison Streets, Chevy Chase, Upper Northwest (1-202 237 0375, www.surlatable.com). Friendship Heights Metro. **Open** 10am-8pm Mon-Sat; 11am-6pm Sun. **Credit** AmEx, Disc, MC, V.

Here you can find hand mixers in a rainbow of colours and all the kitchen gadgets you could possibly want – and some you had never dreamed of. Staff are knowledgeable and happy to help those uncertain of the utility of a rechargeable milk frother.

Tabletop

1608 20th Street, NW, between Q & R Streets, Dupont Circle (1-202 387 7117, www.tabletopdc.com). Dupont Circle Metro. **Open** noon-8pm Mon-Sat; noon-6pm Sun. **Credit** AmEx, Disc, MC, V. **Map** p250 G4.

The owners favour lesser-known designers and makers of playful, clean accessories, such as Klein Reid for vases and Panek Tobin for ceramics. These are sold alongside contemporary lighting and modern jewellery.

Vastu

1829 14th Street, NW, between S & T Streets, U Street Corridor (1-202 234 8344, www. vastudc.com). U Street/African-American Civil

CONSUME

War Memorial/Cardozo Metro. **Open** 11am-7pm Mon-Sat; noon-5pm Sun. **Credit** AmEx, DC, Disc, MC, V. **Map** p250 H3.

Unifying this store is the warm modernism of Steven Anthony upholstered furniture, tables and cabinets by escribaStudio of Brazil, and Babette Holland spun-metal lamps. Vastu also sells Knoll furniture. The cool minimalism of a living room can always be made more cosy with the mobile steel and perspex ecosmart fireplaces, which burn like an eternal flame.

MUSIC

Crooked Beat Records

2116 18th Street, NW, between Belmont & Kalorama roads, Adams Morgan (1-202 483 2328, www.crookedbeat.com). Woodley Park-Zoo/Adams Morgan Metro, then 96 bus. **Open** 1.30-8pm Mon; noon-9pm Tue-Sat; noon-7pm Sun. **Credit** MC, V. **Map** p250 G3.

Crooked Beat and sells in new and used vinyl, especially independent labels or obscure releases from major labels.

Smash Records

2314 18th Street NW, 2nd Floor, between Belmont & Kalorama roads, Adams Morgan (1-202 387 6274, www.smashrecords.com). Woodley Park-Zoo/Adams Morgan Metro, then 96 bus. **Open** noon-9pm Mon-Thur; noon-10pm Fri; 11am-10pm Sat; noon-7pm Sun. **Credit** MC, V. **Map** p250 G3.

Relocated to Adams Morgan from Georgetown a few years ago, Smash specialises in punk and alternative music CDs and vinyl. There's vintage and indie designer clothing too.

Som Records

1843 14th Street, NW, at T Street, U Street Corridor (1-202-328-3345, http://somrecords dc.com). U Street/African-American Civil War Memorial/Cardozo Metro. **Open** noon-9pm Mon-Sat; noon-7pm Sun. **Credit** MC, V. **Map** p250 H3.

You'll find an eclectic mix of music here, on vinyl, with some rare sounds thrown in. Genres include rock, soul, funk, disco, go-go, reggae, samba, salsa, folk, blues, punk and electronica.

SPORT

City Bikes

2501 Champlain Street, NW, at Euclid Street, Adams Morgan (1-202 265 1564, www.city bikes.com). Woodley Park-Zoo/Adams Morgan Metro then 90, 92, 96 bus. **Open** 10am-7pm Mon-Wed, Fri, Sat; 10am-9pm Thur; noon-6pm Sun. **Credit** MC, V. **Map** p250 G2.

Hardcore cyclists frequent City Bikes for its excellent bikes, parts and mechanics. More casual cyclists

show up to rent bicycles for a short ride. This shop (and website) is also a hub for a range of cycling activities; visitors to DC may want to take part. **Other locations** 709 8th Street, SE, Capitol Hill (1-202 688 2099).

Fleet Feet Sports

1841 Columbia Road, NW, between Biltmore Street & Mintwood Place, Adams Morgan (1-202 387 3888, www.fleetfeetdc.com). Woodley Park-Zoo/Adams Morgan Metro, then 96 bus. **Open** 10am-8pm Mon-Fri; 10am-7pm Sat; noon-4pm Sun. **Credit** AmEx, DC, Disc, MC, V. **Map** p250 G3.

Judging by the number of runners that hang around here at weekends, it would seem that athletes can't tear themselves away from the first-rate selection of well-priced shoes to actually go running. You'll find everything here from arch-supporting insoles and sports bras to mp3 players and of, course, the shoes.

Hudson Trail Outfitter

4530 Wisconsin Avenue, NW, at Brandywine Street, Tenleytown (1-202 363 9810, www.hudson trail.com). Tenleytown-AU Metro. **Open** 10am-9pm Mon-Sat; 11am-6pm Sun. **Credit** AmEx, Disc, MC, V.

Hudson Trail offers an extensive array of hiking clothes, shoes and gear, plus bicycles and stuff for climbing, kayaking, snow sports and fly-fishing. In fact, everything you'll need for the great outdoors.

Sports Zone

3140 M Street, NW, at Wisconsin Avenue, Georgetown (1-202 337 9773, www.sprtzone.com). Foggy Bottom-GWU Metro, then 32, 36 bus or Georgetown Circulator bus. **Open** 10am-9pm Mon-Thur; 10am-10pm Fri, Sat; 11am-7pm Sun. **Credit** AmEx, MC, V. **Map** p249 E5.

'Lifestyle' footwear' to get you out running on track or field or road by Ecko, Adidas and Avirex. Sporty but fashionable clothing to go with the shoes. **Other locations** throughout the city.

TICKETS

Tickets for many concerts and other events can often be obtained from the venues. The main booking agency is Ticketmaster (www.ticketmaster.com).

TRAVELLERS' NEEDS

For mobile phones, there are branches of Radio Shack and Best Buy throughout the city; check the Internet for your nearest. For computer repair, try Geeks In Minutes (1-202 629 9804, www.computerrepair.washington.com). Luggage can be bought at most department stores and malls (*see pp115-117*).

Hotels

Hallowed halls and designer gems.

Change has been the buzzword in Washington for the last few years, but it's more than a political mantra. It's indicative of what's been happening throughout the city – and its hotels. That's not to say you won't find those dark, wood-panelled spots with power players wheeling and dealing that DC is known for. Those places still exist, but even some of these, like the historic Hay-Adams (*see p135*) and the grand old Jefferson (*see p142*), have received a makeover in recent years.

Washington has plenty to offer in contemporary hotels too. The W (*see p136*) stamped its own very particular personality on an old Downtown landmark hotel a few years ago now. Among other notable properties, Donovan House (*see p143*) attracts revellers as well as residents to its popular rooftop bar and pool. Indeed, rooftop bars have become quite the thing in DC. New luxury hotel the Capella (*see p150*) has one, with an infinity pool, as does fellow new Georgetown hotel the boutiquey Graham (*see p152*) – although in this case without the pool.

RATES & SERVICES

Except in the smallest hotels, there is no such thing as a fixed rate in Washington. Because many visitors swoop into town on business and leave by the weekend, rooms cost much more from Monday to Friday. All in all, rates vary according to the time of year, the day of the week and what discounts you can wangle. Rates change often and, in addition, it is often possible to find deals and special offers, especially at weekends.

Rates decrease during summer – when locals flee the humidity and visitors decide not to brave the conditions in large numbers – and are rock-bottom around Christmas. They are at their highest in spring, when DC sees an influx of school groups and cherry-blossom gazers; early autumn is another busy time. Bear in mind that taxes are added to prices quoted. In DC this is sales tax of six per cent, plus hotel tax of 14.5 per cent. This adds quite a chunk to any hotel bill.

> **❶** Red numbers given in this chapter correspond to the location of each hotel as marked on the street maps. *See pp248-53.*

You can find lower rates at many DC hotels through websites such as www.expedia.com, or DC-specific site Capitol Reservations (www.capitolreservations.com), although many hotels guarantee that the lowest prices appear on their websites.

As a guide to our price categories, you might find a $250 bargain for a double room at a hotel in the **Deluxe** band, but you'll usually pay $350-$1,000 (plus). **Expensive** hotels run from around $180 to $450 per night. **Moderate** covers a range of around $120 to $250. **Budget** prices are from around $30 for a dorm room to $150 for a private room with bath.

In a town where the term 'presidential suite' might mean just that, there are only a handful of really low-budget options. DC has no campsites or RV/caravan sites. And there is only one official youth hostel in town (**Hostelling International Washington, DC**, *see p145*), but thankfully it's a very good one.

THE WHITE HOUSE & AROUND

Deluxe

Hay-Adams Hotel

1 Lafayette Square, NW, at 16th & H Streets, DC 20006 (1-202 638 6600, www.hayadams.com).

CONSUME

W.

Farragut North or McPherson Square Metro.
Rooms 145. **Credit** AmEx, Disc, MC, V.
Map p250/p252 H5 ❶

This grande dame across from Lafayette Square received a subtle makeover a few years ago to add more contemporary touches to its early 20th-century core. Guest rooms now include in-room safes large enough for laptops and Bose Wave systems with iPod capability. The renovations, which also include a modernised business centre and new fitness room, manage to update the hotel without taking away from its elegant, old-fashioned feel. To really drink in that clubby Washington feel, stop into the hotel's basement bar.
Bar. Business centre. Concierge. Disabled-adapted rooms. Gym. Internet (free wireless). Parking ($45 valet per day). Restaurant. Room service. TV (pay movies, DVD players on request).

★ W
515 15th Street, NW, at F Street, DC, 20004 (1-202 661 2400, www.washingtondc.com). Metro Center or McPherson Square Metro. **Rooms** 317. **Credit** AmEx, Disc, MC, V. **Map** p252 H6 ❷

The venerable old Hotel Washington has had the W treatment, and it's every bit as fabulous as you might imagine. Key historical fittings remain in the lobby, like the old check-in/cash desk, original stucco and chandeliers, incorporated into a reborn and slightly fantastical 'living room'. There's a touch of *Alice in Wonderland* in the check-in desks that are upside- down tables and the big chairs on small rugs. There's a riff on buttoned-down DC masculine power going on, too, with clubby pin-striped chairs meeting their match in hot-red vinyl couches, while big black lamps drip with crystal drops. Upstairs, rooms and suites have all the style and comfort you would expect. For something truly spectacular, the Extreme Wow Suite channels the Oval Office with curved walls and strong, masculine colours, while the Marvelous Suite has an ethereal palette of pales. All rooms have waterfall showers, and iPod docks are among the amenities.

The Bliss spa is, well, blissful, and Jean-Georges Vongerichten's J&G Steakhouse, with chef Philippe Reininger at the helm, delivers a melding of classic steak and fish and clean, modish flavours in surroundings of simple elegance. (Michelle Obama has eaten here with friends.)
Bars (2). Business centre. Concierge. Gym. Disabled-adapted rooms. Internet (wireless, $14.95 per day). Parking ($25 per day). Restaurant. Room service. Spa. TV (pay movies).
▶ *For a review of POV rooftop bar, see p106.*

Moderate

JW Marriott
1331 Pennsylvania Avenue, NW, at 14th Street, DC 20004 (reservations 1-800 393 250, hotel direct 1-202 393 2000, www.marriott.com). Metro Center Metro. **Rooms** 737. **Credit** AmEx, Disc, MC, V. **Map** p252 H6 ❸

Located on Pennsylvania Avenue near the White House, National Mall and the theatres, the JW Marriott sits on a prime location. For a view of the Washington Monument ask for a room facing Pennsylvania Avenue between the third and 15th floors. Those on the seventh and 12th floors have balconies as well. Beyond the fantastic real estate, the hotel recently underwent a $40-million renovation that provided several technological upgrades including a plug-in panel that lets guests split the TV screen so they can check email and watch TV.
Bars (2). Business centre. Concierge. Disabled-adapted rooms. Gym. Internet (wireless, $12.95 per day). Parking ($49.56 valet per day). Restaurants (2). Room service. TV (pay movies, DVD players on request). Spa. Swimming pool (indoor).

★ Sofitel Lafayette Square
806 15th Street, NW, at 16th & H Streets, DC 20005 (1-202 730 8800, www.sofitel.com). McPherson Square Metro. **Rooms** 237. **Credit** AmEx, Disc, MC, V. **Map** p250/p252 H5 ❹

From the outside, the Sofitel looks like a typical big-city American hotel, but there's a clue to some subtle differences: a French flag flying alongside the Stars and Stripes. Inside, contemporary artworks lift the traditional look of the wood-panelled lobby. Rooms also have good, vibrant pictures livening up neutral, comfortable, upscale decor and furnishings. European-style duvets are a welcome continental touch. TVs are high-definition, and marble bathrooms have separate bathtubs and glass-enclosed showers. There's more French influence in the ICI Urban Bistro, where morning coffee comes in a French press (cafetière), and breakfast orders come with a croissant and a pain au chocolat as well as bread. Both the sophisticated Le Bar and the bistro have outside space, which is at a premium in this area. Many of the staff are French too. Vive la différence!

Bar. Business centre. Concierge. Gym. Disabled-adapted rooms. Internet (free wireless, one-time charge of $14.95). Parking ($43 valet per day). Restaurant. Room service. TV (pay movies).

THE CAPITOL & AROUND
Moderate

Hyatt Regency Washington on Capitol Hill

400 New Jersey Avenue, between D & E Streets, DC 20001 (1-202 737 1234, http://washington regency.hyatt.com). **Rooms** 834. **Credit** AmEx, Disc, MC, V. **Map** p253 K6 ⑤

A hotel on a grand scale, guests take an escalator down to the lower-level entrance lobby, which is actually more like a small village, with enough check-in desks for an airline, a comfortable lounge and bar, and

a restaurant space behind a low barrier. Off this expansive open-plan area are facilities including shops, a shoeshine area and a Fed-Ex office. The Hyatt Capitol Hill is the sister hotel of the more styled and expensive Park Hyatt (*see p141*). This one can't be beaten for location, however – it's right beside the Capitol – and its rooms are comfortable, done out in neutral colours and equipped with iPod docking stations. The club floor allows access to a lounge with complimentary continental breakfast and snacks through much of the day. *Photo p138.*

Bar. Business centre. Concierge. Disabled-adapted rooms. Gym. Internet (wireless, $10.99 per day, $14.95 per day premium service). Parking ($48 valet per day). Restaurant. Room service. TV (pay movies).

★ Liaison Affinia

415 New Jersey Avenue, NW, between D & E Streets, DC 20001 (reservations 1-800 638 1116, hotel direct 1-202 638 1616, www.affinia.com). Union Station Metro. **Credit** AmEx, Disc, MC, V. **Rooms** 343. **Map** p253 K6 ⑥

Sofitel Lafayette Square.

Hyatt Regency Washington on Capitol Hill. *See p137.*

Just blocks from the Capitol and Union Station, this former Holiday Inn was transformed into an Affinia hotel, complete with contemporary rooms and the chain's pillow menu. During the summer the rooftop swimming pool and sundeck offer up sweeping views of the city's skyline. Downstairs is Art and Soul, a Southern-food restaurant by Oprah favourite Art Smith.

Bar. Business centre. Concierge, Disabled-adapted rooms. Gym. Internet (wireless, $13 per day). TV (pay movies, DVD player on request).

UNION STATION & AROUND

Expensive

Hotel George
15 E Street, NW, between New Jersey Avenue & North Capitol Street, DC 20001 (reservations 1-800 546 7866, hotel direct 1-202 347 4200, www.hotelgeorge.com). Union Station Metro. **Rooms** 139. **Credit** AmEx, DC, Disc, MC, V. **Map** p253 K6 **7**

The first Kimpton Group property in DC, the George sets the bar high. From the sleek and airy lobby in light sandstone with grand piano to the hip, buzzy bar and excellent restaurant-bistro Bis, it succeeds in creating an urban brand of style. Rooms are generously sized and decorated with refreshing restraint and style – not a floral in sight, and the only flourish is a Warhol-like print of a dollar bill. The gym features high-tech equipment and steam rooms.

Bar. Business centre. Disabled: adapted rooms. Gym. Internet (wireless, free to Kimpton In Touch members – can sign up when a guest). Parking ($45 valet per day). Restaurant. Room service. TV (pay movies).

Moderate

Phoenix Park Hotel
520 North Capitol Street, NW, at Massachusetts Avenue, DC 20001 (reservations 1-800 824 5419, hotel direct 1-202 638 6900, www.phoenixpark hotel.com). Union Station Metro. **Credit** AmEx, Disc, MC, V. **Rooms** 149. **Map** p253 K6 **8**

Despite its location just blocks from the Capitol, this hotel is more green than red, white and blue. Named after a park in Dublin, the Phoenix features standard-sized rooms decorated with Irish artwork and linens. The ground-floor Irish pub, the Dubliner, provides nightly entertainment, an outdoor patio and a welcoming atmosphere.

Bar. Business centre. Disabled-adapted rooms. Concierge. Gym. Internet (free wireless). Parking ($43.66 valet per day). Restaurant. Room service. TV (pay movies).

FEDERAL TRIANGLE

Deluxe

Willard InterContinental
1401 Pennsylvania Avenue, NW, at 14th Street, DC 20004 (reservations 1-800 327 0200, hotel direct 1-202 628 9100, http:// washington.intercontinental.com). Metro Center Metro. **Rooms** 375. **Credit** AmEx, Disc, MC, V. **Map** p252 H6 **9**

There is no DC hotel with more history than the Willard. The current building, completed in 1901, replaced the hotel's first incarnation; together they have hosted every president, either as a resident guest or at a social function, since Zachary Taylor in 1850. The old Willard played a particularly strong

CONSUME

role as a hub of political activity during the Civil War years. The current building closed during the mid 20th-century years of decline, reopening in 1986. The original, restored lobby is a real fin de siècle spectacle, with marble pillars, palms, and gilt-painted stucco on cornices and ceiling. Off the lobby is the iconic and aptly named Round Robin Bar, a real gentlemen's hangout. Follow the grand hallway called Peacock Alley, where tea is served, to learn more about the hotel's past in its History Gallery. Rooms are as comfortable, with furnishings as traditional as one would expect. The Jenny Lind suite has a round window beside the big tub in its bathroom; it catches the Washington Monument directly in its centre. The Café du Parc serves bistro-style cooking in an informal space.

The History Gallery is the hotel's own small museum, with over 100 artefacts and photos tracing the fortunes of the hotel and its many famous guests through the years. Among the collection are

the menu from Lincoln's inaugural lunch – corned beef and cabbage, mock turtle soup, parsley potatoes and blackberry pie – and the bill for his stay at the hotel; he and his family lived at the Willard for a month before moving into the White House. The stay cost $773.

Bar. Business centre. Concierge. Disabled-adapted rooms. Gym. Internet (free wireless). Parking ($42 valet per day). Restaurants (2). Room service. Spa. TV (pay movies).

▶ *For the Round Robin Bar, see p107.*

SOUTH OF THE MALL

Deluxe

L'Enfant Plaza Hotel
480 L'Enfant Plaza, SW, between D Street & Dwight Eisenhower Freeway, DC 20024 (reservations 1-800 635 5065, hotel direct

---

Hotels are Healthy

DC hotels can get you fit.

There's no excuse for being a slouch when you're staying in most Washington hotels. Gyms are pretty standard these days, but some hotels do a lot more to see that their guests keep fit. At the **W** (*see p136*), for instance, guests can work out on one of the cardio machines, use the free weights or strap on boxing gloves and go a few rounds on the heavy bag – and then relax with a massage afterwards.

Throughout the warmer months the **Liaison** (*see p137*) also offers free daily vinyasa-based yoga classes on its expansive rooftop. Yoga mats, bottled water and towels are provided.

Kimpton Group hotels, which include the **Palomar** (*see p146*), **George** (*see p138*) and **Monaco** (*see p142*), along with several others, offer in-room on-demand video workouts and provide yoga mats in rooms. There are in-room spa treatments, too, to help you recover from the exertion. Kimpton's **Topaz** (*see p148*) even offers energy drinks during a morning Power Hour.

The **Park Hyatt** (*see p141*) has a fitness centre with an indoor pool. And guests who want to get out and explore the city and its miles of park and bike trails can take advantage of the Bicycle Valet, which offers a free hybrid bike rental for adults and children. The rental includes a helmet, bike lock, bottled water and map of the area's trails.

The **Mandarin Oriental** (*see p140*), meanwhile, has some of the most extensive fitness facilities to be found in DC hotels, with a 1,400-square-foot gym that includes a heated indoor lap pool and sun deck. Personal training and private yoga classes in the garden are also available. The fitness centre also offers several unique sessions including a facial fitness programme that works to tighten the muscles in your face and neck, a pool-based workout and Cardio-Core-Combo, which incorporates hand-eye coordination, strength and flexibility through cardio drills.

Topaz.

CONSUME

1-202 484 1000, www.lenfantplazahotel.com).
L'Enfant Plaza Metro. **Rooms** 372. **Credit**
AmEx, Disc, MC, V. **Map** p252 J7
A large opulent hotel in an unusual south of the Mall
location that is close to the Capitol. There are great
views from the balconies but the business-heavy
area largely shuts down at night. That said, the hotel
goes out of its way to welcome families: children
under 18 stay in parents' rooms for free, and pets are
allowed in deluxe rooms only for a fee of $25.
Business travellers are also very well catered for,
and the seasonal, heated rooftop swimming pool is
perfect for downtime.
*Bar. Business centre. Concierge. Disabled-adapted
rooms (8). Gym. Internet (free wireless). Parking
($42 valet per day). Restaurant. Room service.
Swimming pool (outdoor). TV (pay movies).*

Mandarin Oriental

*1330 Maryland Avenue, SW, at 12th Street, DC
20004 (reservations 1-888 888 1778, hotel direct
1-202 554 8588, www.mandarinoriental.com/
washington). Smithsonian or L'Enfant Plaza
Metro.* **Credit** AmEx, Disc, MC, V. **Rooms** 415.
Map p252 H7 ⑪
Many Washingtonians raised an eyebrow when
the Mandarin chose a spot surrounded by government office buildings and a seafood market for its
400-room hotel. But managers at the international
chain saw potential in the site – which, in fairness,
is actually only a few blocks from the Mall and two
Metro stations – and went about proving that location isn't everything. The hotel is sumptuous in
every detail, from the gorgeous spa, indoor pool
and top-notch restaurant to the bed linens and

bathroom toiletries. Some rooms have views of
monuments and the Tidal Basin.
*Bar (lobby). Business centre. Concierge. Disabled-
adapted rooms. Gym. Internet (wireless, $14.95
per day, free for Fairmont Gold members).
Parking ($42 valet per day). Restaurant. Room
service (24hrs). Spa. Swimming pool (indoor).
TV (pay movies, DVD players on request).*

Expensive

Residence Inn by Marriott Capitol

*333 E Street, SW, between 3rd & 4th Streets,
DC 20024 (reservations 1-800 228 9290,
hotel direct 1-202 484 8280, www.capitol
marriott.com). Federal Center SW Metro.*
Rooms 233. **Credit** AmEx, Disc, MC, V.
Map p253 K7 ⑫
Opened in January 2005, the first Native American-
owned Marriott is located four blocks south of the
new National Museum of the American Indian and
was built with the same limestone exterior. Inside,
you'll find large suites with full kitchens (but unin-
spired decor) and good service. The hotel is especially family friendly; staff can configure four-
bedroom suites and there are books and games
available in the lobby. Ask for a room on one of the
upper floors to escape the noise from nearby train
tracks and construction. The surrounding area has
few restaurants, so unless you plan to cook, you'll
want to eat before returning to the hotel.
*Business centre (small). Disabled-adapted rooms.
Gym. Internet (free wireless). Parking ($30 per
day). Swimming pool (indoor). TV (pay movies,
DVD players on request).*

CONSUME

Jefferson. See p142.

FOGGY BOTTOM/WEST END

Deluxe

Park Hyatt

1201 24th Street, NW, at M Street, DC 20037 (reservations 1-800 233 1234, hotel direct 1-202 789 1234, www.parkwashington.hyatt.com). Foggy Bottom-GWU Metro. **Rooms** 216. **Credit** AmEx, Disc, MC, V. **Map** p250/p252 F5 ⓫

This luxurious hotel features spacious rooms with thick down duvets, Americana accents such as Shaker wooden boxes and coffee-table books on American culture, and all the most modern amenities. In the rooms and suites, a panel separating the bedroom and living area features a flatscreen TV on one side and a hand-carved chequerboard on the other, as well as spa-inspired bathrooms with large, sunken tubs. On the ground floor is the popular Blue Duck Tavern, which serves contemporary American fare. *Bar. Business centre. Concierge. Disabled-adapted rooms. Gym. Internet (free wireless). Parking ($41.50 valet per day). Restaurant. Room service. Spa. Swimming pool (indoor). TV (pay movies).*

★ Ritz-Carlton, Washington, DC

1150 22nd Street, NW, at M Street, DC 20037 (1-202 835 0500, www.ritzcarlton.com/hotels/ washington_dc). Foggy Bottom-GWU Metro. **Rooms** 300. **Credit** AmEx, Disc, MC, V. **Map** p250/p252 G5 ⓮

Both reassuringly traditional and warmly welcoming, the Ritz-Carlton is definitely a hotel for off-duty enjoyment as well as business stays. Mellow wood panelling greets guests in the public areas, along with careful attention to detail: apples on a platter just so, glorious flowers, and well-placed art and ceramics. Not to mention little touches to make you feel special, like hot apple cider and lemon cookies in the lobby on an autumn Sunday afternoon. Guestrooms are the supremely comfortable affairs that one would expect. Marble bathrooms have separate tubs and shower cubicles; there are iPod docks and HD TVs; furnishings have deco-esque touches. A stay on the club floor allows access to a lounge where complimentary drinks and snacks are served all day. The Westend Bistro (www.westend-bistrodc.com) is a lively, modern restaurant with a menu that mixes bistro classics with a robust, contemporary approach to local food and flavours. *Bar. Business centre. Concierge. Disabled-adapted rooms. Gym. Internet (wireless, $9.95 per day). Parking ($49 valet per day). Restaurant. Room service. Spa. Swimming pool (indoor). TV (pay movies, DVD players & game systems for rent).*

Expensive

Embassy Suites Hotel

1250 22nd Street, NW, at N Street, DC 20037 (reservations 1-800 362 2779, hotel direct 1-202 857 3388, www.embassysuites.com). Dupont Circle or Foggy Bottom Metro. **Credit** AmEx, Disc, MC, V. **Rooms** 318. **Map** p250/ p252 G4 ⓯

Yes, it's a generic chain hotel with identical twins in other cities. But the large, reasonably priced suites make this a good choice for families and business travellers who need room to spread out. The complimentary breakfast is cooked to order, and there's a daily cocktail reception. Plasma-screen TVs and the swimming pool and sauna will help you relax after a day of sightseeing or board meetings. *Bar. Business centre. Concierge. Disabled-adapted rooms. Gym. Internet (wireless, $12.95 per day). Parking ($40 per day). Restaurant. Room service. Swimming pool (indoor). TV (pay movies).*

Fairmont

2401 M Street, NW, at 24th Street, DC 20037 (reservations 1-866 540 4508, hotel direct 1-202 429 2400, www.fairmont.com/washington). Foggy Bottom-GWU Metro. **Rooms** 415. **Credit** AmEx, Disc, MC, V. **Map** p250/p252 F5 ⓰

The Fairmont's sunny, marble-floored lobby, so full of plants it looks like a greenhouse, instantly lifts the spirits. The pool, garden patio and 415 vast, bright rooms do the rest. The fitness centre offers up-to-date machines, a lap pool, squash and racquetball courts, aerobics classes and massages. Everyone, staff and guests alike, seems happy to find themselves here. Pets are also welcome, and owners can get advice on pet-friendly places to take them in DC. The Fairmont Gold, a 'hotel within a hotel', is a club floor with separate check-in, and free continental breakfast, afternoon tea and evening cocktails in the private lounge. *Bar (lobby). Business centre. Concierge. Disabled-adapted rooms. Gym. Internet (wireless, $14.95 per day, free for Fairmont Gold members). Parking ($45 per day). Restaurant. Room service (24hrs). Spa. Swimming pool (indoor). TV (pay movies, DVD player on request).*

River Inn

924 25th Street, NW, between I & K Streets, DC 20037 (reservations 1-888 874 0100, hotel direct 1-202 337 7600, www.theriverinn.com). Foggy Bottom-GWU Metro. **Credit** AmEx, Disc, MC, V. **Rooms** 125. **Map** p250/p252 F5 ⓱

Once a family-friendly lodging that drew primarily government and university types, the River Inn was reinvented as a boutique hotel a few years ago. It now exudes modern elegance, with dark wood and clean lines. The hotel pampers guests with plush robes, a video/CD library and in-room coffee makers; its restaurant, Dish, serves up nostalgic American food. The hotel also offers free bicycle rentals. *Bar. Business centre (small). Disabled-adapted rooms. Gym. Internet (free wireless). Parking ($34 valet per day). Restaurant. Room service. TV (pay movies, DVD players in some rooms).*

CONSUME

Moderate

Hotel Lombardy

2019 Pennsylvania Avenue, NW, at I Street, DC 20006 (reservations 1-800 424 5486, hotel direct 1-202 828 2600, www.hotellombardy.com). Foggy Bottom-GWU or Farragut West Metro. **Credit** AmEx, Disc, MC, V. **Rooms** 140. **Map** p250/p252 G5 ⑱

Formerly a grand apartment building, this 134-unit boutique hotel has managed to retain some of that charm, with old-fashioned touches such as brass fixtures and crystal doorknobs, and a Middle Eastern-style bar. The views over Pennsylvania Avenue are good, but try not to get stuck in a room at the back of the building. There's another old-fashioned touch in the shape of an attendant-operated elevator – when was the last time you saw that in a hotel? Access to the pool at the nearby Washington Plaza Hotel is included.
Bar. Concierge. Gym. Internet (free wireless). Parking ($36 per day). Restaurant. Room service. TV.

St Gregory Luxury Hotel & Suites

2033 M Street, NW, at 21st Street, DC 20036 (reservations 1-800 829 5034, hotel direct 1-202 530 3600, www.stgregoryhotelwdc.com). Dupont Circle or Foggy Bottom-GWU Metro. **Rooms** 154. **Credit** AmEx, Disc, MC, V. **Map** p250/p252 G5 ⑲

A whimsically stylish hotel – there's a life-sized statue of Marilyn in the lobby, skirt up – where each of the 154 rooms and suites look as if they were decorated by a pro. No expense has been spared with the floral displays and high-quality furniture. Many rooms also have full kitchens and some have balconies. The staff more than match the decor, treating everyone like VIPs. Stop by the hotel bar for a mojito during happy hour.
Bar. Business centre. Disabled-adapted rooms. Gym. Internet (wireless or wired, $12 per day). Parking ($35 valet per day). Room service. TV (pay movies, DVD players on request).

THE BEST HISTORIC HOTELS

Hay-Adams
A landmark 1927 Italian-Renaissance style building. *See p135.*

Jefferson
An imposing 1923 Beaux Arts building. *See p142.*

Willard InterContinental
Early 20th-century opulence reflects the optimism of the era. *See p138.*

DOWNTOWN
Expensive

Madison

1177 15th Street, NW, at M Street, DC 20005 (reservations 1-800 424 8577, hotel direct 1-202 862 1600, www.loewshotels.com). McPherson Square Metro. **Rooms** 363. **Credit** AmEx, Disc, MC, V. **Map** p250/p252 H5 ⑳

A Downtown hotel whose luxurious and very traditional feel – just as Founding Father James Madison would have wanted – makes it popular with visiting foreign dignitaries. One of its two restaurants, Palette, is sleek and modern – a departure from the rest of the hotel. The surrounding area is dominated by office buildings and is a little dull after dark, but you can easily walk to the livelier Dupont and Logan Circle neighbourhoods.
Bars (2). Business centre. Concierge. Disabled-adapted rooms. Gym (with steam room). Internet (free wireless). Parking ($50 valet per day). Restaurants (2). Room service. TV (pay movies, Sony PlayStations).

Jefferson

1200 16th Street, NW, at M Street, DC 20036 (1-202 448 2300, www.jeffersondc.com). Farragut North or Farragut West Metro. **Rooms** 99. **Credit** AmEx, Disc, MC, V. **Map** p250/p252 H5 ㉑

Just blocks from the White House, this Beaux Arts building reopened a couple of years ago after a two-year renovation that blends the modern – complimentary Wi-Fi – and the historic, with elegant nods to Thomas Jefferson. Four-poster beds have linens that feature the third president's Monticello home and grounds. Downstairs is a clubby bar, snug library and Plume, an upscale French restaurant nestled under the lobby's barrel-vaulted skylight. *Photo p140.*
Bars (2). Business centre. Concierge. Disabled adapted rooms. Gym (24hr). Internet (free wireless). Parking ($45 valet per day). Restaurants (2). Room service. Spa. TV (pay movies, DVD players on request).

★ Monaco

700 F Street, NW, at 7th Street, DC 20004 (reservations 1-800 649 1202, hotel direct 1-202 628 7177, www.monaco-dc.com). Gallery Place-Chinatown Metro. **Rooms** 183. **Credit** AmEx, Disc, MC, V. **Map** p253 J6 ㉒

The Monaco makes the most of its grand setting – an imposing neo-classical building that was once the main Post Office sorting office. The unusual premises mean irregular shapes, high ceilings and features such as cornicing add an extra touch of originality to the guestrooms, where dramatic furnishings such as black and white print headboards and curtains, with circles and stripes, add further individuality. It's not at the expense of comfort, however: furnishings are top of the range, bathrooms well appointed and rooms

CONSUME

Monaco.

come with CD players and HD TVs. The large lobby/lounge is a stunner: painted a vivid kelly green and furnished with statement pieces, some modern classics, others one-off whimsical designs, that come together to create a gracious whole. There's a complimentary wine hour in the evening. The Monaco is the flagship property of the Kimpton group, which has several hotels in DC and Northern Virginia. Its conversion into a hotel was one step in the process of the regeneration of Downtown.

Bar. Business centre. Concierge. Disabled-adapted rooms. Gym. Internet (wireless, free to Kimpton In Touch members – can sign up when a guest). Parking ($40 valet per day). Restaurant. Room service. TV (pay movies).

▶ *For a review of bar/restaurant Poste, see p108.*

Renaissance Mayflower

1127 Connecticut Avenue, NW, between L & M Streets, DC 20036 (reservations 1-800 228 9290, hotel direct 1-202 347 3000, www.renaissance hotels.com). Farragut North or West Metro. **Credit** *AmEx, Disc, MC, V.* **Map** *p250/p252 G5* ㉓

Near the Washington Convention Center and Verizon Center, this large hotel features 64,000sq ft of flexible function space, a 6,000sq ft fitness centre and a 4,000sq ft spa that offers a variety of therapeutic treatments. For a more intimate vibe, the lobby has several cosy spots where guests can hold small meetings or meet friends. Each of the unique seating areas offers free Wi-Fi and food and beverages.

Bars (2). Business centre. Concierge. Disabled-adapted rooms. Gym. Internet (wireless, wired $12.95 a day, premium $16.95 per day; free in suites). Parking ($46.50 per day). Restaurants (2). Room service. TV (pay movies).

Moderate

Comfort Inn Downtown/ Convention Center

1201 13th Street, NW, at M Street, DC 20005 (reservations 1-877 424 6423, hotel direct 1-202 682 5300, www.choicehotels.com). Mt Vernon Square/7th Street-Convention Center or McPherson Square Metro. **Rooms** *100.* **Credit** *AmEx, Disc, MC, V.* **Map** *p250/ p252 H5* ㉔

A well-appointed hotel, Comfort Inn Downtown provides 100 surprisingly decent and, of course, comfortable rooms in an up-and-coming neighbourhood three blocks from the convention centre. The cheerful staff serve a free continental breakfast every morning.

Business centre. Concierge. Disabled-adapted rooms. Gym. Internet (wireless, wired free). Parking ($30 per day). TV.

★ Donovan House

1155 14th Street, NW, at Thomas Circle, DC 20005 (reservations 1-800 383 6900, hotel direct

CONSUME

*1-202 737 1200, www.donovanhousehotel.com).
McPherson Square Metro.* **Rooms** 193. **Credit**
AmEx, Disc, MC, V. **Map** p250/p252 H5
This contemporary hotel features guestrooms in pur-
ples and browns with hanging egg chairs, cylindrical-
shaped showers and iPod docking stations. Floor-
to-ceiling windows overlook Thomas Circle. The best
views, however, are found people-watching on the
ground-floor Asian fusion restaurant, Zentan, or at
the rooftop bar, with outdoor fireplace and pool.
*Bars (2). Business centre. Disabled-adapted rooms.
Gym. Internet (wireless, free to Kimpton In Touch
members – can sign up when a guest). Restaurant.
Room service. Swimming pool (outdoor). TV
(pay movies).*

Hamilton Crowne Plaza

*1001 14th Street, NW, at K Street, DC 20005
(reservations 1-800 227 6963, hotel direct 1-202
682 0111, www.hamiltonhoteldc.com). McPherson
Square Metro.* **Rooms** 318. **Credit** AmEx, Disc,
MC, V. **Map** p250/p252 H5
The gorgeous Beaux Arts architecture of the
Hamilton dates from the 1920s, the elegant exterior
on Franklin Square complementing the 318 small
but elegantly appointed rooms and suites inside.
Some of the rooms have skyline views. Club Level
guests get the use of a private elevator, plus free
breakfast and use of the club lounge, and there's a
women's floor for female travellers, with full baths,
magazines, fancier toiletries and exclusive elevator
key access.
*Bar. Business centre. Concierge. Disabled-adapted
rooms. Gym. Internet (wireless, $12.95 per day).
Parking ($49.56 valet per day). Restaurant. Room
service. TV (pay movies).*

Hampton Inn Washington, DC-Convention Center

*901 6th Street, NW, at Massachusetts Avenue,
DC 20001 (hotel direct 1-202 842 2500, www.
hamptoninn.com). Gallery Place-Chinatown
Metro.* **Rooms** 228. **Credit** AmEx, Disc, MC,
V. **Map** p251/p253 J5
Affordable, convenient and sparklingly clean, this
chain hotel has earned praise from visitors. Just
two blocks from the Metro, it's convenient for sightseeing. For business guests there are meeting
rooms available. You won't need the Metro to get
to great dining and shopping, though; the immediate area is packed with restaurants and shops. The
guestrooms are unremarkable, but why spend time
in your room?
*Business centre. Disabled-adapted rooms. Gym.
Internet (free wireless). Parking ($34 valet per
day). Swimming pool & hot tub (indoor). TV
(pay movies).*

Budget

Hostelling International Washington, DC

*1009 11th Street, NW, at K Street, DC 20001
(1-202 737 2333, www.hiwashingtondc.org).
Metro Center Metro.* **Rooms** 250. **Credit** MC,
V. **Map** p250/p252 J5
A top-notch, dirt-cheap hostel close to the Metro and
Downtown Washington, Hostelling International
offers 250 beds divided between singles and doubles
and larger dorm-style single-sex rooms or 'family'
rooms of four-, six-, eight- and ten-bed configurations.
Private rooms sleep two hostellers in twin beds.
Most have shared bathrooms, but there are a limited

CONSUME

Donovan House. *See p143.*

number with en suite bathrooms. You can reserve online for a $5 discount – you'll have to forgo the breakfast, but you won't miss it. Kitchens, lockers, a new games room and a laundry (self-service) are all at your disposal during your stay, and the staff arrange group walking tours and theatre outings. Most importantly, there is no lock-out time. We recommend booking well in advance, because large groups often take up most of the beds. Non-members of Hostelling International are subject to a temporary membership fee of $3 per person.

Disabled-adapted rooms. Internet (free wireless on first floor, as well as pay-for stations). TV (in games room).

PENN QUARTER
Budget

Hotel Harrington
436 11th Street, NW, at E Street, DC 20004 (reservations 1-800 424 8532, hotel direct 1-202 628 8140, www.hotel-harrington.com). Metro Center Metro. **Rooms** 242. **Credit** AmEx, Disc, MC, V. **Map** p252 J6 **㉙**

The Hotel Harrington is a family-owned budget hotel, plain and simple. The lobby and rooms are clean but outdated, the staff welcoming and helpful. People choose to stay here for two reasons: price and location. The hotel is surrounded by a neighbourhood where you'll never get bored, and the Smithsonian museums and the Mall are also within easy reach. Family rooms sleep up to six people, and the hotel has a self-service laundry.
Bars (2). Disabled-adapted rooms. Internet (free wireless). Parking ($16 per day). Restaurants (2). Room service. TV.

DUPONT CIRCLE
Deluxe

Mansion on O Street
2020 O Street, NW, between 20th & 21st Streets, DC 20036 (1-202 496 2000, www. omansion.com/hotel). Dupont Circle Metro. **Rooms** 23. **Credit** AmEx, Disc, MC, V. **Map** p250 G4 **㉚**

Discretion exemplified, the 23-room B&B Mansion is hidden away on a quiet residential side street, with no sign to announce its presence. Each room in the three interconnected townhouses has a different theme: the Log Cabin suite, for example, has huge log beams, cow-hide rugs and three Frederic Remington sculptures; prices vary dramatically. The complex serves mainly as a private club and event space, and much of what you see, from the furniture to the wall hangings, is for sale. Some visitors love staying in a private mansion with 30 secret doors; others miss the better (and more accessible) service offered at conventional hotels. There are no 'standard' rooms here; rooms and suites are individually priced.
Bar (2). Business centre. Concierge. Internet (free wireless). Parking ($30 valet per day). Room service. TV.

Expensive

Palomar
2121 P Street, NW, between 21st & 22nd Streets, DC 20037 (reservations 1-877 866 3070, hotel direct 1-202 448 1800, www.hotelpalomar-dc.com). Dupont Circle Metro. **Credit** AmEx, Disc, MC, V. **Map** p250 G4 **㉛**

Palomar.

Madera.

The old Radisson that was on this site bequeathed large-sized rooms, an asset for the sleek, retro-styled Palomar. The spacious guestrooms use a soft palette of taupes, browns and mushroom, with a hint of leopardskin in the taupe jacquard carpet, plus odd flashes of colour. Headboards come in beige leather, and rooms are also equipped with capacious armchairs with footstools. Some, 'Spa Kings', come with Fuji soaking tubs (in serene bathrooms of white marble and dove grey); all have a yoga mat. Rooms also have DVD/CD players and iPod docks. The lobby has a touch of the exotic, with chocolate browns, dark woods and 1960s-style chandeliers.
Bar. Business centre. Concierge. Disabled-adapted rooms. Gym. Internet (wireless, free to Kimpton In Touch members – can sign up when a guest). Restaurant. Room service. Parking ($41 per day). Swimming pool (outdoor). TV (pay movies).

Moderate

Beacon Hotel
1615 Rhode Island Avenue, NW, at 17th Street, DC 20036 (reservations 1-800 821 4367, hotel direct 1-202 296 2100, www.beaconhotelwdc.com). Dupont Circle or Farragut North Metro. **Rooms** 97. **Credit** AmEx, Disc, MC, V. **Map** p250 G/H4 ●
Once the stodgy Governor's House Hotel, the Beacon was completely remade into a boutique-style lodging befitting the trendy Logan Circle neighbourhood. Four nights a week, you can head to the rooftop for great views, designer martinis and appetisers. The Beacon is convenient for Connecticut Avenue shopping and a short stroll to the White House. Passes to the YMCA are available on request. Some suites resemble small apartments, complete with kitchens.
Bar. Business centre. Concierge. Disabled-adapted rooms. Parking ($35 valet per day). Room service.

Internet (wireless, $12 per day). TV (pay movies, DVD players in some rooms).

Dupont at the Circle
1604 19th Street, NW, between Q & Corcoran Streets, DC 20009 (reservations 1-888 412 0100, hotel direct 1-202 332 5251, www. dupontatthecircle.com). Dupont Circle Metro. **Rooms** 11. **Credit** AmEx, Disc, MC, V. **Map** p250 G4 ●
Just off bustling Dupont Circle, this elegant B&B is housed in two connected townhouses dating from 1883. Thickly blanketed beds, a luxurious parlour and a charming family-style dining room make the place feel ritzy but comfy. The owner is friendly and helpful, and guests receive free passes to a nearby fitness centre.
Internet (free wireless). Parking ($20 per day; reserve in advance). TV (certain rooms, some have DVD players).

Madera
1310 New Hampshire Avenue, NW, between N & 20th Streets, DC 20036 (reservations 1-800 430 1202, hotel direct 1-202 296 7600, www.hotelmadera.com). Dupont Circle Metro. **Rooms** 82. **Credit** AmEx, DC, MC, V. **Map** p250 G4 ●
The large and comfortable guestrooms of the Madera have recently been transformed with strong blocks of colour, combined with stripes and patterns, for a vibrant, cheerful look. It's eclectic but not overwhelming and typical of the Kimpton group, which owns other hotels in the DC area, among them the Helix (*see p150*), Donovan House (*see p143*) and the Monaco (*see p142*). The location is hard to beat, and we like the wood and country look of the Firefly bar and restaurant. Speciality rooms include extras

Topaz.

such as exercise equipment and kitchenette. There's a wine hour for guests in the evening.
Bar. Business centre. Disabled-adapted rooms. Internet (wireless, free to Kimpton In Touch members – can sign up when a guest). Parking ($43 per day). Restaurant. Room service. TV (pay movies).
▶ For a review of Firefly, see p109.

Swann House
1808 New Hampshire Avenue, NW, at 18th Street, DC 20009 (1-202 265 4414, www. swannhouse.com). Dupont Circle Metro.
Rooms 12. **Credit** AmEx, Disc, MC, V.
Map p250 G4 **35**
Unlike Washington's townhouse B&Bs, the Swann House, built in 1883, is a freestanding mansion, which means the hallways aren't cramped and the lighting is good throughout. The pleasant rooms, which vary in their colour schemes, are romantic without being twee, and some have working fireplaces and jacuzzis. A small swimming pool nestles in a brick courtyard at the back. Although it's a four-block walk to the nearest Metro station, you are rewarded with a beautiful tree-lined neighbourhood within an easy stroll of the trendy bars on U Street and the hip strip of 17th Street. Room prices include breakfast, afternoon nibbles and an evening sherry. Note: children under 12 are not allowed. A two-night stay is usually required at weekends.
Internet (free wireless). Parking ($16 per day; reserve in advance). Swimming pool (outdoor). TV (DVD player on request).

★ Tabard Inn
1739 N Street, NW, between Connecticut Avenue & 17th Street, DC 20036 (1-202 785 1277,

www.tabardinn.com). Dupont Circle Metro.
Rooms 40. **Credit** AmEx, Disc, MC, V.
Map p250/p252 G4 **36**
Each of the Tabard's 40 rooms is decorated in brilliant colours with a hotchpotch of slightly chipped antiques. Unique and classy, the hotel draws locals, who come to enjoy its excellent restaurant, the garden courtyard in summer and a roaring fire in winter. It's made up of three 19th-century townhouses and is the oldest continuously operated hotel in DC – the floors and doors squeak and there's no lift. Guests can use the nearby YMCA.
Bar. Internet (free wireless). Parking ($38 per day, at hotel next door). Restaurant.

Topaz
1733 N Street, NW, between Connecticut Avenue & 17th Street, DC 20036 (reservations 1-800 775 1202, hotel direct 1-202 393 3000, www. topazhotel.com). Dupont Circle Metro. **Rooms** 99. **Credit** AmEx, DC, Disc, MC, V. **Map** p250/ p252 G4 **37**
A recent redecoration has seen guestrooms done out in calming creams and lilacs in this Kimpton group hotel that focuses on mind, body and spirit. There's a free yoga mat in every room, as well as in-room spa treatments and a morning power hour, with energy drinks served. And the Topaz Bar, recently transformed in Moroccan style, contains a hidden nook called the Zen Den. It's not just for health nuts, though: in the evening, the bar comes to life with a complimentary wine hour, exotic cocktails and dance music.
Bar (with food service). Business centre. Disabled-adapted rooms. Parking ($43 valet per day). Internet (wireless, free to Kimpton In Touch members – can sign up when a guest). Room service. TV (pay movies).

ADAMS MORGAN/ WOODLEY PARK

Expensive

Marriott Wardman Park

2660 Woodley Road, NW, at Connecticut Avenue, DC 20008 (reservations 1-800 228 9290, hotel direct 1-202 328 2000, www.marriott.com). Woodley Park-Zoo/Adams Morgan Metro. **Rooms** 1,314. **Credit** AmEx, Disc, MC, V. **Map** p249 F2 ⊛

A huge and labyrinthine hotel perched on a hill near the Woodley Park-Zoo/Adams Morgan Metro stop. If you get lost (as you inevitably will), ask the friendly staff, who seem to be everywhere. Although the 1918 building is gorgeous and surrounded by luscious greenery, the larger wing of the complex is monolithic and lacks character. Expect to see weddings or conferences here; the hotel has extensive facilities for the latter.

Bar (1). Business centre. Coffee shop. Disabled-adapted rooms. Gym. Parking ($36 per day, $41 valet per day). Restaurants (2). Swimming pool (outdoor). Internet (wireless, wired $12.95 per day; free wireless in public areas). TV (pay movies).

Normandy Hotel

2118 Wyoming Avenue, NW, at Connecticut Avenue, DC 20008 (reservations 1-800 423 6953, hotel direct 1-202 483 1350, www.the normandydc.com). Dupont Circle Metro then L1 bus. **Rooms** 26. **Credit** AmEx, Disc, MC, V. **Map** p250 G3 ⊛

Tucked along a quiet street amid some of DC's most expensive homes is this comfortable boutique hotel. The look is discreetly elegant, rooted in tradition but with some lively modern touches. Rooms have duck-down duvets, entertainment systems and in-room Nespresso machines. There are complimentary wine and cheese evenings on Tuesdays.

Disabled-adapted rooms. Internet (wireless, wired, free). Parking ($30 per day; limited availability, first come, first served). TV (DVD players).

Omni Shoreham

2500 Calvert Street, NW, at Connecticut Avenue, DC 20008 (reservations 1-800 545 8700, hotel direct 1-202 234 0700, www.omnishorehamhotel. com). Woodley Park-Zoo/Adams Morgan Metro. **Credit** AmEx, Disc, MC, V. **Map** p250 F2 ⊕

CONSUME

Helix. *See p150.*

One of Washington's largest and grandest hotels, the Omni Shoreham is located on 11 acres in the pleasant Woodley Park neighbourhood, thus allowing the space for beautiful, formal gardens. The National Zoo, Rock Creek Park, Adams Morgan and the Metro are all within easy walking distance. All this outdoors space makes it a good choice for families with children and the hotel has a programme for child guests. The lobby and restaurant are quite posh, though the hotel is showing its age (75 years) in some places. Many of the bedrooms are former apartments, which means they're among the largest in town.

Bar. Business centre. Concierge. Disabled-adapted rooms. Gym. Internet ($9.95 per day; free in rooms for members of the Select Guest loyalty programme). Parking ($35 valet per day). Restaurant. Room service (24hrs). Spa. Swimming pool (outdoor). TV (pay movies, DVD player on request).

Moderate

Adam's Inn

1746 Lanier Place, NW, at 18th Street, DC 20009 (reservations 1-800 578 6807, hotel direct 1-202 745 3600, www.adamsinn.com). Woodley Park-Zoo/Adams Morgan Metro then 90, 92, 96, bus. **Rooms** 26. **Credit** AmEx, Disc, MC, V. **Map** p250 G2 **④①**

Clean, sunny rooms fill the inn's three 100-year-old townhouses on a quiet and pretty street in Adams Morgan. The welcoming staff and old-fashioned furnishings and fireplaces make for a cosy stay. While the rooms don't have phones or TVs (invaluable for those seeking peace and quiet), there is a common lounge, kitchen and garden patio if you crave company, and nearby 18th Street offers enough bars and restaurants for a week.

Internet (free wireless). Parking ($20 per day; reserve in advance for limited spots). Payphone. TV (in common area).

LOGAN CIRCLE
Moderate

Helix

1430 Rhode Island Avenue, NW, between 14th & 15th Streets, DC 20005 (reservations 1-800 706 1202, hotel direct 1-202 462 9002, www.hotel helix.com). Dupont Circle or McPherson Square Metro. **Rooms** 178. **Credit** AmEx, DC, Disc, MC, V. **Map** p250 H4 **④②**

The lobby may be channelling the Starship *Enterprise*, with flashing light squares and blue plastic check-in stands, and you may enter it through a purple curtain that sweeps open as you approach, but this does nothing to diminish the well-thought-out style and comfort of the roooms. Here, daring colour matches (blue-green velour couch meets brownish-red footstool in a suite, for example) work, and there's a 1950s-slanted attention to detail with

Formica-look walls in the bathroom and curtains in colourful retro prints. Warholesque art on the walls, and a whole-wall black and white surfing mural in some rooms, adds eclecticism. The whole is actually pretty relaxing, in a pop culture kind of way. This is perhaps the Kimpton group's most far-out property (speaking metaphorically not geographically, that is). You'll recognise it by the large Magritte-style painting on the outside. There's a complimentary champagne hour in the evening. *Photo p149.*
Bar (with food service). Business centre. Disabled-adapted rooms. Gym. Parking ($42 valet per day). Room service. Internet (wireless, free to Kimpton In Touch members – can sign up when a guest). TV (pay movies).

Rouge

1315 16th Street, NW, at Massachusetts Avenue & Scott Circle, DC 20036 (reservations 1-800 738 1202, hotel direct 1-202 232 8000, www.rouge hotel.com). Dupont Circle or McPherson Square Metro. **Rooms** 137. **Credit** AmEx, DC, Disc, MC, V. **Map** p250 H4 **④③**

When the theme of your hotel is red, and your material of choice is leather, you're going to end up with something louche and loungey, and the Rouge has those qualities. Just down the road from the Helix (*see left*), this is another distinctive Kimpton hotel. A studded oriental-look doorway leads into a stylish retro lobby. The adjoining Rouge Bar is a dark, red-accented and stylish space that looks built for intrigue. Spacious rooms are a decadent combo of padded red leather ceiling-height headboards, huge lamps and armchairs, some in white leather. They're equipped with HD TVs, PlayStations, Wii and CD players. There's a complimentary wine hour in the evening.
Bar (with food service). Business centre. Disabled-adapted rooms. Gym. Parking ($42 valet per day). Room service. Internet (wireless, free to Kimpton In Touch members – can sign up when a guest). TV (pay movies).

GEORGETOWN
Deluxe

Capella

1050 31st Street, NW, between South Street and Blues Alley, DC 20007 (reservations 1-855 922 7355, hotel direct 1-202 617 2400, www.capella hotels.com/washingtondc). Foggy Bottom-GWU Metro then 31, 32, 36, 38B bus or Circulator bus. **Rooms** 49. **Credit** AmEx, Disc, MC, V. **Map** p249 E5 **④④**

There's been a lot of hype surrounding this new luxury opening along the C&O Canal. Public spaces are a stylish riff on the deeply traditional, with lots of dark, polished wood and marble lifted by flashes of modernity; in the Capella Living Room, for example, the gentlemen's club feel of dark wood panelling is given a twist by a floor-to-ceiling strip of flecked marble surrounding a modish fireplace. Elsewhere, well-placed pieces of contemporary art have a similar effect. Guestrooms continue the dark wood theme, with sophisticated furnishings in cream, taupe and brown. Bathrooms are very well appointed. The rooftop bar has stunning views of Georgetown and the city; there's an infinity pool here too.

Bar (2). Business centre. Concierge. Disabled-adapted rooms. Gym (24hrs). Internet (free wireless). Parking ($48 valet per day.) Restaurants (1). Room service (24 hrs). Swimming pool (outdoor). TV (DVD player on request).

Four Seasons

2800 Pennsylvania Avenue, NW, between 28th & 29th Streets, DC 20007 (reservations 1-800 819 5053, hotel direct 1-202 342 0444, www.four seasons.com/washington). Foggy Bottom-GWU Metro then 30, 32, 34, 35, 36 bus or Circulator bus. **Rooms** 222. **Credit** AmEx, Disc, MC, V. **Map** p249 F5 ⓯

One of DC's most comfortable hotels, the Four Seasons has long attracted VIP guests. The health

spa is both serious and sybaritic, and good art is displayed throughout. Even if you're not lucky enough to be staying here, you can at least treat yourself to afternoon tea on the Garden Terrace. If you can stump up the money for a reservation, ask to stay in the east wing, where a $40-million renovation a few years ago enlarged the rooms and updated the decor.

Bar. Business centre. Concierge. Disabled-adapted rooms. Gym. Internet (wireless or wired, free). Parking ($52 valet per day). Spa. Swimming pool (indoor). Restaurants (2). Room service. Satellite TV (pay movies, DVD players).

Ritz-Carlton, Georgetown

3100 South Street, NW, at 31st Street, DC 20007 (reservations 1-800 241 3333, hotel direct 1-202 912 4100, www.ritzcarlton.com/hotels/georgetown). Foggy Bottom-GWU Metro then 30, 32, 34, 35, 36 bus or Circulator bus. **Rooms** 86. **Credit** AmEx, Disc, MC, V. **Map** p249 E5 ⓰

With just 86 guestrooms – about a third of which are executive suites – the Ritz's Georgetown property is more intimate than its Foggy Bottom sister hotel (*see*

Capella.

p141). Located near the Potomac River waterfront, the hotel is housed in a renovated red-brick building with a 130ft smokestack. The industrial architecture makes a striking backdrop for the chic modern furnishings. Some rooms have views of Downtown and the river. The building also houses a cinema, spa and coffee shop, as well as a restaurant (Fahrenheit) and martini lounge (Degrees). The upmarket neighbourhood is not near the Metro, but there's plenty going on in the area to keep you entertained.

Bar. Business centre. Concierge. Disabled-adapted rooms. Gym. Internet (wireless, $9.99 per day). Parking ($39 per day). Restaurant. Room service. Spa. TV (pay movies, DVD players).

Expensive

Graham Georgetown
1075 Thomas Jefferson Street, NW, between M & K Streets, DC 20007 (reservations 1-855 341 1292, hotel direct 1-202 337 0900,

Monaco Alexandria.

www.thegrahamgeorgetown.com. Foggy Bottom-GWU Metro then 31, 32, 36 bus or Circulator bus. **Rooms** 57. **Credit**. AmEx, Disc, MC, V. **Map** p249 F5 ⑰
In the property that was the old Monticello, the new Graham is a sophisticated take on a boutique hotel. The look is restrained, with lots of taupes, browns and marble in the public areas. Rooms and suites – all with CD players/radios – use greys, with carefully chosen splashes of colour, and checks and patterns that blend well and are never loud. The expansive rooftop bar, the Observatory, has great views and is set to be a major asset.

Bars (2). Business centre. Concierge. Disabled-adapted rooms. Gym. Internet (free wireless). Parking ($48 valet per day). Restaurant. Room Service. Spa. TV.

Moderate

Georgetown Suites
1111 30th Street, NW, between K & M Streets, & 1000 29th Street, NW, at K Street, DC 20007 (reservations 1-800 348 7203, hotel direct 1-202 298 7800, www.georgetownsuites.com). Foggy Bottom-GWU Metro then 30, 32, 34, 35, 36 bus or Circulator bus. **Rooms** 222. **Credit** AmEx, Disc, MC, V. **Map** p249 F5 ㊽
This all-suites hotel, divided into two buildings, is on a quiet street off the main drag of M Street. Formerly full condominiums, each suite is well equipped with full kitchens and some units have patios. It's well situated for forays into Georgetown and along the Potomac River. The rooms are bright and spacious – some are absolutely huge.

Business centre. Concierge. Disabled-adapted rooms (1). Gym. Internet (free wireless). Parking ($30 per day). TV (DVD player on request).

SOUTHWEST
Moderate

Capitol Skyline
10 I Street, SW, between South Capitol Street & Half Street, DC 20024 (1-202 488 7500, www.capitolskyline.com). Metro Navy Yard. **Rooms** 203. **Credit** AmEx, Disc, MC, V. **Map** p253 K7 ㊾
This space-age looking hotel with a honeycomb exterior sits in the shadow of the Capitol and the Nationals ballpark in the up-and-coming Navy Yard neighbourhood. The rooms are pretty standard; it's the pool that draws a crowd. Surrounded by neon pink and orange Adirondack chairs, the pool attracts families during summer mornings and adults looking for a Miami vibe in the afternoon and evenings.

Bar (2). Business centre. Concierge. Disabled adapted rooms. Gym. Internet (free wireless). Parking ($25 per day). Restaurant. Swimming pool (outdoor). TV (pay movies). Room service.

Morrison House.

ALEXANDRIA, VA
Expensive

★ Monaco Alexandria
480 King Street, Alexandria, VA 22314 (reservations 1-800 368 5047, hotel direct 1-703 549 6080, www.monaco-alexandria.com). King Street Metro then 10min walk. **Rooms** 241. **Credit** AmEx, Disc, MC, V.
The Monaco Alexandria makes a bold design statement with its lobby/lounge. Walls and pillars are a glowing, striking blue, and there's just a touch of Old Shanghai in the gold on black patterned walls behind the red padded-leather reception desk. Furnishings here are a happy mixture: lots of shades and patterns are thrown together to great effect, with hints of whimsy in a leopardskin-painted fire surround. Bedrooms continue the bold theme. They're luxurious, many with brown-khaki walls, and lots of black and white in comfortable armchairs and chaises longues. Some feature bathrooms with two-person soaking baths. There's an indoor swimming pool in the third-floor fitness centre.
Bar. Business centre. Disabled-adapted rooms. Gym. Internet (wireless, free to Kimpton In Touch members – can sign up when a guest). Parking ($25 valet per day). Pool (indoor). Restaurant. Room service. TV (pay movies).

Morrison House
116 S Alfred Street, Alexandria, VA 22314 (reservations 1-866 834 6628, hotel direct
1-703 838-8000, www.morrisonhouse.com). **Rooms** 45. **Credit** AmEx, Disc, MC, V.
A graciously appointed, intimate hotel in Old Town Alexandria, Morrison House is part of the Kimpton group, representing its take on traditional, Colonial style. Colours are subtle in the gleaming public rooms, their furnishings revealing just tiny hints of a modern design ethos. We like the quiet sitting room with polished parquet floor and wood panelling. In the guestrooms, discreet contemporary artwork mediates the yellows and peaches and Colonial-style furniture. Beds in some rooms are four-posters (with steps to help you climb in). There's a complimentary wine hour in the evening.
Bar. Business centre. Disabled-adapted rooms. Internet (wireless, free to Kimpton In Touch members – can sign up when checked in). Parking ($25 valet per day). Room service. TV (pay movies).

ARLINGTON, VA
Moderate

Key Bridge Marriott
1401 Lee Highway, at Wilson Street, VA 22209 (reservations 1-800 228 9290, hotel direct 1-703 524 6400, www.marriott.com). Rosslyn Metro. **Rooms** 582. **Credit** AmEx, Disc, MC, V.
You won't find a better view of the Washington skyline at night than from the top of the Key Bridge Marriott. A large and luxurious hotel built for conventions (it has 17 meeting rooms), it's about a mile from Arlington National Cemetery and a quick walk across the bridge to Georgetown. The Metro, too, is nearby. Be sure to request a room with a city view.
Bar. Business centre. Gym. Concierge. Disabled-adapted rooms. Parking ($19 per day). Restaurant. Swimming pools (indoor/outdoor). Room service. Internet (free wireless). TV (pay movies).

BETHESDA, MD
Moderate

Hyatt Regency Bethesda
1 Bethesda Metro Center, 7400 Wisconsin Avenue, at Old Georgetown Road, MD 20814 (1-301 657 1234, www.bethesda.hyatt.com). Bethesda Metro. **Rooms** 390. **Credit** AmEx, Disc, MC, V.
Children will adore this luxurious hotel for its rooftop pool (there's also a whirlpool and sauna), thrilling 11-storey atrium lobby and three speedy glass elevators. Each of the 390 rooms has huge desks and black and white photographs of the city's monuments. Another perk: the Metro station is directly underneath the hotel.
Bar. Business centre. Concierge. Disabled-adapted rooms. Gym. Internet (wireless, $9.95 per day). Parking ($20 per day). Restaurants (2). Room service. Swimming pool (indoor). TV (pay movies).

CONSUME

Arts & Entertainment

Children

Nation's capital, children's playground.

Walk along the National Mall, especially on a summer day or at the weekend, and you'll find children everywhere. It's the museums and monuments that are the attraction. They're some of the world's finest, and most – including the Smithsonian museums – are free, a major boon for parents. The museums take care not to neglect their younger visitors, with special exhibits or trails to hold their attention.

DC is an easy city to get around with babies and young children too. It's pedestrian-friendly, and Metro stations all have lifts.

ARTS & ENTERTAINMENT

To get a taste of the major sights, consider taking a hop-on hop-off trolley tour (http://www.viator.com/tours/Washington-DC), which offers the chance to travel by open-air trams. Family walking tours, such as those offered by **Washington Walks** (1-202 484 1565, www.washingtonwalks.com), can be very enjoyable for children. The tour of 'Washington's Most Haunted Houses' may be right up their street. Since most tours last approximately two hours, they may be more suitable for older children.

BABYSITTING

Childcare in Washington is not cheap, but most large hotels and those with concierge services can provide it, using in-house services or local companies. Last-minute requests can usually be accommodated (with extra fees), but it's best to book ahead. Childcare agencies include **White House Nannies** (1-800 266 9024

Virginia and Maryland, 1-703 250 0700 in Washington DC, www.whitehousenannies.com), a well-respected service that uses thoroughly screened, independent carers at a flat fee. **Mothers' Aides Inc** (1-800 526 2669, www.mothersaides.com) offers a similar service and charges a $70 agency fee per day plus the caregiver's hourly wage (normally $15-$20 per hour).

ENTERTAINMENT

The listings below focus on attractions in or near central DC. For places further afield and in the suburbs buy a copy of *Going Places with Children in Washington, DC* or *Around Washington, DC with Kids*, both excellent specialist guides.

Eating out

Children are welcome at all but the fanciest restaurants – where you're unlikely to want to take them anyway. For quick budget meals, fast-food restaurants are plentiful and easy to find, but if your offspring aren't fussy eaters, you might want to try one of the many moderately priced ethnic restaurants such as the Ethiopian choices found along Adams Morgan's 18th Street or Shaw's 9th Street. The food court in the Pavilion at the **Old Post Office** (1100 Pennsylvania Avenue, NW, between 11th & 12th Streets) is near the Museums of Natural History and American History, while the **National Gallery of Art** (*see p33*) has a nice self-service café with plentiful seating. Famished families at

Union Station (*see p46*) on Capitol Hill can find sustenance at the food court in the station, where a branch of the 1950s-style burger joint Johnny Rockets is a favourite.

If a trip to the zoo develops their appetites, the **Lebanese Taverna** (2641 Connecticut Avenue, NW, 1-202 265 8681, www.lebanese taverna.com) introduces children to the taste of Middle Eastern food in bite-sized nibbles.

In the Dupont Circle neighbourhood, **Firefly** (*see p109*) takes a child-friendly approach, with a 'lil' kid's' menu and a 'big kid's' meal, featuring the likes of hamburgers and BLTs. Each small child gets an unbaked cookie at the beginning of the meal that can be decorated and baked.

Museums

All Smithsonian museums offer at least a few exhibits geared towards children, though three are consistently highly rated: the **National Air & Space Museum** (*see p32*), the **National Museum of American History** (*see p37*) and the **National Museum of Natural History** (*see p37*). Others making a special effort for children are the **National Building Museum** (*see p61*), the **International Spy Museum** (*see p60*) and the **Museum of the American Indian** (*see p37*). And though it's not a museum per se, don't miss the **Bureau of Engraving & Printing** (*see p49*). Children are fascinated by its 35-minute tour, where they can look at currency being printed.

Three more child-friendly museums:

National Geographic Museum at Explorers Hall
17th & M Streets, NW, Downtown (1-202 857 7588, www.nationalgeographic.com/museum). *Farragut North Metro.* **Open** 10am-6pm daily. **Admission** $11 adults; $7 5-11s; free under-5s. **Credit** AmEx, Disc, MC, V. **Map** p252 H5.

Filled with hands-on, science-oriented exhibits for the younger visitor, this museum-from-the-magazine offers free family programmes each Friday morning.

National Postal Museum
2 Massachusetts Avenue, NE, Capitol Hill (1-202 633 5533, www.postalmuseum.si.edu). *Union Station Metro.* **Open** 10am-5.30pm daily. **Admission** free. **Credit** AmEx, MC, V. **Map** p253 K6.

More than 35 interactive games and screens make the mail fascinating for even the most technology-addled youngsters. Myriad stamp collections and a 'personal postcard' machine complete the experience.

★ Newseum
555 Pennsylvania Avenue, NW, Judiciary Square Area (1-888 639 7386, www.newseum.org). *Archives-Navy Memorial-Penn Center Metro.* **Open** 9am-5pm daily. **Admission** $21.95; $12.95 7-18s; free under-7s. **Credit** AmEx, MC, V.

Thoughtful, interactive entertainment is a hallmark of this museum dedicated to journalism and free speech. In the Interactive Newsroom, junior reporters can step in front of the cameras and file reports from a variety of backdrops, while touch-screen Be A Reporter and Be A Photographer games send kids on a quest to break stories and meet deadlines.

Animals & the outdoors

Within the District, the best outdoor activity for children, bar none, is a trip to the **National Zoo** (*see p70*) – and what's more, it's free. Particularly popular are the zoo's two giant pandas, the prairie dog community and the 11.30am daily sea lion feeding and training. Survival tip: the zoo slopes steeply downhill to Rock Creek from the entrance on Connecticut Avenue, so to avoid a long, hot climb at the end of your visit, plan a circular route that gets you back to the entrance before you run out of energy.

ARTS & ENTERTAINMENT

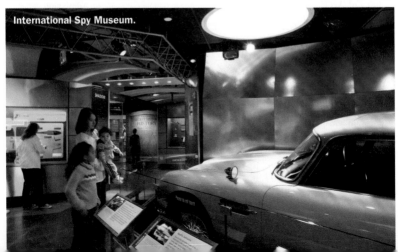
International Spy Museum.

★ Rock Creek Nature Center & Planetarium

5200 Glover Road, NW, at Military Road, Upper Northwest (1-202 895 6070, www.nps.gov/rocr/ naturecenter). Friendship Heights Metro then E2, E3 bus. **Open** 9am-5pm Wed-Sun. **Admission** free.

Rock Creek is a great place for cycling, skating, horse riding and exploring the old mill and the site of the Civil War battle at Fort Stevens. As well as the Nature Center's guided hikes, there's the highly entertaining Creature Feature programme (4pm Fri), which takes a close look at the park's wildlife. Inside Peirce Barn, kids can try on period clothing and play with 19th-century toys. The planetarium (on the park's western edge) hosts several free shows: check the website for details.

Cycling

Washington is a fantastic city for bike riding, with miles of family-friendly trails. Try the picturesque **C&O Canal Towpath** (www. nps.gov/choh, *see p186*) – where mule-drawn barge rides are also available – or the beautiful **Mount Vernon Trail** river ride (www.nps. gov/gwmp/mvt.html). The latter ends at George Washington's estate, where a tour is offered that younger children enjoy hugely (*see p200*). Also great are the 11 miles of the **Capital Crescent Trail** (*see p186*) and the loop through East Potomac Park. For maps and details, contact the Washington Area Bicyclist Association (*see p186*). For bike rental, *see p186*.

Theatre & the arts

The Weekend section of Friday's *Washington Post* (www.washingtonpost.com) has a kids' page that covers the current week's events and activities in and around DC. Other institutions that occasionally offer art and theatre programmes include the **National Gallery of Art** (*see p33*), the **Corcoran Museum of Art** (*see p40*), the **Hirshhorn Museum & Sculpture Garden** (*see p31*) and the **National Building Museum** (*see p61*).

Arthur M Sackler Gallery/ Freer Gallery of Art

1050 Independence Avenue, SW, between 11th & 12th Streets, The Mall & Tidal Basin (1-202 633 4880, www.asia.si.edu). Smithsonian Metro. **Open** 10am-5.30pm daily. ImaginAsia times vary. **Admission** free. **Map** p252 J7.

The Sackler and Freer galleries offer ImaginAsia, a family programme with a special guided tour for children aged six to 14, who must be accompanied by an adult. They are given an activity book before entering the exhibition and the tour ends with the opportunity to create arts and crafts inspired by what they have seen. There is also a children's activity on most

weekends. Traditional Asian festivals are celebrated here, giving children the chance to participate.
▶ *For more on the galleries' collections, see p43 and p44.*

Glen Echo Park

7300 MacArthur Boulevard, at Goldsboro Road, Glen Echo, MD (1-301 492 6229, www.glenecho park.org). Friendship Heights Metro then Ride-On Bus 29. **Carousel** May-Aug 10am-2pm Wed-Fri; noon-6pm Sat, Sun. *Sept* noon-6pm Sat, Sun.

Until 1968, Glen Echo was a popular amusement park just a trolley ride from Downtown. Today, it is preserved by the National Park Service (2pm weekend tours) and run by a non-profit group as a site for theatre, art and dance. It also has a playground, picnic tables, plenty of places to explore and a charming 1921 carousel. The following are highlights of the activities on offer:

Adventure Theatre *1-301 320 5331, www. adventuretheatre-mtc.org. See website for showtimes and tickets.*

One-hour plays for fours and over based on fables, fairy tales, musicals and children's classics, using puppets and actors.

Living Classrooms *1-202 488 0627, www.glenechopark.org/living-classrooms.*

From a former stable building, this programme offers hands-on outdoor activities in the park, including live animal encounters for children up to 15.

Puppet Company Playhouse *1-301 634 5380, www.thepuppetco.org. See website for show times, but usually 10am, 11am Thur, Fri; 11.30am, 1pm Sat, Sun. Tiny Tots shows 10am.*

Plays for all ages, most of them adaptations of classic stories for children such as *Cinderella* and *The Jungle Book*. Reservations recommended.

Kennedy Center

2700 F Street, NW, at New Hampshire Avenue & Rock Creek Parkway, Foggy Bottom (1-800 444 1324, 1-202 467 4600, www.kennedy-center.org). Foggy Bottom-GWU Metro. **Admission** varies. **Credit** AmEx, DC, Disc, MC, V. **Map** p252 F6.

The Kennedy Center offers an amazing variety of dance, music and theatre for youngsters, with subjects as diverse as West African dance and the history of Mexico in song. The National Symphony also presents occasional family concerts here.

Saturday Morning at the National

National Theatre, 1321 Pennsylvania Avenue, NW, between 13th & 14th Streets, Federal Triangle (1-202 783 3372, www.nationaltheatre.org). Metro Center Metro. **Admission** free. **Map** p252 H6.

Free entertainment for both children and adults at 9.30am and 11am, September to April. The one-hour events include theatre, music, dance and magic. From jugglers to ventriloquists and fabulous magic shows, it is a real treat for children. Tickets are distributed half an hour beforehand so arrive early.

Film

More than just multiplexes.

The dominance of multiplexes in the US is mitigated in Washington, DC by the existence of a few independents and other venues screening films from outside the mainstream. In 2010, the **Avalon**, an old movie house dating from the 1920s, was joined by the **West End**. Founded by film-lovers in a previously disused cinema, it aims to be a new outlet for independent, foreign and documentary films. There is also an extensive array of non-commercial repertory film programmes in the city's museums, while the American Film Institute's **Silver Theatre & Cultural Center**, housed in a restored art deco cinema in Silver Spring, also shows the kind of films that you won't see elsewhere.

Most DC-area cinemas, however, show the same formulaic product that's seen from coast to coast (and around the world). Nevertheless, declining returns for Hollywood-made films have had some impact, encouraging the major chains to book more documentaries and independent films.

Local filmmakers often claim that DC has the country's third-largest film industry, after LA and New York, but few features are produced locally. Instead, the emphasis is on documentaries, many of them made for the DC-based Discovery and National Geographic cable channels. There are many local showcases for non-fiction films, including the **Silverdocs** festival every June at the AFI Silver.

Washington has long been a useful location for Hollywood movies, but the crews often spend just a few days in town, filming at conspicuous landmarks before heading back to LA or continuing the shoot in cheaper locales. The Metro doesn't allow violent acts to be staged on its property, so subway scenes in Washington-based action movies are often shot in Baltimore. Still, Hollywood filmmakers keep coming.

THE CINEMAS

The **AMC Loews** chain dominates DC's mainstream cinema landscape. **Landmark**, the leading US arthouse chain, operates the eight-screen **E Street Cinema**, while **Regal** owns the 14-screen **Gallery Place** megaplex. The city currently has two independently owned cinemas, the **Avalon** and the new **West End**.

The E Street and Gallery Place cinemas returned cinema to Downtown, which was once full of opulent movie palaces. But two favourite historic moviehouses are found along Connecticut or Wisconsin Avenues, the major commercial arteries of the city's affluent west side.

TICKETS AND INFORMATION

Most cinemas have two or three screenings a night (usually between 7pm and 7.45pm, and 9pm and 9.45pm) and often a late show at the weekend. All have matinées. Landmark E Street and Bethesda Row sometimes do weekend cult-film midnight shows. Filmgoers usually don't book in advance, although it's advisable to do so for the opening of big new movies. Advance tickets for AMC Loews cinemas are available at www.moviewatcher.com. Purchase tickets for Regal Gallery Place at www.fandango.com.

INSIDE TRACK
EXORCIST STAIRS

The Exorcist was filmed in Georgetown: the university features, and so do some now-notorious outdoor stairs – the 75 steep steps down which Father Damien Karras threw himself to his death after the demon left Regan's body and entered his. Now popularly known as the Exorcist Stairs, they link Prospect Street with M Street below.

ARTS & ENTERTAINMENT

MAINSTREAM FILMS

AMC Loews Georgetown
3111 K Street, NW, between 31st Street &
Wisconsin Avenue, Georgetown (1-202 342 6033,
www.amctheatres.com). Bus 30, 32, 34, 35, 36, 38,
D2, D4, D6, G2, DC Circulator. **Tickets** $10-$12.
Credit AmEx, Disc, MC, V. **Map** p249 E5.
This 14-screen cinema, part of a complex that incorporates the old Georgetown Incinerator, has a large,
dramatic lobby. The theatres, the biggest of which
have 300 seats, are standard stadium-seating houses,
with large screens and clear views. Right nearby is
the recently revamped Georgetown Waterfront Park.

AMC Mazza Gallerie
5300 Wisconsin Avenue, NW, at Jenifer Street,
Upper Northwest (1-888 262 4386, www.amc
theatres.com). Friendship Heights Metro. **Tickets**
$9-$11. **Credit** AmEx, Disc, MC, V.
The seven-screen cinema was the city's first with stadium seating, boasting large screens and excellent
sightlines. Alcoholic beverages and an expanded
snack menu are available in the two 'club cinemas'.
The latter auditoriums are restricted to viewers over
21, although that doesn't guarantee that the movie
shown will be suitable for adults.

AMC Loews Uptown
3426 Connecticut Avenue, NW, between Porter
& Ordway Streets, Cleveland Park (1-202 966
5400, www.amctheatres.com). Cleveland Park
Metro. **Tickets** $9-$11. **Credit** AmEx, Disc,
MC, V. **Map** p249 F1.
With the destruction of the last of the Downtown
movie palaces in the 1980s, what was once just an
average neighbourhood theatre became the city's
premier cinema. The 1936 art deco movie palace –
with 1,500 seats it's the city's largest – now shows
blockbusters and would-be blockbusters. Not everyone applauds the curved screen, originally installed
in the 1960s for Cinerama movies.

Regal Gallery Place
701 7th Street, NW, at G Street, Downtown
(1-202 393 2121). Gallery Place-Chinatown
Metro. **Tickets** $9-$11. **Credit** AmEx, Disc,
MC, V. **Map** p253 J5.
Across the plaza north of Verizon Center and up two
flights of escalators awaits a sparkling new but otherwise standard contemporary megaplex, with 14
auditoriums. A rowdy scene on weekend nights.

FOREIGN & INDEPENDENT FILMS

★ Avalon
5612 Connecticut Avenue, NW, at McKinley Street,
Chevy Chase (1-202 966 6000, www.theavalon.org).
Friendship Heights Metro or E2, E3, E4, E6, L1,
L2, L4 bus. **Tickets** $8.25-$11.50. **Credit** MC, V.
Abandoned by its corporate operator, the city's oldest surviving moviehouse was rescued and restored
by a neighbourhood group. Both inside and out, the
1923 structure has more charm than any number of
the cookie-cutter megaplexes that have sprouted like
mushrooms in the suburbs. It now shows a mix of
foreign, independent, documentary and Hollywood
fare, as well as classic and children's films. The small
second screen upstairs is nothing special.

Landmark E Street Cinema
555 11th Street, NW (entrance on E Street),
Downtown (1-202 452 7672, www.landmark
theatres.com). Metro Center or Gallery Place
Metro. **Tickets** $8.50-$11.50. **Credit** AmEx,
Disc, MC, V. **Map** p252 J6.
The eight-screen Landmark is the city's leading arthouse. Screens are big, even in the smallest of the
auditoriums. This is one of only three DC cinemas
with a liquor licence; other amenities include
upscale concessions and an espresso bar.
Landmark also operates the roomier Bethesda Row
in suburban Maryland, which also shows artsy
flicks, but the Downtown theatre's bookings tend
to be more adventurous.
Other locations 7235 Woodmont Avenue,
Bethesda, MD (1-301 652 7273).

★ West End Cinema
2301 M Street, NW, at 23rd Street, Foggy Bottom
(1-202 966 6000, www.westendcinema.com).
Foggy Bottom-GWU Metro or 31, 32, 36, 38B,
Circulator bus. **Tickets** $8.46-$10.34. **Credit**
AmEx, MC, V. **Map** p250/252 F5.
Opened in late 2010, the city's newest arthouse
reclaims a three-screen cinema abandoned by a
national chain in 2004. The theatres are small, but
the equipment is state-of-the-art and the projection
excellent. Early offerings have been heavy on documentaries, but also include films by Gaspar Noe,
Jean-Luc Godard and Woody Allen. Upscale snacks
and alcoholic drinks are available. *Photo p162.*

REPERTORY

Washington no longer has any commercial
repertory cinemas. It does, however, possess
one of the country's most extensive non-
commercial rep film scenes. Keeping abreast
of the programmes at these venues is a major
undertaking, but not an expensive one: most
of the screenings are free.

Among the many other local institutions
that frequently screen films are the **National
Archives** (documentaries from its collection
or that use its footage, 1-202 501 5000); the
Goethe Institut (films about Germany,
1-202 289 1200); the DC Jewish Community
Center (Jewish-related films, tickets 1-800 494
8497, information 1-202 518 9400 ext 229); the
National Museum of Women in the Arts

Essential Washington Films

The city is the backdrop to some very different films.

All the President's Men.

ENEMY OF THE STATE
TONY SCOTT (1998)

Will Smith and Gene Hackman star in a tense political thriller that is like a re-imagining of Francis Ford Coppola's *The Conversation* – with car chases. In both films Hackman plays a reclusive surveillance expert. Director Tony Scott winds the political paranoia up to the max.'

MR SMITH GOES TO
WASHINGTON
FRANK CAPRA (1939)

James Stewart's young Wisconsin senator exposing corruption and upholding true American values in a Senate riddle with graft is quintessential Capra – popular wish fulfillment served up with such comic panache that you don't have time to question its cornball idealism.

THE EXORCIST
WILLIAM FRIEDKIN
(1973)

A young girl is staying with her mother in Georgetown. Something is clearly wrong when she starts levitating, projectile vomiting green bile and saying unspeakable things to the priests called by her desperate mother to perform an exorcism. The climax sees a death on the 'Exorcist' stairs (*see p159*).

HEARTBURN
MIKE NICHOLS (1986)

Adapted from Nora Ephron's book about her marriage to Carl Bernstein, *Heartburn* follows the relationship of food writer Rachel Samstat (Meryl Streep) and political columnist – and serial philanderer – Mark Forman (Jack Nicholson) as they fall in love, marry, renovate a Georgetown house, have a child and finally part.

ALL THE PRESIDENT'S
MEN
ALAN PALUKA (1976)

Robert Redford and Dustin Hoffman are *Washington Post* journos Woodward and Bernstein, set on uncovering dirty goings-on at the Nixon White House. Visual set-ups are extraordinary, mixing light and shadow, and engulfing the pair in monumental buildings to stress the enormity of their task.

PRIMARY COLORS
MIKE NICHOLS (1998)

John Travolta portrays a familiar womanising president in this *film à clef* based on Clinton's 1992 campaign. Young Democratic idealist Henry Burton joins President Harry Stanton's campaign staff but soon finds himself mired in a world of secrets, lies and deals springing from his boss's indiscretions.

West End Cinema. See p160.

(films by women or linked to current exhibits, 1-202 783 7370); and several foreign embassies. See www.reeldc.com or the *Washington Post* for listings.

AFI Silver Theatre & Cultural Center

8633 Colesville Road, at Georgia Avenue, Silver Spring (1-301 495 6720, www.afi.com/silver). Silver Spring Metro. **Tickets** $8.50-$11.50. **Credit** AmEx, Disc, MC, V.

The American Film Institute opened this handsome, state-of-the-art complex in 2003. The largest of the three houses is a restored (and reduced) version of the Silver, a 1938 art deco cinema. It tends to show first-run foreign, indie and documentary films. But it still hosts retrospectives of directors and stars, overviews of national cinemas, and series devoted to African and Latin American cinema.

Freer Gallery of Art

Meyer Auditorium, Jefferson Drive, SW, at 12th Street, Mall & Tidal Basin (1-202 357 2700, www.asia.si.edu). Smithsonian Metro. **Tickets** free in person 1hr before screening, or through Ticketmaster (www.ticketmaster.com) for $2.75 per ticket and $1.25 per order. **Screenings** usually 7pm Fri; 2pm Sun. **Map** p252 J7.

The films shown here come from the countries represented in the gallery's collection, predominantly Asia and the Middle East. It is one of the best places in town to see movies from India and Iran, but arrive early – the theatre soon fills up with émigrés from those countries.

Hirshhorn Museum & Sculpture Garden

7th Street & Independence Avenue, SW, Mall & Tidal Basin (1-202 357 2700, www.hirshhorn. si.edu). L'Enfant Plaza Metro. **Tickets** free. **Screenings** usually 8pm Thur, Fri. **Map** p253 J7.

The Hirshhorn showcases work by upcoming and experimental directors, often fresh from their successes on the international film festival circuit. Highlights from several alternative festivals are shown annually and filmmakers sometimes show works in progress.

Letelier Theatre

3251 Prospect Street NW, upper courtyard, near Wisconsin Avenue, Georgetown (1-202 338 5835, http://leteliertheater.com). Foggy Bottom-GWU Metro then 32, 36 bus or Circulator bus. **Tickets** free-$20. **Map** p249 E5.

That this is not a mainstream cinema is evident from its name, a tribute to the Chilean exile assassinated by Pinochet's agents in Washington in 1976. The 85-seat theatre has no in-house programmer, but is used regularly for film series and special events. The Alliance Française screens new and classic French films and Global Lens shows features from the developing world; documentaries (often with a political edge) are frequently scheduled.

National Gallery of Art

East Building Auditorium, 4th Street & Constitution Avenue, NW, Mall & Tidal Basin (1-202 842 6799, www.nga.gov). Judiciary Square or Archives-Navy Memorial Metro. **Tickets** free. **Screenings** afternoon Sat, Sun, some weekdays. **Map** p253 J6.

This auditorium has one of the biggest screens and some of the most interesting programming in the city, as well as the most leg room. Film series are sometimes linked to major exhibitions, but the museum also hosts major retrospectives. Documentaries about art and related topics are shown on weekdays.

FILM FESTIVALS

The largest local annual festival is **Filmfest DC** (www.filmfestdc.org), which shows about 75 films, most of them international, during a two-week period beginning in late April. Its organisers also sponsor an annual overview of Arab films, usually in October. In October and November, the American Film Institute (www.afi.com) presents the European Film Showcase, introducing new films that recently premiered at the continent's leading festivals.

Other festivals include the **Environmental Film Festival** (www.dc.environmentalfilm fest.org) in March; **Reel Affirmations** (www.reelaffirmations.org), the gay and lesbian film fest, in April and May; and the **Jewish Film Festival** (www.wjff.org) in December. Check the *Washington Post* listings for details.

Gay & Lesbian

The gay city at play.

Washington's gay and lesbian scene has been inching further east ever since it first staked its claim in Dupont Circle decades ago. Then it reached 14th Street, Logan Circle and Shaw, and it's still heading north- and eastwards, now making its presence felt in Columbia Heights, Petworth and over towards North Capitol Street and H Street.

The gay community's activists – who once received a great deal of attention by staging a 'nude-in' on the Mall – have found that they get even more respect with their clothes on. The AIDS crisis and its need for loud voices and charismatic leaders took the perennial outsiders off the city's streets and planted them inside the Capitol. Gays transformed themselves from a marginalised minority into a mainstream force to be reckoned with, complete with a smart headquarters for the lobbying organisation, the Human Rights Campaign. The strength of the city's gay voice was demonstrated in March 2010, when DC became the sixth jurisdiction in the US to permit same-sex marriage.

THE LOCAL SCENE

After a hard day's lobbying, the District's gays and (to a lesser extent) lesbians can take advantage of a steady stream of bars and clubs that keep them occupied after dark, and often right up until dawn.

As one would expect in a town that has become increasingly partisan over the last decade, divisions abound in Washington's gay community as well. Bears and bikers and those who love them frequent **Blowoff** and the **DC Eagle**, while DC's D&G crowd are more likely to be found in the other dance venues. Race tends to be another divider.

Finding places that separate the men from the boys might be easy enough but sadly the same can't be said for the District's lesbian bars; one would find it much easier to point to where the girls aren't, rather than are in this town. **Phase One** and **Lace** remain the only nightly options for women. Phase One has done much to move beyond its image of a place where gals shoot pool and watch the Redskins. Live performances dot its calendar, and even if it's not the glitziest place in town, it is the city's longest running gay bar, making it worthy of a visit.

For news about the scene, try *Metro Weekly* (www.metroweekly.com) and the *Washington Blade* (www.washingtonblade.com).

★ Blowoff

9:30 Club, 815 V Street, NW, at 9th Street, U Street Corridor (1-202 393 0930, www.930.com, www.blowoff.us). U Street/African-American Civil War Memorial/Cardozo Metro. **Dates** see website. **Admission** varies. **Credit** AmEx, MC, V. **Map** p251 J3.

In the main room of the 9:30 Club, Bob Mould and Rich Morel's 'diva-free' dance party pumps some real muscle into the District's nightlife. Expect anything from Black Legend to Madonna to Secret Machines to Mould and Morel's own remixes and compositions. Check the website for dates and times.. *Photo p164.*

DC Eagle

639 New York Avenue, NW, between 6th & 7th Streets, Downtown (1-202 347 6025,

INSIDE TRACK PRIDE

Washington's annual **Capital Pride** celebrations take place in May or June, with the usual parties, pageants and parades. It's joined by the three days of concerts, films, workshops, games and awards that is **Black Pride**. For both, *see p22.*

ARTS & ENTERTAINMENT

www.dceagle.com). Mount Vernon Square/ 7th Street-Convention Center Metro. **Open** 4pm-2am Mon, Tue, Thur, Sun; 4pm-3am Wed, Fri, Sat. **Admission** free. **Credit** MC, V. **Map** p253 J5.

Those familiar with the Eagle standard, set in clubs across the country, will know what to expect. DC's version of the popular club offers the usual trappings – pool, pinball and a rock/industrial dance mix. However, what the unfamiliar might find most surprising is the lack of pretence and attitude among the bar's patrons. A great, but dimly lit, club for those who love men in leather (or just the smell of them).

Fireplace

2161 P Street, NW, at 22nd Street, Dupont Circle (1-202 293 1293, www.fireplacedc.com). Metro Dupont Circle. **Open** 1pm-2am Mon; 1pm-3am Fri, Sat. **Admission** free. **Map** p250 G4.

It's very much a case of upstairs and downstairs at this place; upstairs is for dance and attracts a younger African American crowd, while downstairs, where the actual fireplace is, attracts an older, racially mixed clientele. Some say its cliquey and seedy, others love it. In any case, it's a DC fixture.

Green Lantern

1335 Green Court, NW, behind lot at 1335 L Street, between 13th & 14th Streets, Downtown (1-202 347 4533, www.greenlanterndc.com). McPherson Square Metro. **Open** 4pm-2am Mon-Thur; 4pm-3am Fri, Sat; 1pm-2am Sun. **Admission** free. **Credit** MC, V. **Map** p252 H5.

The Green Lantern still draws the same burly types that it always has, especially on Thursday nights when 'shirtless men drink free'. HUMP: Live Exotic Dancers on Wednesday and karaoke on Sunday and

Monday nights add variety to the regular entertainment provided by pool tables, the dancefloor and video screens. There are special-event dance nights, too, but the real action is the cruising.

JR's

1519 17th Street, NW, at P Street, Dupont Circle (1-202 328 0090, http://jrsbardc.com). Dupont Circle Metro. **Open** 4pm-2am Mon-Thur; 4pm-3am Fri; 1pm-3am Sat; 1pm-2am Sun. **Admission** free. **Map** p250 G4.

Bar staff move at lightning speed to serve customers in this tight space. Nightly happy-hour specials and singalongs on Mondays, not to mention occasional seasonal events (such as the annual Easter bonnet contest), keep the crowd entertained. Videos and pool tables are the main entertainment – aside from cruising, that is – as there's no dancefloor.

Lace

2214 Rhode Island Avenue, NE, at South Dakota Avenue, Brookland (1-202 832 3888, www.lace dc.com). Rhode Island Avenue Metro then 83, 84, 86 bus. **Open** 11am-midnight Mon-Thur; 11am-3am Fri; 4pm-3am Sat. **Admission** free. **Credit** AmEx, MC, V.

Linda McAllister arrived in Washington expecting to find a plethora of lesbian bars, but instead encountered a rather barren nightlife scene. She opened Lace in late 2008, as a restaurant and lounge. The clientele is mostly (not entirely) African American, and if your brother is straight, he's welcome too. Decor is unmistakeably feminine, though.

MOVA Lounge DC

2204 14th Street, NW, between Florida Avenue & W Street, Logan Circle (1-202 629 3958, www. movaloungedc.com). U Street/African-American

Blowoff. *See p163.*

Civil War Memorial/Cardozo Metro. **Open** *Apr-Oct* 4pm-3am Mon-Sat; 4pm-2am Sun. *Nov-Mar* 5pm-3am Tue-Sat; 5pm-2am Sun. **Credit** AmEx, MC, V. **Map** p250 H4.

MOVA is a smart, sleek cocktail bar (its cucumber ginger martini came top in a recent *Washington Blade* readers' poll for best cocktail). DJs turn up the volume later in the evening, and weekly events include College Night on Thursdays, and the Curtain Call show tunes night on Saturdays.

★ Nellie's Sports Bar

900 U Street, NW, at 9th Street, U Street Corridor (1-202 332 6355, www.nelliesdc.com). U Street/ African-American Civil War Memorial/Cardozo Metro. **Open** 5pm-midnight Mon-Thur; 5pm-3am Fri; 11am-3am Sat; 11am-midnight Sun. **Credit** MC, V. **Map** p251 J3.

A gay-friendly sports bar? *Mais oui*, with karaoke on Tuesdays, Smart Ass Trivia Night on Wednesdays, board games galore, and a roof patio; along with ten HD TVs and one giant screen for game days – in the more traditional, sports-bar sense of the word. Nellie's, named after the owner's great- and great-great-grandmother, has all the accoutrements of a regular sports bar (wings, nachos, burgers), along with a mixed crowd, a serious take on sports, and Latin-themed *arepas* and *empanadas* from the Venezualan co-owner.

Phase One

525 8th Street, SE, between F & G Streets, Capitol Hill (1-202 544 6831, http://phase1 dc.com). Eastern Market Metro. **Open** 7.30pm-2am Thur, Sun; 7pm-3am Fri, Sat. **Admission** free. **No credit cards**. **Map** p253 M8.

Phase One has done its best to overcome its image of a rough-gurl hangout where fist-flying bar brawls were the norm, though you're still most likely to find the place packed out when the Redskins game is projected on to a gigantic screen. The bar recently celebrated its 40th anniversary, no mean feat in a business where operations come and go with alarming regularity. Phase One now hosts occasional open mic events, jello wrestling and even the odd dance night. It also stands alone in presenting drag king shows.

Town Danceboutique

2009 8th Street, NW, at U Street, Shaw (1-202 234 8696, www.towndc.com). U Street/African-American Civil War Memorial/Cardozo Metro. **Open** 6pm-4am Fri; 10pm-4am Sat. Event times vary. **Credit** MC, V (admission only). **Map** p251 J3.

One of the city's most popular and packed dance clubs, with two floors and multiple rooms, Town also has a performance space hosting drag shows every weekend, plus a comfortable lounge. A 'DC Bear Crue' happy hour takes place Fridays 6-11pm. Occasional theme parties (superheroes was a recent one) are a popular draw.

Nellie's Sports Bar.

Ziegfields/Secrets

1824 Half Street, SW, at T Street, Southwest (1-202 863 0670, www.secretsdc.com). Navy Yard Metro. **Open** *Secrets* 9pm-2am Wed, Thur, Sun; 9pm-3am Fri, Sat. *Ziegfields* 9pm-2am Fri, Sat. **Credit** MC, V.

Resurrected from the dead in 2009 – it was closed to make way for construction of the ballpark – Ziegfields is now back to doing what it does best: regular, uproarious drag nights with hostesses Ella Fitzgerald and Destiny B. Childs. Nude male dancers perform Wednesday through Sunday nights after 9pm. Upstairs, Secrets has DJs and occasional amateur dance contests.

GYMS

Bodysmith

1622 14th Street, NW, at Corcoran Street, Logan Circle (1-202 722-0001, www.bodysmithdc.com). Shaw-Howard University Metro. **Open** varies. **Credit** AmEx, MC, V. **Map** p250 H4.

Bodysmith's personal trainers are well qualified and, judging by the look of the patrons, they do their job well. Best to book ahead, however, as appointments go fast at this small personal training facility. There are no independent workouts here, only clients and their trainers. If you like a challenge you could always sign up for the ominously named 'boot camp series'.

Crew Club

1321 14th Street, NW, between N Street & Rhode Island Avenue, Logan Circle (1-202 319 1333, www.crewclub.net). McPherson Square Metro. **Open** 24hrs daily. **Rates** Day membership $10;

30-day membership $15. Extra charges for some rooms & lockers. **Credit** AmEx, MC, V. **Map** p250 H4.

A licensed nudist facility, Crew Club caters to those looking for a workout that's uninhibited – or at least undressed. Showers, lockers and towels are all available, as are condoms. There's a TV room too.

VIDA Fitness

1612 U Street, NW, between 16th & 17th Streets, U Street Corridor (1-202 939 2577, www.vida fitness.com). U Street/African-American Civil War Memorial/Cardozo Metro. **Open** 5am-11pm Mon-Fri; 7am-9pm Sat, Sun. **Map** p250 H3.

VIDA pumped millions into renovating the warehouse building that formerly housed Results the Gym, adding spa features, two endless pools, a 'Fuel Bar', and a rooftop pool and lounge. The luxe, gay-friendly gym chain has been taking over the city in recent years, and now operates locations in Penn Quarter, Logan Circle, NoMa, and in the Renaissance Hotel downtown, among others.
Other locations throughout the city.

RESTAURANTS & CAFÉS

There really aren't any restaurants that are exclusively gay in the District. But there are joints where the community tends to congregate as much for the scene as for the sustenance.

Annie's Paramount Steak House

1609 17th Street, NW, between Q & Corcoran Streets, Dupont Circle (1-202 232 0395, www.anniesdc.com). Dupont Circle Metro. **Open** 10am-11.30pm Mon-Wed; 10am-1.30am Thur; 11.30am Fri-11pm Sun. **Main courses** $10-$22. **Credit** AmEx, Disc, MC, V. **Map** p250 G4.

A DC institution: having served DC's gay community for more than 50 years, it's worth grabbing a burger at Annie's just to say 'I was there'. There's nothing remarkable about the decor or the service – or the food, for that matter. Many of the patrons seem to come to reminisce about the glory of their youth, giving the restaurant even more of a neighbourhood feel. Midnight brunch is served at weekends and holidays, and the kitchen remains open round the clock from Friday night until Sunday night.

Duplex Diner

2004 18th Street, NW, at Vernon Street, Adams Morgan (1-202 265 7828, www.duplexdiner.com). Dupont Circle Metro then 42 bus. **Open** 6-11pm Mon; 6pm-12.30am Tue, Wed; 6pm-1.30am Thur; 6pm-2am Fri, Sat; 11.30am-11pm Sun. **Main courses** $9-$15. **Credit** AmEx, Disc, MC, V. **Map** p250 H3.

The Duplex Diner, or the 18th & U as it's also known, has the casual feel of the 1950s eateries it emulates and a reputation for *au courant* cocktails. Some nights attract more patrons than others; for instance, the Thursday night bar and club crowd often relies on the Duplex as its opening act. The menu lists diner favourites – burgers and fries, natch – but the real draw is the neighbourhood feel.

Dupont Italian Kitchen (DIK)

1637 17th Street, NW, at R Street, Dupont Circle (1-202 328 3222, www.dupontitaliankitchen.com). Dupont Circle Metro. **Open** 11am-11pm Mon-Thur; 11am-1am Fri; 10.30am-1am Sat; 10.30am-11pm Sun. **Main courses** $6-$16. **Credit** AmEx, Disc, MC, V. **Map** p250 H4.

It's not the food that keeps this place in business, but rather the prime vantage point it offers for viewing the 17th Street flora and fauna. The meals are modestly priced and the mood is casual. It's a great place to spend a lazy afternoon outside, or to socialise on a warm summer night. But note that when patrons get a seat here, they're not likely to give it up in a hurry, and table turnovers can be few and far between. Upstairs is a favourite hang of those of a certain age who don't fancy the loud, late club scene.

L'Enfant Café

2000 18th Street, NW, at corner of U Street & Florida Avenue, Adams Morgan (1-202 319 1800, www.lenfantcafe.com). Dupont Circle Metro then 42 bus. **Open** 6pm-midnight Mon-Thur; 6pm-1am Fri; 10am-1am Sat; 10am-midnight Sun. **Main courses** $12-$21. **Credit** AmEx, Disc, MC, V. **Map** p250 H3.

L'Enfant does its best to deliver decent French stalwarts, like boeuf bourguignon, at a reasonable price with reasonable speed. Dimly lit but welcoming and warm, it's an ideal spot to spend a winter afternoon; in spring and summer, its outdoor patio gets lively.

Duplex Diner.

Nightlife

Time to stay up late.

Vibrant nightlife may not be something immediately associated with Washington DC. But if you forget politics and instead focus on DC as a young, energetic and cosmopolitan city, with a creative drive and a distinctive indigenous music scene, then it's easier to imagine why its nightlife might be memorable. Here we list some of the city's best dance clubs, along with lounges with DJs and live music.

At various times, Washington has been known for bluegrass, hardcore punk and the syncopated funk known as go-go (*see p169* **Washington's Own**). But the local music 'scene' has always actually been a patchwork of scenes. How could the hometown of Al Jolson, Duke Ellington, John Philip Sousa, Marvin Gaye and Henry Rollins be limited to any one sound? Punk no longer dominates, but the subculture it created – with its preference for easygoing all-ages clubs – still defines the live rock scene.

For bars with music, *see pp106-114.*

CLUBS & LOUNGES

Information on club nights and parties can be found in the *Washington City Paper* and the *Washington Post*'s 'Night Watch' column in Friday's 'Weekend' section. Natural-born scruffs should note that some of the DC scene operates a dress code: think smart. Access to upscale joints will be denied those wearing jeans, sneakers or hats.

In addition to the places below, check out **Little Miss Whiskey's** on H Street (*see p96* **A Taste of H Street**) for beers and dance parties, and **Josephine** (1008 Vermont Avenue, NW, between K & L Streets, Downtown, 1-202 347 8601, www.josephinedc.com) for cocktails and more dancing.

Bravo! Bravo!

1001 Connecticut Avenue, NW, between K & L Streets, Downtown (1-202 223 5330, www. bravobravodc.com). Farragut North Metro. **Open** 11am-9pm Mon, Tue, Thur; 11am-4am Fri, Sat. **Admission** $10-$15. **Credit** AmEx, DC, Disc, MC, V. **Map** p252 G5.

For over ten years this unassuming bar and nightclub three blocks from the White House has been attracting upwards of 400 polished dancers for Latin music on Friday and Saturday nights. The mood is flirty; the music is a combination of Spanish-language club hits and up-tempo remixes. This is one of the few 18-and-over dance nights in the city. Lighting is harsh and security tight.

Bukom Café

2442 18th Street, NW, between Belmont & Columbia Roads, Adams Morgan (1-202 265 4600, www.bukom.com). Woodley Park-Zoo/ Adams Morgan Metro then 96 bus or walk. **Open** 4.30pm-2am daily. **Admission** free. **Credit** AmEx, Disc, MC, V. **Map** p250 G3.

The crowd is West African and African American but everyone's welcome to get lost in the sway. The Ghanaian menu is reason alone to visit, but arrive after 10pm and it's standing room only: be prepared to dance with whoever's next to you. Nightly bands play reggae, soca and funk.

Chi-Cha Lounge

1624 U Street, NW, between 16th & 17th Streets, U Street Corridor (1-202 234 8400, www.chichaloungedc.com). Dupont Circle or U Street/African-American Civil War Memorial/ Cardozo Metro. **Open** 5.30pm-1.30am Mon-Thur, Sun; 5.30pm-3am Fri, Sat. **Admission** usually free. **Map** p250 H3.

Ecuadorean entrepreneur Mauricio Fraga-Rosenfeld has taught DC to relax to a Latin beat. Since opening

Chi-Cha, he's expanded to Dupont Circle (Gazuza), Georgetown (Mate) and Arlington (Gua-Rapo). All follow the same formula: deep velvet couches, candlelight, Andean tapas, sangría, Latin jazz and hookah pipes filled with honey-cured tobacco. Chi-Cha hosts live bands from Sunday to Thursday; on these nights there's a $15 minimum consumption fee. No hats, ties or sportswear. That's right, no ties.

Eighteenth Street Lounge

1212 18th Street, NW, between M Street & Jefferson Place, Dupont Circle (1-202 466 3922, www.eighteenthstreetlounge.com). Farragut North or Dupont Circle Metro. **Open** 5.30pm-2am Tue-Thur; 5.30pm-3am Fri; 9.30pm-3am Sat; 9pm-2am Sun. **Admission** $5-$10. **Credit** AmEx, MC, V. **Map** p250 G5.

Love it or hate it, ESL remains the city's trendiest and most exclusive lounge, widely renowned (or notorious) for its strict door policy. Should your attire (or your connections) please the notoriously fickle doormen and you're granted entrance through the unmarked wooden door, you'll find hipsters mingling and dancing to live jazz or down-tempo electronic music spun by the city's best DJs.

▶ *For more on the Eighteenth Street Lounge as a bar, see p109.*

Fur

33 Patterson Street, NE, at North Capitol Street, Northeast (1-202 842 3401, www.furnightclub. com). New York Avenue/Florida Avenue-Gallaudet U Metro. **Open** 10pm-3am Fri; 10pm-4am Sat. **Admission** $10-$25. **Credit** AmEx, Disc, MC, V. **Map** p253 K5.

Dress up and wait in line at the city's latest superclub. What makes Fur different from DC's other multi-level venues? All boast chic interiors, VIP rooms, leading names and vast dance spaces. But what sets Fur apart is its intimate lounges, which provide a haven from the audio-visual show pulsating from the dancefloors. They have louche names like the Mafia Room and the Mink Room. Theme nights are frequent so check the website in advance.

Habana Village

1834 Columbia Road, NW, between Biltmore Street & Mintwood Place, Adams Morgan (1-202 462 6310, www.habanavillage.com). Woodley Park-Zoo/Adams Morgan Metro/ 90, 92, 96 bus. **Open** 6.30-10pm Wed; 6.30-11pm Thur; 6.30pm-1am Fri, Sat; 5-10pm Sun. **Admission** varies. **Credit** MC, V. **Map** p250 G3.

Latin dance-lovers come here to drink mojitos and get sweaty to a live band. Three storeys of music inspire dancers from all nationalities and all levels of proficiency to grab a stranger's hand and get swinging. Expect live merengue, salsa, and bachata on the top floor, and crowded dance rooms with fans going at full blast.

Patty Boom Boom.

Heaven & Hell

2327 18th Street, NW, at Kalorama Road, Adams Morgan (1-202 667 4355, www.clubheavenand helldc.com). Woodley Park-Zoo/Adams Morgan Metro then 96 bus or walk. **Open** 5pm-2am Tue-Thur, Sun; 5pm-3am Fri, Sat. **Admission** $5 (includes 1 drink). **Credit** AmEx, DC, Disc, MC, V. **Map** p250 G3.

The gimmick here is that there are two bars on the premises. Upstairs, Heaven has nightly dance parties, while Hell (down below, obviously) is a basement bar with beer and pool. Dance music in Heaven tends towards mainstream house and techno, with a changing roster of DJs. Downstairs, music has a harder edge (punk, maybe, or hip hop), and the walls have spooky decor of skeletons and the like.

Love

1350 Okie Street, NE, at New York Avenue, Northeast (1-202 636 9030, http://lovetheclub. com). **Open** 9pm-2am Wed, Thur; 8pm-3am Fri, Sat. **Admission** $10-$40. **Credit** AmEx, MC, V.

Love is still one of the hottest dance clubs in town, but it's a nightmare to reach (best to drive or take a cab, as there's no Metro nearby and the area can be dangerous). A refurbished four-storey warehouse in an industrial neighbourhood off New York Avenue, the club is an evening's commitment. But dress to impress and it's worth it. Inside are myriad bars, rooms pumping hip hop, R&B, house and trance. Fridays is International Embassy Fridays. On Saturday it's Tainted Saturdays.

Patty Boom Boom

1359 U Street, NW, at 14th Street, U Street Corridor (1-202 629 1712, www.pattyboom boomdc.com). U Street/African-American Civil

War Memorial/Cardozo Metro. **Open** 8pm-2am Wed, Thur; 8pm-3am Fri, Sat. **Admission** free. **Credit** AmEx, MC, V. **Map** p250 H3.

The outpost of the Eighteenth Street Lounge/Thievery Corporation empire is dedicated to two Jamaican products: patties (spiced meat or veggies in pastry) and reggae. Bands perform at this laid-back venue, but DJs dominate; they pump roots, rock steady, dub and dancehall through a 21-speaker sound system that doesn't stint on the bass. The food and music draw a Jamaican clientele. The place opens for lunch; the music starts at 9pm.

Pure

1326 U Street, NW, between 13th & 14th Streets, U Street Corridor (1-202 290 7058, www.pureloungevip.com). U Street/African-American Civil War Memorial/Cardozo Metro. **Open** 6pm-2am Tue-Thur; 6pm-3am Fri; 9pm-3am Sat; 6pm-2am Sun. **Admission** free, except for special events. **Credit** AmEx, DC, MC, V. **Map** p250 H3.

Pure Lounge has a sleek, space-age look, with a Miami-style white lounge. The two levels feature different DJs, with music that ranges from hip hop, house and soul to soca, Afropop and reggae. The venue draws a diverse clientele. Thursdays and Sundays are reggae nights.

U Street Music Hall

1115 U Street, NW, between 11th & 12th Streets, U Street Corridor (1-202 588 1880, www.streetmusichall.com). U Street/African-American Civil War Memorial/Cardozo Metro. **Open** 10pm-2am Mon-Thur, Sun; 10pm-3am Fri, Sat. **Admission** free-$10. **Credit** AmEx, MC, V. **Map** p250 J3.

This bare-bones basement club, which emphasises music over luxury, arrived just in time for the economic downturn. The vibe is closer to a rock club than a 'bottle service' lounge, and rock bands perform live. But the club's founders, local DJs Will Eastman and Jesse Tittsworth, built the room for dancing: the 1,200sq ft hardwood dancefloor floats on a cork foundation, and the 20,000-watt sound system is modelled on those in top London clubs. Recent guest DJs include Simian Mobile Disco, Tensnake, Richie Hawtin and Amon Tobin. Ages 18 and over.

Ultrabar

911 F Street, NW, between 9th & 10th Streets, Downtown (1-202 638 4663, www.ultrabar dc.com). Gallery Place-Chinatown or Metro Center Metro. **Open** 10pm-2am Thur; 9.30pm-3am Sat, Sun. **Admission** $10-$15; sometimes free by signing up via the website. **Credit** AmEx, MC, V. **Map** p253 J6.

The last club standing on what a decade ago was a bustling late-night block, Ultrabar is an upscale, four-level venue in a former bank building. The management promises 'a slice of Miami', with different styles of dance music on each level. Theme nights include Carnival Night, Bikini Night and 'Little Black Dress' parties; check the website for dates and details. Seats at tables require bottle service ($100 and up), and a 'dress to impress' code is enforced. Ages 18 and over only. *Photo p170.*

Zengo

781 7th Street, NW, at H Street, Downtown (1-202 393 2929). Chinatown/Gallery Place Metro. **Open** 5-11pm Mon-Thur; 5pm-3am. **Admission** free. **Credit** AmEx, MC, V. **Map** p253 J5.

Washington's Own

Go-go is DC's very own brand of funk.

Washington is not a hip hop desert: the city and its more urban suburbs are home to such rappers as Tabi Bonney, Wale and DJ Kool. But the beat of black Washington remains go-go, the heavily syncopated big-band funk pioneered in the 1970s by Chuck Brown and the Soul Searchers. This style has scored a few national hits, notably EU's 1988 'Da Butt', but most Americans have heard go-go only in the samples beneath such hits as Nelly's 'It's Hot in Herre' and Beyoncé's 'Crazy in Love'.

Go-go and hip hop have grown closer over the years. Today's go-go bands rely more on keyboards and samplers, and less on the horn sections and multiple percussionists of such classic go-go outfits as EU, Rare Essence and Troublefunk. But go-go retains such distinctive (and African-rooted) elements as chattering polyrhythms, call-and-response shout-outs to the audience and grooves that can extend for hours.

It's fundamentally live music, which is why few go-go acts release studio recordings any more. (The venerable Chuck Brown, who had a street named for him in 2009, is an exception.) When Wale records, he works with such producers as British hitmaker Mark Ronson; but when he plays live, he's usually backed by a go-go band.

Go-go is an insular scene, whose shows are not publicised to outsiders, and whose venues can be sketchy. Listings for local shows can be found at www.gogobeat.com and www.tmott gogo.com, but the safest course would be to experience the music at a more mainstream hall, such as the 9:30 Club (*see p170*).

Ultra Bar. *See p169.*

A sleek Latin-Asian lounge where the pricey cocktails are actually worth the money (try the Mojito De Mango), Zengo's drinks, vibrant atmosphere and food from renowned chef Richard Sandoval make it a favourite among the trendy crowd.

COMEDY & CABARET

Improv

1140 Connecticut Avenue, NW, between L & M Streets, Downtown (1-202 296 7008, www.dc improv.com). Farragut North Metro. **Open** *Shows* 8.30pm Tue-Thur; 8pm, 10.30pm Fri, Sat; 8pm Sun. **Admission** $15-$35. **Credit** AmEx, MC, V. **Map** p252 G5.

The most common assessment of Improv is that the service is disappointing but the material hysterical.

MUSIC VENUES

Rock, roots & R&B

From small rooms to large arenas, DC's stages host every type of rock and pop performance imaginable, including the pretty bog standard. As well as venues listed below, some clubs and lounges, such as the **Eighteenth Street Lounge** (*see p168*) also host live music, while mammoth acts head for the **Verizon Center** (*see p189*) and, occasionally, the **RFK Stadium** (*see p189*). Outdoor pop concerts and all-day rock festivals use such suburban venues as Maryland's **Merriweather Post Pavilion** (www.merriweathermusic.com) and **Fedex Field** (www.fedex-field.com).

Folk, country and bluegrass music acts are now generally booked into rock clubs as well, although the **Birchmere**, **Iota Club & Café** and **Jammin' Java** have more than their share of unplugged acts.

Whatever you're going to see, get tickets well in advance. Younger punters should check venues' admissions policies: many require patrons to be 21 or over, though **9:30 Club**, **Black Cat** and smaller punk-rooted venues admit any age group (no alcoholic drinks served to under-21s).

You can find information on what's on at www.showlistdc.com and www.thrillcall.com/live-music/Washington-dc.

★ 9:30 Club

815 V Street, NW, at 9th Street, U Street Corridor (1-202 265 0930, 393 0930, www.930.com). U Street/African-American Civil War Memorial/Cardozo Metro or 66, 68, 70, 71, 90, 92, 93, 96, 98 bus. **Open** varies. **Admission** varies. **Credit** AmEx, MC, V. **Map** p251 J3.

Once a tiny art-scene dive on F Street, renowned for its heat (and smell), the 9:30 relocated in 1996. It now boasts state-of-the-art sound and ventilation, as well as a healthy slate of microbrews. A few long-lived (or reunited) punk and post-punk bands have played both incarnations, among them Wire, the Feelies and Mission of Burma, but these days you're as likely to see George Clinton, Jane's Addiction, Andrew Bird, the Magnetic Fields, Snoop Dogg, Patti Smith or the Walkmen, and Adele has performed here too. The open floor and balcony layout is supposed to guarantee unrestricted viewing of the stage from anywhere in the club, and for the most part it succeeds. However, arriving early, scoping out the best vantage point and then standing your ground for the rest of the night is the best way to ensure a good view.

Birchmere

3701 Mount Vernon Avenue, between W Reed Avenue & Russell Road, Alexandria, VA (1-703 549 7500, www.birchmere.com). Pentagon Metro then 10A or 10E bus. **Open** from 6pm on gig nights. **Admission** $15-$45. **Credit** AmEx, MC, V.

Originally a bluegrass, folk and country institution, the Birchmere is one of these venues artists can't bear to outgrow. Patty Loveless might play a couple of nights here in the autumn before heading to Wolf Trap in the spring, and Merle Haggard's annual gigs always sell out. Now the Birchmere also serves up the kind of pop, smooth jazz and world music that appeals to an over-30s crowd. The Band Stand area has a dancefloor, but most of the shows are in the larger Music Hall. This is a listeners' club, not some chicken-wire honky-tonk, and a few house rules apply in the table-service Music Hall: no standing, no smoking, no recording, no talking. Rowdier patrons can head for the bar and the pool tables. Coming up at the time of writing were Macy Gray, Rachel Yamagata and Dr John, and recent acts include Graham Parker, Aimee Mann, Dar Williams and Steve Earle.

★ Black Cat

1811 14th Street, NW, between S & T Streets,
U Street Corridor (1-202 667 7960, www.black
catdc.com). U Street/African-American Civil War
Memorial/Cardozo Metro. **Open** 8pm-2am Mon-
Thur, Sun; 7pm-3am Fri, Sat. *Red Room Bar*
8pm-2am Mon-Thur, Sun; 7pm-3am Fri, Sat.
Admission $8-$20. **No credit cards** (ATM
in club). **Map** p250 H3.
As famous for having Foo Fighter Dave Grohl as a
backer as it is for the bands it books, the Black Cat
has picked up where the old 9:30 left off when it
comes to hosting less mainstream acts. Opened in
1993, the Black Cat began with the Fall, Stereolab
and Slant 6 and has been continuing pretty much
along those lines ever since. The vibe is dark and
homey. A downstairs area – Back Stage – hosts
greener local and out-of-town bands, as well as DJ
nights that range from '80s retro to bhangra. Acts
set to perform at the time of writing included Gold
Panda, the Thermals and Wire.

Comet Ping Pong

5037 Connecticut Avenue, NW, at Nebraska
Avenue, Upper Northwest (1-202 364 0404,
www.sashalord-presents.tumblr.com). Van
Ness/UDC Metro then L2, L4 bus. **Music**
takes place until 2am Fri, Sat, with occasional
shows other nights. **Admission** free-$8.
Credit AmEx, MC, V.
The underground rock scene that bounced around
several funky Downtown venues – some legal, some
maybe not – has now landed at this gourmet pizza
joint in an affluent residential neighbourhood not
famed for nightlife. Music begins as the pizza ovens
start to cool, most Fridays and Saturdays, with the
focus on indie rock, mostly touring acts. Funk, reggae and electronica can sometimes be heard. Recent
acts include Mykii Bianco, Golden Grrls and the
Babies. Check Comet's Facebook page for information on upcoming acts.
► *For a restaurant review of Comet Ping Pong,*
see p103.

DC9

1940 9th Street, NW, at U Street, U Street
Corridor (1-202 483 5000, www.dcnine.com). U
Street/African-American Civil War Memorial/
Cardozo Metro. **Open** 8pm-2am Mon-Thur, Sun;
7pm-3am Fri, Sat. **Admission** $5-$15. No advance
tickets. **Credit** MC, V. **Map** p251 J3.
This club's long, thin, vintage-looking first-floor
bar leads to an oddly shaped upstairs performance
space. It showcases the same sort of local and touring indie bands that play Galaxy Hut, Velvet
Lounge and the Red & the Black, but has a larger
capacity. Mostly alt-rock, although the Very Best
made its DC debut to a packed house here. At the
time of writing, the Men and Tera Melos were due
to perform.
► *The rooftop bar here is also popular.*

Fillmore

8656 Colesville Road, Silver Spring, MD (1-301
960-9999, www.fillmoresilverspring.com). Silver
Spring Metro. **Open** hours vary. **Admission**
varies. **Credit** MC, V.
After many delays, the 2,000-capacity club in the
suburbs (the latest franchise from famed San
Francisco promoter Bill Graham) opened with a sold-
out Mary J Blige show in September 2011. So far it's
been hard to pin down exactly where the Fillmore
fits into the region's music scene; acts have been all
over the map, including classic rock (Cheap Trick)
and jam bands (Trey Anastasio). Acts on the 2013
schedule have included Olly Murs, Rancid and
Flogging Molly.

Galaxy Hut

2711 Wilson Boulevard, between Danville &
Edgewood Streets, Arlington, VA (1-703 525
8646, www.galaxyhut.com). Clarendon Metro.
Open 5pm-2am daily. **Music** Mon, Sun.
Admission generally $5.
This petite bar offers up-and-coming acts (mostly
indie-rock) for a small cover charge. With a capacity
of only 48, the place fills up easily, but in good
weather you can watch the bands from outside,
through the picture window. As of 2012, the restaurant here went all-vegetarian.

Hole in the Sky

2110 5th Street, NE, at Rhode Island Avenue,
Northeast (no phone, www.holeintheskydc.com).
Rhode Island Avenue Metro. **Open** 8pm-midnight
on show nights. **Admission** $1-$10 donation. No
advance tickets. **No credit cards. Map** p251 L3.
The latest place to enter the storied history of DC
artspaces/punk venues is this multi-purpose, second-storey loft in a light-industrial neighbourhood.

Black Cat.

Rock & Roll Hotel

The non-profit collective hosts five to ten shows a month, mostly various forms of punk. Local bands predominate, although Brooklyn's Shellshag and San Francisco's Street Eaters were there recently. Enter through the alley between 4th and 5th Streets, and if you expect to be thirsty, bring your own beverage.

Howard Theatre

620 T Street, NW, between 7th & Witteberger Streets, Shaw (1-202 803 2899, http://the howardtheatre.com). Shaw-Howard University Metro. **Open** varies. **Admission** varies. **Credit** AmEx, MC, V. **Map** p251 J3.

A place with a starred history (it was dubbed 'the largest colored theater in the world' when it opened in 1910), the Howard hosted most of the jazz greats in its heyday, among them Duke Ellington, Ella Fitzgerald, Billie Holliday, Louis Armstrong and Cab Calloway. Shuttered since the 1980s, it has now been creatively restored and features performances from R&B, gospel and soul bands and singers, among them Alexander O'Neill, Brian McKnight and Sheila E. There are regular Sunday gospel brunches too.

IOTA Club & Café

2832 Wilson Boulevard, between Edgewood & Fillmore Streets, Arlington, VA (1-703 522 8340, www.iotaclubandcafe.com). Clarendon Metro. **Open** 5pm-2am Mon-Sat; closes midnight Sun. **Admission** $10-$15. **Credit** AmEx, MC, V.

IOTA has an intimate atmosphere that makes it an excellent place in which to hear singer-songwriters such as the child-friendly Dan Zanes or the all-grown-up Ron Sexsmith. Unfortunately, the surroundings can be a little too intimate and it's not unknown for patrons to be asked to shut up or leave the premises – sometimes by the performers themselves – as even the slightest whisper can interfere with the music. The artist-comes-first policy has its benefits: Norah Jones and John Mayer played their first DC shows here. The layout of the tiny tiny club doesn't provide many optimum vantage points, so early arrival is advised. Recent performers include Holly Golightly, the Weathervanes and Lambchop.

Jammin' Java

228 Maple Avenue, East Vienna, VA (1-703 255 1566, https://jamminjava.com). **Open** 3pm-1am Mon-Wed; 9am-1am Thur, Sun; 9am-2am Fri, Sat. **Admission** $10-$22. **Credit** AmEx, MC, V.

A Christian coffeehouse bought out and turned secular, Jammin' Java has earned a place on the folk, blues and roots circuits, with fare ranging from Bert Jansch, Pegi Young and the Mekons to regular open mic nights. Owners Luke and Daniel Brindley also occasionally take the stage as pop-rock duo the Brindley Brothers.

★ Rock & Roll Hotel

1353 H Street, NE, between 13th & 14th Streets, H Street Corridor (1-202 388 7625, www.rockandrollhoteldc.com). Gallery Place Metro then X2 bus. **Open** 6pm-2am Mon-Thur; 6pm-3am Fri, Sat. **Admission** $10-$25. **Credit** MC, V. **Map** p248 M5.

Downstairs, this is a basic rock bar, but the upper floor plays on the hotel theme with private rooms that can be rented by small groups. (No beds; it's not that kind of hotel.) Since opening in 2006, the 400-capacity club has scored numerous booking coups, including utterly sold-out shows by Sleigh Bells, Best Coast and Phoenix. Recent acts include Jamie Lidell, the Cave Singers and the Meat Puppets. DJs rule upstairs, and occasionally below.

State Theatre

220 N Washington Street (Lee Highway/Route 29), Falls Church, VA (1-703 237 0300, www.the statetheatre.com). East Falls Church Metro then 2A, 3A bus. **Open** 7pm on show nights; closing time varies. **Admission** $10-$30. **Credit** AmEx, Disc, MC, V.

Another converted movie theatre, the State is a favourite haunt of jam bands, blues and reggae artists – and lots of tribute bands – from near and far. Recent acts include Buddy Guy, the Smithereens and Soul Asylum.The club has ample seating in the back and upstairs, plus a raked floor for good sight-lines throughout the room. It may feel like a hike to get out there, but it's only a 10-minute bus journey from the East Falls Church Metro station.

Essential DC Albums

City Sounds.

BUSTIN' LOOSE
CHUCK BROWN & THE
SOUL SEARCHERS (1979)

The 'godfather of go-go' and his fellow funksters the Soul Searchers give us a dose of the distinctive, syncopated, rhythm-heavy brand of funk that is Washington's very own. It's title track was a dancefloor hit, sampled decades later by Nelly in 'Hot in Herre'.

MASTERPIECES
BY ELLINGTON
DUKE ELLINGTON (1950)

Native son, composer, pianist, big band leader and jazz legend, Duke Ellington began his career in his hometown and performed in Washington many times. With a career spanning 60 years there's a lot to choose from. This album features 'Mood Indigo', 'Solitude and 'Sophisticated Lady'.

TUBULAR BELLS
MIKE OLDFIELD (1973)

Mike Oldfield's classic prog rock debut album, recorded in England and released when he was just 19, found a Washington connection when its mesmerising and eerie opening section, beginning with a single soft minor-key piano line, was used as the soundtrack for DC-set horror film *The Exorcist*.

MOVING TARGET
GIL SCOTT-HERON (1982)

We're back in the dark days of early '80s Washington with Gil Scott-Heron's polemic track about the wrongs of having 'citizens of poverty barely out of sight' of the monuments supposed to symbolise democracy. As the man says, 'It's a mass of irony for all the world to see/ It's the nation's capital, it's Washington DC.'

THE RICHEST MAN
IN BABYLON
THIEVERY
CORPORATION (2002)

Formed in Washington's Eighteenth Street Lounge, Thievery Corporation is a true DC outfit. *The Richest Man* exemplifies their audacious mixing of genres (reggae, rap, dance, Indian music) and languages (English, French, Portuguese, Spanish and Persian), backed with a heavy bass.

REPEATER
FUGAZI (1990)

DC's Dischord Records and its bands, especially Fugazi, whose frontman Ian MacKaye also co-owned the label, established an ethos of fierce independence, social activism and anti-commercialism that still influences local musicians. *Repeater* exemplifies its particular brand of lean, vehement, political post-punk.

ARTS & ENTERTAINMENT

Velvet Lounge

*915 U Street, NW, between Vermont Avenue &
9th Street, U Street Corridor (1-202 462 3213,
www.velvetloungedc.com). U Street/African-
American Civil War Memorial/Cardozo Metro.*
Open 8pm-2am Mon-Thur, Sun; 8pm-3am Fri, Sat.
Admission $5-$15 **Credit** MC, V. **Map** p251 J3.
Often the province of local bands and DJs – and their
friends whooping them on from the audience – the
Velvet Lounge also books indie-rockers from far outside the Beltway, including such cult acts as Damo
Suzuki and the Homosexuals. The place still has the
feel of a neighbourhood bar that just happens to have
a small stage upstairs. A good place to drop in after
attending a show at the nearby 9:30 Club (*see p170*).

Jazz

Washington has a rich jazz history, claiming
the legendary likes of Duke Ellington and
Shirley Horn as its own, though you wouldn't
know it from the relatively few clubs hosting
the music. But with jazz enshrined as 'American
classical music', the **Kennedy Center** (*see
p176*), particularly its KC Jazz Club, and the
Smithsonian (*see p177*) help pick up the slack.

Blues Alley

*1073 Wisconsin Avenue, NW, at M Street,
Georgetown (1-202 337 4141, www.blues
alley.com). Foggy Bottom-GWU Metro then 31,
32, 36, 38B, Circulator bus.* **Open** 6pm-12.30am
daily. **Admission** $16-$50. **Credit** AmEx, DC,
MC, V. **Map** p249 E5.
Some patrons consider the cover charges here outrageously high, especially as there is also a two-
drink minimum per person for each set, which
usually lasts just under an hour. Others are just so
thankful that they have a small space where first-
rate acts such as Mose Allison or Pieces of a Dream
will perform that money is not an object. Acoustics
are as top-notch as the talent on the stage. Recent
acts include Earl Klugh, Karrin Allyson and Afro
Bop Alliance.

Bohemian Caverns

*2003 11th Street, NW, between U & V Streets,
U Street Corridor (1-202 299 0800, www.
bohemiancaverns.com). U Street/African-
American Civil War Memorial/Cardozo Metro.*

INSIDE TRACK ID ALERT

If you're going to a club or music venue
where alcohol is served, always carry ID.
Most places will card you no matter how
old you look. Even venues that admit
under-21s are strict about not serving
them alcohol.

Open 6pm-1am Tue; 8pm-2am Wed; 9pm-2am
Thur; 9.30pm-3am Fri, Sat. **Credit** AmEx, MC, V.
Map p250 J3.
After being shuttered for 30 years, the legendary
Bohemian Caverns reopened in 2000. While it has not
quite restored the glory days of U Street single-
handed, it has found a place among the revitalised
nightlife in the historic African-American corridor.
Christian Scott, Benny Golson and the Young Lions
have played here recently.

HR-57

*1007 H Street NE, between 10th & 11th
Streets, H Street Corridor (1-202 253-0044,
www.hr57.org). Metro Center or Gallery Place-
Chinatown Metro then X2 bus.* **Open** phone for
details. **Admission** varies. **No credit cards**.
Map p248 M5.
This unassuming club recently upgraded to a larger
spot – a former church on H Street – after migrating
to the corridor from 14th Street a few years back.
The principal attraction here is jazz and blues;
the place is named after the US House of
Representatives' resolution recognising jazz as a
national treasure. You won't find big names here,
unless they stop in to jam after local concert-hall
gigs, but you will find huge talent. The cover charge
is usually only a few dollars, and along with
Southern food like greens and beans you can bring
your own wine for a $3 corkage fee – a popular move.
Hit it on a good night, and you've got the best din-
ner-and-a-show value in town.

Twins Jazz

*1344 U Street, NW, between 13th & 14th Streets,
U Street Corridor (1-202 234 0072, www.twins
jazz.com). U Street/African-American Civil War
Memorial/Cardozo Metro.* **Open** 6pm-midnight
Tue-Thur, Sun; 6pm-1am Fri, Sat. **Credit** AmEx,
MC, V. **Admission** $10-$30. **Map** p250 H3.
The twins here are owners Kelly and Maze Tesfaye,
and their well-worn jazz club regularly feature locals
(Lenny Robinson, Michael Thomas) and national
(David 'Fathead' Newman, Eddie Henderson) players.
The headlining cuisine is that of the twins' native
Ethiopia, with Caribbean and American dishes round-
ing out the menu. Like with most jazz clubs, there's a
cover charge and a two-drink minimum.

Utopia

*1418 U Street, between 14th & 15th Streets, U
Street Corridor. U Street/African-American Civil
War Memorial/Cardozo Metro.* **Open** Closed for
renovations at press time; expected to reopen
sometime in 2013. **Map** p250 H3.
One of the first places to open as part of the regeneration of the Shaw neighbourhood, this small space
has settled into a regular schedule of local jazz and
blues. Exhibits by local artists and a international
cuisine (lunch and dinner) all go towards making
Utopia a sophisticated but relaxed local joint.

Performing Arts

A vibrant theatre scene and a broad spectrum of music.

The stage scene in Washington is in a state of rude health and, like any theatre town worth its greasepaint, DC can point to posh troupes with a roster of distinguished directors as well as scrappy little outfits that get by on foundation grants and volunteer sweat. Glittering, glass-fronted new halls for the Shakespeare Theatre Company and Arena Stage (for both, *see p181*) represent both landmarks on the classical theatre scene and new challenges for the companies that inhabit them.

In terms of music, while the National Symphony Orchestra has never been considered one of the country's best, the city has an unusually active schedule of choral and chamber music concerts, and a growing array of venues, some of them quirky and unusual such as the Sixth & I Historic Synagogue (*see p180*). The Kennedy Center (*see p176*) is DC's landmark arts centre and is home to theatre, as well as the Washington National Opera and the National Symphony Orchestra. It also has free shows in its Millennium Stage series.

LISTINGS AND INFORMATION

The free weekly *Washington City Paper* has good music and theatre listings. The *Washington Post* has an extensive 'Weekend' section on Fridays. *Express*, a free commuter paper owned by the *Washington Post* and available at most Metro and bus stops, offers entertainment previews on Thursdays. (It's also at www.readexpress.com.) For theatre, also see the Helen Hayes Awards site (www.helenhayes.org). And for lively discussions of the local theatrical landscape, there's http://DCTheatreScene.com.

Tickets for most performances can be bought direct from the venue. Ticket agencies such as **Ticketmaster** (www.ticketmaster.com) allow you to order online but add high surcharges.

Music: Classical & Opera

Washington DC's classical music and opera scene can reflect the 'by the book' mentality of the city when it comes to the arts. Everything is professional and top-notch, of course, but there's not a lot that could be considered daring. Still, there are numerous embassies here with

active cultural departments, offering an incredible number of opportunities to hear musicians from around the world. Many such events – held in the embassies or in venues around town – can be found at www.embassyseries.com and www.culturaltourismdc.org. If you're around in June, be sure to catch a few of the concerts put on by the volunteer-run Washington Early Music Festival (www.earlymusicdc.org).

COMPANIES

Choral Arts Society

1-202 244 3669, www.choralarts.org. **Tickets** $17-$50. **Credit** AmEx, Disc, MC, V.
Under the direction of Scott Tucker, this 190-member chorus has a very popular subscription series for its performances at the Kennedy Center. Occasional international appearances are also part of its itinerary, and it routinely performs locally with the National Symphony Orchestra. Not bad for a bunch of volunteers.

National Symphony Orchestra

1-202 416 8100, www.kennedy-center.org/nso. **Tickets** $40-$75. **Credit** AmEx, DC, MC, V.
The National Symphony, which performs mainly in the Kennedy Center Concert Hall, tries to live up to

INSIDE TRACK CHEAP TICKETS

Try Ticketplace (1-202 638 2406, www.ticketplace.org), at 407 Seventh Street, NW, for last-minute half-price tickets; check theatre-company websites for all kinds of cheap-seat offers, from rush tickets to hefty under-35 discounts.

its name by offering something for everyone. Music director Christoph Eschenbach, a German whose previous gig was in Philadelphia, arrived in 2010. Overall, the NSO delivers a variety of engaging performances throughout the year, including composer-themed festivals.

Washington National Opera

1-202 295 2400, www.dc-opera.org. **Tickets** $45-$290. **Credit** AmEx, MC, V.

The Washington Opera, resident at the Kennedy Center Opera House, is one of the city's best national performing arts groups. After Placido Domingo ended his 15-year tenure as director in 2011, French conductor Phillipe Auguin took the reins as music director. Recent productions strayed from the purely operatic with a spectacular *Showboat*. Wagner's *Tristan and Isolde* and Verdi's *The Force of Destiny* are on the schedule for later in 2013. The season usually sells out to subscribers but there is the chance that a call to the KenCen's box office will result in a lucky score of tickets. All productions have English subtitles.

Main venues

Folger Shakespeare Library

201 East Capitol Street, SE, Capitol Hill (1-202 544 7077, www.folger.edu). Capitol South or Union Station Metro. **Open** *Library* 10am-4pm

Mon-Sat. **Performances** times vary. **Tickets** vary. **Credit** AmEx, MC, V. **Map** p253 L7.

The Globe isn't, though the convincing back-lit canopy does manage to convey the appearance of an outdoor theatre from Shakespeare's time. The Folger Consort ensemble presents period recitals of medieval, Renaissance and baroque chamber music. Interesting for the casual fan and a must for anyone with a passion for lyres and lutes.

★ Kennedy Center

2700 F Street, NW, at New Hampshire Avenue & Rock Creek Parkway, Foggy Bottom (tickets & information 1-800 444 1324, 1-202 467 4600, office 1-202 416 8000, www.kennedy-center.org). Foggy Bottom-GWU Metro (free shuttle 9.45am-midnight Mon-Fri; 10am-midnight Sat; noon-midnight Sun). **Box office** 10am-9pm Mon-Sat; noon-9pm Sun. **Peformances** times vary. **Tickets** vary. **Credit** AmEx, MC, V. **Map** p252 F6.

The John F Kennedy Center for the Performing Arts – the national cultural centre of the United States – hosts a great variety of music, particularly on its free Millennium Stage. However, its primary focuses are classical and jazz. A welcome addition is the slate of intimate KC Jazz Club shows scheduled in the Terrace Gallery. The Center has five auditoriums. The Concert Hall is where the National Symphony Orchestra and Washington Chamber Symphony (among others) perform; its acoustics are first class. The Opera House hosts dance and ballet, Broadway-style musical performances, and is the home of the Washington Opera. Productions in the Eisenhower Theater tend to have more of an edge, while the Theater Lab and Terrace Theater are the Center's most intimate spaces.

▶ *Specially priced tickets (SPTs) are sold for many performances for 50% of the face value. Full-time students, over-65s and those with disabilities are among those eligible.*

Kennedy Center.

Lincoln Theatre. *See p180.*

FREE **National Academy of Sciences**

2100 C Street, NW, at 21st Street, the Northwest Rectangle (1-202 334 2415, concert information at www.cpnas.org). Foggy Bottom-GWU Metro. **Performances** times vary. **Tickets** free. **Map** p252 G6.

A favourite of chamber ensembles, this space hosts groups such as the Jupiter Symphony Chamber Players and the Mendelssohn String Quartet. The performances are free but the seating is on a first-come, first-served basis. Navigating the one-way streets around the Academy can be tricky so either take a cab or study your map before you set out.

OTHER VENUES
Museums & galleries

Phillips Collection

1600 21st Street, NW, at Q Street, Dupont Circle (1-202 387 2151, www.phillipscollection.org/music). Dupont Circle Metro. **Performances** *Oct-May* 5pm. **Tickets** concert included with museum admission. **Credit** AmEx, Disc, MC, V. **Map** p252 G4.

The Phillips, as it's known locally, carries with it a certain status that seems to lift it above the other smaller venues in Washington. Its Sunday afternoon concerts are thus fittingly first-rate as well. If it's name-recognition you're looking for, however, you won't always find it on the bill. But if it's an excellent performance of chamber music in an environment where such things are truly appreciated that you're seeking, then you won't be disappointed. The Phillips Camerata, the ensemble-in-residence with a rotating roster, is now in its second season.

Smithsonian Institution

Various buildings of the Smithsonian Institution (1-202 357 2700, www.si.edu).

As part of its varied programme, the Smithsonian regularly sponsors music events that can range from jazz performances and chamber music recitals to the two-week Folklife Festival that takes place

in late June and early July. Call ahead for the locations as they can change depending upon the seating required. Also of interest to music-lovers are the performances on the early instruments that are part of the permanent collection in the Museum of American History (*see p37*) and the Friday evening IMAX Jazz Café at the Museum of Natural History (*see p37*).

Churches

Several of the city's churches, cathedrals and synagogues open their doors for special performances. Others are known for the calibre of the choirs at their weekend services. In addition to those listed below, the **Church of the Epiphany** (1317 G Street, between 13th & 14th Streets, NW, Downtown, 1-202 347 2635) has an outstanding lunchtime musical programme.

FREE **Basilica of the National Shrine of the Immaculate Conception**

400 Michigan Avenue, NE, at 4th Street, Northeast (1-202 526 8300, www.nationalshrine. com). Brookland-CUA Metro. **Performances** times vary. **Tickets** free. **Map** p251 L1.

Occasional choral performances, or carillon and organ recitals, which are healthily attended.

FREE **St Augustine's Church**

1419 V Street, NW, at 15th Street, U Street Corridor (1-202 265 1470, www.saintaugustine-dc.org/music.html). U Street/African-American Civil War Memorial/Cardozo Metro. **Map** p250 H3.

As the Mother Church of the local African American Roman Catholic community, St Augustine's is best known for its wonderful Easter vigil service. The Sunday 12.30pm mass is also popular. Led by the more sedate choir and choral group, the latter complete with ensemble accompaniment of bass, guitar and drums, the service becomes a mix of Gospel, old-time revival and traditional mass.

Crystal Palaces

Bold, beautiful modern theatres reflect a healthy performance culture.

When they made the announcement, the city arched an eyebrow: **Arena Stage** (see p181), that cornerstone of the Washington theatre establishment, wouldn't be relocating to one of DC's resurgent downtown neighbourhoods. Instead, it would sit tight in the capital's Southwest quadrant, down on the Potomac waterfront, in a woebegone district that hadn't had much life since a botched urban renewal scheme turned it into a beige concrete wasteland back in the 1950s.

But Arena wouldn't simply be sitting still. Instead, the company would gut its two vintage theatres and enclose them in a curvaceous glass wrapper under a soaring, swooping sail of a roof. The architect's drawings were breathtaking.

And then, for years, the project went nowhere. Announced back in 2000, Arena's new campus wouldn't actually welcome its first patrons until a decade later. In the interim, the **Shakespeare Theatre Company** (*see p181*) had planned and then opened the gleaming, glass-fronted Sidney Harman Hall, an $85 million second home for the city's second-largest troupe, around the corner from its Lansburgh Theatre in the Penn Quarter neighbourhood. And across the river, the **Signature Theatre** (*see p183*) built a $16 million, two-theatre space; if its own glass curtain wall looks

out on to one of those prefabricated suburban 'downtowns' that have been popping up across the American landscape, it's still a pleasing, sophisticated gathering place, and one that represents a step into the big league for a company that got its start in a grotty industrial garage.

Arena's plans – laid as the dot-com boom of the late 1990s collapsed in the bust of the early 2000s, and clung to tenaciously even as the capital shuddered in the wake of the 9/11 terrorist attacks – took longer to realise. For a while, observers wondered if they'd happen at all. But then the fundraising effort got a jolt in 2006, when philanthropists Gilbert and Jaylee Mead bumped up their original giving plans to an eye-popping $35 million. And once ground was broken in 2008, construction went swimmingly, with the complicated $135 million undertaking coming in on time and, astonishingly, under budget.

And the result? Worth the wait: a dream of a space, airy and substantial at once. Massive wooden columns, tall as yews and slanted like a ship's bowsprit, hold up that 450-foot blade of a roofline, and a surprising wickerwork basket of a new theatre – a 200-seater called the Cradle, designed specifically to provide shelter for the development of plays too risky for Arena's bigger houses – provides a focus

Arena Stage.

Multi-use venues

Atlas Performing Arts Center
*1333 H Street, NE, between 13th & 14th Streets
(1-202 399 7933, www.atlasarts.org/event-types/
music). Union Station Metro then X2, X8 or X9
bus.* **Tickets** vary. **Credit** AmEx, DC, MC, V.
Opened in 2006, this four-theatre venue incorporates
the long-abandoned Atlas, an art moderne cinema
built in 1938. The programing emphasises drama
and dance, but the centre also hosts resident companies such as the Capital City Symphony and
Congressional Chorus, while the Library of Congress
and Washington Chorus often drop by.

Clarice Smith Performing Arts Center
*University of Maryland, College Park, MD (1-301
405 2787, www.claricesmithcenter.umd.edu).
College Park/U of Maryland Metro, then
University of Maryland shuttle bus.* **Tickets**
vary. **Credit** AmEx, DC, MC, V.
The centre majors in 'the unfamiliar, the unpre-
dictable and the developing'. There are all kinds of
theatre, dance and music performances. Music programing includes lots of student performances, but
also the likes of Laurie Anderson, the Kronos Quartet
and the DC area's first Bang on a Can Marathon.

FREE Coolidge Auditorium,
Library of Congress
*Independence Avenue, between 1st & 2nd
Streets, SE, Capitol Hill (1-202 707 5502,
www.loc.gov/ rr/perform/concert). Capitol
South Metro.* **Performances** times vary;
most begin 8pm. **Tickets** free. **Map** p253 L7.
The problem with some Washington venues is that
standards of architecture and acoustics don't always
match – with monumental structures yielding muf-
fled sound. But this auditorium in the Jefferson
Building rises to the occasion on both counts.
Programming is intriguing and intimate, running
from classical to country to world music, with recent
bookings ranging from the Moscow Sretensky
Monastery Choir to folksters Noel Stookey, Ramblin'
Jack Elliott and Jimmy LaFave, performing for the
Woodie Guthrie centennial celebration.

George Mason University
Center for the Arts
*Roanoke Lane & Mason Drive, Fairfax, VA
(1-703 993 8888, ww.cfa.gmu.edu). Vienna/
Fairfax Metro then Cue Gold, Cue Green
bus.* **Tickets** $17.50-$84. **Credit** AmEx,
Disc, MC, V.
It's a shame that one of the area's best concert facilities is located so far from the District. But this venue
on the George Mason campus offers some of the best
in music, experimental drama and modern dance.
The main hall seats nearly 2,000 and has hosted
artists from the Canadian Brass to Dr John to the
Dresden Philharmonic. The university's 10,000-seat

for it all. The lobby has that excellent
and elusive quality, flow; it draws
audiences in, up a wide stair, across a
sloping expanse and up another stairway
to a terrace with splendid views of trees
and river and sky. Architecture critics
greeted it ecstatically, anointing its
creator, Vancouver-based Bing Thom,
with their choicest adjectives. Theatre
critics pronounced themselves delighted
with both the feel of the new Cradle and
the way the renovation addressed longstanding acoustical anxieties in the
Arena's old four-sided Fichandler theatre.

The Mead Center for the American
Theater, the whole package is called,
and it's a capstone on more than a
decade of theatrical monument-making
in the nation's capital. It's a material
statement, too: like Harman Hall and
the Signature space – the glass atrium
at the centre of the **Studio Theatre**
complex (*see p182*), completed in 2004
– the jewel box that is Arena Stage's
home speaks of openness, invitation
and occasion all at once. They're
event buildings, all of them, not just
performance spaces; they're reminders
that theatres were once shrines. They're
public comments, too, on the maturity
and substance of the Washington
theatre scene.

ARTS & ENTERTAINMENT

stadium, the Patriot Center, hosts basketball games but also big-name musical acts like REM, Green Day and Neil Young.

Lincoln Theatre

1215 U Street, NW, between 12th & 13th Streets, U Street/ Corridor (1-202 328 6000, www.the lincolntheatre.org). U Street/African-American Civil War Memorial/Cardozo Metro. **Tickets** $10-$50. **Credit** AmEx, MC, V. **Map** p250 H3.
Washington's one-time answer to Harlem's Apollo Theatre, this magnificent structure is most often the site of neo-'Chitlin Circuit' theatre. The underused Lincoln is frequently dark, but over the years it has hosted Paul Weller, King Sunny Ade and the Smithsonian Jazz Orchestra. *Photo p177.*

Lisner Auditorium

730 21st Street, NW, at H Street, Foggy Bottom (1-202 994 6800, www.lisner.org). Foggy Bottom-GWU Metro. **Tickets** vary. **No credit cards**. **Map** p252 G5.
Located in George Washington University, Lisner hosts dance troupes, Latin music and the Gay Men's Chorus of Washington. Author readings and rock shows are scheduled as well, sometimes on the same night, as when Dave Eggers split the bill with They Might Be Giants. This is the most likely DC site for shows by prominent African performers, including Youssou N'Dour, Salif Keita and Ladysmith Black Mambazo.

Sixth & I Historic Synagogue

601 I Street, NW, at 6th Street, Chinatown (1-202 408-3100, www.sixthandi.org). Gallery Place-Chinatown Metro. **Tickets** vary. **Credit** MC, V.
Rededicated as a synagogue in 2004 after five decades as a church, this Byzantine Revival temple is non-denominational and has no permanent congregation. While many of the activities here are religious, the striking, intimate two-storey sanctuary has also become a significant concert venue. It's hosted a wide range of big names in recent years, including Adele, Bryan Adams and Fiona Apple. Comedy shows (with big names like Lewis Black) are also popular.

Strathmore

5301 Tuckerman Lane, North Bethesda, MD (1-301 581 5100, www.strathmore.org). Grosvenor-Strathmore Metro. **Tickets** vary. **Credit** AmEx, Disc, MC, V.
This suburban competitor to the Kennedy Center Concert Hall features a blond-wood interior that suggests a huge sailing ship. Part of a larger arts complex, Strathmore books jazz, rock and contemporary music, from Randy Newman and Bauhaus to Kenny G and the American première of Steve Reich's *2x5*. But it's designed for acoustic music, best heard in performances featuring such visiting classical soloists as Joshua Bell and Hilary Hahn. The venue is a second home for the Baltimore Symphony.

Folger Theatre. *See p182.*

Warner Theatre

13th & E Streets, NW, The Federal Triangle (1-202 783 4000, www.warnertheatre.com). Metro Center Metro. **Tickets** vary. **Credit** AmEx, Disc, MC, V. **Map** p252 H6.
Built in 1924, the Warner Theatre has seen a variety of acts on its stage. The early deco design of the auditorium gives it either a decadent gaudiness or a stately individuality, depending on the performance. Comedians, dance troupes and Broadway plays dominate, but music acts still surface now and then.

Wolf Trap

1645 Trap Road, Vienna, VA (1-703 255 1900, www.wolftrap.org). West Falls Church Metro then Wolf Trap shuttle bus. **Tickets** $10-$70. **Credit** AmEx, Disc, MC, V.
Calling itself 'America's National Park for the Performing Arts', Wolf Trap consists of two essentially separate performance spaces – the Barns and the Filene Center. Don't let the name 'Barns' fool you. Yes, the space is rustic, but that doesn't mean you'll be sitting on a milking stool. The acoustics here are top-notch, as are the seating and facilities. The Filene Center is the sprawling outdoor concert facility with lawn and pavilion seating. The scope of the perform-

ances at both spaces is broader than that at many venues in the District that also use the name 'national'. Note that the shuttle bus runs only in summer.

Theatre

The biggest players (the likes of **Arena Stage**, the **Studio Theatre** and the **Shakespeare Theatre Company** are not the only ambitious outfits in DC. Over on Capitol Hill, the **Folger Theatre** plays host to Shakespeare and Shakepeare-oriented productions, while the brash and brilliant **Woolly Mammoth** continues to push theatrical boundaries.

MAJOR VENUES

Arena Stage
1101 6th Street, SW, at Maine Avenue, Southwest (1-202 488 3300, www.arenastage.com). Waterfront-SEU Metro. **Box office** 10am-8pm Mon-Sat; noon-8pm Sun. **Tickets** $30-$85. **Credit** AmEx, Disc, MC, V. **Map** p253 J8.
The city's theatrical grande dame and a pioneer in the American resident theatre movement, Arena has emerged from more than a decade of torpor. Blessed (and cursed) with an affluent establishment audience, artistic director Molly Smith disappointed some critics by programming unchallenging audience-pleasers. A two-season exile made the company's work feel more uneven still, but a triumphant homecoming to a glamorously rehabbed facility, complete with a lovely 200-seat new-play incubator space, marked a change. Among the works lined up for 2013 are a world premiere, *Love in Afghanistan*, from resident playwright Charles Randolph-Wright, as well as classic drama with Brecht's *Mother Courage and Her Children*, with Kathleen Turner, which runs until March 2014.
▶ *For more on the new theatre building, see p178 Crystal Palaces.*

Kennedy Center
2700 F Street, NW, at New Hampshire Avenue & Rock Creek Parkway, Foggy Bottom (1-800 444 1324, 1-202 467 4600, www.kennedy-center.org). Foggy Bottom-GWU Metro then free shuttle 9.45am-midnight Mon-Fri; 10am-midnight Sat; noon-midnight Sun. **Box office** 10am-9pm Mon-Sat; noon-9pm Sun. **Tickets** $25-$150. **Credit** AmEx, DC, MC, V. **Map** p252 F6.
As part of its broad-spectrum programming, the national cultural centre puts on a full theatre season each year. It's tilted toward imports and tours, with an emphasis on musicals, but now and again the imports are remarkable. (Dublin's Gate Theatre brought its celebrated *Waiting for Godot*; Declan Donnellan staged *Twelfth Night* and *Three Sisters*, both in Russian, for a 2010 Chekhov festival.) The handsome Kennedy Center Family Theater space

hosts originals and adaptations by the likes of movie star Whoopi Goldberg and Japanese American dramatist Naomi Iizuka. And with ex-Covent Garden guru Michael Kaiser at the helm, the centre has sponsored a series of ambitious festivals celebrating artists from Shakespeare to Sondheim; an international theatre festival is taking place in 2014. A Kennedy Center production of Hungarian play *The Guardsman*, by Ferenc Molnár, ran in 2013.

National Theatre
1321 Pennsylvania Avenue, NW, between 13th & 14th Streets, The Federal Triangle (1-202 628 6161, www.nationaltheatre.org). Metro Center or Federal Triangle Metro. **Box office** *When show is playing* 10am-9pm Mon-Sat. *In weeks preceding show* 10am-6pm Mon-Sat; noon-6pm Sun. **Tickets** $15-$75. **Credit** AmEx, DC, Disc, MC, V. **Map** p252 H6.
One of the city's oldest theatres (it dates from 1835), the National has a history as a Broadway tryout house – productions have included the flamingly awful jukebox musical *Hot Feet*, which went on to an ignoble 97 New York performances in 2006. But in recent decades it has been home mostly to touring fluff – when it doesn't sit empty, that is. A new Broadway-bound musical *If/Then* runs from November 2013.

★ Shakespeare Theatre Company
450 7th Street, NW, between D & E Streets, Penn Quarter (1-202 547 1122, www.shakespearetheatre.org). Gallery Place-Chinatown Metro. **Box office** *Performance days* 10am-6pm Mon; 10am-6.30pm Tue-Sat; noon-6.30pm Sun. *Non-performance days* 10am-6pm Mon-Sat; noon-6pm Sun. **Tickets** $12-$120. **Credit** AmEx, Disc, MC, V. **Map** p253 J6.
Led for 27 years by noted director Michael Kahn and hailed by the *Economist* as 'one of the world's three great Shakespearean theatres', the Shakespeare Theatre is unquestionably the top classical company in the US – and now it's added an $85-million second house to its portfolio, the better to produce plays in rep and host visiting troupes. (Helen Mirren's *Phèdre*, the Tricycle Theatre's *The Great Game: Afghanistan* and National Theatre of Scotland's *Black Watch* have all played at the company's sleek new Sidney Harman Hall.) The STC stages its own season of major works, of course, serving up not just intelligent, inventive Bardolatry (*Coriolanus* and *A Winter's Tale* in 2013), but classics from the likes of Ben Jonson (an uproarious *Silent Woman*), Eugene O'Neill (a titanic *Mourning Becomes Electra*) and Aeschylus (*The Persians*). The company also makes a speciality of Tennessee Williams and Oscar Wilde, while experimenting with rarities by such writers as Alfred de Musse and Pierre Corneille – which is why it regularly attracts big-name directors (Chicago's Mary Zimmerman, Australian Gale Edwards, rising American light Ethan McSweeny, who launched his

career here) and actors (Keith Baxter, Kelly McGillis, Marsha Mason, Hal Holbrook). Friedrich Schiller's *Wallenstein*, directed by Michael Kahn, ran in 2013.
▶ *For more on the new theatre building, see p178 Crystal Palaces.*

Studio Theatre

1501 14th Street, NW, at P Street, Logan Circle (1-202 332 3300, www.studiotheatre.org). Dupont Circle or U Street/African-American Civil War Memorial/Cardozo Metro. **Box office** *Performance days* 10am-6pm Mon, Tue; 10am-9pm Wed-Sat; noon-8pm Sun. *Non-performance days* 10am-6pm Mon-Fri. **Tickets** $35-$75. **Credit** AmEx, Disc, MC, V. **Map** p250 H4.

Slick productions, smart directors and substantial plays (occasional upmarket musicals, too) make the Studio Theatre a serious player on the capital city's dramatic scene. In the Bush era, it was home to the first DC production of the docudrama *Guantanamo* (then-Defense Secretary Donald Rumsfeld didn't attend). Bright young playwriting lights from Tarell Alvin McCraney to Annie Baker have been introduced to DC audiences in the three intimate 200-seat spaces here. (There's a cosy black box, too, and an acting conservatory.) Co-founder and artistic director Joy Zinoman retired in 2010, handing off an almost absurdly healthy organisation to the gifted, cerebral young director David Muse, whose earlier work for the house had included a rapturously reviewed production of Bryony Lavery's *Frozen*.

OTHER THEATRES & COMPANIES

Folger Theatre

201 East Capitol Street, SE, between 2nd & 3rd Streets, Capitol Hill (1-202 544 7077, www.folger. edu). Capitol South Metro. **Box office** noon-4pm Mon-Sat. **Tickets** $15-$45. **Credit** AmEx, MC, V. **Map** p253 L7.

The Folger's regular directors (including British actor Richard Clifford) produce solid, intelligent Bard-oriented fare. It was here that Lynn Redgrave developed what became the Broadway hit *Shakespeare For My Father*, and here that mischievous DC Shakespearean Joe Banno dramatised Hamlet's internal debates by splitting the title role into four parts – and casting women in three of them. An Edwardian-costumed *Twelfth Night*, directed by Robert Richmond, was running at the time of writing. *Photo p180.*

Ford's Theatre

511 10th Street, NW, between E & F Streets, Downtown (1-202 347 4833, www.fords theatre.org). Metro Center or Gallery Place-Chinatown Metro. **Box office** 10am-6pm Mon-Fri. **Tickets** $27-$50. **Credit** AmEx, Disc, MC, V. **Map** p252 J6.

President Abraham Lincoln's assassination – in 1865, during a performance of *Our American Cousin*

– shuttered this house for a century, but crusading producer Frankie Hewitt helped bring its stage back to life in the late 1960s. For decades, much of what Ford's offered was easy-to-swallow fare, but now and again producers surprise theatergoers with an edgy imported offering. Since Hewitt's death in 2003, Alley Theatre veteran Paul Tetreault has steered the house gingerly in the direction of more substantial fare – including an admirable production of August Wilson's devastating *Jitney* and (to reopen the house in 2009 after a major renovation) an ambitious Lincoln commission called *The Heavens Are Hung in Black*. From September to October 2013, *The Laramie Project* by Moisés Kaufman and Members of the Tectonic Theater Project is being staged as part of the Lincoln Legacy Project. The play is a complex portrait of a community's response to the 1998 murder of Matthew Shepard, a young gay man living in Laramie, Wyoming.
▶ *For the Ford's Theatre Museum and the Center for Education & Leadership, see p55.*

Olney Theatre Center

2001 Olney-Sandy Spring Road (Route 108), Olney, MD (box office 1-301 924 3400, information 1-301 924 4485, www.olneytheatre.org). **Box office** 10am-6pm Mon-Fri; noon-5pm Sat, Sun. **Tickets** $26-$54. **Credit** MC, V.

It's a hike, but the hour-long drive to this suburban Maryland house can be worth the trouble. Founded as a summer theatre in the 1930s, it saw performances by a startlingly starry roster over the decades: Helen Hayes, Tallulah Bankhead, Olivia de Havilland, Hume Cronyn, Jessica Tandy, Uta Hagen and Ian McKellen are just a few of the names who've toured there. More recently, Olney's season has been largely subscriber-friendly fluff, and a fiscal crisis that nearly bankrupted the place in 2009-10 hasn't helped. But now and again artistic director Jim Petosa will offer up something gratifyingly bold. A newish 440-seat main-stage completes a campus with no fewer than four performance spaces – one of them a casual outdoor stage.

Round House Theatre

Bethesda *7501 Wisconsin Avenue, at Waverly Street, Bethesda, MD (box office 1-240 644 1100, information 1-240 644 1099, www.roundhouse theatre.org). Bethesda Metro.* **Box office** noon-5pm Mon-Fri. **Tickets** $25-$60.

Silver Spring *8641 Colesville Road, between Georgia Avenue & Fenton Street, Silver Spring, MD (1-240 644 1099, www.roundhouse theatre.org). Silver Spring Metro.* **Box office** noon-5pm Mon-Fri. **Tickets** $15. *Both* **Credit** AmEx, MC, V.

An established company successful enough to have opened not one but two new spaces in recent years, Round House was home to the world première of *Columbinus*, a thoughtfully disturbing response to the Colorado school massacre. (It went on to get a

Shakespeare Theatre Company. *See p181.*

well-received production off-Broadway.) Its main home is in the close-in suburb of Bethesda, but it also offers a regular slate of performances (including a cabaret series) near the other end of the Metro's Red Line, in a black-box space at the AFI Silver complex in Silver Spring. At Bethesda, new comedy *Seminar* by Theresa Rebeck is being staged in early 2014, followed by Pulitzer-winning August Wilson's *Two Trains Running*, a poignant, humorous portrait of African American life in the 1960s.

Signature Theatre

3806 South Four Mile Run Drive, at Oakland Drive, Arlington, VA (1-703 820 9771, www.sig-online.org). **Box office** 10am-6pm Mon-Fri; noon-6pm Sat, Sun. *During performances* 10am-6pm Mon-Fri; 10am-8.30pm Tue-Fri; noon-8.30pm Sat, Sun. **Tickets** $15-$85. **Credit** AmEx, Disc, MC, V. Signature's signature is first-rate Sondheim – the hit musical *Company* features in 2013 – and if its instincts for straight plays aren't always as keen, it's still an ambitious outfit. Landmark productions in past seasons have included the first *Assassins* to be staged outside New York, a *Passion* that put the house on the map with national critics, and a world-première Van Gogh musical (*The Highest Yellow*) from Tony-nominated composer Michael John LaChiusa. *Miss Saigon* is playing in mid 2013, joined by *Gypsy*, inspired by the memoirs of Gypsy Rose Lee (late 2013-early 2014). And there's straight drama with the DC première of Philip Ridley's new play *Tender Napalm* in March-May 2014.
▶ *For more on the Signature's $16 million, two-theatre complex, see p178 Crystal Palaces.*

Woolly Mammoth Theatre Company

649 D Street, NW, at 7th Street, Penn Quarter (1-202 393 3939, www.woollymammoth.net). Archives/Navy Memorial or Gallery Place/Chinatown Metro. **Box office** 10am-6pm

Mon-Fri. *Performance weeks* 10am-6pm Mon-Fri; noon-6pm Sat, Sun. **Tickets** from $35. **Credit** AmEx, MC, V. **Map** p253 J6.
This brash and often-brilliant company has been pushing boundaries (both theatrical and personal) for a quarter-century, most recently in a superb $7-million, 265-seat Downtown home. Notable playwrights who've called Woolly home include *Six Feet Under* scribe Craig Wright, Pulitzer Prize finalist Sarah Ruhl (*The Clean House*) and that poet of neurosis, Nicky Silver. In the pipeline at the time of writing was *Stupid Fucking Bird*, an irreverent, contemporary remix of Chekhov's *The Seagull*, directed by Woolly artistic director Howard Shalwitz. *Photo p184.*

SMALL COMPANIES

Washington is a terrific theatre town: there are far too many fringey, flaky, fearless small companies to list here. But look for anything involving the Forum Theatre (smart, politically aware stuff from contemporary writers and 20th-century giants, www.forumtheatredc.org), Longacre Lea (fearsomely intelligent, and fun to watch, www.longacrelea.org – but on hiatus in 2013), Synetic Theater (gorgeous movement-based theatre, www.synetictheater.org), WSC Avant Bard (scrappy, www.wscavantbard.org) and Solas Nua (www.solasnua.org).

For the following companies, fixed addresses are given where possible; for information about performances by roving companies, call the number listed or check the website. Note that box office hours have not been given; it's generally a case of leaving a message on the answerphone for the company to call you back.

GALA Hispanic Theatre

3333 14th Street, NW, between Park & Monroe Streets, Columbia Heights (1-202 234 7174,

www.galatheatre.org). Columbia Heights Metro.
Credit AmEx, MC, V. **Map** p250 H1.
Ensconced in the Tivoli Theatre in Columbia Heights, Teatro GALA stages Spanish-language classics such as Calderón de la Barca's *La Dama Duende* and García Lorca's *Blood Wedding*, plus modern plays by writers such as Venezuela's Gustavo Ott (*Evangélicas, Divorciadas y Vegetarianas*) and the occasional Latin-flavoured musical – at the time of writing the Helen Hayes Awards-recommended *DC-7: The Roberto Clemente Story* was playing. Performances are generally in Spanish with a supertitled translation.

Rorschach Theatre
Information 1-202 452 5538,
www.rorschachtheatre.com.
The rambunctious Rorschach company, now with a base at the Atlas Performing Arts Center (*see p179*), applies its nervy vision to some great plays. For the most part, it's a success (Rorschach productions have been nominated for six Helen Hayes Awards); the company serves up everything from Serbian wunderkind Biljana Srbljanovic (*Family Stories: A Slapstick Tragedy*) to the sprightly Amy Freed (*The Beard of Avon*). Other past outings have included a solid staging of Tony Kushner's Nazi-era fever-dream *A Bright Room Called Day* and a smart take on *The Arabian Nights*, the sexy, swoony fable by German playwright Roland Schimmelpfennig. A 2012 production of *A Maze*, by Rob Handel, featuring a dysfunctional cartoonist and the maze he creates in his work, won good reviews.

Woolly Mammoth. *See p183.*

Theater Alliance
H Street Playhouse, 1365 H Street, NE, between 13th & 14th Streets (www.theateralliance.com).
Gallery Place-Chinatown Metro then X2 bus.
Map p248 M5.
Once the sort of company that would take a playfully kinetic pass at Salman Rushdie's *Haroun and the Sea of Stories* or introduce Washington audiences to the hugely ambitious writer Naomi Wallace (with a gob-smackingly bold *Slaughter City*), the Theater Alliance grew less ambitious as it went through leadership changes and the broader economy went south. By 2010-11, things were looking shaky, but the Theater Alliance began a new chapter in 2012, under the leadership of artistic director Colin Hovde. It has since mounted six full-scale productions, among them Fin Kennedy's *How to Disappear Completely and Never Be Found.*

Washington Stage Guild
The Undercroft Theater at Mount Vernon Place United Methodist Church, 900 Massachusetts Avenue, NW, between 9th & 10th Streets (1-240 582 0050, www.stageguild.org). Mount Vernon Square or Gallery Place Metro. **Tickets** $40-$50.
No credit cards. **Map** p250 H3.
Forced out of its longtime lodgings by DC's downtown redevelopment, and then rocked by the death of its much-loved founding artistic director, this tight-knit 25-year-old ensemble went dark for a couple of seasons, but resurrected itself and found a new home. In an over-educated city where knotty dramas play out in each day's headlines, it draws a loyal crowd with smart stagings of Shaw (a politically well-timed *On the Rocks* in 2004 is remembered as a high point) and other literary-minded fare. The 2012-13 season lineup included Shaw's *Pygmalion*, and *The Elder Statesman* by TS Eliot.

WSC Avant Bard
Artisphere, 1101 Wilson Boulevard, Arlington, VA (1-703 418 4808, www.washington shakespeare.org). Rosslyn Metro. **Credit** AmEx, MC, V.
With a name change to reflect its wider repertoire and avant garde thinking, this highbrow-on-a-shoestring troupe formerly known as the Washington Shakespeare Company has 20-plus seasons of the Bard – not to mention Beckett, Marlowe, Stoppard, Albee and more – under its scruffy belt. It's sometimes quite good (a 2004 *Waiting for Godot* unearthed all the prodigious tenderness in that bleak play) and always ambitious: what company with a bare-bones budget tackles *The Royal Hunt of the Sun* and *Death and the King's Horseman* within a twelvemonth? A naked *Macbeth* drew worldwide attention back in 2007. *Caesar and Dada*, by DC playwright Allyson Currin, is premièring in June 2013. The play follows an acting troupe rehearsing *Julius Caesar* as they seek to challenge and change the audience's expectations and experiences.

Sport & Fitness

Get out and play – or watch the professionals.

Washington gained a new string to its sporting bow with the opening of Nationals Park, a state-of-the-art ballpark for the Washington Nationals Major League baseball team in 2008. But this city isn't all about baseball, of course, not with the Washington Redskins on the football field and the Wizards on the basketball court, both teams with great track records and devoted fans.

Away from professional sports and big stadiums, the superb natural landscapes surrounding the city provide a perfect environment for outdoor activities. Some of the Washington area's most famous city sights and beautiful rural spots can best be seen while in-line skating, biking, boating – or even on a Segway. Or check out the National Mall or Rock Creek Park in the spring and summer for pick-up games. So grab a baseball glove, kayak or football, and go out and play.

Participation Sports

BOATING & FISHING

In March and April, when the cherry blossoms are in peak bloom, a popular way to see the sights is on a paddleboat on the calm Tidal Basin. **Tidal Basin Paddle Boats** (1501 Maine Avenue, SW, 1-202 479 2426, www.tidalbasinpaddleboats.com) rents out paddleboats from mid March to mid October. It's $12 an hour for a two-seater and $19 for a four-seater. Advanced reservations are available online.

Annapolis (*see p199*), about a 45-minute drive from DC, is on the Chesapeake Bay, the largest estuary in the US. **South River Boat Rentals** (Sunset Drive, Edgewater, MD, 1-410 956 9729, www.annapolisboatrental.com) rents out sailing boats and power boats for a day on the bay. **J World Annapolis** (213 Eastern Avenue, 1-410 280 2040, www.jworldannapolis.com) and the **Annapolis Sailing School** (7001 Bembe Beach Road, 1-800 638 9192, www.annapolissailing.com) offer sailing classes.

Annapolis is also a great place to go seafishing. **Chesapeake Bay Charter Fishing** (4160 Mears Avenue, Chesapeake Beach, 1-301 855 8450, www.rodnreelinc.com, www.cbresortspa.com) is among several companies that offer fishing excursions for groups in the spring, summer and autumn. It's best to call several days in advance in order to be sure of reserving yourself a spot. Below are companies hiring boats in DC and the immediate area.

Fletcher's Boathouse

4940 Canal Road, NW, at Reservoir Road, Upper Northwest (1-202 244 0461, www.fletcherscove.com). **Open** *early Mar-Nov* 7am-5pm daily (boats returned by 6pm). **No credit cards. Map** p248 B3.
Fletcher's rents out boats, canoes, bicycles and fishing equipment, and is convenient for the Potomac River and the C&O Canal.

Key Bridge Boathouse

3500 Water Street, NW, under Francis Scott Key Bridge, Georgetown (1-202 337 9642, www.keybridgeboathouse.com). Foggy Bottom-GWU Metro *then 38B bus.* **Open** *noon-7pm Mon-Fri; 8am-7pm Sat, Sun. Hours can vary by season.*
On the premises that was formerly Jack's Boathouse, this place rents out canoes, kayaks and stand-up paddleboards. Rates from $10 to $30.

Thompson Boat Center

2900 Virginia Avenue, NW, at Rock Creek Parkway, Foggy Bottom (1-202 333 9543, www.thompsonboatcenter.com). Foggy Bottom-GWU Metro. **Open** 6am-8pm Mon-Sat; 7am-7pm Sun. *Boat rentals* spring-autumn 8am-5pm daily. *Bike rentals* spring-autumn 8am-6pm daily. **Credit** MC, V. **Map** p252 F5.

Rowing on the Potomac. See p185.

ARTS & ENTERTAINMENT

Canoes, kayaks and bikes for hire during the warmer months. Rowing lessons are also available.

Washington Sailing Marina

1 Marina Drive, off George Washington Memorial Parkway, Alexandria, VA (1-703 548 9027, www. washingtonsailingmarina.com). **Open** *Summer* 9am-6pm daily. *Winter* 10am-5pm daily. *Boat rentals* weekends only, spring-mid Oct. **Credit** MC, V.
This outfit hires out two types of sailboats: the smaller Aqua Fin, which comfortably accommodates two people ($15 per hour or $40 for three hours) and the 19ft Flying Scot, which costs $23 per hour (minimum two hours, maximum five people). You must be certified or pass a written test to hire.

CYCLING

Paved bicycle trails abound in Washington. They're easy to spot, being marked clearly with a green sign with a picture of a bike on it. But for rougher terrain you'll have to leave the city environs. Check out Scott Adams's *Washington Mountain Bike Book* – available at local bicycle shops. Trail maps and on-street bike route maps can be found at bike shops. Also, the **Washington Area Bicyclist Association** (1803 Connecticut Avenue, NW, 1-202 518 0524, www.waba.org) has an informative website with maps and other resources for cycling enthusiasts; the website www.bikewashington. org is also a valuable resource on local trails. Metro riders note that you can take your bicycle on the trains only during off-peak hours – between 10am and 2pm and after 7pm during the week, and all day at weekends and holidays. Below are a list of popular cycling trails.

C&O Canal Towpath

A 184-mile gravel path that starts at the corner of the Pennsylvania Avenue, NW, ramp of the Rock Creek Parkway (which is near the Foggy Bottom Metro stop) and finally ends up in Cumberland, Maryland. For a popular biking trip, take the trail 19.9 miles to Great Falls Park in Maryland.

Capital Crescent Trail

This trail makes its way from the Thompson Boat Center on the Potomac in Georgetown all the way up to Silver Spring in Maryland. The 11-mile trail also links with the Mount Vernon Trail (*see below*). The paved section terminates in Bethesda, Maryland, but more advanced cyclists can take the crushed stone Georgetown Branch Trail to Silver Spring.

Mount Vernon Trail

An asphalt trail that takes riders along the Potomac River. It starts out on Theodore Roosevelt Island in Rosslyn, Virginia (near the Rosslyn Metro stop), and travels 18.5 miles through Old Town Alexandria, ultimately terminating, as the name suggests, at George Washington's historic home.

Rock Creek Park Trail

Miles of biking, from the Lincoln Memorial up through the park to Maryland. The southern section follows a narrow, rather bumpy paved path. There's a better option on weekends, when the two-lane Beach Drive is closed to cars but open for cyclists between Military and Broad Branch roads.

Rentals & tours

In addition to the companies listed below the Capital Bikeshare scheme, with bikes available at 175 stations around the DC area, has been in operation since 2010. For details, *see p229*.

Big Wheel Bikes

1034 33rd Street, NW, at Cady's Alley, Georgetown (1-202 337 0254, www.bigwheel bikes.com). Dupont Circle Metro then Circulator

bus or Foggy Bottom-GWU Metro then 31, 32, 36, 38B bus. **Open** 11am-7pm Tue-Fri; 10am-6pm Sat, Sun. **Credit** AmEx, MC, V. **Map** p249 E5.
A basic bicycle is $7 an hour or $35 a day (the minimum rental time is three hours). A range of different models is available.
Other locations 3119 Lee Highway, Arlington, VA (1-703 522 1110); 6917 Arlington Road, Bethesda, MD (1-301 652 0192); 2 Prince Street, Alexandria, VA (1-703 739 2300).

Bike & Roll

Tour starts at the Old Post Office Pavilion, 1100 Pennsylvania Avenue, NW, Downtown (1-202 842 2453, www.bikethesites.com). Federal Triangle Metro. **Hours** vary by season but usually start at 9am. See website for details. **Bike rentals** from $10-$20 for 2hrs. **Credit** AmEx, MC, V. **Map** p252 H7.
See Washington on two wheels. A variety of tours is available, including Monuments@Nite and cherry blossom rides. They range from four-milers to longer treks of around 20 miles. Tours usually cost $40 for adults and $30 for children, including bike and helmet hire. The company also runs a bike-hire service.
Other locations Union Station, *see p46* (1-202 962 0206); 1 Wales Alley, Old Town, Alexandria, VA (1-703 548 7655).

GOLF

There are three public golf courses in the area on National Park Service land. Golf equipment, such as carts and rental clubs, can be hired at the clubs, which are all open from dawn to dusk daily. Rates vary based on location, time of week; senior and junior discounts apply. See www.golfdc.com for more information.

Langston Golf Course

2600 Benning Road, NE, at 26th Street (1-202 397 8638). X2 bus.

East Potomac Golf Course

972 Ohio Drive, SW, between 15th Street & I-395 (1-202 554 7660).
Two courses are available here, along with a driving range and miniature golf.

Rock Creek Golf Course

1600 Rittenhouse Street, NW, at 16th Street, Upper Northwest (1-202 882 7332). S2, S4 bus.

GYMS

Gold's Gym

409 3rd Street, SW, between D & E Streets, Southwest (1-202 554 4653, www.goldsgym.com). Federal Center SW Metro. **Open** 5am-11pm Mon-Thur; 5am-10pm Fri; 8am-8pm Sat; 9am-6pm Sun. **Credit** AmEx, Disc, MC, V. **Map** p253 J7.

Gold's has branches throughout DC and its suburbs; this location offers classes. Call ahead to register. At the time of writing, an introductory complimentary one-day pass could be downloaded from the website.

National Capital YMCA

1711 Rhode Island Avenue, NW, at 17th Street, Dupont Circle (1-202 862 9622, www.ymca nationalcapital.org). Farragut North Metro. **Open** 5.30am-10.30pm Mon-Fri; 8am-6.30pm Sat; 9am-5.30pm Sun. **Rates** YMCA members $10 per day. **Credit** MC, V. **Map** p250 G5.
Good equipment, a pool and fitness classes. Non-members can download a three-day guest pass at www.ymcadc.org.

Washington Sports Clubs

1835 Connecticut Avenue, NW, between Florida Avenue & T Street, Dupont Circle (1-202 332 0100, www.mysportsclubs.com). Dupont Circle Metro. **Open** 5.30am-11pm Mon-Thur; 5.30am-10pm Fri; 7am-8.30pm Sat, Sun. **Rates** vary, phone for details. **Credit** AmEx, MC, V. **Map** p250 G3.
Popular with locals, this sports club offers classes, machines, weights and squash courts. There are branches all over the city, including in Columbia Heights (3100 14th Street, NW, 1-202 986 2281) and Gallery Place (787 Seventh Street, NW, 1-202-737-3555)

HIKING

Virginia and Maryland's sumptuous scenery makes for popular hiking territory, and the District has its own expanse of green in Rock Creek Park (which stretches into Maryland). A few well-known trails are listed below, but see www.trails.com or *60 Hikes Within 60 Miles: Washington, DC* by Paul Elliott for more.

Appalachian Trail

www.patc.net.
The AT, as it is known, stretches 2,168 miles from Georgia to Maine, making it a bit long for a day trip. But there are lots of shorter walks that take you along parts of the trail in Virginia and Maryland.

Catoctin Mountain Park

www.nps.gov/cato.
Tucked away in Thurmont, Maryland, the park has 25 miles of trails with scenic mountain views. Check out the 78ft plummet at Cunningham Falls.

Rock Creek Park

www.nps.gov/rocr.
A good starting point for the park's 25 miles of trails is the seven-mile hike from Meadowside Nature Center (5100 Meadowside Lane, Rockville, MD, 1-301 258 4030). You can also pick up trails at Lake Needwood (15700 Needwood Lake Circle, Rockville, MD, 1-301 924 4141) or on Beach Drive in Northwest DC.

ARTS & ENTERTAINMENT

SKATING

For ice skaters, parks and area town centres often set up ice rinks in the winter months, usually from late October through to March. In DC, the popular rink with added scenic value is in the sculpture garden at the **National Gallery of Art** (*see p33*). A new outdoor rink also opened in winter 2013 along the Georgetown waterfront in the Washington Harbour complex.

While many of the bike paths listed on p186 are fair game also for in-line skaters, they're often too narrow and crowded. As an alternative, try Beach Drive, north of Blagden Road in Rock Creek Park, on weekends when it's closed to traffic. Visit www.skatedc.org for more information on where to roller-skate.

SEGWAY TOURS

Segway Human Transporters are like self-balancing scooters that automatically respond to your body's movements. They're popular in DC and a good way of seeing the city. **City Segway Tours** (502 23rd Street, NW, at E Street, Foggy Bottom, 1-877 734 8687, http://dc.citysegwaytours.com) and **Capital Segway** (1350 I Street, NW, at 14th Street, Downtown, 1-202 682 1980, www.capitalsegway.com) run guided tours.

SWIMMING

Cooling off on a hot day in DC is easy – there are nearly three dozen indoor public swimming pools in the area (the gem of which is the Wilson Aquatic Center in Tenleytown), as well as public outdoor pools. Outdoor pools are usually open from Memorial Day (late May) to Labor Day (early September). The best are **East Potomac Pool** (972 Ohio Drive, SW, 1-202 727 6523) and **Francis Pool** (25th & N Streets, NW, 1-202 727 3285). For more options, check out www.dpr.dc.gov. Non-DC residents must pay ($7 per visit for an adult) to visit a city pool. Some local gyms have pools that are open to the public for a fee.

TENNIS

Aside from these public facilities, check out parks and schools for outdoor-only courts. It's first come, first served, so be prepared to wait for a spot and cut your playing time to 30 minutes or an hour if others are in line.

East Potomac Tennis Center

1090 Ohio Drive, SW, at Buckeye Drive, SW (1-202 554 5962, www.eastpotomactennis.com).

Smithsonian Metro then 20min walk. **Open** 7am-10pm daily. **Rates** check website for revised rates. **Credit** MC, V. **Map** p284 H8.
A public facility at Hains Point that has 24 courts, including ten clay and 14 hard. There's also a pro shop and you can call in advance to set up a lesson.

Rock Creek Tennis Center

16th & Kennedy Streets, NW, Upper Northwest (1-202 722 5949, www.rockcreektennis.com). S2, S4 bus. **Open** 7am-11pm Mon-Thur; 7am-8pm Fri-Sun. **Rates** hard courts $10-$12/hr, clay courts $20/hr. **Credit** MC, V.
The club has 25 outdoor courts, five of which can be covered. Racquets and a ball machine are available for hire too.

Spectator Sports

Tickets for nearly all professional sporting events in Washington are sold by **Ticketmaster** (1-301 808 4300, www.ticketmaster.com). There is a service charge for all ticket purchases.

BASEBALL

The opening of **Nationals Park** (*see above* **Inside Track**) in 2008, a home for Major League team the Washington Nationals, highlighted the game in DC. Things didn't go to plan at first, though, with a mixed record and declining attendances. But things looked up in the 2012 season. In September the Nationals beat the Los Angeles Dodgers, becoming the first Washington team to advance to the postseason in 79 years. They went on to clinch the National League East division.

Washington Nationals
*Nationals Park, 1500 South Capitol Street, SE
(1-202 640 7000, www.washington.nationals.
mlb.com). Navy Yard Metro.* **Tickets** vary.
Map p253 K9.

BASKETBALL

Both men's and women's basketball are popular
in DC. The **Washington Wizards** of the NBA
is the men's team. The women's team is the
Washington Mystics. Tickets are usually
relatively easy to get hold of and cost $10-
$775 for the Wizards, or as little as $5 for the
Mystics. Both teams play in the Verizon Center,
the men from November to May, the women
from May to September.

Verizon Center
*601 F Street, NW, at 7th Street, Downtown
(1-202 628 3200, www.mcicenter.com). Gallery
Place-Chinatown Metro.* **Map** p253 J6.
This multi-use arena cost $200 million to build and
seats nearly 20,000 fans.

FOOTBALL

Three-time Super Bowl winners the
Washington Redskins play in Landover,
Maryland at FedEx Field. All tickets at FedEx
Field are season tickets, so you can't just walk
up, buy tickets and watch a game – there's a
decades-long waiting list. If you're keen to see a
match, try the Ticketmaster website (*see p188*).
There are tickets for sale direct from season-
ticket holders on its NFL Ticket Exchange
facility. Or try Craigslist.org or eBay.

If you travel to Baltimore, you have a better
chance of seeing some American football action.
The **Baltimore Ravens**' season tickets go on
sale in August. Phone 1-410 261 7283 or check
www.baltimoreravens.com for information. The
football season runs from August to January.

ICE HOCKEY

American ice hockey is now well and truly
back in the picture as one of the big four
North American spectator sports after the
catastrophic National Hockey League strike
that cancelled the entire season back in 2004-5.
The **Washington Capitals** have had award-
winning attendances at their games but it
should be possible to obtain tickets at short
notice, though early booking keeps the price
down. Tickets cost $25-$355. Phone or check
the website of the Verizon Center (*see p57*) for
match information. Tickets are available from
Ticketmaster (*see p188*).

SOCCER

Washington's **DC United** have proved
themselves to be a talented squad.

RFK Stadium
*22nd & East Capitol Streets, NE, Northeast (office
1-202 547 9077, DC United office 1-202 587
500, www.dcsec.com). Stadium-Armory Metro.*
Open 8.30am-5.30pm Mon-Fri. **Tickets** vary.
Credit MC, V.
Tickets are available from DC United (1-202 587
5000, www.dcunited.com) or through the ubiquitous
services of Ticketmaster (*see p188*).

Soccer on the Mall. See p185.

ARTS & ENTERTAINMENT

Escapes & Excursions

Escapes & Excursions

Political history and stunning scenery within easy reach of DC.

Head out of the city in almost any direction and you'll find something worth seeing. To the north is Baltimore, a city where redevelopment has made a mark on a gritty reputation, and which is host to a number of first-class museums. To the south are the Shenandoah Valley and the Blue Ridge Mountains, where the natural beauty is staggering and outdoor activities abound. And to the east is Chesapeake Bay, America's sailing capital and, at 7,000 square miles, the largest estuary in the United States.

This chapter offers a guide to the best sights and experiences in these three destinations, and also explores the area's historic homes that were once owned by America's Founding Fathers (*see p200* **Presidents in Residence**).

TRANSPORT

The best (and just about only) way to visit Shenandoah and Chesapeake Bay is by car. Traffic can be extremely heavy during commuting hours, especially on I-66 or the Beltway that circles the city. The national car rental companies all have chains in Washington, both in the city and at major airports (*see p226*). Baltimore is more friendly to people without cars; trains depart daily from Union Station (50 Massachusetts Avenue, NE, at North Capitol Street). For more information, see the Getting There section for each destination.

Spirit of Washington Cruises (Pier 4, Water Street, SW, at 6th Street, SW, 1-202 554 8000, 1-866 211 3811, www.spiritofwashington.com) operates boat trips from the city to Mount Vernon, site of George Washington's historic home, between March and October. Departure is at 8.30am and the trip takes about six hours, including three and a half hours to tour Mount Vernon ($38, $31-$36 reductions, free under-6s, price includes the admission to Mount Vernon).

BALTIMORE

Baltimore is one of the earliest true cities in America, a thriving port from the very beginning of the country and later an important manufacturing center. It was even briefly the seat of government of the fledgling nation. Things went wrong, however, and not so long ago it was known mostly for crime and post-

industrial grit, and lived very much in the shadow of the nation's capital 40 miles to the south. But since the 1980s, the 'Charm City', as Mayor William Donald Schaefer dubbed it back in the 1970s, has been undergoing a resurgence. Washingtonians not only visit Baltimore for its many attractions; many have made the Charm City their home, commuting each day to jobs in the nation's capital.

Inner Harbor

Baltimore's revitalisation is nowhere more apparent than around the Inner Harbor. No longer a depressing urban jungle of run-down factories and warehouses, the Inner Harbor has been transformed into Harborplace, a lively civic centre bursting with interesting shops and restaurants. Glass-walled offices in the new high-rise business district form a bright, modern backdrop. For a view of the city from above, take the lift to the 27th-floor observation deck of the **World Trade Center** (aka the Top of the World); at 423 feet it's the world's tallest pentagonal building (401 East Pratt Street, 1-410 837 8439).

For a trip in the opposite direction visit the world-class **National Aquarium in Baltimore**, with aquatic delights including a daily dolphin show (501 East Pratt Street, 1-410 576 3800, www.aqua.org).

The **Baltimore Maritime Museum** (Pier 3, East Pratt Street, 1-410 396 3453,

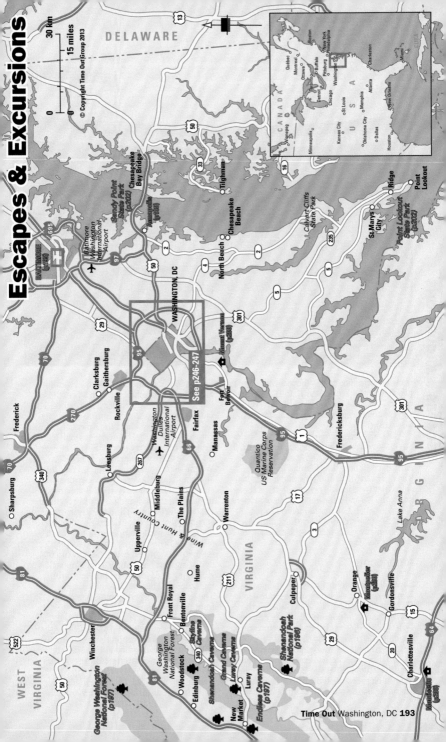

Escapes & Excursions

DELAWARE

CANADA

U S A

Baltimore (p185)

Baltimore Washington International Airport

Sandy Point State Park (p202)

Annapolis (p185)

Chesapeake Bay Bridge

Tilghman

Chesapeake Beach

North Beach

Calvert Cliffs State Park

St Mary's City

Ridge

Point Lookout

Point Lookout State Park (p202)

WASHINGTON, DC

See p246-247

Mount Vernon (p200)

Fort Belvoir

Frederick

Clarksburg

Gaithersburg

Rockville

Washington Dulles International Airport

Fairfax

Manassas

Quantico US Marine Corps Reservation

Fredericksburg

Leesburg

Middleburg

The Plains

Warrenton

Sharpsburg

Upperville

Wine & Hunt Country

Hume

Lake Anna

Orange

Montpelier (p200)

Gordonsville

Culpeper

WEST VIRGINIA

Winchester

Front Royal

Bentonville

Skyline Caverns

George Washington National Forest

Woodstock

Edinburg

Shenandoah Caverns

Grand Caverns

Luray Caverns

Luray

New Market

Endless Caverns (p197)

Shenandoah National Park (p196)

VIRGINIA

Charlottesville

George Washington National Forest (p197)

Blue Ridge (p197)

30 Km
15 miles

© Copyright Time Out Group 2013

Time Out Washington, DC **193**

Camden Yards.

www.historicships.org) is the mooring place for
two veterans of World War II, the Coast Guard
cutter *Taney*, the last survivor of Pearl Harbor,
and the submarine that fired the last torpedo of
the conflict.

The USS *Constellation* (Pier 1, 301 East Pratt
Street, www.constellation.org) is the last Civil
War-era vessel still afloat. It patrolled the
African coast near the mouth of the Congo
River between 1859 and 1861 and intercepted
ships that were illegally engaged in the slave
trade (the US made the importation of slaves
illegal in 1808). The fourth historic ship, the
Light Ship, served as the floating lighthouse
that for many years marked the entrance to
Chesapeake Bay.

Americana

Baseball is the national pastime, and no one
looms larger in the history of the game than
the legendary Babe Ruth. The **Babe Ruth
Birthplace & Museum** (216 Emory Street,
1-410 727 1539, www.baberuthmuseum.org)
is a cramped rowhouse in the scruffy
neighbourhood that was home to the young
'Sultan of Swat', a hero to American men and
boys during the 1920s and '30s for his home
run-hitting prowess on the field. (He was a
legendary boozer and lecher off it.) It sits in

the shadow of **Camden Yards**, a beautiful
Major League baseball stadium where the
Baltimore Orioles play their home games. The
museum stays open until 7pm on game days.

For the history behind the American national
anthem, which kicks off every baseball game,
visit **Fort McHenry** (end of East Fort Avenue,
1-410 962 4290, www.nps.gov/fomc). During the
War of 1812, Americans fought off the British
attempt to take the fort, which guards the
entrance to Baltimore Harbor. Bombarded
throughout the day and night of 14 September
1814, the fort held out and the British ships
eventually withdrew. Francis Scott Key, a
young lawyer who happened to be aboard
one of the British ships to negotiate the
release of a captured friend, was inspired
by the sight of his country's badly torn flag
still flying at dawn on the 14th and wrote
the lyrics of 'The Star-Spangled Banner'.
The expanded fort now on the site dates
from the Civil War.

It was Mary Pickersgill who stitched the
stars and the stripes on to the huge flag that
flew tattered over Fort McHenry during the
1814 British bombardment. Her 1793 home
is now the **Star-Spangled Banner Flag
House** (844 East Pratt Street, 1-410 837 1793,
www.flaghouse.org). There are guided tours
of the house, furnished with appropriate

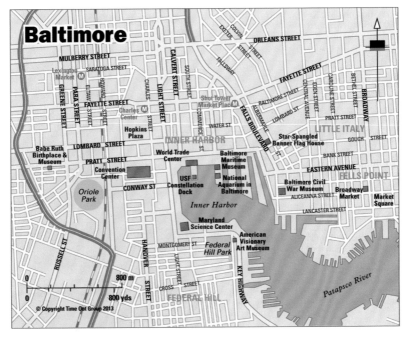

Federal-period antiques and a museum. The actual banner underwent painstaking restoration at Washington's Smithsonian Institution before it was returned to public display at the National Museum of American History in 2006 (*see p212* Profile).

While not the birthplace (Boston was), Baltimore is the burial site of **Edgar Allan Poe**, the master of the macabre who first won national acclaim with his poem 'The Raven'. He died in 1849 at age 40. His final resting place is Westminster Hall & Burying Ground, the cemetery of the First Presbyterian Church (West Fayette Street & Greene Street). Visit the churchyard on your own, or call for a guided tour of the catacombs conducted on the first and third Friday of each month from April to November (1-410 706 2072, www.eapoe.org/balt/poegrave.htm).

The **Reginald F Lewis Museum of Maryland African American History & Culture** (830 East Pratt Street, 1-443 263 1800, www.africanamericanculture.org, closed Mon) is the largest African American museum on the East Coast. Exhibits are divided into three major areas: community; slavery and labour; and art and intellect. Call or visit the website for information about special exhibitions. Exhibits at the **Baltimore Civil War Museum** (601 President Street, open 10am-5pm Sat, Sun)

highlight the city's ambivalent role in the bitter 1861-65 struggle between North and South. Baltimore was a station on the 'underground railroad' by which fugitive slaves escaped to the North, but it was also home to many Confederate sympathisers. There were riots when Union troops passed through the city. The museum closed in 2007 but has since reopened on a part-time basis with limited weekend hours, with the help of volunteers from a group of interested museum supporters, the Friends of President Street Station.

Art

The **Walters Art Museum** (600 North Charles Street, 1-410 547 9000, www.the walters.org, closed Mon, Tue) is one of the best fine art museums in the US, with a collection including medieval, Renaissance, 18th- and 19th-century, Islamic and Asian art. Works on show include Raphael's *Madonna of the Candelabra*, Bernini's statue of the *Risen Christ* and El Greco's depiction of *St Francis Receiving the Stigmata*. The **Baltimore Museum of Art** (10 Art Museum Drive, 1-443 573 1700, www.artbma.org, closed Mon, Tue) has a notable collection of modern paintings and sculpture from Van Gogh to Warhol and Rodin to Nevelson. At the **American Visionary**

Art Museum (800 Key Highway, 1-410 244 1900, www.avam.org, closed Mon) across the harbour in South Baltimore, the focus is on untrained but inspired artists working outside the norms.

Where to eat & drink

Woodberry Kitchen (2010 Clipper Park Road, No. 126, 1-410 464 8000, www.woodberry kitchen.com, closed lunch Mon-Fri, mains $12-$31) has garnered praise for its big flavours and dedication to local ingredients, including Chesapeake oysters.

Phillips (301 Light Street, 1-410 685 6600, www.phillipsseafood.com, main courses $17-$30) is a large and popular restaurant with a great harbour view, terrace dining in season and seafood. Rusty Scupper (402 Key Highway, 1-410 727 3678, www.select restaurants.com/rusty, $19-$50), across Inner Harbor from Harborplace, also does seafood, plus prime rib and the like.

Though in a rather bleak location, Della Notte (801 Eastern Avenue, 1-410 837 5500, www.dellanotte.com, mains $22-$39) is highly rated. Finally, the area of Fells Point is known not only for its antiques shops but also for drinking establishments. Head to the funky Point for a drink or dinner.

Tourist information

Baltimore Area Convention & Visitors Association 401 Light Street (1-877 225 8466, www.baltimore.org). Open 9am-6pm daily.

Getting there

By car

Baltimore is about an hour's drive from Washington. Take I-95 north to I-395, exit 53, which quickly becomes Howard Street (take care not to shoot off to the left on Martin Luther King Jr Boulevard). Continue north on Howard a short distance (a football stadium and the Camden Yards baseball stadium are on your left) to Pratt Street. Turn right and continue past Charles and Light Streets to Harborplace.

By train

Amtrak (1-800 872 7245, www.amtrak.com) and Marc (1-410 539 5000, www.mtamaryland.com) both run services to Baltimore from Washington's Union Station. Amtrak trains to Baltimore's Penn Station take 35-45mins and run until after midnight (most last trains depart Penn Station at 12.40am); Marc trains run into Penn Station and Camden Station, and take a little over an hour. Last trains are at 10.45pm and as this is a commuter service there is no service at weekends.

USS Constellation.
See p194.

SHENANDOAH

More than a million people pass through Shenandoah National Park (1-540 999 3500, www.nps.gov/shen) and the surrounding area each year, making it the undisputed outdoor playground for Washingtonians. Straddling Virginia's Blue Ridge Mountains for more than 100 miles, the park takes its name from the valley and river just to its west. Skyline Drive follows the crest of the mountain range for the entire length of the park. There are 75 overlooks where motorists can take in the valley views.

The crowds begin to descend on the park in the spring, as the azaleas and dogwoods bloom. By summer, Skyline Drive can begin to feel like a clogged freeway. But the busiest time may be in the final weeks of October, when the changing foliage adorns the park in a resplendent display of colour. Current accessible areas and other information can be picked up at park entrances and several visitors' centres along Skyline Drive.

Taking to the trails

A visit to Shenandoah is not complete without setting foot on one of the national park's 500 miles of trails. Trail maps published by the Potomac Appalachian Trail Club can be purchased ($6) when entering the park. (Some maps can be downloaded at www.nps.gov/shen/planyourvisit/mapshiking.htm.) From **Skyline Drive**, there are an endless number of hikes. Many include sections of the **Appalachian Trail**, an idea first conceived by a conservationist named Benton MacKaye as an antidote to the rapid urbanisation and hectic pace of life in the northeastern US. Completed in 1937, the trail extends 2,174 miles from Maine to Georgia. Of these 101 run through **Shenandoah National Park**. Waterfalls are Shenandoah's feature attraction. The challenging nine-mile **Whiteoak Canyon Trail** (mile 45.6 off Skyline Drive) passes six of them and is one of the most popular routes. For a shorter hike, try the four-mile **Rose River Loop** (mile 49.4), which runs past a waterfall that drops more than 60 feet.

Vistas are another reason to take to the trails. The **Mary's Rock** (mile 31.6) trail climbs 1,210 feet and ends at a rock outcropping with a view of Thornton Gap. Legend has it that Mary Thornton, a 15-year-old former park resident, hiked the two miles to the top and returned with a bear cub under each arm. For a shorter hike with a big payoff, try **Stony Man** (mile 41.7). It's less than a mile to the 4,011-foot summit, the second highest in the park. If you can, take in the valley at sunset.

Luray Caverns.

Shenandoah's most popular hike is **Old Rag Mountain**. At 3,200 feet it offers a breathtaking view of the valley. Near the summit of the mountain, the trail gives way to massive boulders. Scaling these rocks (or sliding between or under them) requires a sturdy pair of hiking boots and, on occasion, a friend's helping hand. The non-adventurous need not apply. Be forewarned: arrive at sunrise on weekends. Parking spaces fill up quickly, and in some cases you may need to hike before you even reach the trail.

To avoid the crowds, nearby **George Washington National Forest** (1-888 265 0019, www.fs.usda.gov/gwj) is less visited but has great scenery and hundreds of miles of trails. **Signal Knob Trail** leads to the top of a mountain that Confederate forces used to send messages during the Civil War. There are two overlooks before the summit – Buzzard Rock and Fort Valley. The ten-mile loop marked with yellow blazes starts just north of Elizabeth Furnace Campground off State Road 678.

A shorter option is the **Big Schloss Trail**, which starts at Wolf Gap Campground off State Road 675. The hike is about two miles one way and leads to a rock outcropping, which offers a panoramic view of the forest below. Peregrine falcons have been released into the wild here.

Going underground

Shenandoah is home to hundreds of caves, where summer temperatures hover around a cool 55 degrees fahrenheit (12 degrees centigrade) – a great way to beat the heat. Many are accessible to the public. **Luray Caverns** (970 US Highway 211 West, 1-540 743 6551, www.luraycaverns.com, $24 adults, $12 6-12s, free under-6s, incl tour) has paved, well-lit walkways and a Disneyland feel. Its main feature is a stalacpipe organ. Outside the caverns is a garden maze where the children can have fun getting lost ($6, $5 reductions, free under-6s).

Other options include **Endless Caverns** (1800 Endless Caverns Road, New Market, 1-800 544 2283, www.endlesscaverns.com), where the fossilised tooth of a woolly mammoth was found in 1996, and **Shenandoah Caverns** (261 Shenandoah Caverns Road, 1-540 477 3115, www.shenandoah caverns.com), which has a calcite crystal formation called the Diamond Cascade. Some crystal caverns were closed at the time of writing because of a fungus affecting bats, so it might be a good idea to check before visiting.

Civil War soldiers during a break in the fighting autographed the walls of **Grand Caverns** (Grand Caverns Drive, Grottoes, 1-888 430 2283, www.grandcaverns.com), and locals hosted dances in a 5,000-square-foot chamber called the Grand Ballroom. **Skyline Caverns** (10344 Stonewall Jackson Highway, Front Royal, 1-800 296 4545, www.skyline caverns.com) has rare white-spiked ceiling formations called anthodites.

Reel talk

Herbert Hoover, the 31st president (1928-32), was one of the first Washingtonians to flee the humidity of the nation's capital for Shenandoah. He chose for his presidential retreat a spot along the Rapidan River, largely because he loved to relax with rod and reel. Fishing, he wrote, 'is the chance to wash one's soul with pure air, with the rush of a brook, or with the shimmer of the sun on the blue water'.

Hoover had 13 cabins, three of which have been restored to their former glory, including the president's grand abode. Hike two miles down to the cabins along the Mill and Laurel Prong loop (mile 52.7) and meet up with a tour, or catch a van from the Harry F Byrd visitor centre at Big Meadows. Tours are three hours long and have a 13-person limit. Check the schedule and make reservations by phone on 1-540 999 3500 or in person at the Byrd Visitor Center.

If Hoover inspires you, grab a reel and rod yourself (the president loved trout, particularly with bacon and eggs for breakfast). Brook trout,

smallmouth bass, brown trout; fly-fishing or conventional fishing; the options are well-nigh limitless. Guides provide equipment and can find the best holes. Harry Murray of **Murray's Fly Shop** (121 Main Street, Edinburg, 1-540 984 4212, www.murraysflyshop.com) and his son Jeff grew up fishing Stoney Creek, which flows by his store in the valley and into the North Fork of the Shenandoah River.

You'll need a Virginia fishing licence, which you can purchase and print out online (www. dgif.virginia.gov/fishing/regulations). It's $14 for a freshwater licence for five consecutive days.

Riding the river

Take your pick, from canoe, kayak, raft or tube – many outfitters are ready to set you up for a whitewater adventure or a leisurely float. Reservations are essential; trips can fill up quickly. Front Royal bills itself as the 'Canoe Capital of Virginia'. Head to **Front Royal Canoe Company** (8567 Stonewall Jackson Highway, 1-800 270 8808, www.frontroyal canoe.com). In Luray, try **Shenandoah River Outfitters** (6502 South Page Valley Road, 1-540 743 4159, www.shenandoahriver.com). And in Bentonville, there is **Downriver Canoe Company** (884 Indian Hollow Road, 1-800 338 1963, www.downriver.com).

Shenandoah National Park.

Where to eat

Thornton River Grille (3710 Sperryville Pike, Sperryville, 1-540 987 8790, www.thornton rivergrille.com, closed Mon, mains $10-$29) can fill up quickly for dinner thanks to its delicious burgers and crab cakes. Make a reservation. The **Joshua Wilton House** (412 South Main Street, Harrisonburg, 1-888 294 5866, www.joshuawilton.com, closed Mon, Sun, mains $21-$30) is more upscale. The outdoor patio is a good place to wind down after a day of outdoor fun. The menu is seasonal and reservations are recommended. To stock up on a few treats before hiking, head to **Cranberry's Grocery & Eatery** (7 South New Street, Staunton, 1-540 885 4755, www.gocranberrys.com).

Where to stay

Planning ahead is essential, with some places getting booked up a year in advance in peak season. **Skyland Resort** (Mile 41.7, Skyline Drive, 1-800 778 2851, closed Dec-Feb, doubles $142-$186) is located at the highest point (3,680 feet) on Skyline Drive. It has lodge suites, rustic cabins, a decent restaurant and spectacular views. **Big Meadows Lodge** (Mile 51.2, Skyline Drive, 1-800 778 2851, doubles $149-$188) has traditional-style rooms, some with fireplaces, in the beautifully panelled main lodge and another 72 in multi-unit lodges and rustic cabins. Its restaurant offers 'ladies high tea' ,which still uses the recipes dating from the era when the likes of Eleanor Roosevelt visited. **Lewis Mountain Cabins** (Mile 57.5, Skyline Drive, 1-800 778 2851, doubles $82.25-$117) is a more outdoorsy option.

Information about all three can be found at www.nationalparkreservations.com/shenandoah_cabins.php.

Tourist information

Woodstock *Shenandoah County Tourism, Suite 101, 600 North Main Street (1-540 459 6227, 1-888 367 3965, www.shenandoahtravel.org).* **Open** 8.30am-5pm Mon-Fri.
New Market *Shenandoah Valley Travel Association, 277 West Old Cross Road, PO Box 1040 (1-540 740 3132).* **Open** 9am-5pm daily.
Edinburg *George Washington National Forest – Lee Ranger Forest District, 109 Molineu Road (1-540 984 4101/933 6171).* **Open** 8am-4.30pm Mon-Fri.

Getting there

By car

Of the several entrances to the park, the most convenient from Washington is at its northern tip,

Annapolis.

90mins or less via I-66 to exit 6, then south three miles on US 340 to Front Royal.

CHESAPEAKE

Sailboats dotting the bay, gentle bay breezes, life at a languid pace. There is no shortage of reasons to visit picturesque Chesapeake Bay and embark on a vacation from your vacation. **Annapolis** is the jewel of the Chesapeake and has been Maryland's capital since 1695. A modern city has grown up around the colonial core, but the historic city is largely preserved. The narrow streets surrounding the old harbour are lined with what is claimed to be the largest concentration of Georgian houses in the country. Annapolis is no longer the busy port it once was, but the sea remains very much part of its identity. Marinas, sailing schools and charter services make it a recreational center. Several tours, self-guided and otherwise, of the whole Annapolis historic area are also available. Check at the City Dock information booth for details.

South of Annapolis, the Chesapeake's less publicised West Shore stretches more than 100 miles to Point Lookout, where the Potomac River flows into the bay. Cross over the Bay Bridge from Annapolis to reach the Chesapeake's Eastern Shore.

Presidents in Residence

Four of the first five US presidents were Virginians.

Thomas Jefferson's **Monticello** is a two-and-a-half-hour drive from Washington, but worth the journey. To understand Jefferson – the author of the Declaration of Independence and third president (1801-09) – you must first understand Monticello, or so the saying goes. Jefferson was a Renaissance man, an architect and inventor who dabbled in archaeology, paleontology and astronomy. All of his pursuits are on display here. Jefferson designed and oversaw the construction of the house, a neo-classical gem befitting a Founding Father. He selected all the furnishings, many of which he purchased while serving as a diplomat in France. Tours of the three-storey, 21-room house are conducted continuously each day. In the entrance hall, Jefferson created a mini-museum of European art and artefacts from explorers Lewis and Clark's celebrated Western expedition, which he commissioned as president. Tours also include Jefferson's sitting room, library, bedroom, dining room and a guest bedroom. Visitors can wander through the wine and beer cellars in the basement on their own. Jefferson had a lifelong interest in botany and agriculture; his restored gardens can be explored in daily tours between October and April. There are a variety of other tour and event options, including archaeology open houses; see website for details.

If you visit Monticello, be sure to also drop in on Jefferson's former neighbours. **Montpelier** is the former home of James Madison, the fourth president. Also designed by Jefferson, the house embodied his classical vision. Later owners, including the immensely wealthy Du Pont family, expanded and significantly altered the original structure. An extensive restoration that began in 2003 sought to restore the house to its original size and Federal-period appearance. It was completed in 2008.

James Monroe, the fifth US president (1817-25), owned **Ash Lawn-Highland** plantation. Though without the size or scope of Monticello, it too has breathtaking views. Just 14 miles south of DC along the George Washington Memorial Parkway (which ends at the visitors' entrance), **Mount Vernon** is the most celebrated and visited historic home in the country. George Washington has gone down in history as a soldier and statesman, but he devoted the greater part of his life to improving the estate he had inherited from an older half-brother, seeking to re-create an English manor house on the banks of the Potomac. The faithfully restored plantation house contains original furniture and many of the first First Family's belongings. The gardens have been planted in colonial style.

A major project in recent years has been the re-creation of a colonial-era farm where crops of Washington's day are raised using the simple implements of the time. It includes an ingenious octagonal threshing barn he devised, revealing him as a true agricultural innovator. An orientation centre and museum, tactfully concealed under a meadow, further fleshes out Washington – literally, in the case of a forensically reconstructed statue of him at age 19. Traditional treasures shine alongside, notably Jean-Antoine Houdon's terracotta bust from life – the most accurate likeness of Washington ever created.

There are a couple of appealing ways to reach the estate: by car down the elegant George Washington Parkway (which set the scenic-drive standard in 1932); or by traditional excursion boat, with regular

Monticello

Mount Vernon

Naval gazing

Annapolis is the home port of the **US Naval Academy**, which was founded in 1845 and educates future naval and marine officers. The 4,000 students (or midshipmen, as they're known) stride around town conspicuously in their white uniforms. The academy is open to the public. Picture identification is required to enter the campus for anyone over 16. Visiting hours are generally 9am-5pm. Visitors may observe the noon formation of midshipmen held Monday to Friday, weather permitting, during the academic year. Guided tours are available at the **Armel-Leftwich Visitor Center** (52 King George Street, 1-410 293 8687). The visitor centre also has naval and astronautical memorabilia, such as the *Freedom 7* space capsule and an exhibit on John Paul Jones.

Jones is America's pre-eminent naval hero from the Revolutionary War, best known for the words he uttered on 23 September 1779. As Jones fought the HMS *Serapis* on the North Sea off Flamborough Head, his ship, the *Bonhomme Richard*, came under fire and began to sink. When the opposing captain called for Jones to surrender, he allegedly responded, 'I have not yet begun to fight!' Jones then proceeded to board the *Serapis* and captured it. In 1792, Jones died in Paris. But in 1905, his remains were unearthed, and he was reburied in a crypt in the basement of the Naval Academy's chapel. Today, the crypt is surrounded by artefacts from Jones's life, such as the gold medal Congress awarded him in 1787.

A collection of 108 ship models is one of the highlights of the **United States Naval Academy Museum** (Preble Hall, 1-410 293 2108, www.usna.edu/museum). The museum also has artefacts from the USS *Constitution* and other ships, artwork depicting naval battles and memorabilia from significant naval figures.

Bay breezes

Annapolis has been called the 'sailing capital of the world', which should be incentive enough to take to the water. Call ahead for reservations and prices. Two-hour cruises usually run for around $30 per person. The *Woodwind* (1-410 263 7837, www.schoonerwoodwind.com), a 74-foot schooner, departs from the Annapolis Marriott Waterfront Hotel and offers two-hour rides, including sunset sails. On Tuesdays, the captain offers up a selection of beer from microbreweries for tasting. He'll even let you take the wheel or help hoist the sails. If power boating is more your speed, **Watermark Cruises** (1-410 268 7601, www.watermark cruises.com) has 90-minute and full-day tours. Full-day tours head to St Michaels or the

departures from Washington and Alexandria. An alternative route is by Huntington Metro station and then Fairfax Connector bus 101 or 102.

Monticello
State Route 53 (1-434 984 9822, www. monticello.org). **Open** *Mar-Nov* 9am-5pm daily. *Dec-Feb* 10am-4pm daily. Longer hrs on some weekends & holidays. **Admission** $24; $8 reductions; free under-6s.

Montpellier
11407 Constitution Highway, State Route 20 (1-540 672 2728, www.montpelier.org). **Open** *Apr-Oct* 9am-5.30pm Tue-Sun. *Nov-Mar* 10.30am-4.30pm Wed-Sun. **Admission** $18; $7-$9 reductions; free under-6s.

Ash Lawn-Highland
Route 795 (1-434 293 9539, www. ashlawnhighland.org). **Open** *Apr-Oct* 9am-6pm daily. *Nov-Mar* 11am-5pm daily. **Admission** $12; $5-$11 reductions.

Mount Vernon
George Washington Memorial Parkway (1-703 780 2000, www.mountvernon.org). **Open** *Apr-Aug* 8am-5pm daily. *Mar, Sept, Oct* 9am-5pm daily. *Nov-Feb* 9am-4pm daily. **Admission** $17; $8-$16 reductions; free under-6s.

ESCAPES & EXCURSIONS

Sandy Point State Park.

fishing village of Rock Hall. Ninety minutes will get you to Thomas Point Lighthouse, a National Historic Landmark, among other destinations.

Chesapeake Bay was once filled with so many oysters that Maryland and Virginia fishermen actually resorted to violence as they argued over where the rightful boundary was between the two states. To revisit the bay when the oyster was king, set sail for a two-hour cruise on the *Rebecca T Ruark* (1-410 829 3976, www.skipjack. org), built in 1886 and currently the bay's oldest working skipjack. Captain Wade Murphy will demonstrate how skipjacks dredged for oysters before he does some dredging of his own.

Captain Ed Farley offers two-hour cruises on *HM Krenz* (1-410 745 6080, www.oystercatcher. com). Farley helped author James Michener in his research for *Chesapeake*, the epic historical novel about the bay. Check beforehand as many river trip operators are closed out of season.

Beach life

Chesapeake's strands may not rival Miami's South Beach or Southern California's Laguna Beach, but they do attract a faithful following because of the many different activities on offer. More than a million visitors each year descend on Annapolis's **Sandy Point State Park** at the western terminus of the Bay Bridge (1100 East College Parkway, 1-410 974 2149, www.dnr.state.md.us/publiclands/southern/sandypoint.asp). The site of a pre-Civil War resort, the park has a mile-long beach and offers the chance to swim, fish, go crabbing, rent a rowboat or motorboat (call the marina

for prices and availability, 1-410 974 2772), have a picnic, or hike along nature trails. But maybe the best attraction is watching traffic back up on the Bay Bridge. For those not interested in this perverse pleasure, there are sailing regattas and sea-bound ships to ogle.

Calvert Cliffs State Park (Lusby, 1-301 743 7613, www.dnr.state.md.us/publiclands/southern/calvertcliffs.asp) features 100-foot cliffs that loom over a small beach. More than 600 species of fossil have been discovered on the beach and cliffs. From the parking lot, the hike to the beach is about two miles. **Point Lookout State Park** (11175 Point Lookout Road, Scotland, 1-301 872 5688, www.dnr.state.md.us/publiclands/southern/pointlookout.html) is nothing if not picturesque. A beach three-quarters of a mile long overlooks the point where the Potomac River flows into Chesapeake Bay. Rent motorboats or canoes, go fishing, hiking or swimming. A museum explains the park's history as a Civil War prison camp for more than 50,000 Confederate soldiers.

Getting crabby

Forget fancy napkins, highbrow wine lists and a maitre d' in tails. Maryland crab houses are all about the crab. The tables are paper-covered and the utensil of choice is a wooden mallet. No trip to Chesapeake is complete without tasting the local delicacy, but be warned: this isn't fast food. There's lots of labour necessary to get at the succulent meat.

Maryland's blue crabs spawn in southern Chesapeake Bay once the brackish water starts to warm in June, moving up the bay and its 150 tributaries, periodically shedding their shells as they grow. A crab caught during the first few hours between shedding its old shell and growing a new one is called 'softshell', capable of being cooked and devoured in its entirety. 'Hardshells' over the legal minimum size are a decidedly different dish. The cycle ends in late autumn. Don't be afraid to ask for a tutorial in how to open and slice up your crab, but whatever you do, don't eat its organs. Most crab shacks also offer a selection of shrimp, clams, mussels, calamari and fish, for those who are not crab crazy.

Jimmy Cantler's Riverside Inn (458 Forest Beach Road, 1-410 757 1311, www. cantlers.com, mains $8-$29) is a short drive from downtown Annapolis and the local favourite. Set against Mill Creek, Cantler's has outdoor seating. For another local favourite visit **Mike's Bar & Crab House** (3030 Riva Road, Riva, 1-410 956 2784, www.mikescrabhouse.com, mains $15-$31). Established in 1958, Mike's has a deck with views of the South River. **Cheshire Crab Restaurant** (1701 Poplar Ridge Road, Pasadena, 1-410 360 2220, www.pleasurecove marina.com/cheshirecrab, mains $11-$25, closed Jan-Mar & Mon all year round) has an outdoor deck that overlooks the Pleasure Cove marina, where watermen can tie up and head inside for a quick bite to eat before returning to the waves. On the east side of the Bay Bridge is **Harris Crab House** (433 Kent Narrows Way N, Grasonville, 1-410 827 9500, www.harris crabhouse.com, mains $11-$25), which has a rooftop deck with a view of the Kent Narrows. Housed in an 1830s building first used as an oyster shucking shed (check out the authentic bar ceiling joints), **St Michaels Crab House** (305 Mulberry Street, St Michaels, 1-410 745 3737, www.stmichaelscrabhouse.com, mains $15-$25) has a waterfront patio that overlooks a marina off the Miles River. And finally, **Waterman's Crab House** (Sharp Street Wharf, Rock Hall, 1-410 639 2261, www. watermanscrabhouse.com, mains $14-$28) has a deck that overlooks Rock Hall Harbor and the Bay Bridge. The sunsets from here can be pretty spectacular.

Tourist information

Annapolis & Anne Arundel County Conference & Visitors Bureau 26 West Street (1-888 302 2852, www.visit-annapolis.org). **Open** 9am-5pm daily.
Maryland Department of Natural Resources 580 Taylor Avenue (1-410-260-8367, www.dnr. state.md.us). **Open** 9am-5pm Mon-Fri. This office can provide hiking, camping and fishing information.

Jimmy Cantler's Riverside Inn.

In Context

History

DC began life as a planned city, but its people shaped its destiny.

Symbolically, Washington is the heart of American democracy. More than 200 years after its founding, however, democracy for its own residents is only partial: DC's citizens can participate in presidential elections, but have no voting representation in the US Congress. This awkward circumstance is rooted in the city's founding, which was a political compromise between Northern and Southern states. The Revolutionary War left the North with substantial debts that it pressed the new federal government to assume. In exchange, the Northerners abandoned their hopes of locating the government in a large Northern city such as New York or Philadelphia, each of which served as capital for a time. Instead, they agreed to construct a new city on the border between North and South. The actual choice was left to President George Washington, who chose a spot less than 20 miles from his Virginia plantation, Mount Vernon.

THE NEW CAPITAL

The first president was not the first person to recognise that the confluence of the Potomac and Anacostia rivers was a natural crossroads. The area was an Indian meeting place a millennium before the Federal City was conceived. ('Potomac' may mean 'place where people trade' in the Algonquin language.) Still, the people who lived in the area when Europeans first arrived in the early 17th century left little besides place names.

Within the new city were two port towns that had been founded around 1750: Georgetown on the Maryland side and Alexandria in Virginia. Both were incorporated into the new District of Columbia, a diamond-shaped 100-square-mile precinct that took 70 square miles from Maryland and 30 from Virginia.

But the new capital, which came to be known as Washington, would be built from scratch on land that was originally mostly farmland or forest – contrary to the popular belief that the city is built on a swamp. Washington hired a former member of his army staff, Pierre-Charles L'Enfant, to design the new city.

Construction of the White House and Capitol began in 1792-93, but neither was finished when John Adams, the country's second president, arrived in 1800. Adams and other members of the new government were but the first to notice the gap between the grandeur of L'Enfant's baroque street plan and the reality: a muddy frontier town of a mere 14,000 inhabitants, most of them living in Georgetown and Alexandria.

After 1801, residents of the District of Columbia lost their right to vote in Maryland or Virginia. The Constitution specified that Congress alone would control 'the federal district', although it's unclear that the document's drafters actually intended to disenfranchise the District's residents. The city of Washington was incorporated, with an elected city council and mayor appointed by the president. In 1820, the city's residents were allowed to elect the mayor as well. This was the first of the many tinkerings with the local form of government that were to follow.

What progress had been made in creating the new capital was largely undone during the War of 1812. In 1814, after defeating local resistance at the Battle of Bladensburg, British troops marched unopposed into the city and burned most of the significant buildings. President Madison fled the White House for the **Octagon** (*see p51*), the nearby home of Colonel John Tayloe. It was there that he ratified the Treaty of Ghent, which ended the war. Among the things destroyed by the British was the original collection of the Library of Congress, which didn't yet have its own building; former president Thomas Jefferson had sold the nation his library as the basis for a new collection.

AFTER THE 1812 WAR

After the War of 1812 established American sovereignty, European guests began to arrive to inspect the new capital. They were unimpressed. Visiting in 1842, Charles Dickens provided the most withering sobriquet for pre-Civil War Washington: 'the city of magnificent intentions'. It was another Englishman, however, who made the greatest impact on the city in this period. In 1829, James Smithson, a professor of chemistry at Oxford who had never even visited the United States, left his estate to the new nation for the founding of an educational institution. Congress was so bewildered by this bequest that it didn't act on it for more than a decade, but the Smithsonian Institution was finally founded in 1846. Its original building opened in 1855.

While the Smithsonian laid one of the earliest foundations for Washington's contemporary position as an information hub, the city showed few signs of becoming a centre of commerce. In an attempt to increase trade, the Chesapeake & Ohio Canal was built, paralleling the Potomac River for 185 miles to Cumberland, Maryland. Ground was broken in 1828, and the canal's Georgetown terminus opened in 1840. The canal continued to operate into the early 20th century, but its importance was soon diminished by the Baltimore & Ohio Railroad, the country's first

IN CONTEXT

railway, which began operation in 1830 and arrived in Washington in 1835.

The other event of this period that had long-term significance for Washington was the 1846 retrocession to Virginia of the southern third of the District; this area now encompasses Arlington County and part of the city of Alexandria. Among the grievances of the area's residents was Congress's refusal to loan money to construct a Virginia-side canal connecting Alexandria to the west. The Virginia state government was more inclined to support the project than Congress, which has always been reluctant to spend money on people without any voting representatives in the Capitol. (The canal project was ultimately reduced to an aqueduct connecting Alexandria to the C&O Canal.) An underlying issue, however, was some Virginians' anticipation that Congress would soon restrict the slave trade in the District.

AFRICAN AMERICAN CITY

From its founding, Washington had a large African American population. By 1800, around one-quarter of the city's population was African American, and most of those were slaves. By 1840, the ratio of white to black was similar, but there were almost twice as many free blacks as slaves. Free blacks and runaway slaves arrived in Washington to escape the horrors of life on Southern plantations, and quickly set up institutions to help their compatriots. Washington became a more attractive destination in 1850, when Congress did ban slave trading (but not slavery itself). A year before Abraham Lincoln's 1863 Emancipation Proclamation, Congress abolished slavery in the District.

Despite the presence of some relatively prosperous free blacks, Washington was hardly a safe haven for former slaves. African Americans were sometimes kidnapped off the city's streets and sold into slavery, the papers certifying their free status having been destroyed by their captors. Those who escaped this fate still had to live under the onerous 'black codes' adopted by Congress from the laws of Virginia and Maryland. These restricted African Americans' property

ownership, employment and trades, public meetings and even use of profane language. Being arrested for an infraction of these laws could result in a permanent loss of liberty, since jail wardens were authorised to sell their black prisoners to pay the cost of their incarceration.

CIVIL WAR CONSEQUENCES

The Civil War transformed Washington from a sleepy part-time capital into the command centre of an energised country – the first (but not the last) time that a national crisis actually benefited the city. New residents flooded into town, and such DC inhabitants as photographer Matthew Brady became nationally known for their war work. Among the new Washingtonians was poet Walt Whitman, who initially came to care for his wounded brother and then became a volunteer at the makeshift hospitals in the converted Patent Office and Washington Armory. (Whitman remained in the city for 12 years, working as a clerk at various federal agencies; he was fired from the Bureau of Indian Affairs when the new secretary of interior deemed *Leaves of Grass* to violate 'the rules of decorum & propriety prescribed by a Christian Civilization'.)

Several Civil War battles were fought near Washington, notably the two engagements at Manassas, now a local commuter-rail stop. A string of forts was built to protect the District, but only one saw action: Fort Stevens, site of an 1864 skirmish. The city's most significant war-related incident, the 1865 assassination of President Lincoln at Ford's Theatre, actually occurred five days after the South surrendered.

Following the end of the war, a Congress dominated by 'radical Republicans' made some efforts to atone for the sins of slavery. The Freedman's Bureau was established to help former slaves make the transition to freedom and in 1867 Howard University was chartered for African American students. All adult male residents of Washington were granted local suffrage in 1866, and 9,800 white and 8,200 'colored' men registered to vote.

Profile The Star-Spangled Banner

The story of a song (and a flag).

In 1814, the fledgling American nation was in crisis. Only 30-odd years after its hard-won independence, and the British were back. After British troops burned down the White House and Capitol building they set their sights on Baltimore, bombarding Baltimore Harbor's Fort McHenry with rockets and bombs for 25 hours.

Lawyer Francis Scott Key was on a boat out at sea. As dawn came at the battle's end, he looked towards land and was just able to make out an American flag still flying over the fort. He returned home inspired to write a song (or, to be accurate, song lyrics) and the rest – as they say – is history.

This is a familiar story to Americans, but now they – and the rest of the world – can see the flag that inspired the song that was to become the American national anthem, in an exhibition that follows its journey both as physical artefact and national symbol.

The garrison flag, measuring a huge 30 by 42 feet, was made by professional flag-maker Mary Pickersgill, her teenage daughter and nieces, and a 13-year-old African American indentured servant named Grace Wisher. After the battle, the flag stayed in the possession of the commander of Fort McHenry and his family for 90 years. Snippets, including one of the 15 original stars, were given away from time to time as patriotic keepsakes.

This may seem like careless treatment, but in the early 19th century flags were official emblems with little cultural significance. Buy by giving the flag a name and telling a story Francis Scott Key helped turn it into a symbol of national identity.

By 1907, when it was lent to the Smithsonian, the flag had gone from personal keepsake to national treasure. The loan became a gift a few years later, but it wasn't until 1931 that 'The Star-Spangled Banner' was declared the official national anthem of the United States of America.

IN CONTEXT

ON VIEW
The restored flag is on display in a special, climate-controlled chamber in the **National Museum of American History** (*see p36*).

Yet Congress did not address Washingtonians' lack of Congressional representation. In 1871, it reclassified the city as a territory, but quieted the latest round of rumours that it intended to move the capital west by authorising the construction of the massive State, War & Navy Departments Building directly west of the White House. A prominent local real-estate developer, Alexander Shepherd, was appointed to the territory's Board of Public Works, which he soon dominated. 'Boss' Shepherd began an ambitious programme of street grading and paving, sewer building and tree planting, transforming the city but also unfortunately quickly bankrupting it.

Only three years after establishing the territorial government, Congress abandoned it, putting the city under the control of three presidentially appointed commissioners. Local voting rights were eliminated, a move that one local newspaper welcomed as ending the 'curse' of African american suffrage. President Grant, still a Shepherd supporter, nominated the 'Boss' to be one of the three new commissioners, but the Senate wouldn't confirm him. In 1876, Shepherd moved to Mexico, leaving behind a city that was beginning to look something like modern Washington.

The next major round of civic improvements was inspired in 1881 by severe flooding. A land-reclamation and flood-control project built Hains Point and West Potomac Park, quite literally creating the ground that would become the home of such Washington landmarks as the Lincoln and Jefferson Memorials. That same year, President Garfield was shot at the Baltimore & Potomac Railroad station (now the site of the National Gallery of Art) by a disgruntled job-seeker. Garfield died two months later in New Jersey, where he had been taken for the supposedly rehabilitative effect of the sea air.

Following Shepherd's modernisation of the city, many improvement projects were undertaken. The Washington Monument was finally finished in 1885, and electric streetcars began operation

Lincoln Memorial.

in 1888, opening the areas beyond Boundary Street (now Florida Avenue) to development. In 1889, the National Zoological Park was founded in Rock Creek Park, which was officially established the following year.

NEW CENTURY AND THE NEW DEAL
Washington's 1900 centennial brought major plans to remake the city. Under the influence of the City Beautiful movement, the Congressionally chartered McMillan Commission proposed restoring the primacy of the oft-ignored L'Enfant Plan and developing the neglected Mall and nearby areas along the river. Some of the city's poorest and most dangerous neighbourhoods were to be removed to create a grand greensward, and such unseemly intrusions as the Baltimore & Potomac station were to be banished from the Mall. The result of the latter dictum was Union Station, which upon its 1908 opening consolidated the

city's several downtown railroad stations on a site north of the Capitol. In 1910, the Fine Arts Commission was established to ensure the aesthetic worthiness of new federal structures, and an act was passed to limit the height of buildings.

A practical challenge to the McMillan Plan came with World War I, which prompted another Washington building boom. Dozens of 'temporary' structures were erected, including some built on the western part of the Mall. Many of these buildings were used not only during that war but for World War II as well. The last of them was torn down in 1971 and part of the space they occupied became Constitution Gardens, which opened in 1976.

'Federal government agencies were rigidly segregated, as were most of the capital's public facilities.'

The large numbers of sailors and soldiers demobilised in Washington after World War I are often cited as one of the root causes of the terrible race riots that convulsed the city in the summer of 1919. Nine people were killed in the worst disturbance, which began after false rumours spread that a black man had raped a white woman. Much of the violence spread from the Navy Yard into the predominantly African American neighbourhoods nearby in Southwest.

Race relations were strained by the riots, but they were precarious even before them. Most of the advances for African Americans in the post-Civil War era had been turned back by the early 20th century; President Woodrow Wilson, hailed as a visionary in foreign policy, was a reactionary on matters of race. Federal government agencies were rigidly segregated, as were most of the capital's public facilities – although its

libraries, trolleys and buses, and baseball stadium (but not the teams that played there) were integrated.

In 1922, when the **Lincoln Memorial** (*see p32*) opened, the man who freed the slaves was commemorated by a racially segregated crowd; Tuskegee Institute president Robert Moten, an official invitee, was ushered to the negro section. Three years later, 25,000 hooded Ku Klux Klansmen marched down Pennsylvania Avenue, although the founding of a local Klan chapter drew little support. In 1926, the local superior court upheld the legality of voluntary covenants that were designed to prevent black people from buying property in predominantly white neighbourhoods.

Women won the vote in 1920, although not if they were DC residents. Meanwhile, separate and unequal African American Washington boomed, with the Harlem Renaissance mirrored on U Street, known as the Great Black Way. The Howard and other theatres frequently presented such performers as Ella Fitzgerald, Eubie Blake and Washington native Duke Ellington. The city's African American neighbourhoods were swelled by dispossessed Cotton Belt agricultural workers, and the Depression was soon to send more Southern blacks to town.

In central Washington, the work begun by the McMillan Commission continued. Beginning in 1926, the construction of the Federal Triangle displaced the city's Chinatown and one of its roughest neighbourhoods, 'Murder Bay', while creating an area of monumental federal office buildings unified by their Beaux Arts style. Other events boosted the capital's national prestige: in 1924 and 1925, the Washington Senators baseball team made the first two of three trips to the World Series. (They won only in 1924, and disappeared altogether in 1973.) In 1927, the first Cherry Blossom Festival was held, calling attention to the city's new ornamental riverfront.

The Depression soon ended the major civic improvement projects and made Washington the focus for a different sort of national attention. In 1931, a group called the Hunger Marchers arrived in the city; they were followed by some 20,000 jobless World War I veterans who became known as the Bonus Army. They encamped at various places around the city, sometimes with their families, waiting for Congress to pass legislation awarding them back pay. Eventually, troops under the command of General Douglas MacArthur dispersed the camps with bayonets and tear gas. During this action four people were killed, two of them young children.

In 1932, Franklin D Roosevelt was elected president. When his New Deal created new programmes and jobs, Washington again benefited from national adversity. Local construction crews began to work once more, erecting the **National Archives** (see p47) and the **Supreme Court** (see p45), both finished in 1935. Meanwhile, some of the president's cabinet members and top advisers discovered Georgetown, which fitted the 1930s vogue for the colonial style; the old port town, which then had a large African American population, became the first Washington neighbourhood to go down the road towards gentrification.

The New Dealers took a more liberal stand on racial issues. Although Roosevelt was reluctant to antagonise segregationists with major changes, he did sometimes invite black leaders to receptions – and black musicians to perform – at the White House. In 1939, when the Daughters of the American Revolution refused to let famed African American contralto Marian Anderson perform at the group's Constitution Hall, Secretary of the Interior Harold Ickes immediately approved a concert at the Lincoln Memorial. Anderson performed there for an integrated crowd of 75,000.

World War II added to the city's bustle, as thousands of workers and volunteers arrived to further the war effort. National Airport opened in 1941, and the **Pentagon** (see p77), still the nation's largest federal office building, was rapidly constructed for the military command. (The Pentagon was built with separate bathrooms for white and black employees, but after FDR protested, signs distinguishing the facilities were never added to the doors.)

Also opening in this period were two less martial structures, the **Jefferson Memorial** (see p32) and the **National Gallery of Art** (see p33). The arts kept a low profile for the remainder of the war, however, as such institutions as Dumbarton Oaks were requisitioned by wartime agencies.

Despite fears of a post-war depression, the city continued to boom in the late 1940s. As the Korean War began, the 1950 census put the District's population at 800,000, its highest point. Washington's new position as an imperial capital was emphasised by a series of controversial hearings on alleged Communist infiltration of the federal government. There were also two attacks by Puerto Rican nationalists: gunmen tried to shoot their way into Blair House to kill President Truman (he was living at the property, normally used for visiting dignitaries, during renovations to the White House). And then, soon after, attackers wounded five Congressmen on the floor of the House of Representatives.

In the 1950s, suburbanisation began to transform the land around Washington, most of it farms or woodland. Aided by new highways and federally guaranteed home mortgages, residential developments grew rapidly in the inner suburbs, followed by commercial development. Congress authorised the Interstate Highway System and supported plans for an extensive system of urban freeways for Washington that would destroy neighbourhoods and overwhelm the proportions of L'Enfant's plan.

The automobile, petroleum and rubber interests that worked quietly to destroy public transit systems in other American cities had no need for such subtlety in DC, which still had no elected local government. Corporate envoys influenced law makers to eliminate trolleys in favour of 'modern' cars and buses. Under Congressional pressure, streetcar lines were abandoned throughout the decade, with the final routes cut in 1962. While the suburbs grew, Congress turned again to remaking embarrassing examples of poverty in the vicinity of the Capitol. Thousands of working-

Parallel Lives

Washington played a crucial role in black American culture.

Black history – as a concept – was born in Washington in 1926, when Dr Carter G Woodson launched Negro History Week to counter the assumption that his race didn't have any. Soon afterwards, Howard University professor Alaine Locke sparked the New Negro cultural revival. In the 1930s the New Negro Alliance broke significant legal ground, with action by pickets forcing Washington businesses to desegregate. Meanwhile, native son Duke Ellington was playing his progressive jazz to audiences nationwide. The Harlem Renaissance may be better known, but Washington arguably played a broader and deeper role in stirring African American consciousness between the wars.

Sheer population numbers had helped establish Washington as a hub of black America. During the Civil War, DC's blacks were joined by thousands of freedmen from the South. Evidence of the influx remains in the dwellings known as alley houses – cheap, tiny houses thrown up by developers in the spacious alleys providing rear access to homes. Remaining alleys include Rumsey Court, at the 100 block of First Street, SE; Terrace Court, behind the Supreme Court, at the 200 block of A Street, NE; and Archibald Walk, at the 600 block of E Street, SE.

Congress ruled that the city's expanding black population should be educated – though not, needless to say, alongside whites. The result was free public schools that were arguably the only genuine 'separate but equal' schools in the nation. With its federal funding, Howard University (*see p64*) offered the best black higher education in the country. Fom this core grew an affluent, sophisticated African American elite of merchants and professionals, a virtually separate city within a larger, racially segregated Washington.

After World War II, Howard alumni and faculty were prominent in the legal war against racial discrimination. As legal director of the NAACP, former HU law professor Thurgood Marshall argued the case against segregation in the Supreme Court in Brown vs Board of Education, the landmark case that led to the desegregation of public schoools; in 1967 he became the first black Supreme Court justice.

It's hard to overstate the destructive impact of the 1968 riots, driving middle-class African Americans out of wrecked neighbourhoods, and marking the end of an era for black Washington.

Today, however, DC's eminence as a centre of African American culture gets the attention it deserves. Virtually every local jurisdiction distributes free black history maps or booklets. The African American Heritage Trail at www.culturaltourismdc.org consists of a free booklet, a database and 19 neighbourhood trails.

IN CONTEXT

class inhabitants were displaced from Southwest Washington in a process called 'urban renewal'. (Critics called it 'urban removal'.) Southwest also became a focus for federal development, with massive new headquarters buildings erected near the new L'Enfant Plaza.

RIGHTS AND RIOTS

The city's white population began to decline precipitously in 1954, after the Supreme Court outlawed racial segregation. While many jurisdictions resisted the ruling, Washington quickly came into compliance. It was soon a majority black city, with a poverty rate that mortified federal officials. Under Presidents John F Kennedy and Lyndon Johnson, the capital became both the symbolic focus and a conspicuous test case of the civil rights movement and the 'war on poverty'.

In 1963, Martin Luther King Jr led a 200,000-person March for Jobs and Freedom to Washington, and delivered his 'I have a dream' speech at the Lincoln Memorial. Neither race relations nor inner-city economies improved significantly in the mid 1960s, and some feared the capital would soon experience the same sort of riots that had already scarred other major cities. Upon the 1968 assassination of Martin Luther King Jr, Washington and other cities erupted in flames. Twelve people were killed as rioters burned many small businesses in predominantly black sections of the city.

Congress had already made tentative steps toward enfranchising Washington residents. In 1961, a Constitutional amendment gave Washington residents the right to vote in presidential elections, and in 1967, Congress restored the mayor and council system of government, but with all officials appointed by the president. Despite post-1968 fears that Washington would explode again, progress in establishing an elected local government was slow. Finally, in 1975, Walter Washington became the city's first elected mayor of the 20th century and its first African American one.

The 'Free DC' battle for local voting rights was rooted in, and interconnected

with, the larger civil rights movement. Many of the city's first elected officials – notably Marion Barry, who began the first of four terms as mayor in 1979 – were civil rights veterans. Almost as important, however, was the anti-freeway campaign. An ad hoc citizens' group managed to stop most of the proposed highways through the city. Protests halted a planned freeway bridge across the Potomac River, and the slogan 'white men's roads through black men's homes' halted an eight-lane thoroughfare through Upper Northeast.

Local activists preferred a mostly underground rapid-rail system, which had already been discussed for half a century. Congress funded the system that would become the Metro, but influential Congressmen held up financing until residents also accepted the freeway system. They never did, and the Metro finally opened its first section in 1976.

In the 1970s, Washington served as a backdrop for several national struggles, notably the one over the Vietnam War. President Richard Nixon, who recognised his local unpopularity, stressed 'law and order' – considered code words for racial fears – and painted the majority-black city as the nation's 'crime capital'. Then five burglars working indirectly for Nixon were arrested during a break-in at the Democratic National Committee campaign headquarters in the Watergate office building, and 'Watergate' gradually became synonymous with Washington and the corruption of the political system. Nixon resigned the presidency in 1974.

The city's reputation was supposed to be bolstered by the 1976 celebration of the nation's bicentennial, but most people skipped the party, perhaps frightened by reports of crowds that never materialised. Still, the year saw the opening of the **National Air & Space Museum** (*see p33*), which soon became the country's most popular museum.

The following year, members of a small black Islamic group, the Hanafi Muslims, seized the District Building, the B'Nai Brith Building and the Washington Islamic Center in a protest against an obscure film depicting the prophet Mohammed. In the attack on the District Building,

IN CONTEXT

the headquarters of the mayor and the city council, a journalist was killed and councilman Marion Barry was wounded.

Faced with pressure from the DC statehood movement, in 1978 Congress passed a Constitutional amendment that would have given the District voting representation in both the House and the Senate. The amendment was ratified by only 16 of the necessary 35 states, however, and it expired in 1985.

In 1981, Ronald Reagan became president and, that same year, survived an assassination attempt outside the Washington Hilton Hotel. Reagan was ideologically opposed to big government and temperamentally averse to Washington. Nonetheless, after surviving the major recession of Reagan's first term, the region enjoyed a building boom, as new office buildings rose in both the city and its suburbs, especially Virginia. Tenants of the latter were known as 'Beltway bandits', after their proximity to the circumferential highway completed in 1964, which has become the main street of Washington's suburbs; many of them were government contractors who enjoyed the Reagan administration's large military build-up.

Although the city benefited from the tax revenues flowing from the new developments, Barry spent much of the money on assuring his political invulnerability. Years of rumours about the mayor's nocturnal activities were validated in 1990 when Barry was arrested after being videotaped smoking crack. Many Barry supporters were angered by the FBI sting, however, charging entrapment. When brought to trial, Barry was convicted of only a misdemeanour, making him eligible for office at the end of his jail term.

DC IN THE 1990S

Barry did indeed run again in 1994, winning re-election in a vote polarised along racial and class lines. He showed little interest in the job, however, and Congress had no patience for the notorious mayor. With revenues diminished by the early 1990s real-estate slump, the city was at great fiscal risk. Congress took advantage of the crisis to seize control of the city, putting a financial control board in charge of most municipal business.

When Barry was replaced by the sober, low-key Anthony Williams in 1999, Congressional leaders backed off. The pro-business Williams antagonised many residents, but his administration met the requirement to produce three years of balanced budgets, thus causing the financial control board to disappear in 2001.

IN CONTEXT

Reagan assassination attempt, 1981.

2001 AND BEYOND

On 11 September of that year, a hijacked airliner smashed into the Pentagon in nearby Virginia, killing 184. Although overshadowed by the much greater death toll in New York, the Pentagon attack – and the likelihood that a fourth plane was supposed to hit the Capitol or the White House – put the federal government on high alert, where it essentially remains. Security was tightened, barriers went up around federal buildings, and permanent new crowd-control methods were hastily put in place.

Aside from this horrific event, probably the biggest story in DC in the 21st century is changing demographics and regeneration. The 2005 census put DC's population at 582,000. In 2012, the US Census Bureau estimated the District's population at 632,323, a 5.1 per cent increase since the 2010 census. The increase continues a growth trend since 2000, following a half-century of population decline. The city's racial composition has also changed, with middle-class blacks leaving for the suburbs and young, white fans of urban living moving into the city, along with Asians and Latinos. In the 1970s, Washington was around 70 per cent black. Now this figure is around 50 per cent. This new affluent population brought with it regeneration on a large scale.

It's hard to imagine now that Downtown, Logan Circle and U Street were poor, neglected and crime-ridden as recently as the mid '90s. While change has been slow in the city's easternmost precincts – although H Street, NE, has recently been transformed – areas along Metro's Green Line are rapidly gentrifying as DC continues to dodge the worst of the recession. Over in Southeast, a new ballpark, Nationals Park, opened in 2008, with hopes that that area, too, would experience renewal.

Gentrification remains controversial, though, and the battle lines were revealed by the 2010 mayoral race. One-term mayor Adrian Fenty was defeated by City Council Chariman Vincent Gray, whose political base is east of the Anacostia, the river that divides most of the city from some of its poorest precincts. Both candidates are black but some suggested that Gray would drag Washington back to the bad old days personified by former mayor Marion Barry.

The eyes of the world were on Washington in 2009 for the inauguration of the nation's first African American president. Barack Obama went on to win a second term in 2012.

Barack Obama's inauguration, 2013.

IN CONTEXT

Architecture

Built from a neo-classical base.

TEXT: MARK JENKINS

Despite some forays into modernism, architecture in Washington remains at heart about neo-classicism. DC's two best-known buildings, the Capitol and the White House, symbolise American government and, specifically, Congress and the president. They also exemplify the city's dedication to a formal, low-rise style at odds with most American cities.

Although Washington was the first major Western capital designed from scratch, it never occurred to its creators to build a city free of classical precedents. Such founding fathers as Thomas Jefferson (an avid, if self-educated, architect) insisted on architectural styles that recalled democratic Athens and republican Rome. George Washington hired Pierre-Charles L'Enfant to design a baroque street plan, which became known as the L'Enfant Plan. The plan is a rectangular street grid with broad diagonal avenues radiating from ceremonial circles and squares and from two essential structures, the White House and the Capitol. Washington also mandated that the new capital's structures be built of brick, marble and stone, thus giving a sense of permanence to a city – and a country – that in its early days seemed a bit wobbly.

FIRST BUILDINGS

The city's oldest buildings actually precede Washington's founding. The river ports of Georgetown and Alexandria existed prior to their incorporation into the District of Columbia, and they contain most of the area's examples of 18th-century architecture. The city's only surviving pre-Revolutionary War structure is Georgetown's **Old Stone House** (3051 M Street, NW, 1-202 426 6851), a modest 1765 cottage with a pleasant garden.

Georgetown may have the feel of a colonial-era village, but most of its structures date from the 19th and early 20th centuries. Many are Victorian, but some are in the Federal style, a common early 19th-century American mode that adds classical elements like columns, pediments and porticoes to vernacular structures usually made of brick or wood.

Across the river in the Old Town district of Alexandria, which was once but is no longer part of DC, there are some larger pre-Revolutionary structures, including **Carlyle House** and **Christ Church** (for both, *see p75*), a Georgian-style edifice where George Washington was a vestryman. Like Georgetown, however, most of Old Town is of 19th- and 20th-century vintage.

Further south is George Washington's plantation, **Mount Vernon** (*see p200* **Presidents in Residence**), now a museum about the first president and the life of colonial-era gentry. This Georgian estate (including a dozen outbuildings) is one of the finest extant examples of an 18th-century American plantation. Next to Arlington National Cemetery is **Arlington House** (also known as the Lee-Custis House), a neo-classical mansion that was once the home of another Virginia aristocrat, Confederate general Robert E Lee.

Washington's two most metonymic structures, the White House and the Capitol, were both first occupied in 1800 and have been substantially remodelled and expanded since. James Hoban was the original architect of the **White House** (*see p42*), but Thomas Jefferson, who lost the competition to design what was

'Despite its grander scale, the Capitol remains true to the original neo-classical conception.'

originally called simply the President's House, tinkered with the plans while in residence during 1801-09; the most significant additions were new monumental north and south porticoes, designed in 1807 by Benjamin Latrobe but not built until the 1820s. Many additions followed, with some of the more recent ones (for offices and security equipment) out of sight. The structure apparently got its current name after it was whitewashed to cover the damage that resulted from being burned in 1814 by British troops, although the sandstone façade was first whitewashed in 1797 while still under construction.

The **US Capitol** (*see p45*), at the centre of the city's grid, has grown dramatically from William Thornton's modest original design. Since the cornerstone was laid in 1793, virtually every visible part of the structure has been replaced, from the dome to the east and west façades. The last major renovation of the exterior was done in 1987; the most recent update has been the construction of a new underground visitor centre. Despite its grander scale, the Capitol remains true to the original neo-classical conception, with Corinthian columns making the case that the building is a temple to democracy.

Other buildings that survive from the Federal period are less august, although one of them takes a singular form. Built in 1800 as the city home of the prosperous Tayloe family, the **Octagon** (*see p51*) gives a distinctive shape to the Federal style. Actually a hexagon with a semi-circular portico, the house was designed by Capitol architect Thornton. Both the **Sewall-Belmont House** (144 Constitution

Avenue, NE) and **Dumbarton Oaks** (*see p68*) are fine examples of the Federal style, although they've been much altered since they were built in, respectively, 1790 and 1801. (The earliest part of Sewall-Belmont House dates to about 1750.) Dumbarton Oaks is most notable for its elegant gardens and its scenic location on the edge of Rock Creek Park. All three structures are now museums.

Washington's first business district developed around the intersection of Pennsylvania Avenue and Seventh Street, NW, and there are still some examples of pre-Civil War vernacular architecture in this area. The buildings near the intersections of Seventh Street with Indiana Avenue, E Street and H Street in nearby Chinatown all offer examples of the period. Also noteworthy is the 500 block of 10th Street, NW, whose most imposing structure is the 1863 **Ford's Theatre** (*see p55*), site of Abraham Lincoln's assassination.

The government buildings erected in the first half of the 19th century generally adhered to the Greek Revival style, which modelled itself on such Athenian edifices as the Parthenon, rediscovered by European architects in the mid 18th century. Two of these structures, the **Patent Office** and the **Tariff Commission Building** (part of which also functioned as the General Post Office), face each other at 7th and F Streets, NW. Both are early examples of the city's official style – also known in the US and especially in DC as neo-Grec – and both were designed at least in part by Robert Mills, best known for the Washington Monument. In 2002, the long-neglected Tariff Building became the Hotel Monaco. The Patent Office, home to the National Portrait Gallery and the Smithsonian American Art Museum, reopened in July 2006 after extensive renovations.

Mills also designed the **US Treasury Building** (15th Street & Pennsylvania Avenue, NW), with its 466-foot Ionic colonnade along 15th Street. In the first major divergence from the L'Enfant Plan, this edifice was placed directly east of the White House, thus blocking the symbolic vista between the building and the Capitol. Construction began in 1836 and wasn't completed until 1871, but that's speedy compared to the progress of Mills's **Washington**

IN CONTEXT

Arts & Industries Building. *See p220.*

IN CONTEXT

Monument (*see p30*). Started in 1845, it was completed (after a 20-year break due to lack of funds) in 1884. The highest structure in the world at its completion, the 600-foot monument is unusually stark by the standards of 19th-century Washington architecture. That's because the colonnaded base of Mills's plan was never built, leaving only a tower modelled on an Egyptian obelisk. Other notable examples of the pre-Civil War era are **St John's Church** (1525 H Street, NW, 1-202 347 8766), designed in 1816 by Benjamin Latrobe, the architect of the Capitol's first expansion, but subsequently much altered; **Old City Hall** (now occupied by Superior District Court offices, 4th & F Streets, NW); and the modest but elegant Georgetown **Custom House & Post Office** (1221 31st Street, NW), derived from Italian Renaissance *palazzi* and typical of small US government buildings of the period.

AFTER THE CIVIL WAR

The more exuberant styles that came after the Civil War are presaged by the first **Smithsonian Institution** building (1000 Jefferson Drive, SW), designed by James Renwick in 1846. Its red sandstone suits the turreted neo-medieval style, which has earned it the nickname the Castle. Fifteen years later, Renwick designed the original building of the **Corcoran Gallery** (now the Renwick Gallery, *see p40*). Modelled on the Louvre, it is the first major French-inspired building in the US. The Renwick is a compatible neighbour to a more extravagant Second Empire structure, the **Eisenhower Office Building** (17th Street & Pennsylvania Avenue, NW, 1-202 395 5895). The lavish interior of the structure, originally the State, War and Navy Building, is open to tours by appointment on Saturdays. After the war, Adolf Cluss designed the **Arts & Industries Building** on the Mall (1881, *see p41*), also in red-brick neo-Gothic style and part of the Smithsonian. The building fell into decline in the early 2000s but is currently under restoration.

The Civil War led directly to the construction of the **Pension Building** (5th & F Streets, NW), designed by

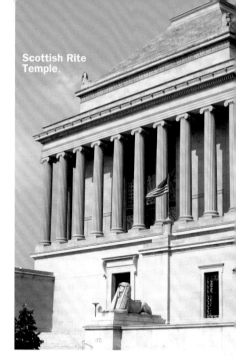
Scottish Rite Temple.

Montgomery Meigs in 1882 to house the agency that paid stipends to veterans and their families. Now the **National Building Museum** (*see p61*), the structure was based on Rome's Palazzo Farnese, but is twice the size. Outside is a frieze that depicts advancing Union Army troops; inside is an impressive courtyard, featuring the world's largest Corinthian columns. The atrium was once essential to one of the building's marvels, its highly efficient passive ventilation system, now supplanted by air-conditioning.

The Eisenhower Building and the Pension Building were disparaged by both classicists and modernists, who often proposed razing them. Equally unpopular was the **Old Post Office** (1100 Pennsylvania Avenue, NW, 1-202 289 4224), which now houses shops, restaurants and offices. The 1899 building is an example of the Romanesque Revival, which adapted the rounded arches, dramatic massing and grand vaults of 11th- and 12th-century Northern European cathedrals. The structure contrasts strongly with its Federal Triangle neighbours, all built in a more sedate style in the 1920s, and was threatened with demolition in the 1920s and again in the 1960s.

Second Empire, Romanesque Revival and other ornate styles are still well represented in the Logan Circle, Dupont Circle, Sheridan Circle and Kalorama Triangle areas. Many palatial homes were built in these areas in the late 19th and early 20th centuries, and some survive as embassies, museums and private clubs. Among those open to the public are the **Phillips Collection** (*see p62*) and **Anderson House** (2118 Massachusetts Avenue, NW, 1-202 785 2040), home to the Society of the Cincinnati, a group founded by Revolutionary War veterans. The survival of the **Heurich Mansion** (1307 New Hampshire Avenue, NW, 1-202 429 1894), a Victorian house museum that was once home to a German-born beer mogul, is now in question.

One of the city's most remarkable architectural fantasies is the **Scottish Rite Temple** (1733 16th Street, NW, 1-202 232 3579), finished in 1915 and modelled on the mausoleum at Halicarnassus, one of the seven wonders of the ancient world. It was designed by John Russell Pope, later the architect of some of the city's most prominent buildings. His work includes the **National Archives** (*see p47*), the neo-classical temple that holds the country's most fundamental documents.

The Archives is the tallest structure erected during Washington's first large urban renewal project, which during the 1920s converted one of the city's most notorious precincts into the government office district known as the Federal Triangle. The Triangle's massive structures provided the headquarters for most of the executive-branch departments, and reiterated the federal government's preference for classicism. The project, which stretches from 6th to 15th Streets between Pennsylvania and Constitution Avenues, NW, was interrupted by the Depression, and its completion was then debated for 50 years. Finally the government committed to a design for the final structure, the **Ronald Reagan Building** (14th Street

& Pennsylvania Avenue, NW), a hulking mediocrity that opened in 1998. It, too, is in classical drag, albeit with some tricky angles to show that it's the work of the prominent architectural firm of Pei Cobb Freed.

Pope went on to design several more neo-classical temples, including the 1941 original (now called West) building of the **National Gallery of Art** (*see p33*) and the 1943 **Jefferson Memorial** (*see p32*). The latter is partially derived from Rome's Pantheon, while its 1922 predecessor, the **Lincoln Memorial** (*see p32*), is modelled on the Athens Parthenon.

These contemplative edifices' bustling cousin is **Union Station** (*see p46*), the 1908 structure whose Daniel Burnham design borrows from two Roman landmarks, the Arch of Constantine and the Baths of Diocletian. Dramatically remodelled before reopening in 1988, the building's interior still features many of its original architectural details – including statues of centurions whose nudity is hidden only by shields – but now incorporates shops, eateries and a cinema. Most of the train-related

Museum of the American Indian.
See p223.

functions have been moved to an undistinguished new hall to the rear.

Other notable neo-classical structures of the period are the 1928 **Freer Gallery of Art** (see p31) and the 1932 **Folger Shakespeare Library** (see p43), an example of Paul Cret's art deco-influenced 'stripped classicism'.

THE ARRIVAL OF MODERNISM

Modernism reached Washington after World War II, but couldn't get comfortable. One dilemma was (and is) the city's Height Limitation Act, which bans skyscrapers. Various subterfuges have been employed to get an extra storey here or there, but no 'inhabitable' space is allowed to go above the 150-foot limit.

In the 1950s, modernist notions of design and planning were applied to an urban-renewal project, the New Southwest, with awkward results. Modernism also guided the nearby **L'Enfant Plaza**, a mammoth office, hotel and retail complex (bordered by Independence Avenue, 9th Street and various freeway approaches); its masterplan was the first of several bad Washington designs by IM Pei, later one of the namesakes of Pei Cobb Freed. This ironically named assault on the L'Enfant Plan was followed by many stark, bleak buildings in Southwest, most of which were rented to the federal government.

In the 1960s and '70s, modernist architects designed some of the city's least popular structures, including the **J Edgar Hoover FBI Building** (see p57), a brutalist concrete fortress finished in 1972. Perhaps more damaging to the style's reputation, however, was the profusion of mediocre office buildings in the 'New Downtown' along K Street and Connecticut Avenue, NW. Built with little consideration for Washington's distinctive street plan and without strategies for adapting the Bauhaus-derived American skyscraper style to the city's height limitation rules, these blank-walled knock-offs look like New York office blocks inexplicably stunted at the 12th floor.

Most of these buildings were designed by local architects, but nationally renowned modernists and postmodernists have also done work in Washington, including Marcel Breuer's 1976 pre-cast concrete **Hubert H Humphrey Building** (2nd Street & Independence Avenue, SW). Mies van der Rohe's 1972 black-box **Martin Luther King Jr Memorial Library** (see p56) has recently been listed on the National Register of Historic Places.

One of modernism's local successes is actually far from the District: **Washington Dulles International Airport**, designed by Eero Saarinen in 1962 and now being expanded in accord with his widely imitated gull-wing scheme. Others include IM Pei's 1978 **National Gallery of Art East Building** (see p33) and Harry Weese's **Metro** system, which applies the same architectural motifs to all its stations. The latter two designs succeed in part because they're sensitive to their Washington context: the East Building's overlapping triangles play off the trapezoidal plot created by the L'Enfant street plan, while Metro's coffered vaults are simply an extreme example of stripped classicism.

The city's response to modernism is rooted in Georgetown, with its Federal-style structures, which became a fashionable neighbourhood when it began to be gentrified in the 1930s, and **Lafayette Square**, which is surrounded by Federal-period houses. In the '60s, when demand for federal office space grew dramatically, replacing these houses with new office buildings was proposed. The eventual compromise was to erect two large structures just off the square, John Carl Warneke's 1969 **New Executive Office Building** (722 Jackson Place, NW) and **Court of Claims Building** (717 Madison Place, NW), which would defer to their older neighbours in form and material, if not in size.

These 'background buildings' set a precedent for design in the city's older districts; several local firms came to specialise in contextual postmodern structures that often incorporated façades of existing buildings. Examples include Shalom Baranes's remake of the **Army-Navy Club** (901 17th Street, NW) and Hartman-Cox's **1001 Pennsylvania**

Newseum.

Avenue, NW, both finished in 1987. Such 'façadomies' were widely criticised, especially when the new construction dwarfed the historic component; one conspicuous example of this is **Red Lion Row** (2000 Pennsylvania Avenue, NW). Yet the technique continues to be employed, with new examples along 7th, 10th and F Streets, NW.

The city's historicist architects are still influential, but no one style currently dominates. An updated, less dogmatic modernism is showcased in such structures as Kohn Pederson Fox's asymmetrical, vaguely industrial 1997 **World Bank** headquarters (1818 H Street, NW, 1-202 473 1806, tours by appointment), and Mikko Heikkinen and Markku Komonen's 1994 **Embassy of Finland** (3301 Massachusetts Avenue, NW, 1-202 298 5824, tours by appointment), which features a trellis façade, dramatic atrium and glass-wall overlook of Rock Creek Park. Such glass curtains are back in favour, notably in the sail-shaped exterior of Graham Gund Architects' near-triangular 2004 headquarters for the **National Association of Realtors** (500 New Jersey Avenue, NW).

On the Mall, 2004 brought a new example of neo-classicism, as well as a novel piece of contextual architecture. Friedrich St Florian's **World War II**

Memorial (*see p37*) is an imperial-style shrine with a circular array of pillars and arches tucked into the vista between the Washington Monument and the Lincoln Memorial. In contrast, the **Museum of the American Indian** (*see p37*), adapted from a design by Douglas Cardinal, is clad in multi-hued limestone with a rough façade to suggest Southwestern mesas.

At the Reynolds Center, joint home of both the **National Portait Gallery** and the **Smithsonian American Art Museum** (*see p52* **Profile**), Norman Foster's curving glass canopy in the building's central courtyard – forming the Kogod Courtyard, opened in 2007 – adds a contemporary, organic dimension to the building's Greek Revival architecture. Pokshek Partnership, the architects of the **Newseum** (*see p58* **Profile**), opened in 2008, designed a building composed of three rectilinear volumes, one behind the other, with a rectangular glass window running most of the height of the Pennsylvania Avenue façade, allowing passers by to view the museum's atrium inside. Very different, but also attracting praise from architectural critics, Arena Stage's new theatre, the **Mead Center for the American Theater** (*see p178* **Crystal Palaces**), by Vancouver-based Bing Thom, is flowing and curvaceous, with vast wooden exterior columns and a glass frontage.

IN CONTEXT

Essential Information

Getting Around

ESSENTIAL INFORMATION

ARRIVING & LEAVING

By air

Three airports serve Washington. **Washington Dulles International Airport**, 25 miles out in the suburbs of Virginia, handles the longer flights into the region, including most international flights. **Baltimore-Washington International Airport (or BWI)** is a lot closer to the first half of its name but easily accessible from Washington by public transport, and is popular for its cheaper fares and more bearable traffic. **Ronald Reagan Washington National Airport** (most people still use the old name 'National') is the closest to DC, located just across the Potomac River from Downtown, and gives a great view of the monuments as you fly in; it's used mostly for short- and medium-haul flights within the US and Canada. The airports have their own official websites, but for general information, including ground transport, shops and services, hotels and maps, go to www.quickaid.com or www.metwashairports.com.

Major airline contact details

Air Canada 1-888 247 2262, www.aircanada.com.
American Airlines 1-800 433 7300, www.aa.com.
British Airways 1-800 247 9297, www.britishairways.com.
Delta Air Lines 1-800 221 1212, www.delta.com.
Southwest Airlines 1-800 435 9792, www.southwest.com.
United Airlines 1-800 241 6522, www.united.com.
US Airways 1-800 428 4322, www.usair.com.
Virgin Atlantic 1-800 862 8621, www.virgin-atlantic.com.

To & from Dulles Airport

1-703 572 2700, www.metwashairports.com.
The quickest and cheapest way to downtown DC is by getting the **Washington Flyer Bus** (1-888 927 4359, www.washfly.com), which operates between Dulles and the West Falls Church Metro stop (20- to 30-minute ride) at the western end of the Orange Line. It costs $10 one way, $18 round trip, and runs at least every half-hour (5.45am-10.15pm Mon-Fri, and between 7.45am and 10.15pm Sat, Sun). From here you can continue your journey into the city on the Metro.
The **Washington Flyer Taxi Service** (1-703 661 6655) has the sole concession to operate out of Dulles (unless incoming passengers have a prearranged pick-up with another cab company). A ride from Dulles to downtown DC costs about $55-$65 plus tip. All Washington Flyer cabs are metered and take credit cards.
Super Shuttle (1-800 258 3826, 1-202 296 6662, www.supershuttle. com) offers door-to-door shared van service between all three airports and anywhere in the area. Price quotes can be obtained online; from Dulles to downtown DC hotels is $28. It's helpful to know the zip code of your final destination.

To & from BWI

1-800 435 9294, 1-410 859 7111, www.bwiairport.com.
Getting to Washington from BWI can often be expensive, a hassle, or both. A cheap combination (best if you have little to haul) to downtown DC is the shuttle-train-Metro option. Take the free shuttle bus (marked BWI Rail, 1-410 672 6169) from the BWI terminal to the train station about a mile away, then catch a MARC ($6 one way, www.mtmaryland.com)) or Amtrak (from $20, www.amtrak.com) train south 25 minutes to Union Station from where you can get on the Metro. BWI is also served by cabs, private car companies and the Super Shuttle (see above), but beware of the long waits for the latter. You can get complete BWI ground transport information from the booth in Pier C or by calling 1-800 435 9294. A cab from BWI to downtown DC costs about $60 plus tip.

To & from Reagan National Airport

1-703 417 8000, www.metwashairports.com.
National Airport is served by the Metro subway system (Yellow and Blue lines). It's about a 20-minute ride to Downtown. Going by cab is another option: signs outside each baggage claim area will direct you to the taxi stand. The taxi stand operator will point you to a particular cab depending on whether you're going to DC, Virginia or Maryland. Virginia-licensed cabs can take you anywhere; DC- and Maryland-licensed cabs can't serve Virginia. Since Reagan National Airport is in Virginia, only cabs registered there will take you to the Downtown area. The fare for Maryland, Virginia and DC cabs is determined by meter. All pick-ups from National Airport add a $1.75 surcharge. A cab to downtown Washington costs about $15-$20 plus tip (Virginia Yellow Cabs, 1-703 522 2222). Reagan is also served by Super Shuttle (*see left*).

By rail

A train from New York City (Penn Station) to Washington DC takes roughly three hours. Fares vary, costing from around $76 each way for a reserved ticket on the slower Northeast Regional train (journey time around three and a half hours). For a reserved seat on the Acela Express service, which takes only two and a half hours, a one-way ticket is approximately $158-$203.
For more information on trains, call Amtrak on 1-800 872 7245 or go to www.amtrak.com. All trains to DC arrive at Union Station, which has its own Metro station.

By bus

The bus journey from New York around five hours, but it's really cheap – starting as low as about $15 booked in advance and going up from there. Greyhound buses (1-800 231 2222, www.greyhound.com) leave from Union Station, and arrive at the Port Authority Bus Station in New York. Popular value lines include Bolt Bus (1-877 265 8287, www.boltbus.com) and DC2NY (1-888 888 3269, www.dc2ny.com).

By car

Washington is served by several major highways, including Interstates 270, 66 and 95. At Washington, the 95 splits into the 495-95 and 95, looping the metropolitan area as the Capital Beltway.

The city is divided into four quadrants – NW, NE, SE and SW – which meet at the US Capitol. North, South and East Capitol Streets, and the National Mall to the west, radiate out from the Capitol and serve as quadrant dividing lines. On one level, the District is completely rational in its layout. Numbered streets run north and south on both sides of the Capitol, with intersecting lettered streets and a few named streets tossed in, running east to west. The higher the number, and the further on in the alphabet the letter, the further away the street is from the Capitol.

But as straightforward as this seems, there is a crucial nuance. Because the naming system radiates from a central point, there are two First Streets (and Second, etc), one on either side of North/South Capitol Street – and ditto for lettered streets, one north and one south of the Mall (aside from A and B Streets, which don't appear in all four quadrants). This means that there can be four different places – one in each quadrant – where, say, a 4th Street and a G Street intersect, so you need to know which quadrant you're aiming for. This is why we have given the quadrant after every address in our listings, and this is also how you should give directions to a taxi driver. Northwest is by far the biggest quadrant.

Street numbers correspond to cross streets; thus 800 C Street will be on C Street at 8th Street (or rather, the eighth block from the US Capitol); 890 C Street will be on the 800 block but closer to 9th Street. For addresses on numbered streets, you can also work out the location. For instance, 400 8th Street will be at the fourth block from the US Capitol. In practice this means you can count up the alphabet – ie 400 8th Street will be at D Street. There are some exceptions to this rule, however: the letter 'B' (or, strictly speaking, the 200 block) is counted even though there are no B Streets in central Washington. Note also that there is no J Street, so it's ignored. For locating yourself, it's useful to remember that E Street is at 500, K is 1000, P is 1500, and U is 2000. Above W Street, the counting depends on the number of blocks, regardless of what the streets are named, although they are generally in alphabetical order.

Woven into the grid of lettered and numbered streets are diagonal avenues, all named after American states – Pennsylvania Avenue, Massachusetts Avenue, and so on –

that can easily cause drivers and walkers severe disorientation. Some diagonals can be a fast way across town, but most hit confusing traffic circles, or run into parks or important buildings (such as the White House) that cause them to dogleg disconcertingly. Note that I Street is often written 'Eye' Street in order to avoid confusion with 1st/First Street.

PUBLIC TRANSPORT

The **Washington Metropolitan Area Transit Authority** runs the entire DC-area public transport network. For information on the Metrorail subway system and buses, call 1-202 637 7000 (6am-8.30pm Mon-Fri; 7am-8.30pm Sat, Sun) or go to its website at www.wmata.com, which features real-time alerts on delays.

Metrorail

The Metrorail (or, more commonly, Metro) subway system is a clean, safe and reliable public transport system. Trains run from 5am Monday to Friday and from 7am on Saturday and Sunday. The system closes at midnight Sunday to Thursday and at 3am on Saturday and Sunday mornings, but the last trains from the suburbs may depart before that. Holiday schedules vary. At busy times, trains come as often as two minutes apart. But even if everything is running on time, the scheduled waits at nights and weekends can be up to 20 minutes. Most signs and announcements use the line's final station as the identifier for platforms and trains – though not all trains go as far as the last station, so you need to know which direction you're heading.

You'll find a Metrorail map on page 256; also use the handy TripPlanner on the Metro website (www.wmata.com), or pick up the Metro Pocket Guide, which usefully lists the nearest Metro station to the monuments and other points of interest. Station entrances are marked on the street by square columns with a big white 'M' on top. Throughout this guide, we've listed the Metro stop nearest to each destination. If the Metro station is some distance away, a bus number is also listed. Metro lines can run deep and the escalators can be very long. The network is, however, wheelchair-accessible via elevators. If the elevators are broken at a particular station, a bus service will run from a nearby station.

Fares & passes

Fares depend on when and how far you travel and can almost double for some rides during rush hours. The minimum price of an off-peak Metro trip is $1.70, the maximum is $3.50; in peak hours journeys cost $2.10 to $5.75. Fares are printed on a big board on the information kiosk in each station. Note that using a paper farecard comes with a $1 surcharge per one-way trip. Up to two under-4s travel free with a full fare-paying adult; each additional child must pay full fare. Payment is by Farecard, SmarTrip® or Rail Pass.

Farecard

Insert your credit card or cash up to the value of $45 into a machine, this will then pop out a flimsy card with a magnetic stripe on the front. Use the card to enter and exit the Metro turnstiles. The price of each trip is subtracted and the remaining amount printed on the card until there's not enough value left to go anywhere. You can then transfer the remaining amount to a new card using the same machines you buy cards from. You can't get into the Metro without at least $1.70 on your card. If you don't have enough to get out at a particular station, use the Exit Fare machines just before the exit turnstiles, which take only $1 or $5 bills. The farecard is usable only on Metrorail.

SmarTrip card

This is a permanent, rechargeable plastic fare card like a credit card that can be purchased for $5 or $10 (with $5 value loaded), at kiosks at Metro stations, vending machines, commuter stores, retail outlets and online at www.wmata.com or www.commuterdirect.com. You can then top up the card with extra money. It is embedded with a special computer chip that keeps track of the amount available on the card. They are usable on either bus or Metro services and are cheaper and more flexible than other passes. A seven-day Fast Pass, valid for seven consecutive days, is available for $57.30. The SmarTrip is becoming the main, integrated system for Metro and buses as paper farecards are slowly phased out. For further information, contact SmarTrip Helpline 1-888 762 7874.

Rail Passes

The **One-Day Pass**, $14, is valid for unlimited trips with no time restrictions.

The seven-day, **Short-Trip Pass**, $35, is valid for seven consecutive days for trips costing up to $3.50 from 5-9.30am and 3-7pm weekdays; or for any trips at other times.

The seven-day **Fast Pass**, $47, is valid for seven consecutive days of unlimited Metrorail travel. Passes are sold at most Metro stations, online at www.wmata.com, some hotels and large grocery stores.

Transit Link Cards

This card offers unlimited Metrorail and Metro bus journeys for a month. It also includes anywhere the Metro runs in Maryland, Virginia and the District of Columbia as well the use of Maryland and Virginia commuter rail lines. TLC cards are available online but not available at Metro Sales Offices. They cost $102.

The lines

Red Line: serves the Maryland suburbs north of DC and runs through the Downtown business district. The Zoo, Union Station and UDC (University of the District of Columbia) are on this line.

Green Line: serves Anacostia, the eastern National Mall area, Chinatown, the U Street district, Howard University and Columbia Heights.

Blue Line: serves Arlington, Alexandria, National Airport, the RFK Stadium and most Downtown memorials and museums. It parallels much of the Orange Line and some of the Yellow.

Yellow Line: serves Fairfax County (Virginia) via Alexandria to the Mall. Includes National Airport.

Orange Line: serves the suburbs from western Virginia to eastern Maryland. Parallels the Blue Line through most major tourist sights.

An extension to the system, the Silver Line, is currently under construction. The new line will run to Dulles International Airport and Tysons Corner, with 29 stations from Route 772 in Loudoun County, Virginia, to Stadium-Armory in DC. The first phase of the new line, running to Reston, Va., is set to open in 2013.

A new 37-mile system of streetcars has also been proposed, and after many delays, construction on the first line is expected to finish by the end of 2013. This debut line will run from Union Station along the H Street NE corridor to the Benning Road Metro station, with eight stops in between. Information about the streetcar project and future plans is available at www.dcstreetcar.com.

Metrobuses

The bus system, also run by the Washington Metropolitan Area Transit Authority, covers the city well and is heavily used by locals. Bus stops are marked by three horizontal stripes in blue, white and red. A good timetable and route tool is available on the Metro website (www.wmata.com/timetables/default.cfm); though the most accurate way to track arrival times is through the online, GPS-based **Next Bus** service (www.wmata.com/rider_tools/nextbus). The greater Washington area is served by different local bus systems. Alexandria and Fairfax Counties in Virginia and Montgomery, Prince George's and Prince William Counties in Maryland each run their own public transport or ride-share systems. To reach these services, call Metro (1-202 637 7000) for phone numbers and information.

Fares

The bus fare system has changed from paper tickets and passes to SmarTrip cards, the prepaid top-up travel cards also used on Metrorail. The Metrobus fare for regular routes is $1.60 using SmarTrip or $1.80 using cash.The fare for express routes is $3.65 using SmarTrip or $4 using cash. Senior/Disabled fare is 75¢ for regular routes, $1.80 on express routes.

Bus passes

The weekly seven-day regional bus pass costs $16 ($7.50 seniors and disabled), purchased online or at Metro Sales Offices. It is uploaded to your SmarTrip card and activated once you start to use the card.

Useful bus routes

One popular area served better by bus than Metro is Georgetown: catch a **31**, **32** or **36** bus marked 'Friendship Heights' running west on Pennsylvania Avenue. The same buses serve the Upper Northwest area along Wisconsin Avenue. For Adams Morgan, including busy 18th Street, take the **90** or **92** (U Street/Garfield line) bus from Woodley Park-Zoo/Adams Morgan Metro, or the **42** (Mount Pleasant line) bus from Dupont Circle Metro. (Adams Morgan is also within walking distance of Columbia Heights Metro).

As its name suggests, the **Circulator** bus operates on circulatory routes; there are five of these, running with distinct red buses and all incorporating

downtown Washington DC. It is a useful system for visitors as it links cultural and entertainment centres to Downtown. Fares are $1 (50c seniors or disabled). Free transfers from Circulator to Circulator, valid for two hours, are available with a SmarTrip card; transfers are not available for cash payments. For route maps and other information visit www.dccirculator.com.

The Circulator has a 'Where's My Bus' service that uses GPS data for bus arrival information and can be accessed from any mobile device with internet access: www.circulator.dc.gov; the system also uses WMATA's Next Bus service (*see left*).

Trains

Both Amtrak and MARC (Maryland Rail Commuter Service) operate out of DC's Union Station. **Amtrak** connects with cities all over the US, including Baltimore, and also has stops at Alexandria in Virginia and at Rockville and New Carrollton in Maryland. There are several trains daily to New York, Philadelphia and Boston, including Metroliner services, on which you're allowed to reserve seats.

MARC is a commuter train running from Union Station to parts of West Virginia and Maryland (including Baltimore). The Penn line goes to Baltimore's northern suburbs and runs from 4.45am to 11.40pm on weekdays (every 30 minutes during rush hour, every hour otherwise). It does not run at weekends. The Camden line stops at Camden Yards (Baltimore's baseball stadium) and runs only during morning and evening rush hours (6.42-8.05am and 4.13-7.35pm). MARC stops at some Metro stations in Maryland. Fares between DC and Baltimore are $7 each way. Both Amtrak and MARC serve the BWI Airport station.

Union Station *50 Massachusetts Avenue, NE, at North Capitol Street (Amtrak 1-800 872 7245, www.amtrak.com, Marc 1-866 743 3682, www.mta.maryland.gov/marc-train). Map p253 L6.*

Taxis

As elsewhere in the States, driving a taxi is a typical job for recent immigrants, so it's not uncommon to get a driver who needs directions.

There are no taxi ranks but you can usually find cabs outside hotels and it's easy to flag down a

DC-licensed cab around most central parts of the city. Cabs for hire have a light on top and the company name on the door. To call a cab in the District, try Diamond (1-202 387 2221, 6200) or Yellow Cab (1-202 544 1212). Cab fares are now metered based on how many miles you travel, with extra charges for additional passengers, rush-hour travel, calling for a cab and travelling during designated snow emergencies. Bear in mind when travelling during rush hour, that time consumed while the taxicab is stopped (or travelling at less than 10mph for longer than 60 seconds) is charged (an extra $15 per hour with Yellowcabs). Baggage charges are usually $1 for each fairly large, grocery-sized bag handled by the driver, after the first one, and $2.50 for each big bag. In reality, some cabbies charge, some don't, depending, it seems, on their mood.

To give an idea of cost, one person, flagging the cab, with no bags, not at rush hour nor in the snow, will probably pay $14-$15 plus tip to travel from Capitol Hill to Dupont Circle.

Note that while taxis have historically been cash-only in DC, requirements for credit card systems for all cars are expected to go into effect in summer 2013. The new laws will also raise base fares from $3 to $3.25.

In Maryland and Virginia, cabs also run on meters. Cabs licensed for these areas can legally only pick up fares in DC on a pre-arranged basis – and only take them to the jurisdiction in which they are licensed. That might be why, no matter how hard you're waving on a DC street, that empty cab goes right on by.

Driving

The Washington area (especially between DC and Virginia) is not a great place to drive. The traffic circles are confusing and some streets, notably Rock Creek Parkway, change direction in rush hours. Read carefully the times posted in the middle of 'Do Not Enter' and 'No Turns' signs; at other times, entrance is allowed. Unless there's a sign saying otherwise, you can make a right turn when the lights are red.

Parking

There are plenty of off-street pay parking lots around town: Monument Parking (1-202 833 9357) has seven locations; Parking Management Incorporated (PMI,

1-202 785 9191) has many more. Street parking ranges from difficult to impossible, especially near the Mall, Downtown and in popular nightlife areas such as Georgetown and Adams Morgan. At metered spaces, it costs $2 per hour to park in high-demand zones. The parking police are notoriously pedantic. Add to this the regular street shutdowns for presidential motorcades and you'll see why nearly a third of District residents don't own a car.

For up-to-the-minute traffic conditions, check the live cameras on www.trafficland.com. Tune into WTOP (103.5 FM) for traffic reports every ten minutes.

Car hire

For getting right out of town, driving is often the best option. Almost every rental agency will require a credit card and matching driving licence, and few will rent to anyone under 25. The price quoted won't include tax, liability insurance or collision damage waiver (CDW). If you already have an insured car in the US, your own liability insurance may cover the rental. Ask about discounts, available to members of the AAA (as well as British AA members), AARP (American Association of Retired Persons) and other organisations.

Zipcar (1-202 737 4900, www.zipcar.com) is a car sharing/rental company that has cars in many locations around the city, available on an hourly or daily basis. Foreign visitors will also be required to join the scheme, which has a fee of $50-$60 for membership plus an application fee of $25 (a drivers' licence and paperwork with information about the prospective member's driving history is required). Once a member, the actual hiring fees are low – around $8 an hour. Metro Rail has linked up with Zip Car to situate car pick-up points at certain rail stations. Call 1-800 745 7433 for information

The following national car rental companies have DC offices:
Alamo 1-800 462 5266, www.alamo.com.
Avis 1-800 331 1212, www.avis.com.
Budget 1-800 527 0700, www.budget.com.
Dollar 1-800 800 4000, www.dollarcar.com.
Hertz 1-800 654 3131, www.hertz.com.
National 1-800 227 7368, www.nationalcar.com.
Thrifty 1-800 847 4389, www.thrifty.com.

Cycling

DC is a great place to cycle. Much of the city, including most of the Mall and Downtown, is flat (though there's Capitol Hill at the eastern end of the Mall). The city has close to 60 miles of marked bike lanes and is building more by the day, while Capital Bikeshare (below) is thriving. The web of bike paths take you to out-of-centre spots, and riding from museum to monument will save your feet hours of ache (though you'll have to lock your bike to a signpost or railings). For more information on biking in and around DC, get in touch with the Washington Area Bicyclist Association (1-202 518 0524, www.waba.org). A helpful map of DC bike lanes is available on the city's transportation website, www.ddot.dc.gov.

Capital Bikeshare

Since the launch of the Capital Bikeshare Scheme in September 2010, the bright red aluminum bikes are increasing in number and becoming a real local presence, with over 1,670 of its signature cruisers at 75 stations throughout the city and suburbs. Each station will begin the day with about ten bikes and five empty docking spaces. Membership is required to rent; daily ($5) or three-day ($15) memberships can be purchased directly at the bike stations, while longer memberships are available online at www.capitalbikeshare.com. Members can check on the website (and its app) for how many bikes are available and how many docking stations are open for returning bicycles at any given moment. Helmets are not provided.

The pricing structure is designed to encourage short journeys rather than longer leisure trips – the first 30 minutes are free and additional costs kick in after that. (You wouldn't want to ride the whole day, for example – for six hours, the price for six hours would be $86.)

If the bike isn't returned within 24 hours, it will be considered stolen and will incur a replacement fee of $1,000.

Walking

Walking is a great way to get around, but remember that summers are hot and muggy, and while the Mall might look like a nice gentle stroll, it's actually two miles long, with a hill at the Capitol end.

ESSENTIAL INFORMATION

Resources A-Z

ADDRESSES

See p78 **Navigating the City**.

AGE RESTRICTIONS

You have to be 21 to drink alcohol in DC, Maryland and Virginia. Note that the law is very strictly enforced, with severe penalties. Be sure to carry ID with you (*see p232*).

ATTITUDE & ETIQUETTE

Washington is unquestionably a major tourist destination, so if you wear jeans, trainers and carry a small rucksack you should feel right at home. It is also, of course, a major business centre, and walking around Downtown you'll see lawyers in suits and other members of a well-dressed workforce.

DC residents usually inhabit their own little niches. They read the *Washington Post* on the Metro, mind their own business on the sidewalk and get upset when tourists stand on the left side of the escalator instead of the right. But if you do stop someone on the street to ask for directions, they will generally be happy to oblige.

BUSINESS

There was a time, not that long ago, when the business scene in Washington could pretty much be covered in one word: government. Not only was the federal presence far and away the dominant industry, but dealing with it was the primary purpose of most private-sector activity. Government is still the 800lb gorilla of the DC jungle, but a number of A-list corporations now

have their headquarters in the Washington area. A high-tech industry has established itself along the so-called Dulles Corridor, turning the expressway linking the city with Dulles International Airport in the Virginia suburbs into something of a Silicon Valley East. The business epicentre is Downtown's K Street, lined with glassy office buildings. DC now has more office space than any other American city aside from New York.

That said, while Washington may have made the big time, standard operating procedures are lower-key than in comparable cities. There are similarities, such as the ubiquitous power lunch, but the overall style is less frenetic. In fact, as viewed from the vantage of New York, Washingtonians have no style.

The idea is to dress down: dark (preferably blue) suits, and ties with a touch of red. In summer, when the heat and humidity threaten to reach meltdown levels, light-hued poplin and seersucker suits are almost a uniform. Year-round, by far the preferred accessory is a neck chain from which dangles a photo-ID card – it's virtually a badge of belonging.

Conventions

Walter E Washington Convention Center
801 Mount Vernon Place, NW, between 7th & 9th Streets, Downtown (1-202 249 3000, www.dcconvention.com). **Map** p253 J5.
The largest single building in the city, its 52,000sq ft ballroom and $4 million art collection make it worth a peek for casual visitors, many of whom stop in at the restaurants and retail outlets on-site.

Couriers

All the major international couriers, in addition to several locally based enterprises, are active in DC. For others, check the internet or the Yellow Pages under 'Air Cargo & Package Express Service', 'Delivery Service', or, for local deliveries, 'Messenger Services'.

Federal Express *1-800 463 3339, www.fedex.com.* **Credit** AmEx, Disc, MC, V.

Skynet Worldwide Courier
1-786 265 4830, www.skynet.net. **Credit** AmEx, Disc, MC, V.

United Parcel Service *1-800 742 5877, www.ups.com.* **Credit** AmEx, MC, V.

Useful organisations

District of Columbia Chamber of Commerce 506 9th Street, NW, at E Street, Downtown (1-202 347 7201, www.dcchamber.org). Gallery Place Metro. Open 8.30am-5.30pm Mon-Fri. Map p252 H5.

Greater Washington Board of Trade *1725 I Street, NW, between 18th & 19th streets, Downtown. (1-202 857 5900, www.bot.org). Foggy Bottom or Farragut West Metro.* **Map** p252 G5.
The Board of Trade functions as a regional co-ordinating organisation for DC, northern Virginia and suburban Maryland.

US Department of Commerce *14th Street & Constitution Avenue, NW, The Federal Triangle (1-202 482 2000, www.doc.gov). Federal Triangle Metro.* **Open** 8am-5.30pm Mon-Fri. **Map** p252 H6.

ESSENTIAL INFORMATION

CONSUMER

Whenever possible, pay with a major credit card so you can cancel payment or get reimbursed if there is a problem (be sure to keep receipts or a form of documentation). Consider travel insurance that includes default coverage to protect yourself against financial loss.

CUSTOMS

A visa waiver form (I-94W) is generally provided by the airline during check-in or on the plane and must be presented to Immigration at the airport of entry to the US. International visitors should allow about an hour in the airport to clear Immigration. For more on visas, *see p237*.

A customs declaration form (6059B) is also provided on international flights into the US; this must be filled out and handed to a customs official after Immigration (keep it handy). Current US regulations allow foreign visitors to import the following duty-free: 200 cigarettes or 100 cigars (Cuban cigars are generally not allowed), 1 litre of wine or spirits (over-21s only), and a maximum of $100 in gifts. You can take up to $10,000 incash, travellers' cheques or endorsed bank drafts in or out of the country. Anything above that you must declare on a customs form, or it risks seizure. It is illegal to transport most perishable foods and plants across international borders. If you are carrying prescription drugs, make sure they are labeled, and keep a copy of your prescription with you. The Customs and Border Patrol website (www.cbp.gov) contains information.

DISABLED

Washington is good at providing facilities for all types of tourists, including the disabled and elderly. Most museums, monuments and memorials are accessible to visitors using wheelchairs and many have other facilities to help disabled travellers. Nearly all streets in the Downtown area have wide sidewalks with kerb cuts for greater accessibility. The Metro has excellent facilities for those with visual and auditory impairments, or mobility problems. All stations are theoretically wheelchair-accessible, although lifts are not always in service. In these cases, a shuttle service is provided.

Information

An extremely useful website is www.disabilityguide.org, which rates Washington's hotels, restaurants, malls and sights according to accessibility. It's run by **Access Information** (1-301 528 8664). The New York-based **Society for Accessible Travel & Hospitality** (1-212 447 7284, www.sath.org) offers advice for disabled travellers throughout the US.

DRUGS

Hard and soft drugs are illegal in Washington, as in the rest of the US. In practice, however, arresting people for the possession of small amounts of soft drugs is not a high priority for DC police.

ELECTRICITY

The US electricity supply is 110-120 volt, 60-cycle AC, rather than the 220-240 volt, 50-cycle AC used in Europe. Plugs are standard two-pins. An adaptor and, in some cases, a voltage converter (available at airport shops and hardware stores) are necessary to use foreign appliances. Check www.voltage valet.com to answer questions about electricity.

EMBASSIES & CONSULATES

Note that most visa offices keep shorter hours than the embassy hours listed. Check online for other embassies.

Australia *1601 Massachusetts Avenue, NW, at 16th Street, Dupont Circle (1-202 797 3000, www.usa.embassy.gov.au). Dupont Circle Metro.* **Open** 8.30am-5pm Mon-Fri. **Map** p250 H4.

Canada *501 Pennsylvania Avenue, NW, at 6th Street, Penn Quarter (1-202 682 1740, www.canadainternational.gc.ca/ washington/index.aspx). Archives-Navy Memorial or Judiciary Square Metro.* **Open** 9am-5pm; *consular services* 9am-noon Mon-Fri. **Map** p252 J6.

Ireland *2234 Massachusetts Avenue, NW, at Sheridan Circle, Dupont Circle (1-202 462 3939, www.embassyofireland.org). Dupont Circle Metro.* **Open** 9am-1pm, 2-4pm Mon-Fri. **Map** p250 F4.

New Zealand *37 Observatory Circle, NW, at Massachusetts Avenue, Upper Northwest (1-202 328 4800, www.nzembassy.com/' usa).* **Open** 8.30am-5pm Mon-Fri. **Map** p249 E3.

United Kingdom *3100 Massachusetts Avenue, NW, at Whitehaven Street, Upper Northwest (1-202 588 6500, http://ukinusa.fco.gov.uk). Dupont Circle Metro then N2, N4, N6 bus.* **Open** 9am-5.30pm Mon-Fri. **Map** p250 F3.

EMERGENCIES

The number to call for fire, police, ambulance and other emergency services is **911** (free from cellphones and public phones).

GAY & LESBIAN

Washington is home to a thriving, well-established gay and lesbian community. For information about groups and what's on, consult the *Washington Blade* (its excellent website is www. washblade.com).

For further information on the local scene, *see pp163-166*.

HEALTH

Accident & emergency

You will be billed for emergency treatment, although emergency rooms are legally only allowed to turn patients away if their injuries are not considered an emergency. However, hospitals will do all they can to ensure they receive payment for treatment. Taking out full medical insurance before you travel is imperative; it's a good idea to call your company before seeking treatment to find out which hospitals accept your insurance.

Children's National Medical Center *111 Michigan Avenue, NW, at First Street (1-202 476 5000, 1-888 884 2327, www.childrensnational.org). Brookland-CUA Metro then H2, H4 bus.* **Map** p251 K2.

Georgetown University Hospital *3800 Reservoir Road, NW, between 38th & 39th Streets, Georgetown (1-202 444 2000, www.georgetown universityhospital.org). Dupont Circle Metro then D6 bus, or Dupont Circle or Rosslyn Metro, then hospital shuttle, every 15-30mins.* **Map** p249 E4.

ESSENTIAL INFORMATION

George Washington University
*Hospital 900 23rd Street, NW,
between I Street & Washington
Circle, Foggy Bottom (1-202 715
4000, www.gwhospital.com). Foggy
Bottom Metro.* **Map** p252 G5.

Howard University Hospital
*2041 Georgia Avenue, NW,
at V Street, Shaw (1-202 865
6100, www. huhealthcare.com)
Shaw-Howard University Metro
then hospital shuttle bus, bus
70, 71,90, 92, 96.* **Map** p251 J3

Contraception & abortion

Several branches of the **CVS** chain
(*see p132*; or call 1-888 607 4287)
are open 24 hours a day. Like other
pharmacies, they sell condoms and
can fill out prescriptions for other
contraceptives. If you need advice
about abortion, call Planned
Parenthood on 1-202 347 8512 or
go to its website, www.planned
parenthood.org. The organisation
has a centre in the Downtown area.

Dentists

DC Dental Society *1-202 547
7613, www.dcdental.org.*
The DC Dental Society can refer
you to a local dentist for treatment.

Doctors

Doctors Referral 1-800 362 8677,
www.1800doctors.com.
Can recommend a local doctor.

HIV & AIDS

Elizabeth Taylor Medical Center
*1701 14th Street, NW, between
R Street & Riggs Place, Logan
Circle (1-202 745 7000, www.
whitman-walker.org). U Street/
African-American Civil War
Memorial/Cardozo or McPherson
Square Metro.* **Open** 8am-8pm
Mon-Thur, 8am-5pm Fri.
Map p250 H4.
Part of the Whitman Walker Clinic
– a pioneering institution offering
services to people with HIV
and other sexually transmitted
diseases – the Elizabeth Taylor
Medical Center provides
counselling to AIDS patients
and their families. The centre's
excellent website contains a
wealth of useful information.

National HIV/AIDS Hotline
*1-800 342 2437,
www.thebody.com.*
Will give information about the
nearest HIV testing centres.

Pharmacies

Several branches of the **CVS**
chain are open 24 hours a day;
see p132 or call 1-888 607 4287.

HELPLINES

Alcoholics Anonymous
1-202 966 9115, http://aa-dc.org.
Auto Impound 1-202 727 5000.
**Mental Health 24hr Access
Helpline** 1-888 793-4357.
Poison Centre 1-800 222 1222.
Rape Crisis Centre 1-202 333 7273.
Substance Abuse Hotline
1-800 784 6776.
Suicide Prevention Centre
1-800 784 2433.

ID

Unless you're driving or drinking
alcohol, there isn't any law that
says you must carry identification
with you, but it makes sense to do
so. Keeping your passport with you
is risky, but a driver's licence is
usually a good idea, as everyone
under the age of 40 seems to get
carded – for entry to nightclubs,
in particular – in DC.

INSURANCE

Non-nationals should arrange
baggage, trip-cancellation and
medical insurance before they
leave home (but first check what
your existing home and medical
insurance covers). Medical centres
and hospitals will ask for details
of your insurance company and
policy number if you require
treatment, so it's a good idea to
keep this information with you.

INTERNET

Most hotels and cafés have
Wi-Fi access, sometimes free and
sometimes for a small fee. Branches
of DC public libraries are great
places to get online free, offering
both Wi-Fi access and computers.
For the central branch, the **Martin
Luther King Jr Memorial
Library**, *see p55*. For other DC
libraries, see www.dclibrary.org.

LEFT LUGGAGE

All three of the area's major airports
have effectively done away with
luggage storage at their facilities in
light of the US Homeland Security
Department's new regulations
following 9/11. The airport may be
able to advise you on other facilities
that may be available.

LEGAL HELP

In the legal capital of the country,
more than one person in seven is
a lawyer. If you can't afford a local
lawyer, stop by the Legal Aid
Society of the District of Columbia,
where legal aid lawyers can provide
free legal assistance.

Legal Aid Society *Suite 350,
1331 H Street, NW, between
14th Steet & New York Avenue,
Downtown (1-202 628 1161,
www.legalaiddc.org). McPherson
Square or Metro Center Metro.*
Open Initial interview hours
12.30-6pm Mon; 12.30-4pm
Thur. **Map** p252 H3.

LIBRARIES

Washington is home to a range
of sites from the endless shelves
of the Library of Congress to
specialised libraries in each
of the Smithsonian museums.
Many national and international
organisations also have their
headquarters in DC, complete
with archives. The city's
universities all have excellent
libraries, and the public library
system (see www.dclibrary.org)
has lots of branches.

Library of Congress
*1st Street & Independence
Avenue, SE, The Capitol &
Around (operator 1-202 707
5000, visitor information 1-202
707 8000, www.loc.gov). Capitol
South Metro.* **Open** varies.
Map p253 L7.
As the central library for the US,
the Library of Congress makes
it its business to have a copy
of almost everything printed.
However, it may take a very long
time to find one small book among
the nearly 100 million items on 535
miles of shelves, even when the
staff do the search for you. The
library is open to the public, but
you must first wait in line for a
library card and an extensive
security check. Take at least one
photo ID. Note that opening times
vary for the different buildings
within the complex.

**Martin Luther King Jr
Memorial Library**
*901 G Street, NW, at 9th Street,
Downtown (1-202-727-1111,
www.dclibrary. org/mlk). Gallery
Place-Chinatown Metro.* **Open**
noon-9pm Mon, Tue; 9.30am-
530pm Wed-Sat; 1-5pm Sun.
Map p253 J6.

LOST PROPERTY

If you leave something on the bus or subway, the chances are you won't see it again, but it's worth calling the Washington Metro Transit Authority Lost & Found on 1-202 962 1195 or submitting a claim online at www.wmata.com. It's also worth checking at the nearest police station to see if it's been handed in.

MEDIA

Washington is the one American city where many people actually watch the political chat shows run every Sunday by the main television networks and offered every day by the growing ranks of cable news channels – notably, the abrasive **Fox News** cable channel, which has been winning viewers at the expense of such operations as **CNN** (part of multimedia superpower Time Warner). There's even a local radio station that carries an audio version of the **C-SPAN** cable channel's Congressional coverage (WCSP, 90.1 FM).

With all the major American news organisations and many foreign ones in residence in DC, news crews are a common sight around town. Newsmakers frequently appear at the **National Press Club** (13th Floor, 529 14th Street, NW, 1 202 662 7500, http://press.org), although only some of these events are open to the public.

Newspapers & magazines

Dailies

The Godzilla of local print journalism is the *Washington Post*, whose clout is the object of some awe and much resentment. Nonetheless, the *Post* has the highest market penetration of any major US daily, although its executives fret, with reason, that its power is waning with younger Washingtonians. The *Post's* coverage exemplifies the inside-the-Beltway mentality, with heavy emphasis on politics and policy, and a poorly concealed scepticism that anything else really matters. By the standards of US newspapers, international coverage is strong, and over recent years the paper has greatly expanded its online presence as well as coverage of business and technology.

By contrast, genuinely local news and the arts are often treated with indifference. On Fridays, however, the *Post* publishes its 'Weekend' section, which runs extensive local arts and entertainment listings.

This, along with the *Washington City Paper (see below)*, is what most Washingtonians turn to for current entertainment information.

Owned by cronies of the Rev Sun Myung Moon, the *Washington Times* offers a right-wing view of events, with front-page stories that are often amusingly partisan. Although some commend its sports coverage, the paper is read principally by paleo-conservatives and people who really, really hate the *Post*.

Although it offers little specifically for Washingtonians, the *New York Times* has a significant DC readership. The paper is most popular on Sundays, when its arts and feature writing trounces the Post's. Most large US newspapers are available in local street boxes.

USA Today, the country's only national general-interest daily, is produced at Tysons Corner, Virginia, but its terse stories, graphics-heavy presentation and middle-American mindset are not much to local taste.

Weeklies

Geographical or cultural subdivisions of the metropolitan area are served by many weekly tabloids, including some suburban ones owned by the *Post*, but the only such weekly of regional significance is *Washington City Paper* (www.washingtoncity paper.com). Founded in 1981 and owned by the *Chicago Reader*, this 'alternative' free weekly has softened its approach over the years. Although it covers local politics, the paper is read mostly for its arts coverage, listings and adverts.

The District's gay community is served by the weekly *Washington Blade* (www.washingtonblade.com), which is a good source of local and national news. *MW* (*Metro Weekly*, www.metroweekly.com) includes listings for bars, clubs, guest DJ spots and parties. It also takes a more gossipy tone than the *Blade*. Both are free and readily available.

Monthlies

The *Washingtonian* is professional although seldom provocative, specialising in consumer journalism and profiles. Two locally published magazines with global agendas are *National Geographic* and *Smithsonian*, which are circulated

to members of their respective organisations and are also sold at newsstands. Their articles on science, history and other subjects of enduring importance – and *National Geographic*'s exceptional photography – exemplify the side of DC that is not consumed by the latest poll numbers.

Outlets

Washington has more newspaper and magazine outlets than you might at first think. Many large office buildings have newsstands, often concealed in their lobbies so that only workers and regular visitors are aware of them. Outdoor newsstands (along with sidewalk cafés) were illegal in Washington for much of the 20th century, and since the ban was lifted in the 1960s most attempts to establish them have failed – which explains why the sidewalks at major intersections are overwhelmed by newspaper vending machines. Among the larger newsstands – and the ones with the best selection of foreign publications – are **News World** (1001 Connecticut Avenue, NW) and **Metro News Center** (1200 G Street, NW). Washington's remaining few Barnes & Noble outlets have extensive periodicals.

Television

Washington's airwaves carry all the usual suspects: **NBC** (WRC, Channel 4); **Fox** (WTTG, Channel 5); right-wing firebrand **Fox News**, **ABC** (WJLA, Channel 7); **CBS** (WUSA, Channel 9) and the **CW Network**. These offer the familiar sitcoms, cop and hospital dramas, and growing numbers (because they're cheap to produce) of news magazine shows. The local news programmes on Washington's commercial TV outlets are supposedly less lurid than in most American cities, although that's hard to imagine. There are also three local public TV stations featuring the customary line-up of *Sesame Street*, British drawing-room dramas and highlights from *Riverdance*: **WMPT** (Channel 22), **WETA** (Channel 26) and **WHUT** (Channel 32). The latter also runs some Spanish-language shows, while a fourth public station, **WNVC** (Channel 56), along with the local cable network **MHZ**, specialise in international programming, from classic Japanese films to the day's news in Mandarin, Polish and French.

ESSENTIAL INFORMATION

On cable, the fare is also commonplace, although it varies slightly among local jurisdictions. National channels based in Washington include **BET** (Black Entertainment Television) and the **Discovery Channel**, as well as the latter's documentary offspring – **Animal Planet**, the **Learning Channel** and the **History Channel**.

Washingtonians watch more **C-SPAN** and **C-SPAN 2** (with live coverage of Congress and other public affairs programming) than most Americans; channels seen only locally include the extensive local news coverage of **NewsChannel 8.**

Radio

World events can change Washington's daily climate rapidly, so visitors would be well advised to keep on top of daily headlines via the city's excellent all-news station, **WTOP** (103.5 FM), which also offers traffic and weather updates every ten minutes. Beyond that, the city is upscale, urban and has a large African-American population, so local radio stations play more classical and hip hop, and less country music than in most parts of the US.

Since the Federal Communication Commission weakened regulations restricting the number of stations that could be owned by large corporations, however, regional diversity in US radio programming is dwindling. Increasingly, stations are tightly formatted to attract a chosen demographic, often with a carefully test-marketed subset of oldies: 'classic rock' (**WARW**, 94.7 FM), 'classic hits' (**WBIG**, 100.3 FM) and 'urban adult contemporary' (**WMMJ**, 102.3 FM). WWDC (101.1 FM) is the area's only 'alternative' station left. 'Urban contemporary' (hip hop and soul) music is heard on **WKYS** (93.9 FM), **WPGC** (95.5 FM) and **WHUR** (96.3 FM). Of the three, **WPGC** is the rowdiest, while **WHUR** goes for a somewhat older audience. The leading Top 40 station is **WIHT** (99.5 FM). **WGMS** (104.1 FM) is the city's commercial classical station. The top two public radio stations, **WETA** (90.9 FM) and **WAMU** (88.5 FM), broadcast much of the news and arts programming of Washington-based National Public Radio (**NPR**). The former also plays classical music; the latter offers weekend folk and bluegrass music.

The once-radical **WPFW** (89.3 FM) still mixes jazz and politics, but has become tamer. The *Post* has a station (107.7 FM) that mixes in-depth stories, feedback from writers and Washington Nationals baseball broadcasts.

College radio, a free-form catalyst in many markets, is insignificant here; the University of Maryland's **WMUC** (88.1 FM) can be received only in the north-eastern suburbs.

MONEY

The United States' monetary system is decimal-based: the US dollar ($) is divided into 100 cents (¢). Coins and dollars are stamped with the faces of US presidents and statesmen. Coin denominations are the penny (1¢ – Abraham Lincoln on a copper-coloured coin); nickel (5¢ – Thomas Jefferson); dime (10¢ – Franklin D Roosevelt); quarter (25¢ – George Washington); the less common half-dollar (50¢ – John F Kennedy) and the 'golden' dollar (depicting Sacagawea, a Native American woman who acted as a guide to 19th-century explorers Lewis and Clark). You may also come across the smaller 'Susan B Anthony' dollar coin, a failed attempt to introduce dollar coins.

Bills, or notes, are all the same size and come in $1 (George Washington); $5 (Abraham Lincoln); $10 (Alexander Hamilton); $20 (Andrew Jackson); $50 (Ulysses S Grant); and $100 (Benjamin Franklin) denominations.

Credit cards

As elsewhere in the US, credit cards are virtually a necessity in Washington. If you want to rent a car or book a ticket over the phone, you will need a major credit card. They are accepted almost universally in hotels, restaurants and shops, though occasionally you will find a gas station, small store or cinema that only takes cash. Visa and MasterCard are the most widely accepted cards, with American Express a distant third. Credit cards are also useful for extracting instant cash advances from ATMs and banks. However, where US account holders pay a flat service charge for getting cash this way, UK companies' charges vary– and you pay interest, of course. Debit cards are also accepted at many shops.

ATMs

Automated Teller Machines (or cashpoints in the UK) are located outside nearly all banks, inside all malls and major shopping areas, and now in many bars and restaurants. They are the most convenient and often the most cost-effective way of obtaining cash – but remember that most charge at least a $2 service fee on top of any charges levied by your home bank. All you need is an ATM card (credit or debit) – and your usual PIN number. Check with your bank before leaving home to find out what the fees will be.

Banks

Bank of America *1501 Pennsylvania Avenue, NW, at 15th Street, White House & Around (1-202 624 4253). McPherson Square Metro.* **Open** 9am-5pm Mon-Thur; 9am-6pm Fri. Map p252 H6.

PNC Bank *Corcoran Branch, 1503 Pennsylvania Avenue, NW, at 15th Street, White House & Around (1-202 835 4502). McPherson Square Metro.* **Open** 9am-2pm Mon- Fri. **Map** p252 H6.

Currency exchange

Some – but not many – banks will exchange cash or travellers' cheques in major foreign currencies. You will need photo ID, such as a passport, to exchange travellers' cheques. The most convenient place for exchange is at the airport when you arrive – but banks often give better rates. Travelex and American Express also exchange currency. Most hotel desks will do the same – handy if you're stuck late at night without any cash and don't want to go out to an ATM.

American Express Travel *The Investment Building, 1501 K Street, NW, at 15th Street. (1-202 457 1300). MacPherson Square Metro.* **Open** 9am-5.30pm Mon-Fri. **Map** p252 H5. Call 1-202 457-1300 for the purchase or refund of travellers' cheques.

Travelex Suite *103, 1800 K Street, NW, at 18th Street, Foggy Bottom (1-202 872 1428, www.travelex.com). Farragut North Metro.* **Open** 9am-7pm Mon-Fri. **Map** p284 G5.

Travelex also has branches at Union Station and Dulles and National airports. The central number is 1-800 287 7362.

Lost/stolen credit cards

In the event of losing your card or having it stolen, call the company immediately to deactivate it and also to request a replacement. Travellers' cheques can be replaced via a local office.

American Express cards
1-800 528 4800.
American Express travellers cheques 1-800 221 7282.
Discover 1-800 347 2683.
MasterCard 1-800 627 8372.
Visa 1-800 847 2911.

Tax

The general consumer DC sales tax is six per cent; it's six per cent in Maryland and four per cent in Virginia. The tax on restaurant meals is ten per cent and is added later to the advertised menu price, while the tax on hotel rooms is 14.5 per cent.

OPENING HOURS

Business hours in DC are generally 9am to 5pm Monday to Friday. Most shops are open 10am to 5pm or 6pm Monday to Saturday and noon to 6pm on Sunday. Even in the business-heavy Downtown area, most shops are open at the weekend. From Monday to Saturday, mall stores usually stay open until 9pm. On the whole, banks open at 9am and close at about 5pm on weekdays only. Restaurants are usually open for lunch from 11am to 2pm and for dinner from 5pm to 10pm, but many are open all day. In Adams Morgan, Georgetown and Dupont Circle, some bars and eateries don't close until 2am or 3am.

POLICE

There are two phone numbers you should know in case you need to reach the police. The first number, **911**, is used in cases of emergencies: if a crime is in progress or has just occurred, or if you see a fire or medical emergency or a major vehicle crash; it is also the number for violent crimes.

The police non-emergency number, **311**, is for minor vehicle crashes, property crimes that are no longer in progress and animal control problems. The **311** number service has been extended to cover other city services.

A good resource for information on police hotlines and other city services is http://dc.gov.

POSTAL SERVICES

Call 1-202 636 2270 or check www.usps.com to find the location of your nearest post offce. Most branches are usually open 8am-5pm on weekdays; some open for limited hours on Saturdays. Mail can be sent from any of the big blue mailboxes on street corners, but if you are sending a package overseas that is heavier than 16oz, it must be sent directly from a post office and accompanied by a customs form.

American Express (*see p235*) provides a postal service for its clients.

General Mail Facility *900 Brentwood Road, NE, at New York Avenue (1-202 636 2270). Rhode Island Avenue Metro.* **Open** 9am-5pm Mon-Fri; 9am-4pm Sat. **Credit** AmEx, MC, V. The city's main postal facility, but it's located quite a way from Downtown. A letter sent Poste Restante (called 'General Delivery' in the US) will end up here; better to have it sent to a specific post office (you'll need the zip code). Mail is held for 30 days.

National Capitol Station Post Office *City Post Office Building, North Capitol Street & Massachusetts Avenue, NE, Union Station & Around (1-202 523 2368). Union Station Metro.* **Open** 9am-7pm Mon-Fri; 9am-5pm Sat, Sun. **Credit** AmEx, MC, V. **Map** p253 K6.

RELIGION

Adas Israel Congregation
2850 Quebec Street, NW, Cleveland Park (1-202 362 4433, www.adasisrael.org). Cleveland Park Metro. **Map** p250 F1. Conservative Jewish.

Basilica of the National Shrine of the Immaculate Conception *400 Michigan Avenue, NE, at 4th Street (1-202 526 8300, www.nationalshrine.com). Brookland-CUA Metro.* **Map** p251 L1. The largest Roman Catholic church in North America, and one of the ten largest churches in the world.

Foundry Methodist Church
1500 16th Street, NW, at P Street, Dupont Circle (1-202 332 4010, www.foundryumc.org). Dupont Circle Metro. **Map** p250 H4.

Islamic Center *2551 Massachusetts Avenue, NW, at Belmont Road, Adams Morgan (1-202 332 8343, www.theislamiccenter.com). Dupont Circle Metro then 96 bus.* **Map** p250 F3.

New York Avenue Presbyterian Church *1313 New York Avenue, NW, between 13th & 14th Streets, Downtown (1-202 393 3700, www.nyapc.org). McPherson Square Metro.* **Map** p252 H5.

St John's Episcopal Church
1525 H Street, NW, at Lafayette Square, White House & around (1-202 347 8766, www.stjohns-dc.org). McPherson Square Metro. **Map** p252 H5.

Washington Hebrew Congregation *3935 Macomb Street, NW, at Massachusetts Avenue, Cleveland Park (1-202 362 7100, www.whctemple.org). Cleveland Park Metro.* **Map** p249 D1. Reformed Jewish.

Washington National Cathedral *Massachusetts & Wisconsin Avenues, NW, Upper Northwest (1-202 537 6200/www.cathedral.org/cathedral). Tenleytown Metro & then bus 30, 31, 32, 34, 35, 36, 37 going south on Wisconsin Avenue.* **Map** p249 E2. Episcopal. *See also p70.*

SAFETY & SECURITY

Apart from the large-scale security concerns and restrictions that come from being the capital of the United States, the areas of DC that are notorious for crime are parts of the Southeast and Northeast quadrants, far from the main (and even most of the secondary) tourist sights. The threat of crime near the major visitor destinations is generally small.

The area around the Capitol is very heavily policed, and Metro trains and stations are also well patrolled and virtually crime-free. Adams Morgan and the U Street/14th Street Corridor are much too heavy with traffic to be considered dangerous, but the sidestreets surrounding them can be dodgy after dark, as can some streets near

Union Station and around Capitol Hill and H Street, NE. Stick to the heavily populated, well-lit thoroughfares when walking in these areas at night.

Generally, as in any big city, you should take the usual security precautions. Be wary of pickpockets, especially in crowds. Look like you know what you're doing and where you're going – even if you don't. Use common sense and follow your intuition about people and situations. If someone does approach you for money in a threatening manner, don't resist. Hand over your wallet, then dial 911 or hail a cab and ask the driver to take you to the nearest police station where you can report the theft and get a reference number to claim insurance and travellers' cheque refunds.

SMOKING

It is illegal to smoke in a public space indoors.

STUDY

While not a full-blown university town like Boston, DC does have its share of colleges and universities. The major ones are listed below, but there are many smaller institutions, branch universities and schools in suburban Virginia and Maryland. Most of these schools conduct summer courses in politics, international relations and other programs directly relating to the city's weighty political scene. For Washington's libraries, *see p232.*

American University *4400 Massachusetts Avenue, NW, at Nebraska Avenue, Upper Northwest (1-202 885 1000, www.american. edu). Tenleytown-AU Metro then M4 bus.* **Map** p248 C1.
Over 11,000 students attend this university in residential DC. It has strong arts and sciences programmes, and a law library.

Catholic University of America *620 Michigan Avenue, NE, at Harewood Road, Northeast (1-202 319 5000, www.cua.edu). Brookland -CUA Metro.* **Map** p251 L1.
Catholic University received a papal charter in 1887. Its diverse programs include architecture, engineering and law.
Georgetown University *37th & O Streets, NW, Georgetown (1-202 687 0100, www.georgetown.edu). Dupont Circle Metro then G2 bus.* **Map** p249 D4.

Georgetown attracts students from all over the world to its prestigious international relations, business, medical and law schools.

George Washington University *I & 22nd Streets, NW, Foggy Bottom (1-202 994 1000, www. gwu.edu). Foggy Bottom-GWU Metro.* **Map** p252 G5.
GWU houses law and medical schools, and has strong programmes in politics and international affairs.

Howard University *2400 6th Street, NW, at Georgia Avenue, Shaw (1-202 806 6100, www. howard.edu). Shaw-Howard University Metro.* **Map** p251 J2.
About 10,000 students attend this historically black university, studying medicine, engineering, dentistry, social work and communications.

University of the District of Columbia *4200 Connecticut Avenue, NW, at Van Ness Street, Upper Northwest (1-202 274 5000, www.udc.edu). Van Ness-UDC Metro.*
UDC was formed in 1974 as a land-grant institution with an open admissions policy. Not as prestigious as most of its neighbours, it nonetheless has a variety of programs, including arts, sciences and law.

TELEPHONES
Dialling & codes

The area code for DC is 202; dial it to make a call within the District. Maryland and Virginia are more complicated. The area codes for the city of Alexandria and the counties of Arlington and Fairfax in Virginia are 1-703 and 1-571. In Maryland, Prince George's County and Montgomery County both use 1-301 and 1-240 area codes. Calls from any one of these area codes to another, as well as within one area code, are classed as local, but you must dial the area code, even if you're dialling from DC. Some calls are treated as local, others long distance. Non-Washingtonians will probably not know which is which, but you will always get through by dialling the '1' first, and if it is a local call you will only be charged for a local rate. For this reason we have included the 1 prefix before all numbers.

Numbers to other parts of the US always require the 1 prefix

before the area code. This is also the case for numbers beginning 1-800, 1-888 and 1-877, which are all toll free within the US, though note that your hotel may still bill you a flat fee. Most are also accessible from outside DC and – at the usual international rates – from outside the US.

Operators & assistance

For local directory assistance within the DC metro area, dial 411. For national long-distance enquiries, dial 1 + [area code] + 555 1212 (if you don't know the area code, dial 0 for the operator). For international calls, dial 011 then the country code (**UK** 44; **New Zealand** 64; **Australia** 61 – check online or see the phone book for others). For collect (reverse charge) calls, dial 0 for the operator. If you use voicemail, note that the pound key is the one marked # and the star key is *.

On automated answering systems, 0 often gets you through to a real-life operator.

Mobile phones

US readers with mobile phones should contact their mobile phone operators about using their phone in Washington. All five UK mobile phone operators have roaming agreements with major US operators, so you should be able to use your mobile in Washington – as long as your phone is a tri-band (and modern phones generally are). All you need do is ensure that the roaming facility is set up before you travel.

Public phones

You'll still find public pay phones, and some of them even work. Phones take any combination of silver coins. To call long-distance or to make an international call from a pay phone you need to go through a long-distance company, such as AT&T. Make the call by either dialling 0 for an operator or dialling direct, which is cheaper. To find out how much it will cost, dial the number and a computerised voice will tell you how much money to deposit. You can pay for calls using your credit card. The best way to make long-distance calls is with a phone card, available from any post office branch and many newsagents and general stores.

TIME

Washington DC operates on Eastern Standard Time (the same time zone as New York and Miami), which is five hours behind Greenwich Mean Time (London) and three hours ahead of Pacific Standard Time (Los Angeles). Clocks go forward one hour on the first Sunday in April to daylight saving time and back one hour on the last Sunday in October.

TIPPING

Cab drivers and waiters are generally tipped 15-20 per cent – more for exceptionally good service. Bartenders expect $1 per drink. Hairdressers get ten to 20 per cent, bellhops $1 per bag and hotel maids $1-$2 per day.

TOILETS

Malls, museums, bookstores and even some grocery stores have toilets; clothes shops almost always do not. In restaurants you may have to buy a drink in order to use them.

TOURIST INFORMATION

DC Chamber of Commerce Visitor information Center *506 9th Street, NW, at E Street (1-866 324 7386, 1-202 638 7330, www. dcchamber.org). Gallery Place Metro, (exit at 9th & G Streets & walk one block south).* **Open** 8.30am-5.30pm Mon-Fri. **Map** p252 H6.
Part of DC Chamber of Commerce, this office supplies tourist maps, city guides, restaurant and hotel information and advice.

Destination DC *4th Floor, 901 7th Street, NW, entrance at I Street,*

Downtown (1-800 422 8644; 1-202 789 7000, www.washington.org). Metro Center Metro. **Open** 8.30am-5pm Mon-Fri. **Map** p253 J5.
Good for general information on the city, largely via the website, which has a calendar of events and many other suggestions for visitors.

National Park Service
1-202 208 6843, www.nps.gov.

Smithsonian information
1-202 633 1000, www.si.edu/visit.
Information on all the Smithsonian's museums.

Traveler's Aid *1-703 572 2536 1127, www.travelersaid.org.*
Network of travel support. This branch is at Dulles Airport; there are others at Union Station (1-202 371 1937) and Reagan National Airport (1-703 417 1806).

VISAS & IMMIGRATION

Some 27 countries currently participate in the Visa Waiver Scheme. If you are a citizen of the United Kingdom, the Republic of Ireland, Australia, New Zealand, Japan or most western European countries (check with your local US embassy or consulate for exact status of your nation), you do not need a visa for stays in the US shorter than 90 days (business or pleasure) as long as you have a machine-readable passport valid for the full 90-day period, a return ticket and authorisation through the ESTA scheme. Visitors must fill in the ESTA form at least 24 hours before travelling (72 hours in advance is recommended); the form can be found on US embassy websites. Canadians will only need visas under special circumstances.

Citizens of other countries or people who are staying for longer than 90 days or who need a work or study visa should contact their nearest US consulate or embassy well before the date of travel (note that visitors requiring visas will also have to submit biometric data). The US embassy in London has a service (020 7499 9000) for all general visa enquiries. The website (http://ukinusa.fco.gov.uk) also has information.

WHEN TO GO

Autumn is a great time to visit, avoiding the humidity and heat of summer and the colder winter weather. April is, in theory, a lovely time to come – early in the month, the cherry blossoms are in flower at the Tidal Basin. However, it's also one of DC's busiest months for tourism. In autumn, the trees turn brilliant shades of orange, red and yellow, and the weather is pleasant.

If you do visit in summer, be sure to drink plenty of water so you don't get dehydrated, and start sightseeing early to avoid long lines. Daytime summer temperatures average 86°F (30.2°C) but feel much hotter because of the high humidity; aim to be inside an air-conditioned building at midday.

Winters are generally fairly mild, but even a light snowfall can still bring the city to a halt. Don't be surprised if there are long periods of bitter weather. Otherwise, winter days can be bright and clear.

If you want to see government in action, remember that in addition to Christmas and Easter breaks, Congress is in recess during August and the Supreme Court from May to September.

NATIONAL HOLIDAYS

New Year's Day 1 January
Martin Luther King Jr Day third Monday in January
Presidents Day third Monday in February
Memorial Day last Monday in May
Independence Day 4 July
Labor Day first Monday in September
Columbus Day second Monday in October
Election Day first Tuesday in November
Veterans Day 11 November
Thanksgiving fourth Thursday in November
Christmas Day 25 December

THE LOCAL CLIMATE

Average temperatures and monthly rainfall in Washington DC.

	High (°C/°F)	Low (°C/°F)	Rainfall (mm/in)
Jan	5.6/42	-3.4/26	69/2.7
Feb	7.3/45	-2.8/27	69/2.7
Mar	13.4/56	2.8/37	81/3.2
Apr	19/ 66	7.8/46	69/2.7
May	24.6/76	13.4/56	94/3.7
June	29.1/84	19/66	96/3.8
July	31.3/88	25.2/71	96/3.8
Aug	30.2/86	21.2/70	99/3.9
Sept	26.9/80	16.8/62	84/3.3
Oct	20.7/69	10.1/50	76/3.0
Nov	14.5/58	5/41	79/3.1
Dec	8.4/47	0.56/31	79/3.1

ESSENTIAL INFORMATION

Further Reference

BOOKS

Non-fiction

All the President's Men
Carl Bernstein & Bob Woodward
The story behind Watergate.
The Beat
Kip Lornell & Charles Stephenson, Jr
Go-go's fusion of funk and hip hop,
DC's music.
Dance of Days
Mark Andersen & Mark Jenkins
Two decades of punk in DC.
**Dream City: Race, Power
and the Decline of
Washington, DC**
Harry Jaffe & Tom Sherwood
An in-depth look at how race and
power-lust corrupted local politics
over several decades.
**Personal History: Katherine
Graham's Washington**
Katherine Graham
The autobiography of the erstwhile
publisher of the *Washington Post*.
Plan of Attack
Bob Woodward
The inside story of the George W
Bush administration's planning for
the 2003 invasion of Iraq, by the
famous reporter.
Ronald Reagan
Dinesh D'Souza
A view from the right: commentator
Dinesh D'Souza puts the case
for viewing the presidency of
conservative hero Ronald Reagan
in a favorable light.
**Shadow: Five Presidents
& the Legacy of Watergate**
Bob Woodward
A thought-provoking bestseller on
how the Watergate affair affected
subsequent presidential scandals.
Washington Goes to War
David Brinkley
The history of Washington during
World War II.

Fiction

Drum-Taps
Walt Whitman
Whitman's war poems were directly
influenced by his work in Civil War
hospitals in Washington.
Echo House
Ward Just
The story of three generations of
a powerful Washington family,
written by a former *Washington
Post* reporter.

Empire
Gore Vidal
A historical novel based on
Theodore Roosevelt's Washington,
Vidal's epic brings America during
the Gilded Age into vivid focus.
King Suckerman
George P Pelecanos
Murder, drugs and the coolest
music in this homage to
blaxploitation.
**Murder in the Map Room
(and other titles)**
Elliott Roosevelt
Series of White House murder
mysteries written by FDR's son,
with First Lady Eleanor Roosevelt
as the problem-solving sleuth.
O: A Presidential Novel
Anonymous
Speculation is rife as to wrote this
Primary Colors-style novel. Set
during the 2008 presidential election
campaign, it features a familiar-
sounding president. The writer is
thought to have personal experience
of the Obama White House.
Primary Colors
Anonymous (Joe Klein)
Guess who's who in this
fictionalised retelling of Bill
Clinton's run for the presidency.
The Tenth Justice
Brad Meltzer
Bestselling thriller based on the
travails of an ambitious young
clerk to a Supreme Court justice.
Thank You for Smoking
Christopher Buckley
Send-up of TV pundits and political
special-interest groups.

Reference

**AIA Guide to the Architecture
of Washington, DC**
Christopher Weeks
Concise descriptions and photos of
DC's notable structures, including
100 built since the mid 1970s.
**Buildings of the District
of Columbia**
Pamela Scott & Antoinette J Lee
Detailed architectural history of
DC, from the Revolutionary War to
post-World War II, with photos,
drawings and maps.
**The Guide to Black
Washington**
*Sandra Fitzpatrick & Maria R
Goodwin*
Places and events of significance to
DC's African-American heritage.

WEBSITES

The following are useful for
information on different aspects
of DC. Websites for venues in the
guide are included in the listings.

Washington Post
www.washingtonpost.com.
The Post makes every word it
prints available online, although
the stories are moved after two
weeks to the archives, access
to which requires the payment
of a fee.

Washington City Paper
www.washingtoncitypaper.com.
Much of this paper's content is not
available online, but its listings and
classifieds are there, however, in a
searchable form.

WTOP News
www.wtopnews.com.
The city's leading all-news radio
station's excellent website includes
breaking news and helpful links to
weather and traffic reports, as well
as a listen-live option.

DCist
www.dcist.com.
Daily digest for the blog generation,
committed to 'documenting the
nation's capital and all its quirks,
one small detail at a time'.

Craigslist
www.washingtondc.craigslist.org.
More than ten million people visit
this exhaustive community clearing
house of jobs, housing, products
and information each month.

DC Watch
www.dcwatch.com.
For outsiders seeking a sense of
the passion and perplexity of civic
affairs in America's 'last colony',
this site gives an exhaustive
introduction.

Congress
http://thomas.loc.gov.
Links to lots of useful
Congressional information,
including days-in-session for the
House and Senate, full text of the
bills that are being considered
and a listing of how congressmen
and -women have voted on specific
issues in the past.

Index

INDEX

INDEX

INDEX

Maps

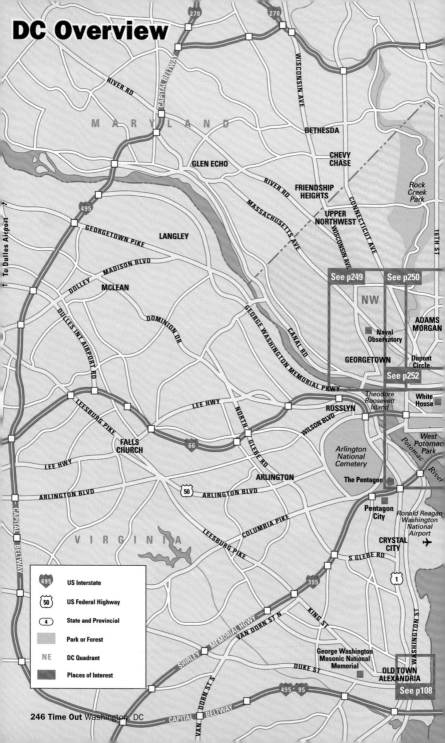

DC Overview

SILVER
SPRING

LANGLEY PARK

COLLEGE
PARK

Sligo Creek
Park

CAPITAL BELTWAY

495

95

295

BALTIMORE AVE

UNIVERSITY BLVD

Greenbelt
Park

WASHINGTON PKWY

TAKOMA
PARK

M A R Y L A N D

BALTIMORE

495

95

NEW HAMPSHIRE AVE

GEORGIA AVE

29

1

BROOKLAND

BLADENSBURG

DISTRICT OF COLUMBIA

JOHN HANSON HWY

CAPITAL BELTWAY

See p251

Catholic
University

Franciscan
Monastery

50

50

RHODE ISLAND AVE

SHAW

NE

Jack Kent
Cooke Stadium

NEW YORK AVE

N CAPITOL ST

National
Arboretum

KENILWORTH AVE

See p253   See p248

214

CONSTITUTION AVE

The National Mall

US Capitol

EAST CAPITOL ST

INDEPENDENCE AVE

RFK
Stadium

CAPITOL
HEIGHTS

East
Potomac
Park

S CAPITOL ST

395

PENNSYLVANIA AVE

SE

PRINCE
GEORGE'S
COUNTY

SW

River

Washington
Navy Yard

Fort
McNair

Anacostia

Cedar Hill

4

295

ANACOSTIA

Anacostia
Museum

St Elizabeth's
Hospital

SUITLAND

PENNSYLVANIA AVE

95

495

BRANCH AVE

ANACOSTIA FREEWAY

MORNINGSIDE

5

95

495

CAPITAL BELTWAY

BRANCH AVE

Andrews Air
Force Base

OXON HILL

0   3 miles

4 kms

© Copyright Time Out Group 2013

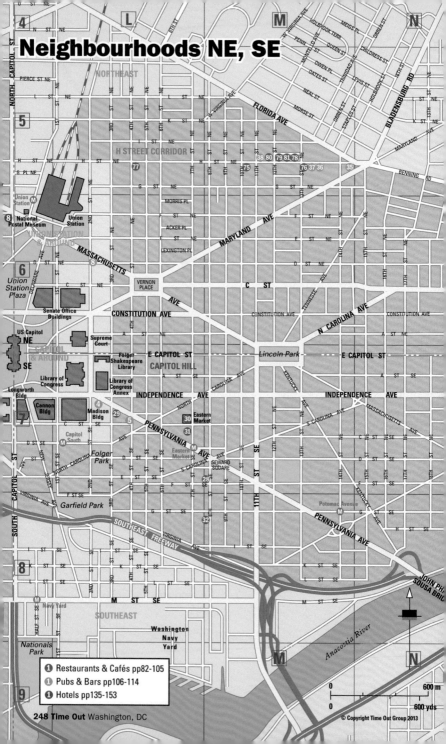

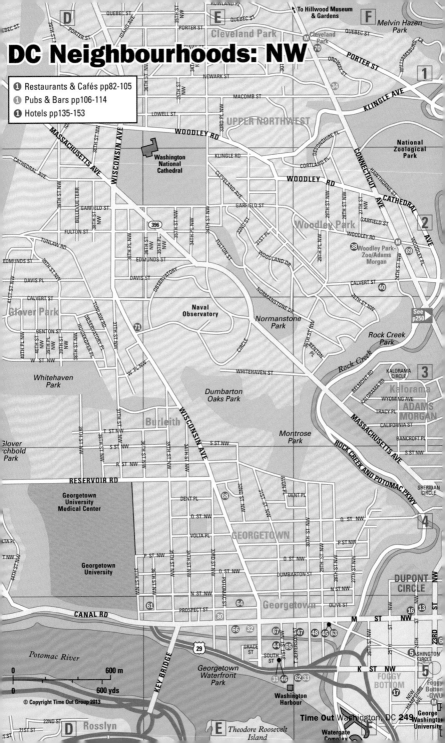

DC Neighbourhoods: NW and NE

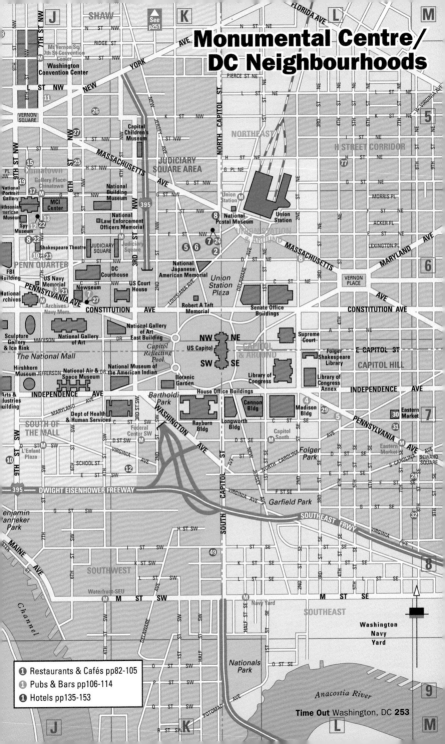

Monumental Centre/
DC Neighbourhoods

Street Index

STREET INDEX

Washington, DC Metro Map

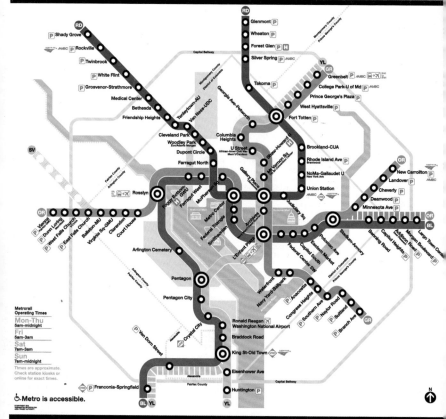